Accounting and Finance Practice Series

ACCOUNTING AND FINANCE PRACTICE SERIES

$\mathbf{A}$nalytical Review

A Guide to Analytical Procedures

Second Edition

Edward Blocher, Ph.D., CPA, CMA
University of North Carolina

John J. Willingham, Ph.D., CPA,
Peat Marwick Main

PRENTICE HALL
Englewood Cliffs, New Jersey 07632

Prentice-Hall International, Inc. *London*
Prentice-Hall of Australia, Pty. Ltd., *Sydney*
Prentice-Hall of Canada, Inc., *Toronto*
Prentice-Hall of India Private Ltd., *New Delhi*
Prentice-Hall of Japan, Inc. *Tokyo*
Prentice-Hall of Southeast Asia Pte., Ltd., *Singapore*
Whitehall Books, Ltd., *Wellington, New Zealand*
Editora Prentice-Hall do Brasil Ltda., *Rio de Janeiro*
Prentice-Hall Hispanoamericana, S.A., *Mexico*

© 1988 by

PRENTICE-HALL, INC.

Englewood Cliffs, N.J.

10   9   8   7   6   5   4   3   2   1

Library of Congress Cataloging in Publication Data

Blocher, Edward.
  Analytical review : a guide to analytical procedures /
Edward Blocher, John J. Willingham.—[2nd ed.]
    p. cm.—(Accounting and finance practice series)
  Includes bibliographies and index.
  ISBN 0-13-033135-X
  1. Auditing, Analytical review.   I. Willingham, John J.
II. Title. III. Series
HF5667.B536 1988   88-7269
657'.3—dc19   CIP

Revised edition of *Analytical Review: A Guide To
Evaluating Financial Statements* by Edward Blocher and
John J. Willingham.

ISBN 0-13-033135-X

PRENTICE HALL
BUSINESS & PROFESSIONAL DIVISION
A division of Simon & Schuster
Englewood Cliffs, New Jersey 07632

PRINTED IN THE UNITED STATES OF AMERICA

Contents

Summary

Preface to the Second Edition

Detailed

Preface to the Second Edition

APPENDIXES

Preface to the Second Edition

This book will help accountants and auditors to use analytical procedures most effectively. It can be used by both external and internal auditors as a guide and a reference for selecting, performing, and interpreting the results of analytical procedures. There are a large number of different uses of analytical procedures in accounting and auditing—the financial audit, the review engagement, the pre-acquisition review, the review of pro forma statements by an auditor, controller or financial analyst, the determination of internal audit scope and priorities, and many more. These procedures can be a very effective and efficient method for auditing and other analysis purposes.

Analytical procedures is the name now used for a variety of techniques the auditor or accountant can use to assess the risk of undetected error in financial records. These procedures involve the analysis of trends, ratios, and reasonableness tests derived from an entity's financial and operating data. The recent Statement on Auditing Standards, "Analytical Procedures," replaces the familiar *analytical review* and *analytical review procedures* vocabulary with the new term *analytical procedures*. The reasoning behind the name change, in part, is to clarify that this type of procedure is used in audit, review, and other types of engagements. Thus, reference to the term *review* is removed from the name of the procedure. The title of our book retains the familiar term *analytical review*, but throughout the book the new term, *analytical procedures*, will be used.

Many accountants and auditors tell us that the full potential of analytical procedures has not been realized. A common explanation for this is that, while the procedures are well known and widely used, there is a general lack of understanding of how they are properly applied and how much they should be relied upon. It is precisely these issues which have motivated us to write this book, and we have prepared it with these issues in mind. It is the objective of this book to show how available, well-known procedures can be used most effectively, rather than only to describe an assortment of techniques which are already familiar to the accountant or to describe an array of state-of-the-art statistical and mathematical approaches which are not now being used and are not likely to be used in the near future.

For the most experienced auditors, the book will be an aid to getting the most benefit from the use of the analytical procedures they are now using. Also, it will help the experienced auditor to identify new applications of analytical procedures. For the less experienced auditor, the book will be useful for training and as a reference to assist in resolving the day-to-day questions which come up on the audit or review engagement. We think the book will be especially useful to the inexperienced auditor, since the effectiveness of analytical procedures is very dependent on the auditor's knowledge and experience, more so than for most other audit procedures.

As our focus is on guidance for the well-known analytical procedures, our approach in the book is to provide a nontechnical presentation of these well-known methods. However, since regression analysis and expert systems are becoming more common in analytical procedure applications, we discuss these methods in a nontechnical manner. The more technical aspects of regression analysis are provided in an appendix.

The basis for the content of this book is our research of analytical procedures in the past seven years. Also, we have used the results of other researchers who are cited frequently throughout the book. This research has identified the judgment biases and mistakes which are commonly made in the use of analytical procedures. The research has also provided some preliminary evidence on the relative effectiveness of different analytical procedures. Our book makes this important research information available to the reader in a nontechnical, easy-to-read form.

Since the first edition was published in 1985, a number of significant changes have taken place in auditing, and particularly in the area of analytical procedures. The most important change is the increasing use of the microcomputer in audit practice. While used in a tentative and limited way when the first edition was being prepared, microcomputers are now widely used in audit practice for an increasing number of tasks of ever-increasing sophistication. Chapters 10, 11, and 12 deal specifically with the opportunities the microcomputer has presented for more effective and more efficient analytical procedures by replacing certain pencil-pushing tasks and by making possible decision aids and statistical analysis which are now far less costly and more accessible to the auditor.

Another important development in recent years includes the issuance of the Statement on Auditing Standards, "Analytical Procedures." This new standard requires the use of analytical procedures at both the planning and review phases of the audit. This book provides guidance to an auditor on what procedures to perform and how to document these procedures, as required by the new standard.

Chapter 1, "The Uses of Analytical Procedures," presents some basic information about the nature of analytical procedures and their role in the independent audit, the internal audit, and other accounting applications. Chapter 2, "Analytical Auditing," addresses the question, "What does it mean to be an analytical auditor?" This is an important topic because of the apparent inconsistency in the two commonly heard observations: (a) most auditors use analytical procedures, and some use it extensively, and (b) many auditors place little or no reliance on analytical procedures and say they have little confidence in their ability to detect financial statement errors. In different words, many auditors seem to say that they use analytical procedures effectively, but that auditors in general do not use them effectively. This suggests it is useful to study the question of what we mean by "analytical" or "analytical auditing." This discussion is presented in the new Chapter 2, which is based on presentation materials one author has used in numerous seminar presentations on analytical procedures.

Chapter 3, "Analyzing and Evaluating Inherent Risk," describes the elements of inherent risk and the analytical procedures which are useful for analysis and evaluation. Chapters 4 through 6 then deal with the three common classes of analytical procedures—trend analysis, ratio analysis, and the reasonableness test, respectively. A particularly important addition to the new edition is the inclusion of an appendix of industry ratios which provide a useful benchmark when analyzing an entity's financial ratios.

Chapter 7, "Using Analytical Procedures for Selected Accounts," explains the approach we suggest for selecting the right procedure for a given account under analysis. Certain procedures are expected to be more effective for certain accounts than others. Also, there is a discussion of the use of analytical procedures for choosing which of many locations to test, given that the auditor is not able to examine all locations.

Chapter 8, "Analytical Procedures at the Completion of the Audit," briefly describes the objectives and procedures for the final review at the completion of the audit. Chapter 9, "Guidance for Using Analytical

Procedures," includes our suggestions for incorporating working paper decision aids and other guidance techniques to enhance the effectiveness of auditor usage of analytical procedures.

A new chapter, Chapter 10, "Analytical Procedures and the Computer," has been added to show the influence of the microcomputer on analytical procedures. The chapter begins with a presentation of mainframe and microcomputer applications of analytical procedures to more clearly show the role of the microcomputer. Also, there are examples of how different types of software—database, spreadsheet, and working paper software—can be used in performing analytical procedures. There are illustrations based on some of the most commonly used software systems.

The new Chapter 11, "Use of Regression Analysis as an Analytical Procedure," is a nontechnical introduction to the application of regression analysis. The more technical details are retained in Appendix F. This chapter should be helpful to any auditor who is interested in learning more about this statistical technique and how it can be used in auditing. The chapter includes an illustration using a microcomputer-based regression analysis software system.

Chapter 12, "Analytical Procedures and Expert Systems," presents an overview and some illustrations of this new area of audit technology. Expert systems are decision aids which are developed to facilitate human judgment in complex areas of decision making. Analytical procedures are particularly well suited to an expert systems approach, in part because of the importance of expert judgment in interpreting properly the findings of an analytical procedure.

The appendixes include relevant portions of professional guidance, a technical reference on regression analysis, and an industry database. We are grateful for permissions received from various publishers to reproduce their material here, especially for the permission given by the firm, Grant Thornton, to use certain of its training materials in Chapter 2 and Chapter 11. We hope you find this book thoroughly interesting and useful.

Edward Blocher
John J. Willingham
January 1988

The Uses of Analytical Procedures

1

§1.01   Introduction

A continuing concern for auditors is the choice of procedures to use in achieving audit objectives. In response to this concern, increasing attention is given to analytical procedures as a means for improving audit efficiency. *Analytical procedures* is a name for a variety of techniques for gathering audit evidence through analyses of expected relationships between an organization's operating and financial data, using ratios, trends, reasonableness tests, and related procedures. An important common characteristic of these procedures is that they require relatively little auditor time or resources. For this reason they are preferable to other audit procedures when they are sufficient to achieve the given audit objective. However, many auditors argue against increased reliance on analytical review until the profession and the individual auditor understand it much better. They point to the unexplained diversity of use for analytical procedures among the largest firms, and to the perceived low precision of the proçedures, as conditions which indicate the need for guidance before the procedures are used more extensively.

Auditors both in practice and in academia are pursuing ongoing research efforts to provide the desired improvement in our understanding of analytical procedures. The research has two thrusts:

1. To develop new and more effective analytical procedures

2. To discover whatever obstacles there might be for auditors in using current procedures effectively and to develop the practical forms of guidance (checklists, decision flowcharts, etc.) to address these obstacles

While both types of research are important, our primary interest is in the latter, that is, helping auditors use available methods more effectively. Moreover, we are specifically concerned with the analytical procedures which are well known and in widespread usage, rather than with the newer mathematical and statistical methods, such as regression and time-series analysis. We feel the greatest overall benefit will come from more effective use of the well-known procedures rather than from the wider use of the new mathematical and statistical procedures.

It is not appropriate here to pursue the arguments supporting or refuting this position, as it would necessarily be a lengthy and probably inconclusive discussion. However, restricting our efforts to the well-known procedures should not limit the utility of this book for most auditors, since these procedures are useful for a wide variety of audit engagements, whereas the utility of the mathematical and statistical procedures may depend on the size of the engagement, the audit history, and the availability of expertise.

§1.02   Objectives of the Book

This book can be used for both instructional and reference purposes. In the first instance, it provides a comprehensive presentation of analytical review which shows the auditor how to use the procedures most effectively. To facilitate quick and lasting learning of the material, illustrations and case examples are used frequently. The focus throughout is on those well-known procedures now used in audit practice, so the terms and concepts will be familiar to most auditors. However, the presentation assumes no prior knowledge of analytical procedures, so the inexperienced auditor or student will find it useful as well.

Since the procedures will be familiar to most auditors, a key aspect of the approach of this book is to highlight the *obstacles* to the most effective use of these procedures. This is done by identifying and explaining the most common judgment mistakes an auditor can make in applying and interpreting the results of an analytical review procedure. This exposition is based in part on the findings of extensive research projects by ourselves and others. Generally, these mistakes involve the use of irrelevant or incomparable data in the process of assessing the reasonableness of some figure. A second aspect of the approach of this book is to develop a strategy for choosing which of the procedures should be used in analyzing a given financial statement account. Again, by reference in part to prior research, we will see that certain procedures are more effective than others for certain accounts, but that no single procedure is preferred for all accounts.

This book does not require an understanding of mathematical and statistical concepts and techniques beyond that level contained in the *Statements on Auditing Standards (SAS)*, the American Institute of Certified Public Accountants guidelines to the profession. However, regression and time-series models are known to be useful in certain applications of analytical procedures, so a thorough presentation of how to develop and apply these statistical models is given in Chapter 11. This chapter explains the proper statistical interpretation of the models, the common mistakes in developing the models, and the conditions for which the models are most effectively applied.

In addition to the instructional objective described above, this book can be used as a reference to guide the auditor's analyses of a given account balance. This use of the book is facilitated by the inclusion of decision flowcharts, outlines, and illustrations which promptly direct the auditor's attention to the needed information.

§1.03   Who Should Use the Book?

This book will assist both the independent auditor and the internal auditor in selecting and in interpreting the results of analytical procedures. Though the overall audit objectives for independent versus internal auditors differ substantially, the role which analytical procedures play in the audit process for each is quite similar. That is, analytical procedures are used to direct the auditor's attention to those areas with the greatest potential for material misstatement, and to provide a basis for allocating effort using this indication of potential for misstatement. Both independent and internal auditors are served by these two uses of analytical procedures.

Examples of uses for the independent auditor: (1) The auditor might use trend analysis to assess which of a set of expense accounts has the highest potential for misstatement, or (2) use a gross profit test to assess the reasonableness of the cost-of-sales/sales relationship, relative to prior years.

Examples of uses for the internal auditor: (1) Suppose a company has several contracts with others to supply goods and services to the company per contract. The internal auditor must choose a sample of these contractors for audit on a periodic basis. An analytical procedures approach would be used to determine which of the contractors might have the greatest potential for error, that is, billing the company for costs not covered by the contract. (2) The internal auditor would use an analytical procedure to determine which of several branch locations of a multilocation company (for example, a bank with many offices) to audit on a periodic basis.

It is useful to distinguish the *financial audit* from the *operational* or *management audit* when considering audit objectives. The financial audit is concerned with the bona fides of the reported amounts, whereas the operational or management audit is concerned with operational efficiency and management compliance with established policies. The independent auditor is primarily associated with the financial audit; the internal auditor can be involved in either type of audit. This book is designed principally for the financial audit, where analytical procedures are most commonly used.

§1.04   Where Analytical Procedures are Used by the Independent Auditor

Analytical procedures can be used by the independent auditor in a variety of situations, including the conventional financial audit engagement. There are five easily identified uses.

The Financial Audit Engagement

In the financial audit, analytical procedures are a substantive auditing procedure which can be used to direct the auditor's attention to areas with the highest potential for material misstatement. Alternatively, it can be used to reduce the scope of other substantive tests in an audit area where risk and materiality are low and where the auditor can be satisfied by the results of the analytical procedure. Also, it can be used as a compensating test in lieu of tests of internal control compliance, and at the final review of the audit working papers to assess the overall reasonableness of the financial statements. The use of analytical procedures in the financial audit is described more fully in Statements on Auditing Standards, *Analytical Procedures (Appendix A)*.

In contrast to its predecessor, SAS No 23, this new SAS requires the use of analytical procedures during the planning and review phases of all audits. Additionally, the new SAS provides somewhat more guidance to the auditor concerning the proper planning and evaluation of analytical procedures. This is accomplished by reference to broad factors that an auditor should consider in assessing the efficiency and effectiveness of a given analytical procedure. These factors include the nature of the assertion being examined by the auditor, the plausability of the relationship underlying the analytical procedure, the reliability of the data used in the procedure, and the precision of the expectation.

The *nature of the assertion* influences the effectiveness and efficiency of an analytical procedure vis à vis other substantive tests, in that analytical procedures tend to be superior in situations which require the tying together of related operating and financial data. A good example is an audit test related to potential ommissions, such as a test of unrecorded sales or unrecorded liabilities. In cases such as this, analytical procedures can provide relatively strong audit evidence. Also, for similar reasons, analytical procedures are particularly appropriate for evaluating accounting estimates and for assessing the issue of an entity's ability to continue in existence, as addressed in recent auditing standards (see below).

The *plausability of the relationship* and *the precision of the expectation* are discussed in Chapter 2 and under the heading **Precision** in Chapter 9. These concepts relate to the inherent predictability of the account or item under examination, and to the relative precision of different types of analytical procedures. We argue that trend analysis is the least precise of the types of analytical procedures, as it relies simply on an examination of prior years' data. The exception to this is the use of regression analysis, which we regard as providing a relatively high level of precision because of the power of the underlying quantitative method. Since ratio analysis is based upon an analysis of related accounts, we view it as providing more precise expectations than trend analysis. Finally, we view reasonableness testing as providing a level of precision higher than that of ratio analysis, because the reasonableness test incorporates operating as well as financial data and is intended to test directly the expected correspondence between related operating and financial data.

The Review Engagement

A review engagement has a narrower scope than that of the financial audit. The auditor expresses only limited assurance that the financial statements do not depart materially from conformity with generally accepted accounting principles. Review procedures consist of certain inquiries and analytical procedures. See Statements on Standards for Accounting and Review Services No 1, *Compilation and Review of Financial Statements* (Appendix B).

Review of Interim Financial Information

When interim financial information is presented together with the financial statements, or is presented alone and purports to conform to the provisions of Accounting Principles Board (APB) Opinion 28, *Interim Financial Reporting,* then certain review procedures and reporting standards apply as described in Statements on Auditing Standards No 36, *Review of Interim Financial Information* (Appendix C). The review procedures consist primarily of certain inquiries and analytical procedures. Review of internal controls and limited tests of details might also be involved.

Special Reports

For the auditor who is involved in an engagement in which scope is limited to certain elements, items, or accounts of a financial statement, the proper test procedures and reporting standards are described in Statements on Auditing Standards No 35, *Special Reports— Applying Agreed Upon Procedures . . .* The SAS does not prescribe the procedures to be applied, but in practice the auditor will find it useful to apply analytical procedures in the planning and testing phases of the engagement. Preacquisition reviews and reviews of creditors' claims are examples of this type of engagement.

Consideration of Going Concern

A recent auditing standard, Statements on Auditing Standards, *The Auditor's Consideration of an Entity's Ability to Continue in Existence,* requires the auditor to consider continued existence in all audits. A principal audit procedure for accomplishing this audit objective is to employ analytical procedures. The *SAS* is shown in Appendix D.

Auditing Accounting Estimates

Statements on Auditing Standards, *Auditing Accounting Estimates* (Appendix E), provides guidance to the auditor on evaluating the reasonableness of accounting estimates, such as the allowance for bad debts, obsolete inventories, losses on purchase commitments, and the like. A primary aspect of the guidance in this standard is the use of analytical procedures for evaluating the reasonableness of the related estimates. Analytical procedures are particularly appropriate in this context, in that they enable the auditor to tie together the relevant operating facts and the related financial data to see if the two are consistent. This approach is the strongest form of audit evidence for evaluating the related accounting estimates.

Budgeting and Short-Run Financial Planning

It is apparent that the use of analytical procedures, which involves an understanding of financial and operating relationships, is in effect an important part of the process of short-run financial planning and budgeting. That is, projecting account balances and relationships between accounts and operating data is an integral part of both analytical review and short-run financial planning. Thus, developing an expertise in analytical procedures should have benefits to the independent auditor both within the audit practice and for that portion of the consulting practice which provides financial planning services for clients.

§1.05   The Nature, Timing, and Extent of Analytical Procedures

Given these different uses for analytical procedures, we are interested in whether there should be differences in the nature, timing, and extent of analytical procedures for each. Also, it appears that the second, third, and fourth applications (review, interim information, and special reports, respectively) are quite similar, since all three require analytical procedures and inquiry to provide limited assurance that there is no material misstatement. Thus, we will use the term "review-type engagement" to refer to these collectively in the following discussion, which contrasts the nature, timing, and extent of analytical procedures for (1) the independent audit engagement, (2) the review-type engagement, and (3) internal auditing (the operational audit excluded).

Nature

Since independent audit, review, and internal auditing are all concerned with financial statement accounts, there is no difference in the nature of analytical procedures between them. That is, the risk analysis or analytical procedure would be applied in the same manner in each case.

Timing

The audit engagement has three principal phases—planning, field work, and final review. During initial planning, analytical procedures are used to evaluate the overall risk of the entity by considering financial liquidity and related measures of the entity's ability to maintain a going concern. The results of this evaluation are important in setting the overall scope of audit testing. In application to individual accounts, analytical procedures help to direct attention to accounts which might be materially misstated by identifying those with unusual relationships or changes relative to the prior period. Also, an analytical procedure can be used to reduce the amount of detail testing in an account, if the auditor is satisfied that the procedure is sufficiently accurate, and if the materiality and risk of the account are low. Since analytical procedures provide negative rather than positive assurance, this work-reducing role of analytical procedures requires careful judgment. When the risk or materiality of an account is high, the auditor may choose to employ a limited use of analytical procedures, or omit it entirely, and rely on detail testing.

Analytical procedures are also employed in the second phase of the audit—the field work. Here they are used to assist in selecting subsegments of the entity, or periods of transactions within an account, for in-depth examination. For example, it is used in selecting branch retail stores for detail work. Second, it is used in those situations in which the auditor must estimate an account balance for the purpose of making an adjustment or assisting the client in making an accrual. For example, the auditor might use an analytical procedures approach to estimate the amount of a contingent liability.

Then, in the final phase of the audit, analytical procedures are applied to assess the overall reasonableness of the financial statements. This use of analytical procedures can lead to additional audit work if an account balance or relationship appears to be unreasonable.

An internal audit activity can be viewed in the same manner, except that the final review phase is generally not applicable, since the internal audit is not typically intended to attest to the reasonableness of the financial statements taken as a whole. Also, it is generally not meaningful to consider phases for the review-type engagement, since it involves limited procedures which do not require extensive planning or review for overall reasonableness.

Extent

The extent of the use of analytical procedures in any engagement depends on many factors—risk, materiality, cost-benefit, applicability of analytical procedures relative to other procedures, and so on. However, the principal factor which determines the extent of analytical procedures to be used in independent audit, review, and internal audit engagements is the availability and effectiveness of substitutable procedures. In the audit engagement, tests of details are the substitute for analytical procedures, whereas in review engagements, the principal substitute is inquiry. The internal auditor may use both inquiry and tests of details in addition to the analytical procedures.

Thus, the chief difference between independent audit, review, and internal audit engagements is the *extent* of the use of analytical procedures and the nature of substitutes, rather than the nature or the timing of the procedures themselves. With this in mind, Chapter 7, Using Analytical Procedures for Selected Accounts, will include a discussion of the relative efficiency of analytical procedures and tests of details for each account in order to assist the auditor in choosing the extent to which analytical procedures should be used for each of the three engagement types. Chapter 8 is relevant only for the independent audit engagement, since it relates to the use of analytical procedures in the final review. The other chapters deal only with the nature of analytical procedures, so they are applicable for all three engagement types.

§1.06 A Frame of Reference for Analytical Procedures

In order to benefit fully from this book, it is important to have a frame of reference for organizing one's thinking about what analytical procedures consist of, and what knowledge, experience, information gathering, and information analysis are necessary to use them properly. The frame of reference we use is the distinction between two general methods for analytical procedures (see Table 1-1). Each of the two methods is a broad category encompassing steps and procedures which produce audit evidence through analysis of relationships between financial and operating data. Together, the methods include virtually all the steps and procedures which have been referred to as analytical procedures. Recognizing that auditors disagree about what should be labeled analytical procedures, our two methods are defined to be very comprehensive. The importance of the distinction between these methods is that they require a somewhat different nature and extent of auditor knowledge and experience. Also, the two methods have somewhat different demands for information gathering, evaluation, and analysis.

The two methods are *overall analysis* and *account analysis procedures*.

1. *Overall analysis* requires the use of extensive accounting and business knowledge and experience to assess the potential for material misstatement in the financial statements taken as a whole. Often, this involves the analysis of financial ratios and indicators or the search for what has been called a "red flag," such as a turnover in key personnel, certain aspects of the audit history, or a change in credit rating. Overall analysis is covered in Chapters 3 and 8.

2. *Account analysis procedures* involve the use of a quantitative procedure to analyze the potential for misstatement in a single account, item, or element of the financial statements. Trend analysis, ratio analysis, and reasonableness tests are the common examples of account analysis procedures. Ratio analysis is any method which involves comparing relationships between financial statement accounts (such as an expense-account-to-total-sales percentage), recognizing that the analysis of ratios often involves also considering the trend for the ratio. Trend analysis is the analysis of the change of an account balance over time. A reasonableness test is any computation used to estimate an account balance. Reasonableness tests usually require nonfinancial data. Account analysis procedures are covered in Chapters 4 through 7.

Table 1-1   Two Principal Analytical Review Methods

Characteristics of the Two Methods	Overall Analysis	Account Analysis Procedures
Primary objective	Analyze the potential for material misstatement in the financial statements taken as a whole.	Analyze the potential for material misstatement of a single financial statement account.
Procedure	Search for a "red flag," for example, turnover of key personnel, that often indicates the potential for material misstatement. Performed by management-level auditor.	Apply one or more of the three computational procedures: (1) trend analysis, (2) ratio analysis, or (3) reasonableness testing. Performed by auditor at the staff-in-charge level.

Required knowledge	A substantial knowledge about (1) the client's organization and business and (2) the financial and operating relationships of the client.	A good working knowledge of (1) the client's organization and business and (2) the financial and operating relationships of the client.
Required information	(1) Client financial and operating data and (2) other client data: correspondence, minutes of meetings, and so on.	Client financial and operating data.
Required evaluation and analysis	Typically negligible.	(1) Simple, though sometimes voluminous, calculations and (2) development of a prediction of what the account balance should be; comparison of this prediction to the reported amount; and analysis of the difference.

What knowledge, experience, and information are necessary to use each of these methods properly? For overall analysis to be effective, it is crucial that the auditor have extensive accounting and business knowledge and experience, since the key aspect of the task is to identify the relevant risk indicators and to interpret them properly. Thus, the analysis and evaluation of data per se is not an important feature of this method. In contrast, account analysis procedures often involve extensive data gathering and analysis and evaluation, as are required, for example, in the trend analysis of the working trial balance accounts. The key aspect of the task is to be able to consistently and correctly apply the procedure and to have the knowledge to interpret the procedure's results properly. Extensive accounting and business knowledge and experience are not as crucial a feature of this method, since the procedures are generally well known and easily understood. In summary, overall analysis can be characterized as an approach which tends to be somewhat open-ended and unstructured, and the judgments required are subjective in nature. On the other hand, account analysis procedures tend to be more well-defined and structured, and the judgments involved are more objective than is the case for risk analysis.

This frame of reference dictates the approach we take in this book. For example, the objective for the presentation of overall analysis in

Chapters 3 and 8 is to describe a comprehensive set of techniques which the auditor can use to assess risk effectively. However, the auditor must use the judgment obtained from knowledge and experience to select and interpret these techniques properly in practice. In contrast, since the calculations for account analysis procedures are well known, the objective for the presentation in Chapters 4 through 7 is to explain methods for facilitating the use of the procedures (computer aids, etc.) and to describe the pitfalls that exist in applying and interpreting the procedures effectively. These chapters will also include suggestions for providing training and supervision of audit staff that will improve usage of analytical procedures.

§1.07   How Much Can the Auditor Rely on Analytical Procedures?

To evaluate the strength of the evidence from analytical procedures, we must consider that analytical procedures provide a negative-type assurance rather than a positive one. That is, although analytical procedures can be a useful technique for detecting a material misstatement, they cannot be relied upon to confirm with positive assurance that a misstatement is *not* present.[1] Positive assurance comes only from the proper application of the appropriate detail test procedures. Thus, the auditor can never rely exclusively on analytical procedures when risk or materiality is high. But, the auditor does obtain reasonable assurance from analytical procedures by making the following four evaluations:

1. The auditor must be satisfied that the analytical procedure is sufficiently *accurate.* That is, the analytical procedure must predict the account balance or relationship with good precision. The accuracy of an analytical procedure is influenced both by the precision of the procedure and by the predictability of the underlying balance or relationship. For example, a statistical prediction (say, using regression) will generally be more precise than a nonstatistical prediction. Also, such account balances as depreciation expense, payroll expense, and interest expense are generally more easily predicted than accounts receivable or inventory. The audi-

---

[1] However, one recent study by Hylas & Ashton, *Audit Detection of Financial Statement Errors,* Account Rev, Oct 1982, at 751-65 has shown that a substantial proportion of errors are initially identified by analytical procedures. This suggests that analytical procedures can be more effective than is generally recognized.

tor uses judgment to assess the precision of each analytical procedures application.

2. The auditor must also evaluate both the materiality and the risk of the account. *Materiality* relates to the potential significance of misstatements in the account, and *risk* relates to the potential that an error occurs and is not detected by the entity's controls. The auditor can obtain reasonable assurance from analytical procedures if both risk and materiality are low.

3. Since the risk of an account is influenced by the quality of the entity's accounting controls, the auditor's reliance on analytical procedures is directly related to the evaluation of *controls.* If the proper controls are in place and are complied with, the auditor can obtain more assurance from the analytical procedures.

4. The nature and effectiveness of *other audit procedures* also influences the auditor's reliance on analytical procedures. If other procedures are effective, and these procedures uncover no significant errors or irregularities, then the analytical procedures can provide reasonable assurance.

Auditor Mistakes and Risks

When considering the degree of reliance to be placed on analytical procedures, it is helpful to understand the types of mistakes the auditor can make, and the related risks. There are two types of mistakes the auditor can make using analytical procedures.

Type 1: The results of the use of analytical procedures indicate to the auditor that a material misstatement is present, when it is not.

Type 2: The results of the use of analytical procedures indicate to the auditor that a material misstatement is *not* present, when in fact it is.

The cost of the type 1 mistake is the unnecessary additional auditing undertaken by the auditor. The type 2 mistake has no immediate cost, but subjects the auditor to the risk of significant later costs if the auditor gives an unqualified opinion and the material misstatement is subsequently detected. A high rate of type 1 mistakes can be related to audit inefficiency, whereas a high rate of type 2 mistakes could be related to ineffectiveness. Avoiding the type 2 mistake is ordinarily the auditor's principal concern because of the potentially high cost of legal liability and related costs.

The chance that an auditor will make the type 2 mistake is called the "risk" of the type 2 mistake. Risk is a percentage or probability between 0 and 1. The extent to which an analytical procedure reduces this risk is a good measure of the usefulness of the procedure and the reliance the auditor can obtain from it.

When one is considering risk and reliance for analytical procedures, it is important to consider the full scope of audit procedures—internal control evaluation and testing, analytical procedures, and tests of details—and the risk that all the procedures will make the type 2 mistake in a given set of circumstances. Audit risk is expressed as the simple product of the individual risk of the type 2 mistake for each of the three procedures. Thus

$$R = IR \times IC \times AP \times TD$$

where
- R = audit risk that a material misstatement is not detected
- IR = risk that a material misstatement occurs (the inherent risk)
- IC = risk that the material misstatement is not prevented or detected by the system of internal accounting controls
- AP = risk that the material misstatement is not detected by analytical procedures
- TD = risk that the material misstatement is not detected by tests of details

For example, if we make the conservative assumption that a material misstatement is present (i.e., $IR = 1.0$), and we assume that the risk of a type 2 mistake for each procedure is 20% (i.e., $IC = AP = TD = .2$), then audit risk can be calculated as the chance of 8 in 1000.

$$R = 1.0 \times .2 \times .2 \times .2 = .008$$

Audit risk is very small because each of the three procedures is assumed to act independently to detect the misstatement, so that the auditor obtains increased assurance, with each additional procedure, that no material misstatement is present. Since the auditor's overall concern is audit risk, rather than its three components, each of the three procedures can be viewed as "compensating" for the risk associated with the other two. Thus, a high risk of the type 2 mistake for internal controls (say, $IC = .5$) can be compensated by a lower risk for tests of details (say, $TD = .08$). Therefore,

$$R = 1.0 \times .5 \times .2 \times .08 = .008$$

This latter example would reflect a case in which the controls are weaker, but the tests of details are stronger, than for the original example.

In summary, since the risk associated with each of the three procedures affects audit risk, and since reduced risk for any one can offset increased risk for any other, the reliance the auditor can place on analytical procedures must be considered together with the evaluation of controls and the planned extent of tests of details. The stronger the other two procedures (low TD and IC), the less the needed reliance on analytical procedures (AP can be high) to achieve acceptable audit risk. Conversely, if the auditor judges the analytical procedures to be strong, then TD or IC can be proportionately higher. The auditor's judgments about the strength of an analytical procedure and about the inversely related risk level are based on the timing, nature, and extent of the procedure. In general terms, the strength of a procedure is proportional to the accuracy, relevance, timeliness, and extensiveness of the data which are used to predict and analyze the account balance or relationship. Each of Chapters 3, 4, 5, and 6 will include a discussion of this judgment process as it applies to the analytical procedure discussed in that chapter.

§1.08   Summary—State of the Art

This chapter has provided an introduction to analytical procedures and to this book. In summary, we now reflect on some of the findings of our research and of other researchers who have studied the practice of analytical procedures. A consideration of these findings will show why and how this book can assist you in using analytical procedures.

The most striking finding of these studies is the lack of consensus among auditors regarding the role and effectiveness of analytical procedures. Though some auditors see analytical procedures as important planning tools, many others prefer using the results of analytical procedures to corroborate other knowledge, rather than to serve as the initial source for audit planning decisions. In effect, they do not consider analytical procedures to be the independent and effective source of audit evidence we have assumed them to be in the previously presented formula for audit risk. Some of the reasons for this view have been expressed as follows:

1. When, as is often the case, analytical procedures are based upon a comparison of financial data across time, a meaningful analysis is frequently not possible because the data are not comparable

owing to significant changes in accounting methods, operating factors, and so on.

2. Certain analytical procedures require operating data and other types of data which are outside the system of internal accounting controls; these data are not ordinarily processed with the same standards of accuracy as financial data are.

3. Many auditors feel that methods relating economic events to financial results are too imprecise, that is, that they often lead the auditor to a wrong conclusion. Further, statistical and other methods which improve this precision are not cost-beneficial.

4. Available auditing literature is inadequate in explaining in a useable fashion how analytical procedures are applied and how to avoid judgment errors which are inherent in using the procedures.

5. Analytical procedures are not well-defined. This leads directly to a lack of consensus among auditors and a lack of consistency for each auditor when applying the procedures. This also leads indirectly to a communication problem between audit team members which conflicts which the effectiveness of the planning, supervision, and review of the engagement.

6. At this point, auditing lacks the important integrative concepts which would help to bring some focus and consensus to the thinking about analytical procedures. For example, the concepts of a "processing cycle" and of a "boundary" have had a key role in the development of improved methods for evaluating internal accounting controls.

7. Commonly used approaches for ratio analysis may not be as effective as desired.[2]

While some of the above difficulties are not easily solved and thus represent a persistent limitation on the usefulness of analytical proce-

---

[2] See particularly studies by Kinney, *Attention-Directing Analytical Review Using Ratios: A Case Study*, Auditing: J Prac & Theory, Spring 1987, at 59-73; Loebbecke & Steinbart, *An Investigation of the Use of Preliminary Analytical Review to Provide Substantive Audit Evidence*, Auditing: J Prac & Theory, Spring 1987, at 74-89; Blocher & Cooper, *A Study of Auditors' Analytical Review Performance*, Auditing: J Prac & Theory, Spring 1988. Together, these three studies utilized case analysis and simulation analysis to show that commonly used analytical procedures (such as the inventory turnover ratio, the receivables turnover ratio, and trend analysis of the accounts) based on annual data can be relatively ineffective at detecting either the presence or absence of financial statement errors.

dures others relate only to a lack of understanding of how to use analytical procedures properly.

This book is intended to address this latter problem. Further, our approach does not accept the belief that a single analytical procedure which is low-cost, which is generally applicable, and which gives the necessary narrow precision is currently beyond our grasp. Rather, we give the auditor a menu of easy-to-use procedures in a reference format.

§1.09 References

Blocher & Cooper, *A Study of Auditors' Analytical Review Performance*, Auditing: J Prac & Theory, Spring 1988.

Hylas & Ashton, *Audit Detection of Financial Statement Errors*, Account Rev, Oct 1982, at 751-65.

Kinney, *Attention-Directing Analytical Review Using Ratios: A Case Study*, Auditing: J Prac & Theory, Spring 1987, at 59-73.

Loebbecke & Steinbart, *An Investigation of the Use of Preliminary Analytical Review to Provide Substantive Audit Evidence*, Auditing: J Prac & Theory, Spring 1987, at 74-89.

Analytical Auditing and the Analytical Auditor

2

---

§2.01 Introduction

In this chapter we step back to look more broadly at what it is we mean by analytical procedures. In the first place, what do we mean by the term *analytical*, what does it mean to be *auditing analytically*, and, finally, can we identify or describe an *analytical auditor*? This chapter addresses each question directly, and invites you to participate through a series of short examples which we think are good illustrations of analytical thinking and analytical auditing. Following this, we cover a number of important topics related to the proper use of analytical procedures, including when to use them and when not to use them, when and how to rely on them, and how to document them, among other related issues.

§2.02   What Does Analytical Mean?

What is your first thought when you see the word *analytical?* Do you think we can apply this term to people such as you and me? If so, do you know of someone whom you would judge to be analytical? Do you think you are an analytical person? Is it good or bad to be so?

What does analytical mean to you? Does it mean a person who:

> Is very smart?
>
> Is generally regarded as an expert?
>
> Has high quantitative ability, as, for example, one who has high math scores?
>
> Is very experienced?
>
> Has a good memory?
>
> Has a certain psychological profile (as measured for example, by the Minnesota Multiphasic Personality Inventory (MMPI) instrument, or by the idea of left brain/right brain, and so on)?

You probably had a hard time deciding which of the above (or some other aspect of intelligence you have added yourself) is the single best way to describe what being analytical is all about. One could argue that each of these attributes is relevant. The problem with them is that they are far too general to be useful. So, we will now give a list of more specific attributes of analytical decision making which we have obtained from research in auditing and psychology. The following attributes are the ones that consistently show up as decision characteristics of expert decision makers in various fields, including accounting and auditing. The analytical decision maker is one who:

> Considers assumptions carefully and explicitly.
>
> Sees interrelationships and patterns more readily than others.
>
> Considers all the alternatives and does not jump to a conclusion, but waits until all the reasonably available information is in. You might say that the analytical person looks beyond the "first right answer" to see if the "second right answer" might be correct.
>
> Is a model builder. In order to see patterns and interrelationships, the analytical person informally (if not explicitly) builds a picture, a "story," structure, or mathematical model of the situation, as a basis for better understanding the decision problem.
>
> Is more creative. Analytical people are better able to come up with novel ideas than others.

Here are some examples to illustrate situations in which analytical thinking was not used. The first example concerns my six-year old son.

I once asked him what he did in school (first grade) that day. He answered that he did some trash, as usual. I was, of course, immediately concerned, and planned to speak to his teacher about it. I later found out that he called his work trash because I threw it out every day after I looked at it. The moral of the story is that there are many explanations for most things. I should have stopped to consider each of them. Also, it taught me not to throw away my son's homework.

A second example deals with a time I was paying the bills and got upset with my spouse about a rather large charge at the local clothing store. I later found out it was for an early Christmas present for me. Again, I had chosen what I thought was the only "right" answer, and had failed to think through the other possible alternative explanations.

You can further illustrate these points to yourself by studying Figure 2-1. Take a few minutes to look at it, and try to think analytically. Look to the next paragraph for the answer when you are ready.

Figure 2-1

What do these items have in common? *

Painted eggs
Fireworks
Champagne
Candy canes
Pranks
John Philip Sousa music
Shamrocks
Jack-o'-lanterns

*Source: R. von Oech, *A Whack on the Side of the Head*, 45 (Warner Books 1983) (reprinted with permission).

The items in Figure 2-1 are each identified with a particular holiday (Easter, July 4, and so on). This is the common element. Were you able to see this relatively quickly?

Try another exercise for more practice. Look now at Figure 2-2. What type of person do you see here? Most often a person seeing this for the first time has a difficult time seeing anything but a young woman. There are also those who have a tough time seeing anything but an old woman. The remarkable thing, which is true for virtually everyone, is that it is difficult to see both the old and the young woman. We have "blinders" on that keep us from perceiving broadly and completely. Of course, it is this ability to see the alternatives quickly which is desirable for analytical thinking and decision making.

An analytical search strategy is both open and systematic. It is open in that it considers multiple possible explanations, and it is systematic in that it considers each of these explanations in a complete and logical

Figure 2-2

manner. In some sense, the analytical searcher knows what he or she is looking for. He or she "predicts" what might be found and then goes looking for it. The idea of taking a predictive approach is central to our concept of analytical procedures, as we will explain in the following section.

§2.03 What are Analytical Procedures?

As defined earlier, analytical procedures are substantive audit procedures for deriving audit evidence through the analysis of interrelationships among financial and operating data. In their simplest form, analytical procedures very closely resemble financial statement analysis, that is, the understanding of financial ratios and other financial analyses which are often taught in accounting and finance courses, or, sometimes, taught as a separate course in business schools. For many auditors, analytical procedures are no more than the ratio analysis, the review of key indicators and other analyses used in financial statement analysis.

Our view of analytical procedures is somewhat broader than that of the basic financial statement analysis. And, in our view, the predictive approach as described in the above exercise is central to a proper understanding and use of analytical procedures. That is, with analytical procedures, the auditor performs the three following steps in sequence: prediction, comparison, and judgment.

Figure 2-3

**Steps in Performing
Analytical Procedures**

FIRST: Prediction
SECOND: Comparison
　　　　　Current Year Amount
　　　　　—Budget
　　　　　—Related Companies
THIRD: Judgment
　　　　　—Business Explanation
　　　　　—Change in Accounting
　　　　　Treatment
　　　　　—Error or Irregularity

The focus on prediction, which is for the most part absent in the various techniques of financial statement analysis, is what makes analytical procedures truly "analytical." As in the above exercise, the predictive approach shows that the auditor knows what he or she is looking for, and is, therefore, more likely to find it. Consider the converse, or non-predictive approach, as would be reflected, for example, in a simple "scanning" of the working trial balance, a procedure which is commonly viewed as an analytical procedure. The difficulty with the simple scanning approach is that it is very inefficient and ineffective. The user of this approach will notice only things which appear to have changed significantly. He or she may then follow up on many "significant" changes which could easily have been predicted from a brief review of the operating facts for the company that year.

Similarly, the scanning approach will not detect those items or accounts which have not changed significantly, whereas a brief review of the relevant operating facts would indicate the item *should have* changed significantly. Only by taking a predictive approach will an auditor be able to detect an item of this type—one which should have changed significantly, but did not. For example, consider the case in which a company, during a low production rate period, used manufacturing labor to assist in the construction of new plant facilities. In this case, it would be difficult to detect an error in which the labor costs were not properly capitalized, since the amount of manufacturing wages would probably look reasonable relative to prior periods. Only by knowing some of the key operating facts, such as the significant decline in production, and using this information to predict the proper manufacturing wage expense, would an error of this type be readily detected.

Prediction of the amount under review is thus the first and most important step in performing an analytical procedure. The prediction is based on the financial, operating, and other external data available to the auditor at the time of the prediction. It is particularly important that the auditor look to the operating data in making the prediction, as it is the comparison of operating facts and reported financial results that is at the heart of the effective use of analytical procedures. In effect, the analytical procedure is one which should provide evidence of whether the company's operating facts and financial results are consistent. In the manufacturing context, the analytical procedures should help answer the question: Do the financial statements reflect what actually happened in terms of units of production, units of manufacturing input, and so on? And, in a retail context, one could ask: Are the financial results consistent with the sales history of the company, the sales capacity, and the influential economic factors affecting this company during the year? Similar questions could be asked about the relationship between operations and financial results for companies in other industry groups. In summary, taking a *prediction first* approach is analytical in that it explicitly draws upon the expected interrelationships among the company's financial and operating data. As in the search for the star exercise above, it is looking for something in a purposeful, efficient way.

The second step in an analytical procedure is to compare the predicted amount to some benchmark value, which can be:

> The current year amount
>
> A budgeted amount
>
> The relevant amount for a related company, or an industry average figure
>
> Management's prediction, financial analysts' predictions, or the prediction of someone else

The crucial element of this second step is to properly choose the desired benchmark. If two or more benchmarks are available, it would be useful to compare the predicted value to each of them for further analytical information. Predictions which might compare well to some benchmarks but not to others could point up areas for further investigation. For example, if the company is experiencing a strong trend in profitability (up or down) which is in the opposite direction of the trend for the industry, or in the opposite direction of that predicted by financial analysts, the auditor should seek an appropriate explanation. The *Equity Funding* case is an example of a situation in which the company's profit performance was at strong variance to that being experienced in the industry as a whole. Sometimes it is necessary to question why the company is doing so well when none of its competitors is experiencing such success, and vice versa.

The final step in an analytical procedure is to make a judgment concerning audit scope, based upon the comparison made in that second step. We will discuss this judgment process in more detail in **§2.05.** The judgment process begins with a determination of a threshold for what constitutes a *significant difference* between the predicted and benchmark amounts. Then, in making the judgment about audit scope, the auditor will consider the three possible interpretations of a significant difference between the predicted amount and the chosen benchmark:

1. There is a reasonable business explanation for the difference, for example, inventory has increased dramatically because of expected future plant closings for renovation, and so on

2. There is a change in accounting treatment for the item, for example, from LIFO to FIFO

3. There is an error or irregularity in the account

While the first two interpretations may require little or no additional audit work, the third interpretation requires a careful consideration of the need for additional audit testing.

A Short Prediction Task

To reinforce the importance of prediction in the performance of an analytical procedure, we offer you the following brief exercise to test your analytical skills at predicting. Our task has to do with basic population data. Suppose we were to ask you for the number of households in the United States in 1980 (the most recent census figures)? You might consider this an unfair question and wonder how you would be able to guess at it. Now, suppose we tell you in addition that the 1980 population was 226,549,000. (Maybe you were ahead of us, and were already asking in your mind for such a "hint" as this.) Now, is it a fair question? Look to the following paragraph for the answer when you are ready.

You may already have come upon a solid analytical approach for answering this question. Try to estimate the number of persons in a household, on the average, and that divided into the total population figure will give you (at least approximately) the right answer. The correct answer is 80,390,000 households, or an average of about 2.8 persons per household. If you were close to being correct on the average number of persons per household, you could have come remarkably close to the correct number of households. The point of this exercise is to emphasize the importance of the predictive approach, and to illustrate how related amounts (or estimates thereof) can be combined to yield useful predictions. Now why don't you try to use this same type of approach to predict the number of marriages, divorces, or the births in the United States in 1980? These predictions will be a little bit harder, because the relationships involved are not as simple. Look to the footnote for the correct answers when you are ready.[1]

A Second Prediction Task

Now that you have a little practice at intuitive predicting, we'll try something a little more challenging. Take a look at the four series of numbers in Figure 2-4 and predict the next number in each of the four series. When you are ready for the answers, look to the next paragraph.

---

[1] 1980 Divorces - 1,189,000; 1980 live births - 3,612,000; 1980 marriages - 2,390,000.

Figure 2-4
Predict the Next Number in Each of the Following Four Series

Series "A"

399,785 367,234 448,590 483,302 402,107 326,936 471,995 _____

Series "B"

444,764 394,350 389,263 435,325 394,644 410,404 440,886 _____

Series "C"

361,936 400,776 518,609 592,314 530,047 648,636 645,901 _____

Series "D"

394,350 478,314 459,298 544,362 545,619 643,091 687,059 _____

The object of this exercise is to point out some of the common prediction biases which affect our ability to predict accurately. Based on a regression best fit, the answer is approximately 420,000 for series A and B and 720,000 for series C and D. Most people will guess too high on series A and B and too low on series C and D. The reason for this is the nature of the four series:

Series A: No trend, high variability from period to period
Series B: No trend, low variability
Series C: Approximately 8% trend, high variability
Series D: Approximately 8% trend, low variability

The results are as noted above because most people, accountants and others, tend to underestimate a trend when it is present, and will tend to see a trend when it is not there. Research studies have shown this fairly consistently.[2]

Also, the prediction errors tend to be greatest for series A and C, which have the highest variability, that is, it is harder to predict something that jumps around more.

These biases lead to prediction errors, and since the research suggests these biases are rather common, the auditor should be watchful for these biases and errors in his or her own intuitive (unaided) predictions.

---

[2] For the related research, see papers by E Blocher, An Investigation of Auditors' Prediction Achievement in An Analytical Review Task (Unpublished workingpaper, The University of North Carolina, Chapel Hill), and Biggs & Wild, An Investigation of Auditor Judgment in Analytical Review, LX Account Rev 607-33 (Oct 1985).

Improving Prediction Performance: The Modeling Approach

Perhaps the most effective way to improve prediction performance is to take a modeling approach. This means the auditor views the amount to be predicted as being related in direct or indirect ways to one or more other amounts. That is, we say there is a functional relationship between the amounts. For example, ordinarily sales commission expense would have a direct relationship to sales and perhaps an indirect relationship to the state of the local economy in which the sales take place.

A model, then, is a systematic structure of the way things interrelate. There are formal models (mathematical and statistical) and there are informal models (using words and simple symbols only). Here we discuss only the latter type of model. Later, in Chapter 11, we will discuss one type of formal model which has been useful in analytical procedures, the regression analysis model.

To discuss the modeling approach properly, we need first to define a few terms.

1. Predicted variable: this is the amount you are trying to predict, say, sales commissions

2. Predictor variable(s): this is the financial data, operating data, or other data which is related to the predicted variable and thus can be used to help predict. For example, sales can be used to predict sales commissions

3. Type of variable: the predicted and predictor variables might move in the same direction (say, sales commissions and sales) or in the opposite direction (say, temperature and heating oil demand)

4. Completeness: the more complete the model, the more precise it is, and, therefore, the more precise and accurate the prediction will be. For example, if we predict sales commissions with sales only, we will probably have a reasonably accurate prediction, since the two variables are strongly related. However, suppose that different products have different commission rates, so that sales mix is an important predictor as well as the total level of sales. Now, the best model is one which includes both sales and sales mix as predictors

5. The nature of the relationships among predictors: sometimes the relationship between the predicted and the predictor variable(s) is simple, and we call it an "additive model." For example, total expense is best predicted as the total of the individual expense

accounts. Other times, the nature of the relationship is more complex, and most often this means the relationship is multiplicative. For example, payroll expense is best predicted as the *product* of the predictor variables: hours, wage rates, and number of employees. The same would be true of interest income or expense. Still other times, the relationship between the predicted and the predictor variable(s) is unknown. In this latter case, it is difficult to employ an informal modeling approach, and a mathematical or statistical modeling approach (such as regression analysis) must be used.

6. Range of the predictor variable: the predictor variable may be either a *numerical variable,* such as a dollar value which can take on any of a potentially long list of possible values, or a *categorical variable,* which usually takes on only two different values (a categorical variable may have three or more values, but rarely more than four). For example, the type of location is a categorical variable. To illustrate, "type 1" is used to represent a store located in a shopping mall, while "type 2" is used to represent a store that is not in a shopping mall.

In developing a model, it is often appropriate to consider a number of predictors. The criterion for including a predictor variable in the model is the determination of whether the addition of the variable will make the prediction more precise and more accurate. The added accuracy has to be weighed against the cost of the additional modeling effort and potential additional data collection. Figure 2-5 shows nine modeling contexts and the potential predictor variables for each. This can be used as a guide to selecting the proper predictor variables for models such as this.

A final point of this section on the modeling approach is to note how the use of informal models as described above can be related to the more general idea of simply "getting the Big Picture" for a particular company. The modeling approach is one in which the auditor is effectively "tuned in" to the interrelationships among financial and operating data for the company, and that is being analytical.

§2.04   What is an Analytical Auditor?

Up to this point, we have looked at what we mean by *analytical,* and we have considered what is meant by *analytical procedures.* Now we consider what is meant by the *analytical auditor.*

As a start, the analytical auditor must be one who understands the use and benefit of analytical audit procedures, and who employs these

Figure 2-5

- Example Predictors for Common Projected Variables

Example Projected Variable	Financial Data	Operating Data	Economic Indicators	Other
1. Sales--account-time analysis	1. Cost of sales 2. Selling expense 3. Advertising expense	1. Units shipped 2. Number of salespeople	1. price level index 2. Index of local economic growth	1. Trend variable 2. Categorical variable for differences in marketing effort
2. Sales--multiple location analysis	1. Cost of sales 2. Selling expense	1. Size of store 2. Store type 3. Store hour open 4. " of salepeople	1. Price level index 2. Index of local economic growth	1. Categorical variable for difference in marketing effort
3. Inventory--multiple location analysis	1. Sales	1. Size of store 2. Store type	1. Price level index 2. Index of local economic growth	1. Categorical variable for difference in management policy
4. Accounts receivable--multiple location analysis	1. Sales 2. Categ. var. for differences to credit sales	1. Store type 2. Index of local in product mix	1. Interest rates 2. Index of local economic growth	1. Categorical variable for difference in credit/collection policy
5. Payroll expense--multiple location analysis	1. Total expenses 2. Sales or cost of goods manufactured	1. Hours worked 2. Categ. var. for difference in labor mix 3. Production level		1. Categorical variable to indicate sig. work stoppage or wage rate difference
6. Payroll expense--account-time analysis	1. Total expenses 2. Sales or cost of goods 3. Production level	1. Hours worked 2. Categ. var. for changes in labor mix		1. Trend Variable 2. Categorical variable for sig. work stoppage or pay rate change
7. Utilities expense--account-time analysis	1. Sales or cost of goods manufactured 2. Production level	1. Average daily temperature additions 2. Categ. var. for plant additions		1. Categorical variable for sig. change in utility rates 2. Trend variable
8. Bad debt expense--account-time analysis	1. Sales 2. Accounts receivable	1. Categ. var. for change in customer mix	1. Interest rates 2. Index of economic growth	1. Trend variable 2. Categorical variable for change in credit/collections policies
9. General expenses--office salaries and supplies, telephone, printing and duplicating, repairs, etc. multiple location analysis	1. Sales 2. Total expenses 3. Net fixed assets	1. Store type 2. Store size 3. Number of employee	1. Index of local price level	1. Age of store 2. Categorical variable for differences in office management-- automation, etc.

procedures regularly. But the analytical auditor should be much more than this. The analytical auditor is one who takes an analytical approach to the performance of the audit—the three-step approach: prediction, comparison, and judgment. The analytical auditor looks for the Big Picture. He or she tries to look behind the reported facts, to see if the financial results and operating facts are consistent. The analytical auditor is always applying logic, knowledge of the client, and a modeling approach to determine whether the observed facts and evidence really make sense.

The analytical auditor is aware of and takes steps to avoid the judgment biases that are common to most people. The biases and errors concerning the effect of trend and variability on prediction performance have already been noted. Here are some additional examples of judgment biases and errors which are commonly observed among auditors and others.

1. Incomplete judgment—the tendency to jump to conclusions. Do you spend more time justifying your decision than you do making the decision? When talking to people, are you listening to them or are you framing your own answer? Complete judgment means you wait until all reasonably available information is present, and then you consider all alternatives. Once you have determined the "first right answer," then you consider what might be the "second right answer," and determine if it might in fact be the correct one.

2. Difficulty aggregating information—true of everyone. We have a tendency to choose a very simple model when we know a more complex and complete one is more appropriate. Ultimately, the choice of models is a matter of cost/benefit—the increased precision of a more complete model versus the added cost of developing and using it.

3. Tendency to use a scanning approach—rather than to use the true analytical approach—prediction, comparison, and judgment. We often simply "go hunting" without a guide.

4. Excessive use of rounding—can cause analytical procedures which are inherently imprecise to be even more imprecise. Rounding should be done carefully and in a limited manner.

5. Objective is not clear—sometimes we don't know what the objective of the procedure is, and so very little is accomplished.

We close this section with some suggestions for helping the auditor to become more analytical. These are shown in Figure 2-6. Many of the suggestions deal simply with the careful use of time, and an intention to be critical of one's own decision processes.

Figure 2-6
The Analytical Approach
- Stop and Think
- Identify and Understand the Assumptions of Your Decision Making
- Self-review Your Work; Take Responsibility for Your Work
- State the Alternatives and Consider Them; Consider That "Second Right Answer"
- Manage Your Time; Take Time to Stop, Think, and Review

§2.05 Use of Analytical Procedures

This section deals with the *why* and *when* of analytical procedures. Four main points are made

1. Analytical procedures are often, but not always, a very cost-effective way to obtain audit evidence
2. It is possible to evaluate the precision of an analytical procedure. Some procedures are more precise than others, and this means the auditor can place greater reliance on them in reducing other tests
3. Investigation criteria—the thresholds for determining the significance of a difference—should be determined prior to employing the analytical procedure
4. The follow-up investigation and documentation of the results of employing the analytical procedure should be of the same high quality as for other substantive tests, and should include the auditor's conclusion

When Does the Auditor Use Analytical Procedures?

Analytical procedures are used at three different stages of the audit:

1. At the planning phase, in determining the proper audit scope, the allocation of audit effort, and the nature, extent, and timing of detail audit tests; this is often termed the "attention directing" role of analytical procedures. The careful use of analytical procedures in the planning phase can enhance audit efficiency, as audit effort is targeted properly to areas of highest risk. Also, the analytical procedures can improve the auditor's overall knowledge

of the client significantly, thereby enhancing the effectiveness and efficiency with which subsequent audit tests are performed.

The procedures employed at this phase would ordinarily include a review of the prior years' financial statements, the interim financial statements, the computation and review of selected financial ratios, obtaining from management key operating data in summary form, reading reports on the state of the client's industry and closest competition within the industry, and review of memos and working papers concerning audit problems and issues in the prior year's audit.

2. During the field work phase, as a substitute for other substantive tests; the objective of the analytical procedures at this phase is to improve the overall efficiency and effectiveness of the audit by replacing relatively more time-consuming detail test procedures with analytical procedures. Additionally, analytical procedures may be more effective than detail test procedures in certain applications, as, for example, in tests for unrecorded transactions. This role of analytical procedures is often termed the "test reducing" role, in that analytical procedures are used to replace detail test procedures. The nature of analytical procedures employed at the field work phase is described in Chapters 6, 7, and 12.

3. At the final review phase at the end of the audit engagement; here, again, analytical procedures are used as an attention-directing device, in a manner similar to the planning phase. The difference is that in the planning phase, the objective of using analytical procedures is to appropriately allocate audit effort, while at the final review, the objective is to provide one check of the reasonableness and fairness of the statements.

Prior to the Statements on Auditing Standards, *Analytical Procedures*, a common perception was that the primary benefit of analytical procedures was their efficiency—they replace relatively time-consuming detail test procedures. Also, analytical procedures were not required, and the auditor used judgment, based in part upon cost/benefit considerations, to determine when analytical procedures should be used. The guidance in the Statements on Auditing Standards, *Analytical Procedures* changes these perceptions and requirements in three significant ways. First, analytical procedures are now required at both the planning phase and at the final review phase of the audit. They are not required as substitutes for detail tests at the field work phase. The extent of use at the field work stage is a matter for auditor judgment, as before.

Second, significant emphasis is now placed on both the effectiveness and efficiency of analytical procedures. There is now a clear recognition that analytical procedures can be more effective (as well as more efficient) than other substantive tests in certain applications. These cases often involve the assertion of completeness in the financial statements, such as audit tests which deal with unrecorded transactions. In these cases, analytical procedures may be far more effective than detail test procedures. To reinforce the point on the relative effectiveness of analytical procedures, recent studies of actual audit engagements have shown analytical procedures to be among the most effective of all audit procedures. For example, Hylas and Ashton studied 152 actual audit engagements and found that approximately 27% of the errors detected in these audits were initially signaled by an analytical procedure, in contrast to approximately 47% initially signaled by detail test procedures.[3] This provides strong evidence for the relative effectiveness of analytical procedures.

Third, together with the requirement of analytical procedures for the planning and review phases, there is a recognition of the difference in reliance the auditor places on analytical procedures in the field work phase relative to the planning or review phase. At the field work phase, the auditor is placing some degree of reliance on the analytical procedures to reduce the amount of other substantive tests. This means the analytical procedures in this case must have reasonably good precision. (The attributes of analytical procedures which the auditor considers in relying on them are discussed in §2.07.) In contrast, when used for a planning or review purpose, analytical procedures do not require the same quality of precision, since the auditor in these cases is not relying on them to reduce the scope of other audit tests. Of course, the higher the precision of an analytical procedure, the more useful it will be in any of the phases of the audit, including planning and review. Generally, the more precise the procedure, the more useful. The important point is that there is a somewhat higher expectation of the quality and precision of an analytical procedure when used at the field work step, since at this phase of the audit, the auditor is relying on the procedure to reduce other tests.

The Test-reducing Purpose: Relative Effectiveness and Efficiency

When are analytical procedures relatively more efficient and effec-

---

[3] Hylas & Ashton, *Audit Detection of Financial Statement Errors,* LVII Account Rev 751-765 (Oct 1982).

tive than other substantive tests? This question is particularly important when analytical procedures are used at the field work stage, for two reasons. First, analytical procedures are not required at this stage of the audit, and they may be excluded if they are not relatively cost/beneficial. Second, since analytical procedures are used as substitutes for other detail tests in this phase, the auditor must choose the best "mix" of analytical and detail audit procedures based on an informed analysis of their relative effectiveness and efficiency.

Analytical procedures may be relatively more effective and efficient to:

1. Identify transactions not captured by the accounting system, such as unrecorded sales or liabilities, since most detail test procedures are limited to the available client financial data

2. Provide a basis to evaluate an entity's ability to continue as a going concern, since this judgment is based on a careful consideration of the profitability, liquidity, and solvency measures of the company which are derived principally from ratio analysis (Chapters 3, 5, and 12 deal with this issue)

3. Provide a basis to evaluate the adequacy of disclosure, since analytical procedures provide a "Big Picture" perspective from which this judgment is more easily made

4. Test completeness of assertions made in the financial statements, for the same reasons as noted above for transactions not captured by the accounting system

On the other hand, analytical procedures may be relatively ineffective and inefficient in:

1. Estimating likely error in a population, which is more properly done through sampling and projecting sample results

2. Testing balances when the underlying assumptions change, and the auditor does not have knowledge of the changes

3. Testing a balance when the amount is influenced by many complex factors

Also, analytical procedures may be relatively more effective and efficient for income statement accounts than for balance sheet accounts, as the income and expense accounts reflect the results of current operations, and, therefore, it is more practical to construct an analytical test based on relevant financial and operating data. In contrast, certain of the balance sheet accounts, cash, for example, have balances which are the result of a number of accounting transactions involving management discretion, different time periods, and a wide range of external influences. For example, the cash account is less susceptible to analytical tests for these reasons. To the extent that inventory and receivables are the results of current operations, these accounts are more easily tested analytically than other balance sheet accounts. Other accounts, because of the small number and large size of transactions in them, are more efficiently and effectively tested by detail test methods.

Management Fraud

Analytical procedures may be particularly effective in detecting cases of management fraud. In cases of fraud, the relationships between the financial results and the operating data for the company will most likely be somewhat distorted, unless the defrauder is able to "cover his tracks" by manipulating both the financial and operating data to show a pattern consistent with prior years. Several well-known fraud cases illustrate the point that the proper application of analytical procedures should have pointed to the fraud more readily than the detail test procedures which were employed in these cases. For example, in the *Equity Funding* case, commission expense was significantly out of line with the reported (fraudulent) commission income. Also, for *Saxon Industries* and *Crown Aluminum,* the reported amount of inventory exceeded the capacity of existing storage facilities. In another example, the *Bar Chris* and *Equity Funding* cases illustrate situations in which these firms were enjoying relative success, while other firms in the respective industries were having very hard times. And finally, in the *Penn Central* case, the maintenance expense account had gotten way out of line with total maintenance and repair costs, indicating improper capitalization of maintenance expense. In each of these cases, it appears that a careful analytical approach to the audit would have more readily detected the fraudulent condition than the typical detail test methods.[4]

§2.06   Types of Analytical Procedures

We have discussed the *when* and *why* of using analytical procedures, and now we will spend a little time with the question of *which* procedures to use. There are three broad categories of analytical procedures.

---

[4] The cited cases were discussed in a paper on analytical procedures presented by Mark P. Connelly to the National Commission on Fraudulent Financial Reporting at their Sept 23, 1986 meeting.

Figure 2-7

Analytical Procedures

- Trend Analysis
- Ratio Analysis
- Modeling
    - — Reasonableness Test
    - — Regression Analysis

Trend analysis is the most familiar type of analytical procedure for most auditors, and also the most widely used. Trend analysis is the comparison of an amount for the current year to the prior year, or to the trend of two or more prior years. A big concern with using trend analysis is that it looks only at the behavior of a single account, and fails to take directly into account what is happening in operations or in related accounts. For example, a relatively large change in an account balance in itself may not be a signal of a problem in the account, since operating facts might show that the large change is quite reasonable. Also, a relatively small change in an account balance does not in itself indicate that the account is error-free. Over all, the trend analysis approach is probably the least precise type of analytical procedure, since it fails to look at anything beyond what is happening to the account balance. Trend analysis is covered in Chapter 4.

Ratio analysis is also very familiar to auditors and widely used, though not to the extent that trend analysis is used. Ratio analysis is the calculation of the ratio of two amounts. Most often, it is the ratio of two dollar amounts which produces a number without a dimension. For example, receivables turnover, the current ratio, or inventory turnover are undimensioned numbers. Also, ratios are obtained from the relationship of a dollar amount and an item of operating data, as, for example, in the ratios *sales per square feet* or *average wage per employee.* The latter type of ratio has a dimension (usually, dollars per unit).

Ratios can be compared to a given benchmark (industry value, etc.) or to the prior year. When ratios are compared over time we will refer to this as ratio analysis as opposed to trend analysis, since the essential difference is the combining of information from two related amounts in ratio analysis, whereas trend analysis as defined above looks only at the behavior of a single amount. Ratio analysis is covered in Chapter 5.

The Modeling Approach is the "true" analytical approach in that, unlike trend and ratio analysis, it follows the three-step analytical process— prediction, comparison, and judgment. It is also the least familiar to auditors and the least used approach, in part because of the required expertise of some of the procedures. There are two principal types of modeling approaches in analytical procedures:

1. Reasonableness tests—the use of operating and other financial data to predict an amount
2. Regression analysis—the use of the statistical regression approach to predict an amount

Reasonableness testing is a relatively simple form of the modeling approach in which the auditor determines relevant predictor variables from other financial and operating data and uses these additional variables to predict the amount under examination. Common applications of this approach include a reasonableness test of interest expense, of depreciation expense, and of payroll expense. Many expense accounts are appropriately tested by means of the reasonableness test, since available operating data can be used to predict the amounts in these accounts with a relatively high degree of precision. In comparison to the trend analysis and ratio analysis approaches described above, the reasonableness test approach is preferred because it is explicitly analytical as noted above, and because it can be performed at a relatively detail level, that is, the depreciation expenses can be estimated at detail asset category levels, and payroll expense can be estimated at various employee levels, and the results of these detail estimates can be aggregated for an estimate of the total expense, which is more precise than could be obtained by a simple ratio or trend analysis. Reasonableness tests are covered in Chapter 6.

Regression analysis is a modeling approach, as is the reasonableness test method, and it has the same important benefits. In addition, the regression approach provides an improved level of precision over the reasonableness test, in that the prediction is derived from an optimizing statistical model. The use of regression analysis in analytical procedures is presented in Chapter 11.

Figure 2-8

Procedure	Ease of Use	Precision of Results
Trend Analysis		
Ratio Analysis		
Reasonableness Test		
Regression Analysis		

In choosing among these procedures, the auditor should keep in mind two key factors: ease of use (including cost of use and required expertise) and the degree of precision derived from the procedures. There are relatively clear trade-offs between these two factors, as illustrated in Figure 2-8. Note that ease of use is greatest for trend analysis, since it is the most familiar and widely used of the procedures, and regression analysis is the least widely used and also the least easy to use in terms of data gathering, calculations, and required expertise. Ratio analysis falls between these extremes and closer to trend analysis, while reasonableness testing falls next to regression analysis.

In contrast, the precision of the prediction derived from the procedure is greatest for regression analysis, and least for trend analysis, for reasons described above. And, again, the precision of the prediction from a ratio analysis or reasonableness test falls somewhere in between. Why is this so? The best argument follows the amount of information contained in each procedure. Trend analysis has information only on one account, while ratio analysis uses information from two or more accounts, thereby extracting the common element and obtaining a more meaningful number. For example, we compute inventory turnover, the ratio of sales to inventory, to recognize that these two accounts move together, and the ratio of the two should stay about the same. This gives a relatively strong basis for comparing the ratio to prior years or to related companies. While we expect the ratio should stay about the same from year to year, we cannot say that about the inventory level itself. Thus, the ratio analysis approach is more informative and more precise than the trend analysis approach.

Going a step further, the reasonableness test approach is more precise and informative than the ratio analysis approach, because it uses two or more predictors, many of which are operating data. So now we have more predictors, and we are able to see whether the operating facts and financial report of these facts are consistent. The reasonableness test is a strong test because it ties in operating facts, whereas ratio and trend analysis typically do not.

Finally, regression analysis provides the greatest precision, because it, like reasonableness testing, provides the integration of operating and financial data, and, in addition, it provides the statistical precision we do not get with a pencil and paper calculation.

The auditor chooses the type of procedure to employ based upon cost/benefit considerations, giving recognition to the fact that some procedures provide greater precision than other procedures. The auditor considers the direct cost of employing the procedure versus the expected future benefit of a more precise procedure, which includes reduced future costs, as the auditor can rely more heavily on the more precise procedures and, therefore, can reduce other tests to a greater extent.

Since we have now opened the topic of reliance on analytical procedures, and how precision relates to this, it is a good time to consider the question of reliance more broadly, and see what other factors should be considered.

§2.07 Factors to Consider in Relying on Analytical Procedures

The purpose of this section is to identify and discuss the various factors which should influence the auditor's decision regarding the degree of reliance to be placed on an analytical procedure. Basically, we are looking at the question of how useful and informative a given procedure is, and what criteria are used in making that judgment. This judgment is necessary for the auditor to be able to select the proper procedure for a given situation and to determine the amount of reduction of other tests, if any, which derives from using the analytical procedure.

Recall that the issue of reliance on analytical procedures is critical principally in the field work application rather than in the planning or review application. As noted above, since the field work use of analytical procedures implies a potential reduction of other audit tests, then the auditor must understand why he or she is relying on the procedure. However, the consideration of reliance factors can be useful in the planning or review phases as well, as this consideration provides a basis for an evaluation of the informativeness and usefulness of the procedures.

There are six factors we will consider in determining the reliance to be placed on analytical procedures.

The Account Detail Level

When applied at a relatively aggregate level, as in total inventory, for example, an analytical procedure will be inherently less precise than when applied at a more detail level, for example, inventory at different locations or inventory in various categories. The reason is that the aggregate figure represents a combination of effects and results of a relatively wide variety of operating and financial relationships and events. The more detail the level at which the procedure is applied, the less complex are these relationships and events, and, therefore, the more likely that the analytical procedure will provide a precise and accurate prediction.

In accordance with the above, the auditor will place more reliance on an analytical procedure which is performed at a relatively detail account level, because of the enhanced precision of the procedure at this detail level.

Figure 2-9
Relying on Analytical Procedures
- Account Detail Level
- Risk
- Materiality
- Objective
- Findings
- Precision

Risk

When the inherent and/or control risk associated with an account or item is relatively high, the auditor will typically not reduce other substantive tests, but instead will use the analytical procedure to provide better focus (the attention-directing purpose) and perhaps to extend the detail test work to respond to the higher risk. The analytical procedure provides an effective means in this case of identifying where audit effort should be applied and extended if necessary.

Materiality

If the dollar amount of an account is relatively high, the auditor will typically use the analytical procedure not to reduce other tests, but to play an attention-directing role, because of the high materiality. In this sense, the effect of high materiality is the same as that of high risk described above. Sometimes the term *exposure* is used to refer to the auditor's joint evaluation of risk and materiality. In summary, when exposure is high, the auditor will tend to use analytical procedures for an attention-directing purpose, and, when exposure is low, the auditor will use analytical procedures for a test-reducing purpose, subject to a consideration of the remaining three factors to be discussed below. If exposure is quite low, the auditor may choose to perform *only* analytical procedures.

Objective of the Analytical Procedure

As explained above, an analytical procedure can have either an attention-directing or a test-reducing objective. The need for reliance is critical under the test-reducing objective only, since here the analytical procedure is taking the place of other audit tests.

Findings

If the findings of the application of the analytical procedure show an unusual or unexpected relationship or amount, then further investigation is needed, leading possibly to additional audit tests. In contrast, if nothing unusual or unexpected is found, the analytical procedure can be relied upon, and no further work may be necessary.

Precision

There are two types of precision which affect the reliance on analytical procedures:

1. The precision of the analytical procedure itself, which was discussed in §2.05. In that section, the point was made that, generally, trend analysis applications have the least precision, and regression analysis has the highest precision. The rank of procedures from most preferred to least preferred in terms of precision is as follows: regression analysis, the reasonableness test, ratio analysis, and trend analysis.

2. The inherent precision of the account or item under examination, that is, how likely is it that a well-designed analytical procedure will be able to develop a precise prediction for this account? The inherent precision of the account is influenced by data reliability and the stability of the account or item over time.
    Data reliability involves the question of whether the data used in the analytical procedure is financial data which is subject to the company's internal accounting controls, which are judged effective. If so, this would enhance the chance of obtaining a precise prediction by way of analytical review. In contrast, if the auditor judges that the financial and/or operating data used in the analytical procedure are not reliable, then the inherent precision of the account and the analytical procedure are limited.
    The stability of the account or item over time is a consideration because some accounts are subject to fluctuating market forces or to management discretion, and are inherently hard to predict as a result. Some examples include the cash account, research and development expenditures, and repair and maintenance expenditures.

Evaluating the Findings of Analytical Procedures

The main objectives here are to point out how the evaluation of the analytical procedure differs depending on whether it is used for a planning, review, or detail test reducing purpose, and to explain the requirements of Statements on Auditing Standards No 47, *Audit Risk and Materiality in Conducting an Audit* in regard to evaluating the findings of analytical procedures.

In the first place, the auditor's evaluation of the analytical procedure at either the planning or review phase has an attention directing purpose, so that the evaluation process is simple and direct. In this case, the analytical procedure is used to identify areas of relatively high risk potential, so that audit effort can be most effectively allocated (or reallocated) to these areas. Since the analytical procedure does not replace other substantive tests, the auditor's evaluation and documentation does not require consideration of the reliance points described above, though such consideration is always advisable. Similarly, used in this way, the analytical procedure is not subject to the SAS 47 requirement regarding the auditor's projection of potential error magnitudes based upon the substantive procedure.[5] That is, the auditor is not in this case relying on the analytical procedure to estimate or project the magnitude of error for an account balance or class of transactions.

In contrast, when an analytical procedure is used for a test reducing purpose, then SAS 47 requires that the procedure should enable the auditor to project error magnitudes. If the analytical procedure does not provide the information needed to project the likely error in the account balance or class of transactions, then the auditor should employ other procedures to do so. Note that the auditor's projection of likely error using a statistical sampling technique is direct and straight forward, as these sampling methods are designed to facilitate the projection of likely error magnitudes. Similarly, regression analysis, which is also a statistical technique, provides a direct and simple way of projecting likely error magnitudes. In contrast, other analytical procedures, such as trends and ratio analysis, do not usually lead to direct measures of likely error. On the other hand, a modeling approach using reasonableness test methods can lead to reasonable error projections. Generally, the ability of an analytical procedure to provide projections of likely error magnitudes is related directly to the degree of precision for the procedure. Recall, as we pointed out earlier, that trend analysis is the least precise procedure, whereas ratio analysis, reasonableness testing, and regression analysis are relatively more precise.

---

[5] SAS No 47, para 27, 28.

§2.08   Choosing an Investigation Rule

In this section, we suppose that the auditor has decided to rely on a given analytical procedure, based upon an evaluation of the six factors described above. It is necessary now to determine an investigation rule which is used in the second step of the analytical process—the comparison of the predicted amount to some benchmark—and which specifies what amount of difference is significant. The investigation rule can be based upon an amount difference, a percentage difference, or some combination of both. An important point here is that the guidance set forth in Statements on Auditing Standards, *Analytical Procedures* requires that this investigation rule be specified before the analytical procedure is performed, that is, the predetermination of the investigation criteria is an integral part of the design of the analytical procedure.

The best way to go about determining an investigation rule is to consider again the six factors described above, that is, the considerations which argue for strong reliance on the analytical procedure would also point to using a smaller, more narrow investigation rule. For example, a 10% threshold might be appropriate when there is low or modest reliance on the analytical procedure, while a 5% threshold would be more appropriate in the case of strong reliance. The argument here is that greater reliance should be associated with an investigation rule that "triggers" smaller differences than would be the case for a weaker reliance level. The reason for the argument is based on conservatism, that is, when the auditor has strong reliance, and plans to make relatively significant reductions in other audit tests, then the investigation rule should be conservative, or such that relatively smaller differences are triggered.

A related question is whether the investigation rule should be in terms of dollar amounts, a percentage amount, or some combination. As a matter of practice, auditors use investigation rules which are derived directly from an assessment of dollar materiality. That is, the auditor determines a planning materiality level per No 47, in dollar terms, and the investigation rule is based on this figure. One study (Blocher, 1984) has shown that auditors typically rely on a dollar amount threshold only in performing analytical review, and another study (Kinney, 1979) has shown that the dollar amount rule outperformed the percentage-based rule in identifying material audit adjustments in a sample of 1441 accounts.[6] The reason for the relative

---

[6] E. Blocher, An Investigation of Auditors' Thresholds When Applying the Attention Directing Role of Analytical Review Procedures, Proceedings of the

ineffectiveness of the percentage-based rule is that it is prone to incorrectly signal a need for investigation when the account under examination has a small dollar amount, and is prone to incorrectly fail to signal a need for investigation for the large dollar amount accounts.

In summary, previous research suggests that the investigation rule be based on a dollar amount threshold, and the auditor should consider adjusting it based upon the degree of reliance taken on the analytical procedure—greater reliance means a lower threshold which would trigger more investigations.

When reviewing the trend of financial ratios, or in comparing these ratios to those of a related company or industry figures, a percentage-based investigation rule is needed. A common percentage in use is 10%, although thresholds of 5% to 15% or 20% are also in use.

Chapter 4 includes further discussion of the choice of an investigation rule as it relates to trend analysis, and Chapter 11 will cover the use of statistically determined investigation rules within the context of regression analysis.

§2.09   Documentation of Analytical Procedures

A proper documentation of the analytical procedure is a crucial part of the overall effectiveness of the procedure. This is particularly true when the analytical procedure is used at the field work stage for the test-reducing purpose. In this case, the quality of documentation is necessary to justify the reliance on the procedure which allows the reduction in other substantive tests.

The standards and methods for proper documentation of an analytical procedure do not differ from those standards and methods which apply for any other type of audit evidence. In general, the documentation must satisfy the broad objectives of completeness, accuracy, and clarity of communication. Additionally, the documentation should describe the work done, by whom it was done, and when it was done. And the working papers should include the auditor's conclusion based upon the use of the analytical procedure.

Some unique aspects of documentation which relate to analytical procedures are as follows:

American Accounting Association Regional Meeting in Baltimore (Apr 1984); and Kinney, *The Predictive Power of Limited Information in Preliminary Analytical Review: An Empirical Study*, Account Res, Supplement 1979, at 140-65.

1. Any assumptions which are relied upon in developing the prediction used in the analytical procedure should be given

2. If the auditor is relying on management statements, this should be so indicated, and procedures undertaken to corroborate these statements, if any, should also be indicated

3. The manner in which the ratios were computed should be described, so that others will know what specific interpretation of the ratio was used (for example, is the inventory turnover ratio based on the average inventory balance or the year-end balance?)

4. Any significant accounting practices which might affect the proper interpretation of the computed ratios, or other analyses, should be described

5. If there was an attempt to take a modeling approach to the analytical procedure, then what predictor variables were considered, and what assumptions were made concerning the relationships among these variables

Specific suggestions for the documentation of analytical procedures in certain accounts are given in Chapter 7, and the issues related to the documentation of a regression analysis application are covered in Chapter 11.

§2.10 Summary

The broad objective of this chapter has been to introduce some ideas regarding what makes an analytical auditor, and to present some considerations for using analytical procedures most effectively. In the next chapter, we look at the analytical procedures that can be used to analyze inherent risk, which is the risk that the account or item has a material error or irregularity in it, prior to the applications of internal accounting controls or audit tests.

§2.11 References

Biggs & Wild, *An Investigation of Auditor Judgment in Analytical Review,* LX Account Rev 607-33 (Oct 1985).

E. Blocher, An Investigation of Auditors' Prediction Achievement in an Analytical Review Task (Apr 1985) (Workingpaper, The University of North Carolina, Chapel Hill).

E. Blocher, An Investigation of Auditors' Thresholds When Applying the Attention-Directing Role of Analytical Review Procedures, Proceedings of the American Accounting Association Regional Meeting in Baltimore (Apr 1984).

Hylas & Ashton, *Audit Detection of Financial Statement Errors,* LVII Account Rev 751-65 (Oct 1982).

Kinney, *The Predictive Power of Limited Information in Preliminary Analytical Review: An Empirical Study,* Account Res, Supp 1979, at 148-65.

Analyzing and Evaluating Inherent Risk

3

§3.01 Introduction

The analysis and evaluation of inherent risk are central to the auditor's development of the scope and plan for an audit engagement. *Inherent risk* is the chance that a material error will occur. Management reduces this risk by employing a sound system of internal accounting controls, and the auditor reduces the risk further by evaluation and testing of the controls and through tests of account balances. The combined risk that the error will occur and not be detected either by the management control system or by the auditor is the audit risk.

Inherent risk is commonly analyzed and evaluated during the planning phase. The analysis has two aspects: (1) the use of selected non-quantitative procedures, which we have described as "risk analysis," and (2) the use of well-known analytical procedures, such as trend analysis and ratio analysis. The elements of risk analysis include assessments of management integrity, an evaluation of the entity's going-concern status, and the like. Trend analysis at this point would focus on the trend in earnings, in selected liquidity measures, and in cash flow. The ratio analysis would be employed to evaluate the entity's liquidity and profitability position relative to other firms in the industry and to the firm's position in prior years. Since there is ordinarily some variability among firms regarding liquidity and profitability, the analysis of these ratios over time is often given priority over the intra-industry comparison.

Upon completion of these analyses, the auditor combines the results to obtain an overall evaluation of inherent risk. This evaluation is the basis for choosing the required scope of audit field work—with greater scope for higher risk. Figure 3-1 summarizes this discussion to show how the audit risk, the phases of the audit engagement, and the two analytical review methods are related in the analysis of inherent risk.

§3.02 Three Aspects of Inherent Risk

Inherent risk has three readily distinguishable aspects which can be analyzed separately. Each aspect is a type of risk, and each is influenced by different factors in the entity's environment. The existence of any of these three risks signals a potential motivation or opportunity on the part of the entity's management or personnel to introduce a material misstatement to the accounting records, whether intentionally or not. And the greater the risk for any of the three, the greater is inherent risk. The common terms for these three risks are operating risk, financial risk, and market risk. Note that each of the three aspects of inherent risk differs in nature from the concept of "business risk," a term which has been used to refer to the risk of loss or injury to the CPA's professional practice, apart from whether or not an undetected material misstatement is present. However, many of the factors which influence inherent risk are among the factors which also influence business risk, so there is some commonality for these risk concepts. We feel the best way to achieve an understanding of the role of analytical procedures in auditing is to consider the three aspects of inherent risk defined above.

Operating risk is associated with the chance that earnings or liquidity position or both will fluctuate unacceptably for reasons related to the nature of the entity's business environment—seasonal or otherwise high-risk products and services, severe competition, general economic conditions affecting the industry, and the like. Many of these factors are not easily controlled by management in the short term; rather, they are managed through diversification and careful long-range planning.

Figure 3-1 Inherent risk, audit risk, analytical review, and the phases of the audit engagement.

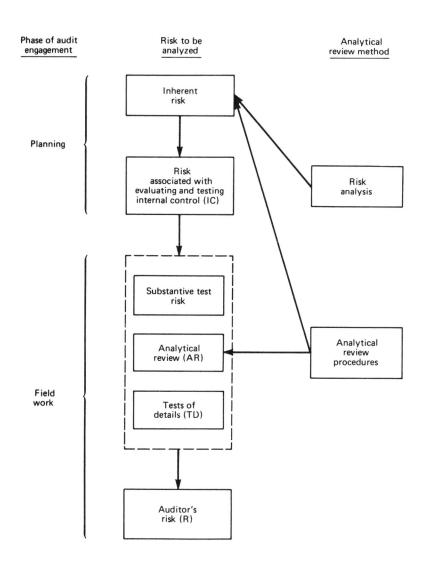

To the extent that these factors threaten the going-concern position of the entity, by eroding earnings or liquidity, risk of material misstatement or the financial statements increases, as does inherent risk.

Financial risk is associated with the entity's ability to meet debt commitments. Because of a desire to achieve a high degree of financial leverage, or because of an inability to obtain acceptable equity financing, a firm might accumulate a high proportion of debt to equity and high interest charges relative to earnings from operations. The amount of debt relative to equity, the portion of debt which is short-term, the nature of credit relationships generally, and the strength of cash flows from operations will together determine whether the firm has significant financial risk. Again, to the extent the financial position of the entity is threatened, financial risk and inherent risk are increased.

Market risk is associated with the variability of the entity's stock prices. Significant fluctuations in an entity's stock price relative to the overall stock market would reflect investors' perceptions that the future returns from the stock are relatively risky. In contrast, stocks with relatively stable prices are associated with relatively lower market risk. Market risk can also be affected by significant changes in stock ownership, by significant inside trading and proxy fights, and the like. Some would say that a high price-to-earnings ratio is an additional sign of relatively high market risk.

Market risk influences inherent risk because it is important in shareholder perceptions of the entity, and thereby can influence management behavior. However, it is not usually associated with the assessment of the going-concern position of the entity, as are operating and financial risk. For this reason it has a lesser impact on inherent risk, and is of lesser concern to the auditor.

On reflection, it is clear that these three risks are not strictly independent. That is, both operating risk and financial risk should influence investors' risk perceptions and thereby influence market risk. Thus, the three risks do not simply "add together" to determine inherent risk, and the auditor's overall evaluation of risk must take this into account. Also, the overall evaluation of inherent risk must include the auditor's assessment of management integrity, apart from the analysis of the three risk factors. That is, a high positive assessment of management integrity could alleviate an otherwise high evaluation of inherent risk. The assessment of management integrity could include an evaluation of ethical standards, the degree of conservatism in income-recognition policy and other accounting matters, and management's openness with internal and external auditors.

The three risk factors and the evaluation of management integrity are combined to obtain the initial assessment of inherent risk. This risk is reduced by management through two levels of controls: (1) controls which simultaneously reduce the risk of misstatement for many or all financial statement accounts, items, or elements and (2) controls which reduce risk for a single account, item, or element. We refer to the former as "organizational controls" and to the latter as "internal accounting controls."[1] We make this distinction to facilitate our discussion of inherent risk. Because of the diversity of types of internal accounting controls for different purposes, we do not attempt to develop in this book an approach for evaluating these controls, and for assessing the extent to which they reduce inherent risk. On the other hand, the review of organizational controls involves a relatively well-defined set of key variables which are common for most organizations. For this reason, the chapter deals with organizational controls only. Additionally, our interest is in analytical procedures, and the review of organizational controls is often considered an analytical procedure, since it is directed to developing an understanding of the entity's business and organization. The relationships among the factors influencing inherent risk are summarized in Figure 3-2.

The following four sections of the chapter will develop a framework for the auditor's use in analyzing operating risk, financial risk, management integrity, and organizational controls, each of which has a major influence on inherent risk. Market risk is not included because it has a relatively less important influence on inherent risk. The chapter concludes with a discussion of methods for aggregating the auditor's evaluation of the three risk types, the organizational controls, and the integrity of management, in order to obtain an overall evaluation of inherent risk.

§3.03   Analyzing Operating Risk

The objective of the auditor's analysis of operating risk is to identify and evaluate those operational characteristics of the auditee's business and organization which contribute to inherent risk. These characteristics may contribute to risk in either of two ways: (1) by motivating the auditee's management or employees to cause and not disclose a misstatement of the accounts or (2) by making it more difficult for management to prevent or detect any misstatement, apart from the effectiveness of the control system employed. The characteristics in

---

[1] Others have used the terms "general" or "administrative" to refer to the type of control we call "organizational" control. We use this term to avoid improper interpretation and to emphasize that this control is "organizational" in scope.

the first case are often those related to the financial performance and position of the auditee, or to the financial need of an employee, while the characteristics in the second case are most often related to the complexity of the organization—diversity and turnover of product lines, decentralization, geographic dispersion, and so on.

The auditor should look for these characteristics in at least five areas, each of which could provide the motivation, opportunity, or both for misstatement:

1. Sales
2. Production and distribution
3. Organizational structure
4. Legal or regulatory matters
5. Other restrictive commitments

A useful approach for this analysis is to use a checklist in the format of the questionnaire that is often used in audit planning, review, and internal control evaluation. The questionnaire would list the relevant characteristics in each of the five areas, and the auditor would indicate the presence and severity of the risk for each characteristic.

Sales

In analyzing the auditee's sales, the auditor is looking primarily for indications of substantial current or near-term deterioration in sales performance. First, the auditor should consider the characteristics of the industry environment in which the auditee firm operates. Does the firm operate in a local, regional, or international market? How do recent and pending governmental regulations and trade agreements, if any, affect the industry? The auditor can find answers to these and related questions through:

1. Advice from industry specialists within the auditor's firm
2. Trade association publications
3. Consultants and economists specializing in the industry
4. Banks and insurance agents who specialize in servicing the industry

From such sources the auditor can determine if there is a significant potential change in sales trend for the industry.

A second level of questions would address the auditee firm's effectiveness in developing a marketing plan. Does the firm analyze its market share in sufficient detail to detect significant regional and local

Figure 3-2. Inherent risk and related factors.

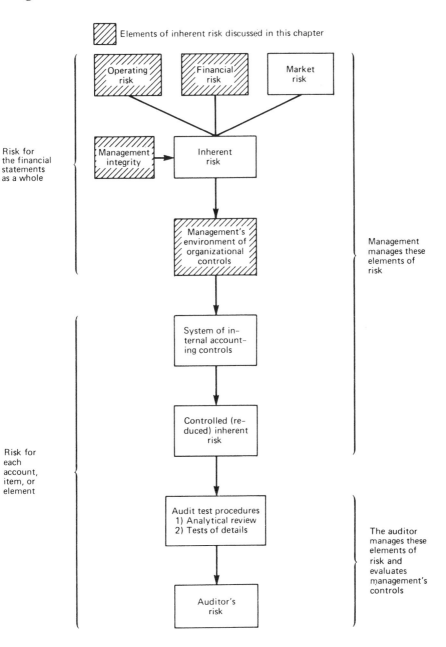

shifts? Are sales forecasts made, and, if so, how are they obtained? How accurate are they? Has management developed an appropriate plan for product diversification? Is there a competitive strategy; that is, has the firm chosen to compete on price, quality, service, or some other factor, and how well has this positioned it in the market? The study of these questions will help the auditor assess the strength of sales performance in coming months.

On a third level, the auditor looks for certain external factors affecting the competitive environment of the firm. Has the firm experienced recent unfavorable publicity because of questions of product quality, safety, or other matters? Has there recently been a substantial shift in marketing strategy in response to competition? In particular, has advertising become more defensive in nature? Do the firm's competitors appear to be gaining a technological edge in product quality, performance, or cost?

On the positive side, the auditor should also take notice of a substantial growth in sales. If the growth outstrips management's span of control, the chance of unintentional misstatement is increased until the accounting system is upgraded. Also, a significant growth in sales that is not explained directly by industry and market conditions should be investigated, especially if management compensation is strongly influenced by sales.

Production and Distribution

As with sales, the auditor studies the firm's production and distribution system in order to detect whether any factors have, or could have in the near term, a damaging effect on the firm's operations. For example, is the availability of necessary materials at reasonable prices assured? Is a change in plant location planned? What is the status of labor relations, and when does the current contract expire? Will a new production process be implemented in the near term? If so, what will be the extent of disruption? Analysis of these questions will enable the auditor to assess the potential for risk associated with production. Similar questions should be asked for the firm's distribution system.

Organizational Structure

Because of their complexity, some organizational structures are inherently more risky than others. For example, firms which grow by internal expansion of facilities, personnel, and management are inherently less risky than those which grow by merger and acquisition. The latter face difficulties of maintaining standards of quality control and maintaining continuity of management policy; they lack goal congruity and consistency in accounting and internal reporting systems, and have related problems. Also, expansion of any type exposes the firm to risks when the new markets are not well understood by management, particularly new international markets. The auditor must assess the risk associated with the expansion by evaluating management's ability to control the incremental activity of expansion, giving special attention to the method of expansion and geographical dispersion.

A second and related issue for organizational structure is the extent of product diversification. As above, the greater the diversification, the greater will be the demand on management's ability to control operations. Does management have the necessary expertise to control and evaluate operations in each line of business? Has management developed a uniform accounting and internal reporting system for all segments? The latter is particularly important because of management's line-of-business reporting responsibility to the Securities and Exchange Commission (SEC), and because of the auditor's related auditing requirements.

The above issues are aggravated by the autonomy of segment managers, which is typically associated with the extensively diversified firm. Also, the accounting for discontinued operations, associated with these firms, contributes to inherent risk because of the unique nature of the accounting transactions.

Legal or Regulatory Matters

In some cases, legal or regulatory matters may represent a significant risk to operations. License, patent, or copyright litigation is one example. Also, pending legislation at the state or federal level could have a substantial impact on competition in the firm's industry. Or, the firm itself may be involved in important litigation with a customer or competitor, the results of which could seriously impact its ability to compete in the industry. The auditor investigates these matters by consulting industry experts, the firm's legal counsel, and the SEC to determine the nature and extent of any pending litigation, regulation, or inquiries. Also, the auditor should stay informed of the progress of relevant state or federal legislation through reference to trade or industry publications and consultants.

Other Restrictive Commitments

Various trade and labor commitments can affect the firm's risk of operations by reducing its flexibility in dealing with competitive pressures within the industry. The auditor should check especially for restrictive commitments in the following areas: (1) lease contracts for facilities or major equipment, (2) labor contracts, and (3) marketing agreements. The best source of this information is usually inquiry of the firm's management, labor union management, and industry consultants.

Evaluating Operating Risk

The above discussion provides a basis for the auditor to uncover several possible indicators of operating risk. To come up with an aggregate

Publication	Publisher
Dun's	Dun's Review 666 Fifth Avenue New York, NY 10019
Sources of Composite Financial Data and Annual Statement Studies	Robert Morris Associates Philadelphia National Bank Building Philadelphia, PA 19107
Quarterly Financial Report for Manufacturing Corporations *Survey of Current Business*	Superintendent of Documents U.S. Government Printing Office Washington, DC 20402
Almanac of Business and Industrial Financial Ratios, by Leo Troy	Prentice-Hall, Inc. Englewood Cliffs, NJ 07632
Compustat Industry Data	Standard and Poor's Compustat Services, Inc. 7400 South Alton Ct. Englewood, CO 80112

evaluation, the auditor should consider whether any of the indicators observed as "negative" (i.e., risky), taken individually, or together with other negative indicators, is so substantial as to require adjustment to the scope of planned audit tests. Additionally, the auditor should prepare an analysis of selected financial ratios for the most current 3 years, as a basis for assessing the trend in these indicators of operating risk. The four ratios most commonly used in evaluating profitability are:

1. Earnings per share
2. Return on assets

3. Return on equity

4. Net profit to sales

A significant deterioration in any of these ratios over the 3-year period would signal increased operating risk. Also, the firm's ratios should be compared with industry statistics relevant for its line of business. Again, significant differences are a signal of operating risk. However, since industry averages are often inappropriate benchmarks for a given firm, because of unique factors affecting the firm, the auditor should place principal reliance on the trend in the ratios and use the industry comparison secondarily.[2] A condensed list of sources of industry statistics is given in the table shown above. For a longer list of sources that offer industry statistics, see Exhibit 2 at the end of Chapter 5. Also, note the industry data in Appendix G.

§3.04   Analyzing Financial Risk

The auditor analyzes the financial structure of the firm to assess the inherent risk associated with its ability to meet debt commitments, primarily short-term debt commitments but also ones in the long term. Hereafter, we will refer to the ability to meet short-term debt as "liquidity" and the ability to meet long-term obligations as "leverage."

The auditor should consider two methods of analysis for financial risk. One method looks at the going-concern question; that is, do we predict the firm will become bankrupt within our planning period? This can be viewed as the extreme or ultimate measure of financial risk and, as such, will be appropriate only in rate instances. The second

---

[2] The auditor should consider whether industry information is reasonably comparable to the information being evaluated. For example, broad industry information may not be comparable to that of an entity that produces and sells specialized products. The lack of comparability may be a very general problem, since research has shown that the financial ratios of firms differ more within broad industry categories than industry average ratios differ among industries, see J. Trapnell, An Empirical Study of the Descriptive Nature of Financial Ratios Relative to Industry Operating Characteristics (1977) (unpublished Ph.D. dissertation, University of Georgia, Athens). Also, the ratios will not be comparable to industry data if the ratios are computed differently among firms within an industry. The lack of uniformity in this context is shown by Gibson, *How Industry Perceives Financial Ratios,* Mgmt Account, Apr 1982). Finally, there is the uncertainty concerning how aggregate industry figures are obtained. Are unusual observations ("outliers") deleted or transformed, and so on?

method of analysis looks at the less severe conditions, which we call "financial distress." This means the firm is in a position which could lead to failure, if not corrected. We assume the means for correction are at hand, however. Each form of analysis is addressed in the following discussion.

Predicting Bankruptcy

The auditor can use either a "key indicator" or a "fundamental analysis" approach to predict bankruptcy. The indictor-based approach is useful for determining whether the firm is at or very near the bankruptcy state, whereas fundamental analysis can provide a meaningful prediction for 2 to 5 years into the future. The fundamental analysis approach is generally less accurate but is more useful since it can predict for a longer period.

Some of the key indicators used by auditors are listed below. The appearance of one or more of these indicators would signal the potential of imminent bankruptcy.

1. Current liabilities greater than current assets

2. Default in loan payment

3. Renegotiation of lease or other debt

4. Projected cash flow from operations which is less than the amount of maturing debt

5. Total liabilities greater than total assets

The auditor should carefully consider the substance behind these indicators. That is, the company may attempt to renegotiate a lease for a good business purpose such as to obtain a lower-cost lease. In this case the event does not indicate pending bankruptcy.

The fundamental analysis approach is based primarily upon the analysis of financial ratios.[3] The two prominent studies of ratios used for bankruptcy prediction are those by Beaver and Altman.[4]

---

[3] The proper use of ratio analysis is covered in more depth in textbooks on financial statement analysis. One of the better books of this type is L. Bernstein, Financial Statement Analysis (1978).

[4] Altman, *Financial Ratios, Discriminant Analysis, and the Prediction of Corporate Bankruptcy,* J Fin, Sept 1968, at 589-609, and Beaver, *Financial Ratios as Predictors of Failure,* J Account Res, Supp 1966, at 71-110.

Table 3-1 Ratios Used to Predict Bankruptcy*

Type of Ratio	Beaver's Ratio	Altman's Ratios
Operating ratios	Return on total assets (2)	Return on total assets (1) Sales to total assets (2)
Leverage ratios	Total debt to total assets (3) Cash flow to total debt (1)†	Market value of equity to total debt (3)
Liquidity ratios	Working capital to total assets (4) Current ratio (5)	Working capital to total assets (5)
Other predictors	(Quick assets—current liabilities) to operating expenses (excluding depreciation)	Retained earnings to total assets (4)

* Adapted from studies by Beaver (1966) and Altman (1968). The ranking of the relative importance of each ratio in each of the studies is indicated in parentheses after each ratio.

†Beaver found this ratio to be the most useful in discriminating between bankrupt and nonbankrupt firms. However, Altman was unable to use a cash flow variable since he did not have depreciation figures and could not compute cash flow, so we cannot know whether this variable would have performed equally well for Altman.

The ratios found to be most predictive of bankruptcy are shown in Table 3-1. These studies applied a statistical methodology to determine the most predictive set of ratios, so the ratios can be viewed as the key variables in identifying potential bankruptcy cases. Note that the results of the two studies are consistent. Operating and leverage ratios are most important, while liquidity ratios are not good predictors. Auditors should consider the significance of this evidence, in part because the conventional wisdom says that the current ratio, the turnover ratios (receivables, inventory), and other liquidity measures are key variables in analyzing financial risk. These results suggest that other ratios are better predictors.

Our classification of ratios—operating, leverage, and liquidity ratios—are among the most commonly used in financial statement analysis textbooks. Table 3-2 shows the 24 most important ratios and how they are computed.

A useful aspect of the Altman model is that it permits the computation of a numerical score of the bankruptcy potential of a firm. It is called the Altman Z-score and is computed as follows:

$$Z\text{-score} = 3.3(\text{return on total assets})$$
$$+ 0.99(\text{sales to total assets})$$

+ 0.6(market value of equity to total debt)
+ 1.2(working capital to total assets)
+ 1.4(retained earnings to total assets)

Table 3-2 Important Ratios and How They Are Computed

Operating ratios

1. Return on sales	$\dfrac{\text{Profits before tax and extraordinary items}}{\text{Net Sales}}$	

2. Return on total assets

$$\frac{\text{Profits before tax and extraordinary items} + \text{interest}}{\text{Average total assets}}$$

3. Return on tangible net worth

$$\frac{\text{Profits before tax and extraordinary items}}{\text{Average tangible net worth}^a}$$

4. Percentage profit change

$$\frac{\begin{array}{cc}\text{Current year's profit} & \text{last year's profit} \\ \text{before tax and} \quad - & \text{before tax and} \\ \text{extraordinary items} & \text{extraordinary items}\end{array}}{\text{Last year's profit before tax and extraordinary items}}$$

5. Percentage sales change

$$\frac{\text{Current year's sales - last year's sales}}{\text{Last year's sales}}$$

6. Sales to total assets

$$\frac{\text{Sales}}{\text{Total assets}}$$

7. Coefficient of variation of net income

$$\frac{\text{Standard deviation of net income}}{\text{Average net income}}$$

Leverage ratios

8. Long-term debt to capitalization

$$\frac{\text{Long-term debt}^b}{\text{Long-term debt} + \text{stockholders' equity}}$$

9. Net tangible assets to long-term debt

$$\frac{\text{Net tangible assets}^c}{\text{Long-term debt}}$$

10. Working capital to long-term debt

$$\frac{\text{Working capital}^d}{\text{Long-term debt}}$$

11. Fixed-charge coverage

$$\frac{\text{Aftertax net income} + \text{interest} + \text{rentals}}{\text{Interest} + \text{rentals}}$$

12. Cash flow to total debt

$$\frac{\text{Cash flow}^e}{\text{Total debt}}$$

13. Total debt to total assets

$$\frac{\text{Total debt}}{\text{Total assets}}$$

14. Market value of equity to book value of debt

$$\frac{\text{Market value of equity}}{\text{Total debt}}$$

15. Interest coverage

$$\frac{\text{Aftertax net income} + \text{interest}}{\text{Interest}}$$

Table 3-2 Important Ratios and How They Are Computed
(Continued)

16. Long-term debt to equity	$\dfrac{\text{Long-term debt}}{\text{Stockholders' equity}}$
17. Tangible net worth to total debt	$\dfrac{\text{Average tangible net worth}}{\text{Total debt}}$

Liquidity ratios

18. Working capital to total assets	$\dfrac{\text{Working capital}}{\text{Total assets}}$
19. Current ratio	$\dfrac{\text{Current assets}}{\text{Current liabilities}}$
20. Quick (acid-test) ratio	$\dfrac{\text{Cash + marketable securities + net current receivables,}}{\text{Current liabilities}}$
21. Liquidity ratio	$\dfrac{\text{Cash + marketable securities + net current receivables}}{\text{Short-term debt/}}$
22. Working capital turnover	$\dfrac{\text{Sales}}{\text{Average working capital}}$
23. Accounts receivable turnover	$\dfrac{\text{Net sales}}{\text{Average receivables}}$
24. Inventory turnover	$\dfrac{\text{Cost of goods sold}}{\text{Average inventory}}$

---

*Tangible net worth = stockholders' equity − intangible assets.

*bLong-term debt = long-term liabilities − (deferred taxes + minority interest).

*Net tangible assets = total assets − (intangible assets + current liabilities + deferred taxes + minority interest).

*dWorking capital = current assets − current liabilities.

*Cash flow = aftertax net income − extraordinary items + depreciation and amoritization + deferred taxes.

*Short-term debt = notes due within 1 year + current position of long-term debt.

SOURCE: Adapted from M. Backer and M. Gosman, *Financial Reporting and Business Liquidity* 119-20 (National Association of Accountants 1978) (reprinted with permission).

The lower the Z-score, the greater the chance of bankruptcy. If the Z-score is less than 1.81, there is a strong potential for bankruptcy within the next 2 years, whereas a Z-score above 2.99 indicates little chance for bankruptcy. In the range between 1.81 and 2.99 there is an increased chance for incorrectly classifying a firm. In computing and interpreting the Z-score, the auditor should be aware that:

1. The Z-score is not accurate beyond 2 years into the future; it is most accurate for a 1-year prediction, least accurate for a 2-year prediction.[5]

2. Three of the ratios—return on total assets, working capital to total assets, and retained earnings to total assets—can be negative, and therefore will be subtracted in obtaining the Z-score.

3. The ratios are entered into the model as decimals rather than absolute percentage terms (for example, sales/assets = 2.0, rather than 200.0 percent).

4. The model assumes that the underlying financial data are reliable.

5. The model applies to manufacturing firms only.

Altman has also created what is called the "four variable" version of the model, which deletes the requirement for the market value of equity from the model. This later model (Altman, 1983) is appropriate for both public and private firms, and for service companies as well as manufacturers. The model is described more fully in Altman and in Kyd.[6] The "grey area" for this model is 1.1 to 2.6 (in contrast to 1.81 to 2.99 for the "five variable" model), and consists of the following:

$$
\begin{aligned}
\text{Z-score} = \ & 6.56 \ (\text{working capital to total assets}) \\
& + 3.26 \ (\text{retained earnings to total assets}) \\
& + 6.72 \ (\text{earnings before interest and taxes to total assets}) \\
& + 1.05 \ (\text{net worth to total liabilities})
\end{aligned}
$$

Predicting Financial Distress

Financial distress is a less severe condition than bankruptcy, but it contributes to inherent risk by creating an environment in which management is motivated to misstate certain financial data. This condition exists when the financing options are limited owing to a downgrading of bonds, deterioration of cash flows, and so on.

---

[5] Altman & McGough, *Evaluation of a Company as a Going Concern*, J Accountancy, Dec 1974, at 50-57. Altman and McGough performed an experiment in which the results show that the Altman model significantly outperformed unaided auditors in predicting bankruptcy.

[6] Altman, *Corporate Financial Distress* (Wiley 1983), and Kyd, *How are You Doing?*, INC, Feb 1987, at 121-23.

As for bankruptcy, the auditor's analysis of financial distress can take either a key indicator or a fundamental analysis approach. One or more of the key indicators in the following list would signal current or near-term financial distress. The first indicator, cash flow, is especially important.

1. Unfavorable trend in cash flows.

2. A low current bond or trade credit rating.

3. A recent downgrade of bond rating or trade credit rating.

4. A bank classification of a loan as substandard.

5. Imminent violation of loan agreement restrictions on cash flow, liquidity, etc.

6. Disruption in relationships with bankers and brokers.

7. Past-due payables or extensions of payment terms. (Note, however, that because suppliers are the least likely to complain about delay of payment, this indicator may not be easily obtained).

By the nature of the markets for these instruments, a downgrading of bonds should be an earlier signal of financial distress than the downgrading of trade credit. Similarly, the downgrading of trade credit should occur before a loan is rated substandard by a bank.

Fundamental analysis has been used to study the relationship between the downgrading of bonds and financial ratios. The results of these studies are shown in Table 3-3. Notice again that operating and leverage ratios are consistently the best predictors of bond downgrading. Liquidity ratios are rarely used. The auditor should then interpret a significant unfavorable trend in any of these ratios as a signal of potential financial distress. The ratios used specifically in financial institutions, utilities, and the transportation industry are shown in Table 3-4.

Table 3-3 Ratios Used to Predict the Downgrading of Bond Ratings

Type of Ratio	Researchers				
	Horrigan	Pogue and Soldofsky	West	Pinches and Mingo	Backer and Gosman
Operating ratios	Return on sales Return on tangible net worth	Return on total assets Coefficient of variation of net income	Coefficient of variation of net income	Return on total assets	Return on sales Return on total assets
Leverage ratios	Tangible net worth to total debt	Long-term debt to capitalization Interest coverage	Long-term debt to equity	Long-term debt to total assets Interest coverage	Long-term debt to capitalization Cash flow to long-term debt
Liquidity ratios	Working capital turnover	None	None	None	None
Other predictors	Subordination status of bonds Total assets	Total assets	Market value of bonds	Subordination status of bonds Years of consecutive dividends Issue size	None

SOURCES: Adapted from Horrigan, The Determination of Long-Term Credit Standing with Financial Ratios, Empirical Research in Accounting: Selected Studies, J Account Res, 1966; Pogue & Soldofsky, What's in a Bond Rating, J Fin & Quantitative Analysis, June 1969; West, An Alternative Approach to Predicting Corporate Bond Ratings, J Account Res, Spring 1970; Pinches & Mingo, A Multivariate Analysis of Industrial Bond Ratings, J Fin, Mar 1973; M. Backer & M. Gosman, Financial Reporting and Business Liquidity (National Association of Accountants 1978) (Reprinted with permission of National Association of Accountants).

Another source for predicting the downgrading of bonds is Standard and Poor's *Credit Watch*, which lists firms whose rating status is currently under review.

Table 3-4 Financial Distress Ratios for Certain Industries

	Financial Institutions	Utilities	Transportation
Operating ratios	Operating expenses to operating revenue	Operating revenue to operating property Operating expense to operating revenue	Operating expense to operating revenue
Leverage ratios	Capital funds to total assets Total deposits to capital	Funded debt to operating property	Long-term debt to operating property
Liquidity ratios	Loans to total deposits	Interest coverage	

Suggestions for Using Fundamental Analysis

The proper use of fundamental analysis based on financial ratios will be facilitated by attention to the following matters:[7]

1.   Ratios should be compared primarily over time, and secondarily to industry benchmarks, for the reasons already cited. Often, there are reasons why a firm's ratios differ from industry standards which do not reflect financial risk.

With further analysis, however, the auditor can obtain useful additional information by comparing the trend of the firm's ratios with the trend of the ratios for the industry group. *Industrial Compustat*, a service of Standard and Poor's Inc., provides aggregate industry data at useful levels of detail to facilitate an analysis of this type. To obtain the analysis in a timely and cost-effective manner, the auditor would maintain the *Compustat* data on computer and develop computer programs to compute and present the desired ratios in an easy-to-use fashion. For example, with proper programming, the auditor-user would be able to input the

---

[7] Baruch Lev and Shyam Sunder present a more thorough discussion of the methodological issues in the use of financial ratios in *Methodological Issues in the Use of Financial Ratios*, J Account & Econ, 1979, at 189-210.

firm's data code number into the computer and receive promptly a preselected analysis of the firm's ratios and the related industry ratios. The ratios could be presented in a columnar format to facilitate the auditor's comparison of firm versus industry trends.

The data available on *Compustat* include approximately 10,500 companies and 215 industry categories for both quarterly (40 periods) or annual (20 years) data. The data are continually updated; thus, they are timely enough for most audit planning purposes.

2.   There is no evidence that any predetermined level for any ratio can be used as a benchmark for assessing financial risk. As above, differences in ratios may not reflect differences in risk. For example, whether the firm is a very new and growing entity and whether it is closely held are among the factors which should affect the interpretation of the ratio. Also, Backer and Gosman found no evidence of the use of ratio benchmarks in their study of bond and trade credit rating decisions.[8] Thus, the use of a single ratio benchmark does not appear to be appropriate. As noted above, it is the *trend* of the ratio relative to the industry *trend* which is useful, rather than the comparison of ratios for 1 year only.

3.   Largay and Stickney in a study of the W. T. Grant Company failure show that ratio analyses did not provide an early signal of bankruptcy, whereas a cash flow analysis would have given an early signal.[9] The ratios did not deteriorate significantly up to the date of failure, while the amount of cash flow generated internally declined steeply for 5 to 6 years before the bankruptcy. This illustrates that ratio analysis by itself is an incomplete fundamental analysis and should be extended by analysis of cash flows, the firm's competitive environment, critical macroeconomic factors for the firm, and so on.

4.   The problem of comparability is enlarged by the variety of accounting conventions which may change within the firm over time. The auditor should watch for consistent treatment of the following:

   a.   Leases—included in long-term debt?
   b.   Minority interest—an element of total capital?
   c.   Subordinated debt—debt or equity?

---

[8] M. Backer & M. Gosman, Financial Reporting and Business Liquidity (National Association of Accountants 1978).

[9] Largay & Stickney, *Cash Flows, Ratio Analysis and the W. T. Grant Company Bankruptcy*, Fin Analysts J, July-Aug 1980, at 51-54.

    d.   Pension reserves—debt or equity?

    e.   Deferred taxes—debt, capital, or asset offset?

    f.   Intangibles—deleted?

5.   The use of ratios is subject to the same limitations as are the underlying financial data, for example:

    a.   Lack of data in constant dollars or current dollars

    b.   Effect of accounting estimates

    c.   Effect of management discretion on inventory levels and unit costs

    d.   Effect of officers' salaries in closely held companies

6.   The untrained auditor may assume incorrectly that, since ratios are numbers, there is a simple linear significance to them; that is, a current ratio of 1.5 is perceived to be "twice as bad" as a ratio of 3.0, when in fact it is many times worse. This is particularly important, for example, when a given ratio approaches the limit set in a loan covenant. If the firm must maintain a current ratio of 2.0 or better, then a deterioration from 2.0 to 1.9 is much more severe than a deterioration from 3.0 to 2.85, though both represent a 5 per cent decline.

7.   Fundamental analysis may be available through purchase from industry specialists or financial analysts. These analyses are produced on a timely basis for stock exchange - listed companies and other large companies.

Evaluating Financial Risk

The auditor's evaluation of financial risk is based upon a review of the distress indicators and of the trend of the financial ratios noted above. If one or more of the indicators or ratios indicate a deterioration of financial position and higher risk, the auditor will consider the significance for audit scope and coverage. In making this evaluation, the auditor should recognize the special importance of evaluating the amount, timing, and certainty of expected cash inflows and outflows. This is one of the most critical factors in financial risk.

It may help the auditor, in making this evaluation, to consider how flexible the firm is in financial matters. How quickly could the firm reduce costs if necessary? Could certain maintenance costs or research and development costs be delayed without serious long-run effects? And, how flexible is the firm's dividend policy? Could dividends be reduced without serious effects? Also, does the firm have a favorable relationship with creditors which would make ready access to short-term loans possible? And finally, could the firm dispose of certain assets for a substantial return, without significantly affecting its ability to operate? Consideration of these questions could provide additional insight into the evaluation of financial risk.

§3.05 Analyzing Management Integrity

Apart from the motivation for misstatement contributed by operating or financial risk, the auditor should evaluate management's propensity to respond with openness and integrity. Does management show a tendency for earnings maximization and manipulation by various means? The auditor will ordinarily have a sense of this from working with the firm's management in planning the audit. Indicators of potential problems include:

1. A decision to change to deferral of items ordinarily expensed
2. A tendency to make transactions or accruals of questionable economic substance
3. Economic trouble in other matters on the part of managers or owners
4. A change in discount policy for unsalable inventory
5. A change in credit policy for uncollectible accounts receivable

Indicators such as the above should heighten the auditor's awareness of the potential effect on inherent risk. For a more complete study of management fraud, see Albrecht et al. and Elliott and Willingham.[10]

§3.06 Analyzing Organizational Controls

Organizational controls are the administrative policies and procedures designed to reduce the chance for a material misstatement in any aspect of the financial statements.[11]

Firm Characteristics Which Make Control Difficult

Before reviewing the elements of a sound system of organizational controls, we consider the characteristics of the firm which generally make controls difficult to implement effectively:[12]

---

[10] W. Albrecht, M. Romney, D. Cherrington, I. Payne, and A. Roe, How to Detect and Prevent Business Fraud (Prentice Hall 1982).

[11] R. Mautz, W. Kell, M. Maher, A. Merten, R. Reilly, D. Siverance, & B. White, Internal Control in U.S. Corporations: The State of the Art, (Financial Executives Research Foundation 1980).

[12] See id 41.

1. Decentralization of any of the functions—production, marketing, finance, controllership

2. Geographic dispersion

3. Rapid growth of the firm or the industry

4. Recent growth by acquisition rather than internal expansion

5. Unsupportive attitude of top management toward the proper control environment

6. Diversity of the firm's operations—products, manufacturing processes

7. High turnover of personnel, especially management personnel

8. Rapid and continual changes in products or services

9. Reporting by operating personnel to nonfinancial managers and a feeling that there is no need to comply with control policies and procedures

10. Resistance by highly technical or creative personnel to control issues

11. Limited staff or budget to support proper control systems

12. Foreign operations

13. Governmental regulations

14. Certain management compensation schemes, based on reported financial results, which create an incentive for biased or incorrect reporting

15. Lack of competence, or a carelessness among record-keeping personnel

16. Large degree of judgment required in accounting records, such as is involved in accounting estimates and in accruals

The auditor can view these characteristics as elements of inherent risk to the extent that management has not developed a responsive set of control policies and procedures.

Elements of a Sound System of Organizational Controls

The policies and administrative procedures which can make up a sound control system are summarized in the following outline. Exhibit 1 at the end of the chapter presents a more extensive checklist for the review of organizational controls.

1. Policies
   a. Top management commitment to the control system
   b. Establishment of clear areas of responsibility
   c. Company code of ethics
   d. Independence of financial and operating functions
   e. Assurance that financial personnel are knowledgeable of company operations
   f. Maintenance of special oversight for:
      (1) Transactions with related parties
      (2) Management-incentive compensation schemes
   g. Assurance that financial personnel have good, up-to-date accounting backgrounds
   h. Thorough contingency planning and management succession planning
   i. Insurance for facilities; bonding and life insurance for key management personnel
   j. Strong and effective internal audit function
   k. Environment of proper stewardship of the firm's property
2. Procedures
   a. Current job descriptions and organization charts
   b. Work plans, schedules, and manuals
   c. Hiring procedures designed to encourage responsible job performance and to detect the potential for unethical behavior
   d. Continuing education programs for employees
   e. Formal promotion and retention procedures
   f. Reconciliation of articulating records
   g. Centralized accounting systems for payroll and other functions
   h. Measurement systems on all functions
   i. Effective operational and financial audit by the internal audit function
   j. Effective audit committee
   k. Restricted access to vulnerable assets and data

Indicators of a Poor Control Environment

Apart from performing an analysis of the characteristics of the firm and its policies and procedures noted above, the auditor can review the firm's audit history and accounting system for indications of a poor control environment.

Audit History. The results of past audits have a strong impact on the auditor's evaluation of risk. A pattern of audit problems would be associated with greater risk. The problems might be difficulty in dealing with management in obtaining necessary records or in resolving questions about required adjustments to the accounts. If management has been informed of control weaknesses in prior audits and has not responded, one could question its commitment to the control system. *Weakness in the Accounting System.* Poor performance of the accounting system can also show lack of commitment to an effective control system. This could be indicated by:

1. Unusually frequent cutoff and accrual errors
2. Lateness or incompleteness of regularly required accounting reports
3. Significant differences between physical inventory and accounting records
4. Inability of accounting personnel to reconcile articulating records or to prepare special analyses (receivables aging, etc.) for the auditor

§3.07 The Overall Evaluation of Inherent Risk

It is difficult to aggregate all the elements of inherent risk to arrive at an overall evaluation. The four elements we have analyzed are not strictly independent:

1. Operating risk
2. Financial risk
3. Management integrity
4. Organizational control environment

Anything which influences one of the risk elements may thereby also influence one or more of the others. With this in mind, the auditor should consider both the significance of each risk element and the influences between them in making the overall evaluation.

The auditor should not have the view that, since each contributes directly to inherent risk, low risk on one element compensates for high risk on another. On the other hand, the effect on inherent risk is increased substantially when two or more of the elements are rated as high risk. Then the auditor is advised to consider the effect of inherent risk explicitly in audit planning and scope decisions.

§3.08   References

Abdel-Khalik, & El-Sheshai, *Information Choice and Utilization in an Experiment on Default Prediction*, J of Account Research, Autumn 1980, at 325-42.

W. Albrecht, M. Romney, D. Cherrington, I. Payne, & A. Roe, *How to Detect and Prevent Business Fraud*, (Prentice-Hall 1982).

E. Altman, *Corporate Financial Distress* (Wiley 1983).

Altman, *Financial Ratios, Discriminant Analaysis, and the Prediction of Corporate Bankruptcy*, J Fin, Sept 1968, at 589-609.

Altman, *Predicting Railroad Bankruptcies in America*, Bell J Econ & Mgmt Sci, Spring 1973, pp. 184-211.

Altman & McGough, *Evaluation of a Company as a Going Concern*, J Account, Dec 1974, at 50-57.

M. Backer & M. Gosman, *Financial Reporting and Business Liquidity* (National Association of Accountants 1978).

Beaver, *Financial Ratios as Predictors of Failure*, J Account Res Supplemental, 1966, at 71-110.

L. Bernstein, *Financial Statement Analysis* (Irwin rev ed 1978).

R. Elliott & J. Willingham, *Management Fraud: Detection and Deterrence* (Petrocelli 1980).

Gibson, *How Industry Perceives Financial Ratios*, Mgmt Account, Apr 1982, at 13-19.

Horrigan, *The Determination of Long-Term Credit Standing with Financial Ratios, Empirical Research in Accounting: Selected Studies*, J of Account Res, 1966, at 44-62.

Kennedy, *A Behavioral Study of the Usefulness of Four Financial Ratios*, J Account Res, Spring 1975, at 97-116.

Kyd, *How are You Doing?* Inc (Feb 1987) at 121-23.

Largay & Stickney, *Cash Flows, Ratio Analysis and the W. T. Grant Company Bankruptcy*, Fin Analysts J, July-Aug 1980, at 51-54.

Lev & Sunders, *Metholodgical Issues in the Use of Financial Ratios*, J Account & Econ, 1979, at 189-210.

R. Mautz, W. Kell, M. Maher, A. Merten, R. Reilly, D. Siverance, and B. White, *Internal Control in U.S. Corporations: The State of the Art* (Financial Executives Research Foundation 1980).

Pinches & Mingo, *A Multivariate Analysis of Industrial Bond Ratings*, J Fin, March 1973, at 1-18.

Pogue & Soldofsky, *What's in a Bond Rating*, J Fin & Quantitative Analaysis, June 1969, at 201-28.

U.S. Small Business Administration, *Ratios Analysis for Small Business* (Management Series, No. 20, 4th ed 1977).

J. Trapnell, An Empirical Study of the Descriptive Nature of Financial Ratios Relative to Industry Operating Characteristics (1977) (unpublished Ph.D. dissertation, University of Georgia, Athens).

West, *An Alternative Approach to Predicting Corporate Bond Ratings*, J Account Res, Spring 1970, at 118-25.

Exhibit 1
Checklist for Review of Organizational Controls

A. Personnel policies and relationships

  1. Attitude and involvement of top management
  2. Hiring and promotion of qualified personnel with integrity and high personal ethical standards
  3. Formal training program for financial and accounting personnel
  4. Separation of duties (e.g., between initiation and approval of transactions)
  5. Close, frequent contact with all financial personnel through conferences and personal visits
  6. Good control climate starting at the top
  7. Promotion of people to financial management from the internal auditing department
  8. Strong dotted-line relationship from CFO of profit centers to corporate CFO
  9. Placement of corporate-trained financial people into profit centers
  10. Confidentiality of divisional controller's communication to corporate controller
  11. Good corporate attitude relating to priorities of soundness, integrity, and proper business ethics in all activities.
  12. For accountants, an independent role related to controls which transcends responsibility to immediate supervisor
  13. One section (or person) controlling or reconciling the activities of another section (or person) within the accounting area
  14. No career auditors in corporate internal audit function
  15. Training and development programs for all levels of financial and operating management
  16. Key senior management with day-to-day operational responsibilities.
  17. Direct reporting to the corporate office by all division controllers
  18. Training for plant controllers and their staffs

B. Special departments, committees, and organizations

EXHIBIT 1 75

1. Systems and methods department
2. Claims and adjusters
3. Short and damage freight clerks
4. Separate review committee for special situations
5. Governmental agencies—Defense Contract Audit Agency (DCAA), Air Force (Contractor Management Evaluation Program), SEC, EPA, DOE, NRC
6. Specialized committee system to review, monitor, and control various functions and activities
7. Committee that monitors compliance with internal control procedures and reports periodically to senior management and the audit committee
8. Insurance policy owners examining committee
9. Ethics committee of board of directors

C. Formal systems and procedures

1. Corporate data processing software developed at parent company and processed by a separate subsidiary
2. Standard cost systems with variance analysis
3. Formal systems of delegating the authority to commit funds
4. Computer cost system
5. Expense budgets
6. Purchasing controls
7. Physical controls
8. Order entry system (provides a control over finished goods inventory and entire production and distribution system)
9. Control of vendor file
10. Capital budgeting system
11. Safety and compliance features
12. Personnel system (controls on hiring and rates of pay)
13. Detailed financial plan
14. Central book account for disbursements originating at offices throughout the United States
15. Strategic and operating management planning and control techniques
16. Plant physical security
17. Strategic, intermediate, and 1-year planning activities

D. Instructions, guides, and manuals
1. Policy statement on internal accounting control
2. Internal accounting control manual
3. Statement of levels of authority to approve types of transactions
4. Operating guidelines for controllers
5. Financial systems and procedures manual
6. Personal actions manual
7. General or corporate policy manual
8. Accounting manual
9. System and procedure documentation
10. Uniform accountancy manual
11. Corporate finance manual
12. Supervisory manual
13. Corporate guidelines for identification of, disposition of, and accounting for obsolete inventory
14. Corporate policy related to the opening and closing of bank accounts, and the approval and control of checks
15. Corporate policy relative to the review and approval of contracts

E. Formal and informal practices bearing on internal control
1. Close examination of personnel reports
2. Close examination of budget variances
3. Close examination of travel and entertainment costs
4. Management involvement in installation, development, maintenance, and use of computer equipment and software
5. Daily inventory of raw material and finished products
6. Quality assurance program in controller's department
7. Two signatures on purchase orders
8. Blind count of merchandise received
9. Dollar limits on cash purchases by stores
10. Corporate controller approval of bad debt write-off by division
11. Recording of out-of-pattern inventory differences and expense accounts of officers and key employees
12. Subjection of operating unit controllers to salary administration by the corporate controller

EXHIBIT 1 77

13. Detailed budgets
14. Observation of internal control of subsidiaries by service people from corporate office
15. Review of results of all internal and external audits by and with subsidiary presidents
16. Joint custody over negotiable securities
17. Presentation of defalcation reports to audit committee
18. Task force teams for special control problems
19. Extensive comparisons with other companies in same business of the same size
20. Management committees
21. Minutes of meetings
22. Audits by outside contractors
23. Close coordination between external and internal auditors
24. Uniform chart of accounts
25. Audits by manufacturer and financial institutions
26. Active audit committee (10 meetings a year)
27. Involvement of EDP auditors with financial and manufacturing system design

F. Regular reviews and representations
   1. Corporate controller's review of operating companies' balance sheets
   2. Internal control questionnaire
   3. Questionable payments review
   4. Representation letters from operating management and controllers
   5. Circularization of findings of internal and external auditors
   6. Annual certification of adequacy of internal control system
   7. Monthly corporate review of divisional operations
   8. Irregular check of all payroll authorizations
   9. Examination of certain employee's and all officers' income tax returns
   10. Monthly management checklist signed by division general managers and controllers
   11. Annual formal report of audit committee (quality, hours, achievements, etc.)

12. Certification concerning misuse of corporate bonds
13. Annual self-audit by each unit manager
14. Certification concerning conflict of interest
15. Quarterly audits by the external auditor
16. Weekly meetings of top management to discuss changes in financial outlook
17. Quarterly and annual detailed analyses of accounts and significant judgment items
18. Quarterly evaluation of investments

G. Special one-time actions
1. Three-year program to review, reevaluate, and document internal accounting controls
2. Analysis and documentation of existing controls

H. Recurring reports
1. Monthly labor ratio reports by operating unit
2. Operating cost reports
3. Activity reports
4. Weekly profit and loss statements
5. Weekly labor utilization reports
6. Weekly raw material yield reports
7. Daily general ledger
8. Internal accounting newsletter

I. Financial policies
1. Specific levels of approval for capital expenditures
2. Bonding of all employees and agents
3. Manual signature of any two of several designated officers for any check over $10,000

Source: Adapted from Mautz et al, *Internal Control in U.S. Corporations: The State of the Art* (Financial Executives Research Foundation 1980) (reprinted with permission).

Trend Analysis

4

"I hold that man is in the right who is most closely in
league with the future."
Letters of Henrik Ibsen

§4.01   Introduction

Trend analysis is the most commonly used of all analytical procedures. It is the analysis of the changes in a given account balance, item,
or element over the past accounting periods, usually annual periods.
In some instances, the analysis is a simple comparison of the prior
year's balance to the current balance. Or, it may involve a more complex analysis of the 12 to 36 or more monthly figures preceding the
current balance. The latter approach usually involves statistical time-
series methods of analysis.

Our objective in this chapter is to deal principally with those types
of analyses which can be done with pencil and paper and require a
dozen or fewer time-series observations. The more complex statistical

methods are identified and explained, and a thorough development of the technical aspects of these methods is presented, in Chapter 11 and in Appendix F.

The most common form of trend analysis is the comparison of current and prior years, based either on the annual figures alone or on a pairwise comparison of the monthly figures in each year. Since this technique is so well known, we will not explain and illustrate it. Rather, the objective of this chapter is to describe a variety of different forms of trend analysis, some of which the auditor may find provide a new and useful approach in certain audit situations. Also, we are concerned about the relative effectiveness of the different types of trend analysis and the potential for judgment errors that might be associated with them. In essence, the objectives of the chapter are threefold.

The first objective is to describe a wide variety of trend analysis procedures, all of which are easy to understand and simple to apply. The auditor's choice of a procedure will depend on the nature and quality of the data available.

The second objective is to provide guidance for the auditor in choosing a cutoff point for determining when the current amount is, or is not, out of line with the past trend. The cutoff can be expressed either as a percentage of the current amount or as a given dollar amount. The choice of a cutoff is based in part upon materiality considerations and upon guidelines of authoritative bodies, such as the AICPA and SEC.

The third objective is to present information from prior research findings about the auditor's tendency to make certain judgment mistakes when using trend analysis. These mistakes often come about because of a lack of understanding of the nature of the actual relationship over time between various financial statement accounts. Also, research has shown that the decision maker's use of time-series data is subject to certain consistent and well-known biases. An awareness of these mistakes and biases can help the auditor to use trend analysis most effectively.

§4.02   Elements of Effective Use of Trend Analysis

Apart from the choice of trend analysis techniques, which we analyze in the following section, the auditor must apply a proper understanding of each of the four elements of effective trend analysis:

Use a Causal Approach

In trend analysis, the auditor uses either a *causal* or a *diagnostic* approach. The causal approach is one in which the auditor answers the question "What should the amount be this year?" That is, the auditor gives a prediction explicitly, basing it upon the trend of the data. In contrast, using the diagnostic approach, the auditor simply compares the current amount with the past trend to determine if it appears to be out of line; no explicit prediction is involved. This is called the "diagnostic" approach because it can be compared to a physician's looking for a symptom of disease; if there is no symptom, then the physician concludes there is no disease. Unfortunately, in accounting and auditing matters, items which may appear OK (i.e., show no symptoms) can be significantly misstated. Thus, a causal approach is recommended. The auditor developes and understanding of what "causes" the trend of the account analyzed, uses this to make a prediction of the amount, and then compares predicted with reported amounts. Only in this way can the auditor detect a potential problem in an account for which there is little or no change from the prior period, but where there should have been a significant change because of changes in the related causal factors.

For example, consider the following hypothetical case. A supplies inventory balance had changed little from the prior year, yet significant quantity increases for these items had occurred. Upon investigation, the auditor discovered that the inventory clerk had failed to include the contents of a new stockroom in the year-end inventory count, thereby significantly understating the supplies inventory and overstating supplies expense. The causal approach probably would have detected the problem, by taking the inventory expansion explicitly into account. The diagnostic approach probably would have missed the problem because of the lack of a "symptom."

Because it requires more effort, the causal approach is more costly, so the auditor considers the cost-benefit of the two approaches, as well as the audit risk and materiality involved, when choosing an audit approach.

Evaluate Prediction Error

The potential for prediction error is implicit in the diagnostic approach but explicit in the causal approach. Trend analysis is fundamentally a process of prediction and judgment, so that the evaluation of prediction error is an important part of the process. As for any financial forecast, the auditor evaluates the potential for error in trend analysis by considering the quality of the process by which the prediction is made:

1. To what extent is an in-depth knowledge of the operating environment of the auditee incorporated in the prediction process? How well does the auditor understand the auditee's business and its operations?

2. How predictable are the operating characteristics of the auditee? The accounts for a mature company in a stable industry are the most easily understood and predicted, while in contrast, the growing company in an unstable industry represents an inherently less predictable situation.

3. Certain trend analysis techniques are more accurate than others because they use more data or more precise statistical procedures.

Our approach for the evaluation of prediction error is presented later in this chapter. As noted above, certain trend analysis techniques offer greater accuracy than others. This in turn allows the auditor greater reliance on the technique and thereby a potentially greater reduction in the extent of other planned substantive texts.

Evaluate Reliability of Data

Because it directly affects the accuracy of the trend analysis, the reliability of the data employed is an important audit concern. Nonfinancial data present a particular problem in this regard since the auditor does not ordinarily evaluate the auditee's controls for the reliability of these types of data. Also, the auditor may use external sources of data for industry for general economic variables. While some of these sources are known to be reliable—such as Standard and Poor's, Dun and Bradstreet, Moody's, Robert Morris Associates, and others—there is little known about the reliability of the many other sources which the auditor may require in any given audit situation. For example, data on local economic activity may be especially relevant for a trend analysis, yet very little may be known about the reliability of the sources for such data (various chambers of commerce, etc). The auditor considers the effect of the untested reliability of these sources on the trend analysis—it enhances the potential for prediction error.

Provide Proper Follow-Up

The final element of an effective trend analysis is the proper follow-up in those cases in which the analysis indicates further investigation is warranted. The follow-up is subject to the same criteria for audit evidence as for any other audit procedure. That is, the follow-up must produce evidence that is relevant and persuasive. The common approach of inquiry of management to explain significant fluctuations is appropriate, but the auditor should consider whether certain of management's assertions should be independently verified.

§4.03   Techniques for Trend Analysis

The techniques for trend analysis can be conveniently categorized as either single- or multiple-variable models. The single-variable model is one such that the predicted amount is based only upon the prior time-series data for that account. The prediction of sales revenue from the prior 36 months' sales figures is an example. In contrast, the multiple-variable model, while providing a prediction for a single variable, will use time-series data for two or more variables in the prediction process. A common representation of the multiple-variable model is the time-series regression model, in which the dependent variable is the predicted amount and the independent variable or variables are the one or more predictors for which time-series data are available. Both models are commonly applied in trend analysis for analytical procedures.

The distinction between these two classes of techniques is important, because the nature of the techniques differs substantially. Thus, the following discussion presents them separately. Greater attention is given to the single-variable model because it is more easily done by the unaided auditor; multiple-variable models often require the use of a computer.

Single-Variable Techniques

In describing the techniques for single variables, we proceed from the simplest to the most complex. The more complex the technique is, the more accurate are its predictions generally. However, more complex techniques will also require a greater commitment of audit resources—auditor expertise and time, data gathering, and so on. Thus, our approach presents a menu of available techniques from which the auditor can choose, according to the needs of each audit situation. There are five types of single-variable techniques:

1. Graphical method
2. Period-to-period change method
3. Weighted average method
4. Moving average method
5. Statistical time-series analysis

Throughout the following discussion we will refer to the account, item, or element that the auditor is predicting as the "predicted variable" or "dependent variable."

The Graphical Method. The first technique attempts to gain insight into the trend of the predicted variable by visual inspection of graphic data. This is done in one of three ways. The simplest of the three is to construct what is called a "scatter diagram" by plotting the data over time. To illustrate, the time-series sales data in column 2 of Table 4-1 is plotted in a scatter diagram in Figure 4-1. Using the scatter diagram, the auditor is able to determine the sales pattern visually and thereby project sales for the coming year. For this illustration, if the auditor feels the overall upward trend in sales will continue, then a prediction for 1989 should lie somewhere between $700,000 and $825,000. The upper and lower dashed lines are used to help predict by showing visually the boundaries within which recent years' sales amounts have fallen. The auditor would then use his or her knowledge of the economic prospects of the firm to come up with a single-value prediction. Using a "freehanded" prediction line as shown, we find that a reasonable prediction for 1989 sales would be $750,000. The $700,000 to $825,000 range can be interpreted as a "confidence interval" for the prediction, to reflect its degree of precision.

This visual-fit approach has three limitations. One is the limited precision of the estimate; unless the pattern of the data is very regular, the auditor's confidence interval is likely to be large, as in the above illustration. Another limitation is the influence on the prediction of one or more very unusual data observations. These could bias the prediction significantly, so the auditor must consider whether these observations are a valid part of the overall pattern of the data. If not, they should be omitted from the scatter diagram.

The final limitation we will discuss is the potential bias due to the auditor's choice of scale for the scatter diagram. For example, Figure 4-2 reproduces the data in Figure 4-1 using a more compressed scale for the sales axis. The visual effect of the two figures is quite different: Figure 4-1 enhances the trend to the data and Figure 4-2 dampens it. The auditor then must consider this "scale effect" in determining the prediction and confidence interval.

One approach to avoiding the scale effect would be for the auditor to use the same type of graph paper on all engagements, and to scale every graph for an engagement in units of the materiality figure used for that engagement.

Table 4-1 DBB Company Sales

Year (1)	Sales, $ (2)	Change in Sales (3)	% Change in Sales (4)	Rank (5)	Weighted % Change* (6)	Weighted Absolute† Change (7)	Exponential Smoothed Sales, $‡ (8)	Exponential Smoothed % Change‡ (9)	Exponential Smoothed Sales, $§ (10)	Exponential Smoothed % Change§ (11)
1982	361,936									
1983	400,776	$ 38,840	1.107	1	1.107	$ 38,840	381,356	—	393,008	
1984	518,609	117,833	1.294	2	2.588	235,666	449,983	1.201	493,489	1.257
1985	592,314	73,705	1.142	3	3.426	221,115	521,149	1.171	572,549	1.165
1986	553,047	−39,267	0.934	4	3.736	−157,608	536,809	1.053	556,947	0.980
1987	668,636	115,589	1.209	5	6.045	577,956	602,722	1.131	646,298	1.163
1988	645,901	22,735	.966	6	5.796	−136,410	624,312	1.048	645,980	1.005
		$283,965	6.652	21	22.698	$779,548				
		÷ 6	÷ 6		÷ 21	÷ 21				
		$ 47,328	1.109		1.081	$ 37,121				

*(6) = (4) × (5).
†(7) = (3) × (5).
‡$\alpha = 0.5$.
§$\alpha = 0.8$.

To add precision to the graphical approach, the auditor can use a simple algebraic calculation to determine the equation for a straight line which fits the data points. This quick calculation frees the auditor from the scale effect and helps to reduce the problem associated with very unusual data observations. The algebraic method also provides a prediction equation which contributes mathematical precision to the prediction. The equation is

$$X = a + b\underline{T}$$

where X = value of the predicted amount—in this case, sales (vertical axis)

   $\underline{T}$ = variable representing the time dimension (horizontal axis)

   a = fixed quantity which represents the value of X when $\underline{T} = 0$ (the intersection of the vertical axis and the straight line.)

   b = slope of the line, that is, the change in sales per unit change in time

Figure 4-1 DBB Company sales—scatter diagram.

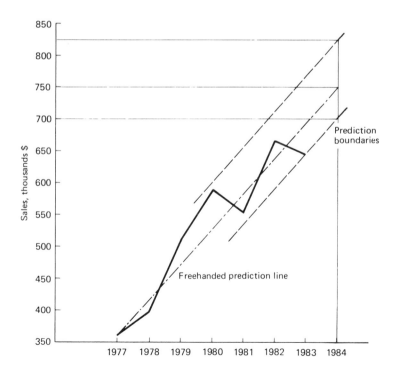

To obtain the equation, the auditor first draws through the data points a freehand line which best fits the overall pattern of the data. An example of this is shown in Figure 4-1. The auditor then chooses two points which are both close to the freehand line and a year or two apart—in this case, the sales amounts for 1983 and 1986 would be a good choice. Then

$$b = \frac{\$553,047 - \$400,776}{5 - 2} = \$50,757$$

(Assume 1986) = year 5 and 1983 = year 2.)

$$a = X - bT = \$553,047 - \$50,757 \times 5 = \$299,262$$
and then $\quad X = \$299,262 + \$50,757T$

Using this equation, the predicted sales for 1989 (year 8) is

$$\text{Sales (1989)} = \$299,262 + \$50,757 \times 8 = \$705,318$$

Upon inspection, it is clear that this algebraic model, since it is linear,

Figure 4-2 DBB Company sales—compressed scatter diagram.

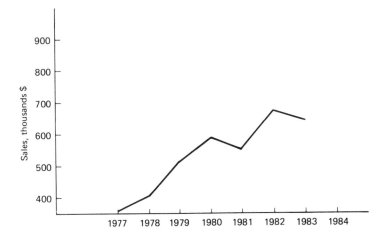

states that the best prediction for sales is a $50,757 increase over the prior year, for any year.

The Period-to-Period Change Method. This method is one of the most commonly used in current audit practice. When properly applied, it can provide very good predictions. It involves an algebraic calculation of the trend in a data series, based on changes between one or more prior periods of data.

It is convenient for us at this point to introduce some mathematical notations to help describe this method:

X_T = *actual* value of the balance, item, or element in period T

X_{T-1} = *actual* value of the balance, item, or element in the period prior to period T

$\hat{X}_{T+1}$ = *predicted* value of the balance, item, or element in the period following period T

$\hat{X}_{T-2}, \hat{X}_{T-3}, \ldots$ are defined in a similar fashion.

Now, the auditor can use either the *absolute amount* of change from prior to current period, or the *rate* of change from prior to current period, to predict the next period, as follows:

$$\hat{X}_{T+1} = X_T + (X_T - X_{T-1}) \qquad \text{(absolute change method)}$$

$$\hat{X}_{T+1} = X_T \left(\frac{X_T}{X_{T-1}} \right) \qquad \text{(rate of change method)}$$

To illustrate, with the data in Table 4-1

Predicted sales
(1989)   = sales (1988) + [sales (1988) − sales (1987)]
       = $645,901 + ($645,901 − $668,636)
       = $623,166 (absolute change method)

or

Predicted sales (1989)   = sales (1988) $\times \dfrac{\text{sales (1988)}}{\text{sales (1987)}}$

      = $645,901 $\times \dfrac{\$645,901}{668,636}$

      = $623,939 (rate of change method

Two aspects of these prediction methods are readily apparent. First, they produce comparable predictions, which is generally the case for these methods. Both models predict well when the underlying time series is approximately linear, though the absolute change model will generally outperform the other. However, when the underlying time series has a trend that is somewhat faster (or slower) than linear, then the absolute change model will underestimate (or overestimate) the correct amount and the degree of error is directly proportional to the extent that the trend departs from the linear in either direction. On the other hand, the rate of change method always overestimates, regardless of trend, and the degree of error is always higher than for the absolute change method. Thus, the auditor will be better served in most cases by the absolute change model; the rate of change method is used only when the auditor's knowledge of the data indicates it is the superior method.

A second observation about the above illustration is that both methods, by construction, cannot "see" the direction of the trend beyond that given by the two most recent data points. Thus, since the two most recent data points in Table 4-1 indicate a downward trend, the predictions for both period-to-period change methods are quite low relative to the predictions of either the visual-fit method or the equation method shown earlier. The auditor can adapt the period-to-period change method to a larger number of data points by averaging the changes over the last few periods, say n periods in general. Then, the predicted amounts are as follows:

$$\hat{X}_{T+1} = X_T + \frac{\sum\limits_{i=0}^{n} [X_{T-i} - X_{T-(i+1)}]}{n+1} \qquad \text{(absolute change method)}$$

$$\hat{X}_{T+1} = X_T \left(\sum\limits_{i=0}^{n} \frac{X_{T-i}}{X_{T-(i+1)}} \right) \frac{1}{n+1} \qquad \text{(rate of change method)}$$

For the data in Table 4-1 (refer to columns 3 and 4)

$$\text{Predicted sales (1989)} = \$645,901 + \$47,328$$
$$= \$693,229 \text{ (absolute change method)}$$

or

$$\text{Predicted sales (1989)} = \$645,901 \times 1.109$$
$$= \$716,304 \text{ (rate of change method)}$$

Finally, the period-to-period change method can also be adopted to account for seasonal fluctuations in the data, should the auditor want a prediction for a month or a quarter. For example, if there is a stable seasonal pattern from year to year, then where the period T is a month

$$\hat{X}_{T+1} = X_{T-11} + (X_{T-11} - X_{T-23}) \qquad \text{(absolute change method)}$$

$$\hat{X}_{T+1} = X_{T-11} \left(\frac{X_{T-11}}{X_{T-23}} \right) \qquad \text{(rate of change method)}$$

These formulas would incorporate both a seasonal effect and an annual trend for a month-by-month prediction.

The Weighted Average Method. The auditor may consider the above approach deficient in some cases because it weights each period's data equally. The auditor may in these cases wish to have the more recent observations weighted more heavily in the prediction, since the more recent data are more relevant. This is easily done once the weights are assigned. Of course, choosing how to assign the weights to the periods is a matter for experienced judgment; there is no single acceptable way to do it. One common approach is simply to rank the periods, 1, 2, . . . and so on from least to most recent. To illustrate, consider again the data in Table 4-1. Columns 5, 6, and 7 illustrate the weighted average method using the simple ranking of years. The predictions are as follows:

Predicted sales (1989) = $645,901 + $37,121 (absolute
change method)
= $683,022
Predicted sales (1989) = $645,901 + 1.081 (rate of change
method)
= $698,219

Note that the predicted sales figures for the weighted average approach are slightly lower than those of the unweighted averaging method shown earlier. The reason for this is that the weighted average methods emphasize the most recent years, and the data in column 2 of Table 4-1 have relatively lower average increases in the most recent years.

The Moving Average Method. Another method for giving greater weight to more recent observations is the moving average method. This method is especially useful when monthly or quarterly predictions are required because it is able to handle seasonal fluctuations conveniently and is easily updated for new data. We consider two ways the auditor can apply a moving average approach:

1. Unweighted moving average
2. Exponential smoothing (weighted moving average)

We illustrate first the unweighted moving average method, again by reference to the data in Table 4-1. A distinguishing characteristic of this method is that it requires the auditor to evaluate the length of any cyclical pattern of the data. For example, by inspecting Table 4-1 or Figure 4-1, the auditor might conclude that, in recent years, there has been approximately a 2-year cycle to the data. That is, there is an up-and-down cycle for the period 1987-1988. The 2-year cycle is then the base for the computation of the unweighted moving average used in the forecast.

$$\text{Predicted sales (1989)} = \$645,901 + \frac{\$115,589 - 22,735}{2} \text{ (absolute change method)}$$

$$= \$692,328$$

$$\text{or, Predicted sales (1989)} = \$645,901 \times \frac{1.209 + .966}{2} \text{ (rate of change method)}$$

$$= \$702,417$$

This approach is called the moving average method because the average for each cycle length includes the most recent data; that is, the average "moves" forward and is updated as new data are added. In effect, this method provides a smoothed prediction by averaging over seasonal and cyclical fluctuations. Again, the averaging period is chosen so as to match the length of fluctuations in the data. If the data are stable with small fluctuations, then the averaging period can be large. In this case we have something that resembles the period-to-period method described earlier. But, if significant fluctuations are present, the averaging period should be short and match the period of fluctuations.[1]

The second type of moving average includes a weighting of past data and is called "exponential smoothing." As we shall see, it also offers certain computational efficiencies over the unweighted approach. A key characteristic of the exponential smoothing method is that a smoothed value must be obtained for both the data series itself and

---

[1] One of the well-known properties of the unweighted moving average method, especially for longer averaging periods, is the tendency to indicate a cyclical pattern to the data where none is present. By a "cycle" we mean a fluctuation which extends over many months, in contrast to a seasonable fluctuation, over a relatively few months. The auditor should keep this in mind when using four or more periods in the moving average.

the trend for the data series; that is, this method separates the two aspects of the data-the trend and the fluctuations about the trend. To continue with the sample data in Table 4-1, the exponential smoothing method forecasts in the following way:[2]

Predicted sales (1989) =   smoothed sales (1988)
                             × smoothed trend (1988)

Our meaning for "trend" is simply the percentage change from year to year, as given in column 4 of Table 4-1. We consider now how the smoothing is done.

The term "smoothing" is used to reflect that this method averages over the fluctuations in the data in such a way that more recent periods are weighted more heavily than later periods. The weighting is done by a geometric series of the following form, where a is the weighting constant:

$$1, (1-a), (1-a)^2,. . .$$

The constant a is a number between 0 and 1, so that weights in the sequence of terms above become progressively smaller. Suppose $a = 0.5$; then the smoothed value of a time series at time T is given by the following, where $S(X_T)$ represents the smoothed value of the series X at time T.

$$S(X_T) = \frac{X_T + 1/2X_{T-1} + 1/4X_{T-2}}{1 + 1/2 + 1/4}$$

The smoothing goes back as many periods as good data are available, each period being weighted less than the one before. Using algebra, we are able to simplify the above equation, to give the following, which is called the smoothing function

$$S(X_T) = aX_T + (1 - a)[S(X_{T-1})]$$

That is, the smoothed value at time T is a linear combination of the actual value at time T and the smoothed value of the prior period. Look again at Table 4-1 for an illustration of the smoothing function. Column 8 shows the smoothed figures for sales using a weighting of $a =$

---

[2] A more in-depth treatment of the exponential smoothing forecasting technique is available in Chisholm and Whitaker, (Forecasting Methods 22-26 Irwin 1971).

0.5. For example, the smoothed sales for 1978 and 1979 are computed as follows:

Smoothed sales (1984)
$$= 1/2 \text{ actual sales (1984)} + 1/2$$
$$\text{smoothed sales (1983)}$$
$$= 1/2 \times \$518,609 + 1/2 \times$$
$$\$381,356$$
$$= \$449,983$$

and

Smoothed sales (1983) $= 1/2 \times \$400,776 + 1/2$
$$\times \$361,936$$
$$= \$381,356$$

The actual sales for 1982 were used in this latter computation since 1982 is the first data period, and thus smoothed sales for 1982 cannot be computed. The smoothing function is applied in a similar manner for all periods, and for the percentage change figures in column 4 as well as for sales. The result is the smoothed figures in columns 8 and 9, which are used to predict sales for 1989.

Predicted sales (1989)
$$= \text{smoothed sales (1988)} \times \text{smoothed}$$
$$\text{trend (1988)}$$
$$= \$624,312 \times 1.048$$
$$= \$654,278$$

The above prediction has used a weighting constant value of $a = 0.5$, which is the midpoint of all possible values, a being between 0 and 1. The choice of this value is part of the prediction process, and it will affect the resulting prediction. The value of a can be compared to the cycle length used in the moving average method. That is, the smaller a is, the greater the impact of distant periods' data on the smoothed prediction. Conversely, the larger a is, the greater the relative impact of more recent observations. Thus, a small a is generally more appropriate for a stable time series, while a large a is more suitable for a time series with significant fluctuations. When a is large, the smoothed prediction responds rapidly to changes in trend.

The auditor may choose to compute the smoothed prediction with two or three different values for a and evaluate the results.[3] If significantly, different predictions are obtained, the auditor may choose to study the time series further to obtain a better understanding of the factors influencing the fluctuations, and then choose the best prediction. To illustrate, if the data in 4-1 for an illustration of the $a = 0.8$, the resulting prediction, using columns 10 and 11, would be:

$$\text{Predicted sales (1989)} = \$645,980 \times 1.005 = \$649,210$$

This prediction differs little from that of the $a = 0.5$ model, so that a small range around $650,000 appears to provide a reasonable precise prediction using the exponential smoothing method.

Statistical Time-Series Analysis. A complete discussion of the available statistical techniques for trend analysis is beyond the scope of the book. Such a discussion would necessarily be quite technical in nature and would presume a high level of understanding of statistical terms, concepts, and techniques. Thus, our approach is to describe these techniques in a general way at this point and to present in Chapter 11 and in Appendix F a more in-depth discussion of one of the techniques, regression analysis. The two statistical techniques available for trend analysis are regression analysis and Box-Jenkins (B-J) time-series analysis.

Regression analysis is a statistical technique for finding a best-fit trend line for a series of observations. It can be compared to the algebra-equation technique illustrated earlier in connection with the graphical method. This technique uses the equation $X = a + bT$, where X is the predicted amount, T is a variable representing time, and the constants a and b are as defined earlier. The algebra-equation technique provides good estimates of a and b, using only two data points. In contrast, the regression method would use all seven data points in the example cited earlier, and thus finds that unique set of constants (a and b) which minimizes prediction error. Therefore, the regression line generally provides a better fit than does the algebra-equation technique.[4] Consult Appendix F for the development of how this is done mathematically.

---

[3] The single best value for a, that which gives the least prediction error over the past data, can be determined by statistical methods such as regression. The regression method is developed fully in Appendix F.

[4] Hogarth & Makridakis, *Forecasting and Planning: An Evaluation,* Mgmt Sci, Feb 1981, at 115-38 compare the performance of simple and complex prediction models, and report that the simple models perform as well as or better than the complex models more often than most forecasters realize. Also, Makridakis & Winkler *Averages of Forecasts: Some Empirical Results,* Mgmt Sci, Sept 1983, at

When regression analysis is applied to the data in Table 4-1, the following equation results, where $T = 7$ means 1988, and so on:

$$\text{Sales} = \$331,312 + 50,787T$$

Thus $\text{Predicted sales (1989)} = \$331,312 + \$50,787 \times 8$
$$= \$737,608$$

The benefit of the regression approach is the mathematical precision of the prediction, since it provides the best-fit prediction line, and the fact that it uses all available data. However, it does not pick up fluctuating patterns and changes in trend as do the period-to-period change and moving average methods. The auditor uses an understanding of the past behavior of the time series to help choose which prediction method to use.

Another statistical approach, which is a good deal more complex than regression analysis but which will pick up fluctuating patterns to the data, is the B-J method. This is a statistical technique which develops very good predictions by extracting the statistical properties of the time-series data over many observations. The B-J method actually consists of many different prediction techniques—simple trend models, smoothing models, and so on. The B-J prediction is based on the best-fitting of all these methods.

Multiple-Variable Techniques

The multiple-variable model is most easily described by reference to our prediction equation, as defined for regression, $X = a + bT$. If we replace T with a series of data for a new variable (X) which is related in some way to the predicted variable (X), then we have a multiple-variable model. The variable Z is called the "independent" (predictor) variable, while X is called the "dependent" (predicted) variable. We then must have data for each variable $(X$ and X) for each of the T time periods. The two types of models are contrasted in figure 4-3.

For example, suppose the sales data in Table 4-1, column 2, represent investment income (X) rather than sales for our audit client. And, we know that the value of investments (Z) is a good predictor of investment income. The data for this new variable are given in the accompanying table. Now, we can obtain our prediction for X by developing the prediction equation.

987-96 show that prediction accuracy can be improved by averaging the predictions of two or more different methods.

$$X_T = a + bZ_T$$

We can find the values for the constants a and b in the same manner as

	Independent Variable (z): Value of Investment, thousands $
1982	6,325
1983	7,001
1984	7,360
1985	7,636
1986	7,215
1987	7,789
1988	8,014

we have for the single-variable cases presented earlier—by the algebra-equation method or through regression analysis. The period-to-period change and moving average methods no longer apply.

Algebra-Equation Method. The values of the constants and b are computed as follows (the data for the years 1977 and 1980 are selected on the basis of an examination of a scatter diagram. Figure 4-4):

Figure 4-3 Illustrations of (*a*) single- and (*b*) multiple-variable analysis.

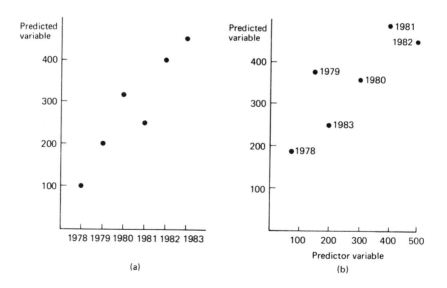

$$b = \frac{592.314 - 361.936}{7636 - 6325} = 0.176$$

$$a = X - bZ = 592,312 - 0.176 \times \$7,636,000 = -\$751,622$$

and
$$X = -\$751,662 + 0.176 \times Z$$

Thus, if 1989 investments are $8,260,000, we would predict investment income as

$$\text{Predicted income (1989)} = \begin{aligned} &-\$751,622 + 0.176 \times \$8,260,000 \\ &= \$702,138 \end{aligned}$$

This figure can be compared with the reported income figure for reasonableness.

Linear Regression Method. Applying a linear regression approach to these data gives similar results. The regression equation computed by the methods described in Appendix F is as follows:

Figure 4-4 Investment income versus investment value.

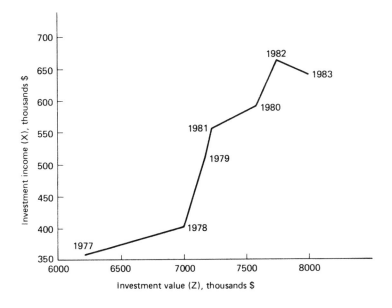

$$X = -\$872{,}955 + 0.192 \times Z$$
$$\text{and} \quad \text{Predicted income (1989)} = -\$872{,}955 + 0.192 \times$$
$$\$8{,}260{,}000$$
$$= \$712{,}965$$

Again, the benefit associated with the regression approach is the greater accuracy of the prediction which comes from the mathematics involved. Also, it is possible when using regression to employ two or more predictor variables rather than the one predictor used in the above illustration. The use of an additional predictor variable can enhance the accuracy of the prediction. For example, the auditor could use data about interest rates as a second predictor variable in the above illustration. Assuming interest rates are relevant, the resulting prediction should be more accurate when both the investment amount and interest rates are used.

Use Care When Making the Prediction. When making the prediction by either the equation or the regression method, the auditor should consider three potential causes of inaccurate predictions:

1. *Inaccurate data.*

2. *Unstable pattern to the data.* If the data fluctuate significantly or do not have a single discernible trend, then neither of these methods will always give good results. In such cases the auditor should avoid placing too much reliance on the prediction.

3. *Improper model.* An improper model is one in which the predicted and predictor variables, which are assumed to be related, are in fact not related at all or are only weakly related. The auditor has chosen the wrong predictor variable for the equation or regression. Also, the relationship might be nonlinear, rather than the assumed linear form. The auditor can avoid such errors by developing a good understanding of the variable being predicted. What other financial and operating data time series are strongly related to the one being predicted? And, what is the proper form of the relationship?

Computer Software

An increasing number of auditors have ready access to a computer or computer service, a situation which makes possible the use of planning and forecasting software for trend analysis. Many of these software packages are available on microcomputers, thus enhancing portability and reducing cost. The auditor can use the packages to complete the complex and tedious arithmetic associated with many of the techniques discussed in this chapter. The packages commonly include such features as moving averages, exponential smoothing, seasonal and cyclical adjustment, regression analysis, and in some cases, the Box-Jenkins time-series analysis. Among the most well known of these packages are the following (there are many others):

STATPRO	Wadsworth Electronic Publishing Company 20 Park Plaza Boston, MA 02116 (617) 423-0420
SMART FORECASTS	Smart Software Inc. 392 Concord Ave. Belmont, MA 02178 (617) 489-2743
MICRO-TSP	McGraw-Hill Book Company 1221 Avenue of the Americas New York, NY 10020 (800) 782-3737
FAST!	Financial Audit Systems 5000 Falls of the Neuse Raleigh, NC 27609 (919) 872-5339
EXEC*U*STAT	Exec*U*Stat Inc. 5 Independence Way Princeton, NJ 08540 (609) 924-9357
STATPAC FORECAST PLUS	Walonick Associates, Inc. 5624 Girard Avenue South Minneapolis, MN 55419 (612) 340-1515

Of course, the auditor may also engage a specialized consultant to develop a forecasting package tailored to the auditor's particular needs.

§4.04   Estimation of Prediction Error

A critical aspect of the effective use of trend analysis is the auditor's explicit consideration of the potential amount of prediction error.

That is, what is the range above and below the predicted amount in which the auditor is fairly confident the actual value will be? This interval will be relatively wide in those cases when the auditor is not very confident of the prediction, and narrower for more confident predictions. The determination of this prediction interval is most often a subjective matter. Only the statistical methods, such as regression, produce objective measures of potential prediction error.[5] Thus, the auditor will most often feel somewhat frustrated trying to estimate the prediction error.

Our approach is to have the auditor express his or her judgment about the potential error, whether in numerical terms or in qualitative terms. For example, the auditor might give the upper and lower values of the interval within which he or she feels the actual value will lie, with some stated confidence. Alternatively, the auditor might simply say the potential for prediction error is "high" or "low." The point of this judgment process is to enhance the auditor's awareness of the importance of incorporating an assessment of potential prediction error in using a trend analysis. The more precise the judgment can be, the better the auditor is able to determine how much reliance to place on it.

§4.05   The Auditor's Decision

This section presents some of the available research about auditor judgment in trend analysis. It should serve as a guide for the individual auditor in using trend analysis more effectively. The discussion focuses on what we know about the tendencies, or "biases," which the auditor, knowingly or not, applies when using trend analysis.

For the purposes of this section, we consider the auditor's decision to be two-phases-(1) whether to investigate any particular account or item (the "attention-directing" function of trend analysis) and (2) how far to push the investigation, once initiated. We do not consider here auditor judgments about reducing tests of details as the result of analytical procedures.

One important consideration when deciding whether to investigate an account or item is determining the "cutoff" dollar amount or per cent difference between predicted and reported amounts beyond which an investigation should be undertaken. This cutoff amount or per cent is generally related to materiality for the engagement. Our

---

[5] In regression, the measure of the confidence interval for the prediction is called the "standard error of the estimate." The computation and interpretation of the standard error of the estimate are presented in Chapter 11 (nontechnical) and in Appendix F.

research on senior-level auditors has shown that a cutoff of 5 per cent of net income before tax or 10 per cent of net income after tax is a good approximation for the rule most commonly applied by these auditors. However, this is an average figure, and auditors differ somewhat on the cutoff applied. On the other hand, each auditor tends to apply a chosen cutoff consistently when going from one audit situation to another.

Our studies also show that the direction of the difference (predicted minus reported) does not seem to affect the auditor's choice of a cutoff. That is, auditors appear to treat the over- and underprediction cases pretty much in an equivalent manner. Also, the auditors tend to base their investigation decisions on the dollar amount differences rather than the percentage difference itself; that is, the amount of the difference (predicted minus reported amount) is the key element of the investigation decision.

Another study has shown that the auditor's determination of a cutoff may be improperly influenced by the current unaudited amount. When determining a prediction interval in which the actual value probably lies, the auditors may center the interval on the unaudited amount rather than the predicted amount. This implies indirectly a bias to accept the unaudited amount, since it is at the center of the prediction interval. It also suggests that auditors are using the unaudited value in making the prediction for the amount, which again biases the auditor to accept the unaudited amount.

This tendency to focus on the unaudited amount is a judgment bias common to many judgment tasks—in business, medicine, and other areas. It has been called the "confirmation bias," since it reflects the decision maker's tendency *not* to seek out disconfirming evidence; that is, a diagnostic approach is taken rather than a causal approach. Time pressure can increase the tendency to this bias, though the natural skepticism displayed by auditors acts to reduce it. In all, the auditor must be alert to the effects of his or her own tendency to the confirmation bias, because research has shown that it is a common human trait.

Another set of studies we have reviewed seems to show that decision makers and auditors have a tendency to perceive a trend to a series of data when no trend is present. Or, when a trend is present, they will overestimate its strength. This also appears to be a common characteristic of human judgment and perception, and auditors should be alert to the effects of the bias in their own trend analysis judgments.

§4.06   References

Albrecht, *Toward Better and More Efficient Audits,* J Accountancy, Dec 1978), at 49-50.

W. Albrecht & J. McKeown, Toward an Extended Use of Statistical Analytical Reviews in the Audit, Proceedings of the University of Illinois Audit Symposium, University of Illinois (1977).

R. Chisholm & G. Whitaker, Jr, *Forecasting Methods* (Irwin 1971).

Geurts & Buchman, *Accounting for "Shocks" in Forecasts,* Mgmt Account, Apr 1981, at 21-39.

C. Gross & R. Peterson, *Business Forecasting* (Houghton Mifflin 1976).

Hogarth & Makridakis, *Forecasting and Planning: An Evaluation,* Mgmt Sci, Feb 1981, at 115-138.

R. Kaplan, Developing a Financial Planning Model for an Analytical Review: A Feasibility Study, Symposium on Auditing Research III, University of Illinois 3-34 (1979).

Kask, *Regression and Correlation Analysis,* CPA J, Oct 1979, at 35-41.

M. Kendall, *Time Series* (Hafner 2d ed 1976).

Kinney, *ARIMA and Regression in Analytical Review: An Empirical Test,* Account Rev, Jan 1978, at 48-60.

Kinney, *the Discriminatory Power of Marco Techniques in Analytical Reviews— Some Empirical Tests,* 17 J Account Res, 148-55 (Supp 1979).

W. Kinney & G. Salamon, The Effect of Measurement Error on Regression Results in Analytical Review, Proceedings of the Symposium on Auditing Research III, University of Illinois 49-64 (1979).

Baruch, *On the Use of Index Models in Analytical Reviews by Auditors,* J Account Res, Autumn 1980, at 524-50.

Makridakis & Winkler, *Averages of Forecasts: Some Empirical Results,* Mgmt Sci, Sept 1983, at 987-96.

J. Neter, Two Case Studies on Use of Regression for Analytical Review, Proceedings of Symposium on Audit Research, University of Illinois (1980).

Stringer, K. W.: *A Statistical Technique for Analytical Review,* 1-13 J Account Res (Supp 1975).

Ratio Analysis

5

§5.01   Introduction

In the previous chapter on trend analysis, we considered the use of various techniques to predict a given account balance as a basis for evaluating the reasonableness of reported amounts. A basic limitation of this approach is that, by focusing on only a single balance, it cannot incorporate the auditor's knowledge about relationships between balances. An alternative approach, ratio analysis, is a potentially more useful approach for analytical procedures because it uses the auditor's knowledge of these relationships. In this manner it also facilitates the comparison of a given firm's financial position with that of other firms. Similarly, it facilitates the comparison of a firm's current performance with the record of past performance. For example, the ratio of cost of sales to sales for most firms is a very stable relationship over time and therefore is useful for evaluating current costs. Also, firms within relatively homogeneous industry groups tend to have similar ratios of this type. Thus, the comparison of a firm's current cost-of-sales/sales ratio with the prior-year ratio or with an industry average ratio can often provide useful information.

The chief benefit of ratio analysis, then, is that it isolates stable (over time) or common (across firms within a given industry) relationships between account balances. Thus, it allows comparisons between firms of different sizes, since even reasonably large size differences often do not affect the relationship; that is, ratios, such as the current ratio or inventory turnover ratio, are expected to be similar for firms over a range of different sizes. Also, such relationships as the current ratio or inventory turnover are not expected to change much over time for a given firm as it grows from year to year. Again, size differences do not affect the usefulness of the ratio. The use of ratios for a given firm over time is often called "times-series analysis," and the comparison of ratios between firms at a given point in time is called "cross sectional analysis." The distinction is illustrated in Table 5-1. We discuss the uses and limitations of each in this chapter.

Table 5-1   Illustration of Financial Ratio Analysis—Time-Series and Cross-Sectional Analysis

| | | Current Ratio for Illustrative Firms | | | | |
		Firm A	Firm B	Firm C	Firm D	Industry Average
	1970	2.1	1.5	2.3	1.8	2.3
	1971	2.0	1.2	2.5	1.7	2.2
	1972	1.9	1.9	2.5	1.5	2.0
	1973	1.7	1.6	1.6	1.7	2.1
	1974	2.0	1.5	1.9	1.6	2.0
	1975	1.9	1.9	1.8	1.4	2.4
	1976	2.3	2.2	1.7	1.8	2.0
	1977	1.9	1.7	2.0	1.7	1.8
	1978	2.5	1.5	2.0	1.6	1.9
	1979	2.3	1.8	2.3	1.7	2.1
	1980	2.3	1.9	1.6	1.6	2.1
	1981	2.4	1.7	1.3	1.9	2.0
Cross sectional → analysis	1982	2.2	2.0	1.5	1.8	2.1

↑
Time-series
analysis

§5.02   Two Methods

Apart from whether a time-series or cross-sectional approach is taken, there are two methods for ratio analysis. Both are commonly used by auditors. The most well known of the two is *financial ratio analysis,* which is based on ratios between financial statement accounts, such as the current ratio or inventory turnover. Another method is to use *common-size statement analysis* (or vertical fluctuation analysis), in which each account balance is shown as a percentage of some relevant aggregate amount, such as total assets, total sales, or total expenses. The common-size statement is most often prepared in the time-series format, as in Table 5-2, but it can also be prepared in the cross-sectional format, as in Table 5-3. The time-series approach allows an analysis of changes in a firm's asset or capital structure over time, as well as a highlighting of important changes in the composition of total expenses. Alternatively, the cross-sectional approach can be used to assess how a firm's makeup of assets, capital structure, and expenses compares with that of other firms in the industry.

Note that above we have considered only ratios among financial statement accounts. Ratios of financial data to selected operating data may also be useful to the auditor. For example, the ratio of total wages to number of employees can be used to assess the reasonableness of the total wages figure. Since this latter type of analysis is best considered a form of reasonableness test, we consider it in detail in the following chapter rather than here.[1] The next section develops an approach for the auditor in using the financial ratio and common-size statement forms of ratio analysis, in both the time-series and the cross-sectional formats. This is followed by a discussion of the problems and limitations in the effective use of the analyses.

---

[1] When operating data are in either the numerator or the denominator of the ratio, we consider this to be a reasonableness test rather than ratio analysis. This does not distinguish the two techniques perfectly, since there are examples in which the ratio of two financial statement accounts is computed as part of a reasonableness test (e.g., interest expense to liabilities; interest income to investments). However, we find it generally true that reasonableness tests employ operating data, whereas "ratio analysis" is typically understood to mean the ratios between financial statement accounts. In a sense, reasonableness tests may be considered a subset of the more general approach, ratio analysis, and we could have treated the two approaches together in this chapter. But the application and interpretation of the two are sufficiently different that we have chosen to cover them in separate chapters.

Table 5-2   Sample Common-Size Statements—Time-Series Approach
DBB Company—Year Ended Dec. 31, 1988

	1985	1986	1987	1988
Common-Size Balance Sheet				
Assets				
Cash	8.2	7.8	7.5	7.8
Accounts receivable	15.1	16.1	17.2	16.8
Marketable securities	10.8	9.2	8.0	8.8
Inventories	18.1	20.9	21.2	20.7
Other current assets	5.6	5.1	4.3	4.8
Investments and other noncurrent assets	13.9	11.9	12.4	11.8
Plant and equipment	28.3	29.0	29.4	29.3
	100.0	100.0	100.0	100.0
Liabilities and equity				
Accounts payable	20.2	19.2	18.1	14.5
Other current liabilities	10.1	9.2	8.6	9.9
Long-term debt	28.6	30.0	30.8	32.4
Deferred tax	4.2	4.4	4.4	4.8
Stockholders' equity	36.9	37.2	38.1	38.4
	100.0	100.0	100.0	100.0
Common-Size Income Statement				
Revenues	97.5	97.1	95.0	96.2
Discounts and allowances	2.5	2.9	5.0	3.8
	100.0	100.0	100.0	100.0
Expenses				
Cost of goods sold	48.2	46.1	47.1	49.4
Marketing, general, and administrative expenses	11.3	18.3	16.5	12.9
Interest expense	15.1	14.8	13.2	13.0
Other expense	8.8	7.2	9.9	11.4
Tax	6.1	5.2	4.8	4.2
Income after tax	10.5	8.4	8.5	9.1
	100.0	100.0	100.0	100.0

NOTE: All figures are percentages.

Table 5-3   Sample Common-Size Statements—Cross-Sectional Approach

DBB Company—Year Ended Dec. 31, 1988

	Regional Competitor A	Regional Competitor B	Regional Industry Average	DBB Company
Common-Size Balance Sheet				
Assets				
Cash	5.1	8.2	6.4	7.8
Accounts receivable	15.8	20.1	17.2	16.8
Marketable securities	10.2	5.1	2.1	8.8
Inventories	22.5	21.3	24.2	20.7
Other current assets	6.1	3.4	3.3	4.8
Investments and other noncurrent assets	8.0	7.9	16.3	11.8
Plant and equipment	32.3	34.0	30.5	29.3
	100.0	100.0	100.0	100.0
Liabilities and equity				
Accounts payable	21.0	21.6	17.2	14.5
Other current liabilities	8.1	12.3	10.1	9.9
Long-term debt	16.1	34.5	22.4	32.4
Deferred tax	12.5	6.4	11.2	4.8
Stockholders' equity	42.3	25.2	39.1	38.4
	100.0	100.0	100.0	100.0
Common-Size Income Statement				
Revenues	98.9	97.2	96.9	96.2
Discounts and allowances	1.1	2.8	3.1	3.8
	100.0	100.0	100.0	100.0
Expenses				
Cost of goods sold	47.3	48.1	45.4	49.4
Marketing, general, and administrative expenses	25.8	10.9	16.0	12.9
Interest expense	7.6	14.2	8.1	13.0
Other expense	8.8	6.5	11.8	11.4
Tax	3.1	6.2	5.8	4.2
Income after tax	7.4	14.1	12.9	9.1
	100.0	100.0	100.0	100.0

NOTE: All figures are percentages.

§5.03   Using Ratio Analysis

This section explains the application and interpretation of ratio analysis in identifying unusual relationships which signal the potential for material misstatement in a given account. Here the focus is on the analysis of individual financial statement accounts in contrast to the use of operating, leverage, and liquidity ratios to analyze the aggregate inherent risk of a client, which we covered in Chapter 3. The two techniques of ratio analysis—financial ratio analysis and common-size statements—are considered separately.[2]

Financial Ratio Analysis

The motivating feature for the use of financial ratio analysis is the utilization of relationships between account balances which the auditor expects to be stable over time or common across related firms or both. For some accounts, these interrelationships are clear, as they are between the marketable securities account and the related investment income account. But for other accounts, there are no clear interrelationships, and therefore a financial ratio approach is inappropriate. This is the case for the cash account balance which represents the net effect of flows from several other accounts. There is no clear one-to-one relationship of cash to another account. With this in mind, we have chosen to illustrate ratio analysis for four balance sheet accounts plus selected revenue and expense accounts which have clear account interrelationships:

1. Accounts receivable
2. Inventory
3. Plant and equipment
4. Current liabilities (and unrecorded liabilities)
5. Revenue and expense accounts

The focus of the discussion is on the use of selected ratios to analyze these accounts. A comprehensive treatment of the analytical procedures for each account is presented in Chapter 7.

---

[2] Five useful references for these techniques are L. Bernstein, Financial Statement Analysis (Irwin rev ed 1978); J. Finnerty, Corporate Financial Analysis, (McGraw-Hill 1986); G. Foster, Financial Statement Analysis (Prentice Hall 1986); S. McMullen, Financial Statements: Form, Analysis and Interpretation (Irwin 1979); and Joel G. Siegel, How to Analyze Business, Financial Statements, and the Quality of Earnings (Prentice Hall 1982).

Accounts Receivable. The most commonly applied ratio for analyzing receivables is the receivables turnover ratio

$$\text{Accounts receivable turnover} = \frac{\text{credit sales}}{\text{average net receivables}}$$

This ratio is a good measure of a company's success in implementing a good credit policy.[3] It can be compared with prior years' results or with relevant industry ratios—the higher the ratio, the better the performance. A ratio that is low relative to prior years or to the industry average might indicate an audit problem related to uncollectibility of certain receivables. A decrease in the turnover ratio might also reflect fictitious credit sales or improper cutoff to improve profitability. Also, a lower ratio could be caused by employee fraud, if collections are not recorded properly to customer accounts. Therefore, a low ratio should be further investigated by having the client prepare a schedule for the aging of receivables, by reviewing the bad debt provisions, and by other means.

In comparing receivables turnover to the industry average, the auditor should consider differences in the nature of the production process between industries. Industries in which the product is durable and has high unit value may be expected to extend credit more freely and for longer periods than industries in which the product is nondurable and of low unit value. This would be reflected in differences in average receivables turnover for these industries.

Other ratios which might bring to light problems in receivables include:

1. *Provision for doubtful accounts to total receivables* or to *credit sales.* If this ratio is significantly smaller relative to prior years or the industry average, this might be an indication of an inadequate allowance for uncollectible accounts.

2. *Customer discounts* to *total receivables* or to *credit sales.* If a client has a policy of giving discounts to customers for early payment of their accounts, this ratio can be used to analyze the effect of the policy, over time and relative to the industry average. Unexpected differences here may reflect audit or management problems

---

[3] The "average collection period," 365 days divided by the receivables turnover ratio, is also in common use. The collection period provides the same information in a different format, and is interpreted in the same manner as the turnover ratio. The auditor may use either, but since they are redundant, there is no need to calculate both.

needing prompt attention. For example, this approach might detect fraud wherein discounts are improperly allowed by a receivables clerk in return for some consideration from the benefited customer.

3. *Largest receivable account balance* to *total receivables*. This ratio, if unusual when compared over time and with the industry average, should cause the auditor to give special attention to analyzing the validity and collectibility of this critical account.

4. *Notes receivable* to *accounts receivable*.

5. Value of *notes receivable renewed this year* to *total notes receivable*. An increase in this ratio, or in the preceding ratio, over time could reflect a collectibility problem. If the ratio is poor relative to the industry average, management attention should be directed to the problem, to reconsider current credit policy.

6. *Accounts receivable* to *current assets*.

7. *Average balance* per *customer*. A relatively high figure for this ratio, or for the preceding one, compared with prior years and the industry average could be an indication of uncollectible accounts.

Inventory. As for receivables, the most commonly used ratio for analyzing inventory is a turnover ratio.

$$\text{Inventory turnover} = \frac{\text{cost of goods sold}}{\text{average inventory}}$$

This ratio measures the relationship between inventory and sales, on the basis that a given volume of sales requires a certain level of inventory.[4] This relationship will differ across industries, and may differ owing to management policy as influenced by seasonal factors, the availability of supply, and so on. The turnover ratio can be compared over time or with the industry average. A high ratio is favorable. A high ratio might reflect more efficient inventory policies, or unrecorded inventory. A low ratio might indicate an audit problem such as obsolete or otherwise unsalable inventory, or overstated inventory valuation. For a manufacturing company, an additional turnover ratio can be computed for raw materials.

---

[4] The "number of days sales in inventory," 365 days divided by the inventory turnover ratio, is an alternative and equivalent ratio in terms of both the information provided and the manner of interpretation.

$$\frac{\text{Raw materials}}{\text{inventory turnover}} = \frac{\text{raw materials issued to production}}{\text{average raw materials inventory}}$$

The latter ratio, if relatively low, might indicate an overstocking or overvaluation of raw materials, or the presence of unusable materials inventory.

The analysis of inventory turnover can facilitate the detection of inventory theft in some cases, especially if the deviation in inventory turnover from one year to the next is due to an unusually large write-down of inventory at year-end. Inventory is normally depreciated, or written off, at year-end owing to normal circumstances of loss and waste during the year. However, an unusually large write-down in one year may simply conceal the theft of inventory in that year, or the intention of theft in the following year. Thus, either a significant improvement or a significant decline in inventory turnover could signal a potential theft.

On the other hand, the failure to make appropriate write-downs of obsolete and unsalable items could have the effect of reducing the ability of the turnover ratio to detect theft. In this case, the high inventory value, including obsolete and unsalable items, could mask shortages in the faster-moving items. Thus, consideration of inventory write-down policy and related analysis of shrinkage rates are a necessary adjunct to the proper analysis of inventory turnover.

The use of the inventory turnover ratio is subject to some important qualifications. The auditor should determine if the ratio is *not* comparable over time or to industry averages for any of three reasons:

1. Differences in accounting methods for valuation of inventory affect the comparability of ratios. All or some portion of inventories may be valued by different methods among firms, or may change over time for the client firm. For this reason, the turnover ratio must be interpreted carefully. Also, industry averages must be evaluated carefully. Do they reflect one method or some mix of methods for the related population of firms?

2. Firms' inventory turnover ratios differ substantially *among* industries. Significant differences in the nature of the production processes among industries lead naturally to different turnover ratios. Thus, the auditor must be confident that the client's ratio is compared with the proper industry average. For example, industries with a long production cycle will generally have high inventories and low turnovers. The book publishing and heavy equipment manufacturing industries are good illustrations.

Large work-in-process inventories and long sales cycles are typical of these industries. Alternatively, industries for which the
product is perishable or subject to rapid obsolescence will generally have low inventories and high turnover. Food products and
newspapers or magazines are good examples here.

3. A properly conceived and implemented management policy may
dictate inventory levels different from the past or from those levels reflected in average industry turnover figures. Such factors
as the availability of supply, seasonal fluctuations in demand,
temporary price fluctuations, and storage costs may be involved
in the management of inventory levels.

With these things in mind, the auditor can use the inventory turnover to identify the potential audit problems noted above. The turnover comparisons will be more informative if they are done by product
line, and if some care is taken that the average inventory figure used
in the ratio is representative of the inventory throughout the year.

Other ratios the auditor might find useful are as follows:

1. *Inventory to current assets.* This has the same use as the turnover
ratio. When compared with prior years or the industry average,
it may indicate an unexpected inventory relationship.

2. *Next year's budgeted cost of sales* to *ending inventory balance.* If available,
the sales budget figures can be used to anticipate the inventory
turnover for the coming year. Is this out of line with the current
year's turnover ratio?

3. *Direct materials* to *total product cost*

4. *Direct labor* to *total product cost*

5. *Overhead* to *total product cost*

On either a unit cost or total manufacturing cost basis, the last three
ratios can be used to analyze the composition of product costs over
time and relative to the industry average. This analysis can be used
to spot the improper classification of cost items, especially in the overhead component. Costs such as past service pension costs, general and
administrative expense, distribution expenses, and "learning curve"
costs may be improperly included in overhead.

Property, Plant, and Equipment. The most commonly used analytical procedure for depreciable asset accounts is a reasonableness test of depreciation expense, which we consider in the following chapter. The audit
concern for which ratio analysis may be appropriate is the consideration of writing down some portion of underutilized assets. If the client

has persistent operating problems leading to an expectation that certain assets will be indefinitely idle, the appropriate accounting treatment is to write down the assets. The ratio of net property, plant, and equipment to net sales should provide a useful measure of the firm's utilization of capacity. Compared across firms or years, if the ratio is unusually high, it may indicate a need to consider a write-down of certain assets.

Accounts Payable and Unrecorded Liabilities. A principal audit objective for accounts payable is to determine whether current liabilities are completely and properly disclosed. The two financial ratios shown below may be useful to this objective since the auditor can use these ratios to analyze the cash needs of the client. If the ratios indicate a severe cash need to support current payables, there may be a motivation for management, among other things, to understate liabilities through intentional cutoff errors or by other means. The two ratios are similar.

$$\text{Acid-test ratio} = \frac{\text{cash} + \text{marketable securities} + \text{receivables}}{\text{current liabilities}}$$

This ratio provides a measure of the immediate availability of current liquid assets to meet current liabilities.

$$\text{Defensive interval} = \frac{\text{cash} + \text{short-term marketable securities} + \text{receivables}}{\text{estimated daily cash operating expenditures (excludes depreciation)}}$$

This ratio is a measure of very short-term liquidity—how many days the most liquid assets could support the operating expenditures of the firm.

If either ratio indicates illiquidity problems, the auditor may consider the risk that the burdensome liabilities may have been understated to improve the overall appearance of the firm's financial position. Of course, critically poor ratios and severe cash needs will have alerted the auditor to audit problems in areas other than payables.

Results of Operations—Revenue and Expense. Three types of ratio analysis are commonly employed to analyze the revenue and expense accounts: (1) common-size statements, (2) the ratios of certain revenue or expense accounts to related assets accounts, and (3) the ratios of certain expense accounts to related income and expense accounts. The first of these, common-size statements, is covered in the following section, while the last two examples are presented here.

Certain expense or revenue accounts are closely related to particular asset accounts, so that the ratio of the accounts is quite meaningful and can be usefully compared over time or with that of other firms. Examples of such ratios include:

1. *Interest expense* to *debt*
2. *Interest income* to *notes receivable*
3. *Investment income* to *investments*
4. *Depreciation expense* to *gross assets subject to depreciation*
5. *Bad debt expense* to the *allowance for bad debts*
6. *Repairs and maintenance expense* to *related property, plant, and equipment*

In some cases, it may be necessary to disaggregate the expense account and related asset account if, for example, it is known that certain investments have substantially different returns from others. Also, the depreciation expense ratio can be computed for major groups of assets wherein depreciation methods are the same. Apart from this, the first four ratios will generally be easy to compute and interpret. Significant deviations from the expected ratio indicate a potential accounting error.

The ratios for bad debt expense and repair and maintenance expense may not be as easily interpreted, however. These relationships are to a significant extent discretionary in nature. Though the ratios should display a predictable long-run pattern (e.g., bad debt expense might be computed as a per cent of credit sales), the ratio may fluctuate in any one period because of differences in management's policies for that period. This is particularly true for maintenance expenses which can be postponed without immediate breakdowns or loss of productivity. The auditor should interpret an unexpected deviation for either of these two ratios with these considerations in mind.

Another type of ratio useful for analyzing the expense accounts is the ratio of certain expenses to related income or expense amounts, for example:

1. *Payroll taxes* to *payroll expense*
2. *Employee benefit expense* to *payroll expense*
3. *Income tax* to *income before tax*

These ratios should have a stable, predictable pattern, especially for the first two. Any significant deviation, if not reflecting a change in tax rates or management benefits policy, would signal the potential for accounting error of some kind. The income tax ratio is less easily interpreted, since it may not be comparable over time because of changes in tax law or because of the tax effects of nonrecurring decisions, such as an unusually large charitable donation in a given year.

Common-Size Statements

Common-size statements are often prepared for both the balance sheet accounts and the income statement accounts. However, the analysis of the income statement accounts tends to be far more useful than does analysis of the balance sheet, since most revenue and expense accounts bear some relationship to total sales, whereas a breakdown of the composition of total assets or total equities is generally less meaningful. For one thing, the balance sheet accounts may include nonoperating items which will reduce the comparability of the common-size percentages, both over time and across firms. Additionally, an analysis of the composition of total assets, liabilities, and equities has value primarily in assessing inherent risk, as we have discussed in Chapter 3, rather than in identifying the potential for error in a given account, as is our subject in this chapter.

The special value of common-size analysis of revenue and expense accounts is that most of the individual accounts bear some relationship to the aggregate—total sales. As sales increase, most expense items increase in a predictable way, and thus the comparison of the common-size percentages over time or across firms can be very meaningful. To illustrate, we discuss the analysis of the common-size percentages for the following four income statement accounts. Other revenue and expense accounts can be analyzed in a similar fashion.

1. Sales returns and discounts
2. Cost of goods sold
3. Selling expense
4. Research and development expenses

The accounts for *sales returns* and *discounts on sales* bear a natural relationship to total sales. Any significant deviation of this percentage, over time within the firm or when compared across firms, provides an indication of potential error in the accounting for these items. For example, a steep increase in the rate of sales returns might be an indication of obsolete or unsalable inventory.

The ratio of *cost of goods sold* to *sales* is among the most common of the ratios used by auditors. For most firms this ratio has a very stable and predictable pattern which makes it very useful for comparison across time or with similar firms. It is most useful when computed by product line since the components of cost and profit margins can vary significantly for different products, and changes in product mix can affect the aggregate rates. In some cases the ratio is used in its equivalent, inverse form, the ratio of gross margin to total sales. The two are interpreted in a similar manner. A significant and unexpected deviation in the ratio for any product line, unless explained by changes in price or productivity, could indicate a lack of consistency in accounting for inventory or in treating a certain component of cost. A cost item might be improperly included in or excluded from product cost, for example.[5]

The cost-of-goods-sold ratio was instrumental in detecting fraud in one case in which cash payments on receivables were taken by a receivables clerk. This left the detail list of customer balances less than the general ledger, but the bookkeeper, thinking the differences were immaterial, made a balancing entry to debit sales and credit receivables. This was done several times through the year, and by year-end, sales were so understated that the cost of sales ratio was significantly increased. Upon investigating the increase, the auditor detected the defalcation.

The ratio of *selling expense* to *sales* should also represent a stable and predictable relationship. To the extent that selling expenses are directly proportional to sales, as for a sales representative's commissions, the ratio is easily interpreted. However, to the extent that some components of selling expense are not related to sales, as for sales representatives' salaries, the ratio has little meaning. Thus, the proper interpretation of this ratio, *as for those of most expense accounts*, requires an understanding of the nature of the underlying cost behavior—is it strictly variable (with sales revenue), strictly fixed, or a mix. The usefulness of the analysis of the ratio, then, is directly proportional to the extent to which the expense item is *strictly variable* in nature. Also, some portion of selling expense might be discretionary, as for nonrecurring special promotion efforts. Items of this nature will also distort the comparability of the ratio to that for prior years.

The ratio of *research and development expenses* to *sales* can provide a useful basis for an analysis of the accounting for ongoing research efforts. However, its interpretation is subject to the same limitations identified above—the distortion due to fixed costs and nonrecurring items. Additionally, research and development expenses are a type of expense in which judgment must be employed to determine what portion of current expenditures is capitalized. Statements of Financial Accounting

---

[5] A detailed statement accounting for variations in cost of goods sold and gross margin is illustrated in L. Bernstein, Financial Statement Analysis 587-90 (Irwin 1978).

Standards No 2, *Accounting for Research and Development Costs,* has limited the bounds for this judgment considerably, but many uncertainties remain as to the proper accounting for these costs. Thus, the analysis of this ratio for a stable and ongoing research effort could be used to signal any change in management's accounting policy for certain of these costs.

§5.04   Problems and Limitations in Using Ratio Analysis

We have just seen that it is very important to know whether a cost item is strictly variable or not when analyzing it through common-size statements. This is one example of many of the problems and limitations in using ratio analysis. These can be conveniently grouped into the following three categories:

1. The effect of different accounting conventions

2. The assumed nature of the relationship underlying the ratio

3. The determination of what is a significant deviation

These three problem areas are relevant for all types of ratio analysis, though different accounting conventions affect intra-industry comparisons far more than they do time-series comparisons. These problems, along with problems in using industry data, are presented later in the chapter, together with some suggestions for using these data most effectively.

Effect of Accounting Conventions

A primary reason why ratios may be noncomparable over time or across firms is the use of different accounting conventions. There are two types of accounting conventions involved, and there may be differences in either: (1) the manner in which the ratio is computed and (2) the accounting policy for recognition and valuation for the related financial statement accounts.

As Gibson and Boyer point out,[6] there is a general lack of uniformity in the manner in which the ratios are computed—what is included in the numerator and in the denominator of the ratio. For example, they point out that two of the principal sources of industry ratios compute inventory turnover in a different manner. Robert Morris Associates

---

[6] Gibson & Boyer, *The Need for Disclosure of Uniform Financial Ratios,* J Accountancy, May 1980, at 78-84.

uses the ratio of cost of sales to inventory, where *Dun's Review* presents net sales to inventory. The latter gives a higher turnover ratio. The auditor must be alert for such differences in using ratio analysis. Additionally, when average ratio figures from trade or industry publications are used, care must be taken that the ratios for each sampled firm were computed in the same manner.

The second type of accounting convention relates to accounting policies which may differ across firms or over time. We list some of the more important potential differences below.

1.   Inventory valuation—LIFO, FIFO, etc.

2.   Differences in management conservatism in making certain accounting estimates, such as the allowance for doubtful accounts or the adjustment for obsolete and unsalable inventory

3.   Differences in the cost accounting methods used, the allocation of overhead, and the treatment of variances

It is clear that consistency for both types of accounting conventions is likely to be greater for a given firm over time than for a comparison across firms or with industry averages. Thus, the auditor must be particularly alert for this kind of problem when comparing a firm's ratios to industry data.

The Assumed Nature of the Relationship Underlying the Ratio

For a ratio analysis to be meaningful, we must be satisfied that the relationship between the numerator and denominator is (1) strictly variable, (2) strictly linear, (3) complete, and (4) stable over time and consistent across firms. Rarely are these assumptions met perfectly in practice, but often they are satisfied sufficiently for the ratio analysis to be meaningful.[7] Consider each assumption.

The Relationship Is Strictly Variable. It is convenient in illustrating this assumption to use certain labels, as follows:

$$R \text{ (the ratio)} = \frac{N \text{ (the numerator)}}{D \text{ (the denominator)}}$$

For example, the ratio of selling expense to sales (R) would be the result of selling expense (N) divided by the sales (D). We start with a

---

[7] A complete, rigorous presentation of the material covered in this section can be found in Lev and Sunder (1979).

very general description of the relationship between sales and selling expense

$$\text{Selling expense} = \text{function of sales}$$

If we assume the relationship is linear, the general linear model with labels would be

$$N = A + RD$$

where A is the intercept of the linear equation. It corresponds to the fixed cost portion of the total selling cost (N), while RD is the total variable cost portion. Thus, the assumption of a strictly linear relationship means that A equals zero, and $R = N/D$. If, however, A is not zero and there is fixed cost, then $R = N/D - A/D$, wherein the last term (A/D) represents bias. Now the ratio R is not comparable for different levels of D because of the bias term. More simply, N/D in this case represents unit variable cost which should be constant for a range of values for D, but A/D will vary with changes in D thus causing the bias.

In summary, the auditor must understand the nature of the relationship between the numerator and denominator of the ratio under analysis, particularly for the ratios of expense to sales involved in common-size income statements. When the fixed component A is present, the comparison among ratios must be interpreted carefully. The auditor can use the cost accounting concept of a *relevant range* to assist when the fixed component is present. That is, the comparability of the ratios is directly proportional to the size of the difference in the denominator for the ratios compared. For example, given the ratios R_1 and R_2, where $R_1 = N_1/D_1$ and $R_2 = N_2/D_2$, if D_1 and D_2 are relatively close, then the comparison of the ratios can be meaningful.

In our studies of auditor judgment, we conducted an experiment to investigate the ability of unaided auditors to apply an understanding of this assumption when interpreting common-size income statements. Only 7 of the 29 auditors differentiated a ratio in which the intercept A was present from one in which the relationship was strictly variable. This suggests that some auditors may not sufficiently understand the importance of this assumption when using ratio analysis.

The Relationship Is Strictly Linear. We have just seen that the analysis of ratios is based on the special case of the general simple linear model with an intercept A equal to zero. It follows then that we are assuming a linear relationship between the numerator and denominator. This assumption is reasonable for many expense categories, especially if we apply the concept of the relevant range. For example, selling expense which is primarily composed of a sales representative's commission of 15 per cent would have an approximately linear relationship with sales. On the other hand, if the commission rate increases or decreases with an increase in sales for the individual sales representative, the relationship is actually nonlinear.

Another example of a nonlinear relationship is the inventory turnover ratio for a firm which employs the economic order quantity (EOQ) formula for optimizing production runs or purchase order size. The simple EOQ model is as follows:

$$EOQ = \sqrt{\frac{2 \times \text{annual sales} \times \text{purchase order cost}}{\text{storage cost}}}$$

As can be seen from the formula, average inventory (approximately EOQ/2) is directly related to the *square root* of sales rather than sales per se. Thus, the inventory turnover ratio does not reflect a linear relationship, and turnover rates for different levels of sales will not be comparable.

As for the "strictly variable" cost assumption above, a response to the problems related to the linearity assumption is to apply the concept of the relevant range. Thus, if the differences in the denominators of the ratios being compared are not significantly different, the ratios will be reasonably comparable.

The Relationship Is Complete. The assumption we address here is that the denominator of the ratio *alone* and no other item of financial or operating data influences the numerator. Consider again the example of the ratio of selling expense to sales. Suppose the relationship between selling expense and sales is best expressed by

Selling expense = function of (sales, sales mix, . . .)

That is, selling expense is now assumed to be influenced by two or more variables, in this case by sales, sales mix, and perhaps other variables. Then the general linear model should be of the following form, where D_1 represents sales, and D_2 represents sales mix (assume A equals zero):

$$N = R_1 D_1 + R_2 D_2$$

Then, the selling-expense-to-sales ratio is biased by the additional variable in the equation:

$$R_1 = \frac{N}{D_1} - \underbrace{\frac{R_2 D_2}{D_1}}_{\text{Bias}}$$

The practical result of this is that two selling expense ratios may not be comparable because of differences in sales mix. Unfortunately, the auditor rarely has enough knowledge of the nature of the relationships affecting the numerator of a ratio to assess the potential for this type of bias. The application of multivariate statistical methods, such as multiple regression analysis, can be used to identify these multiple relationships, but these techniques may be cost-effective on only the largest audit engagements.

The Relationship Is Stable over Time and Consistent across Firms. This is perhaps the most obvious of the assumptions of the nature of the relationship expressed by the ratio. It relates to the nature of the operating and financial structure of the firm. For example, the installation of a computer-based inventory management system should have a significant effect on average inventories. Inventory turnover ratios before and after the development would not be comparable. The same can be said for differences in financial and operating structure across firms.

Determining What Is a Significant Deviation

A basic limitation of the effective use of ratio analysis is the lack of useful guidance in determining a cutoff or threshold for identifying significant deviations. This is largely a matter of auditor judgment, based on knowledge of the client's operations, the quality of the client's controls, and other factors. Our studies of auditor judgment suggest that, without prompting, auditors use a cutoff of somewhere between 5 and 10 per cent of the amount of the ratio, for common-size statement analysis. The thresholds for balance sheet ratios are probably higher, though these were not included in our study.

§5.05   Using Industry Data

This section points out the difficulties in using industry figures for comparison with a firm's ratios. An approach for most effectively using industry data is presented. This approach uses the auditor's knowledge of the client's business to construct a specialized industry index for the client.

The Difficulties

Some of the problems in using industry data have already been explained. In Chapter 3 we discussed the problems in using industry leverage, liquidity, and operating ratios in analyzing the financial risk component of inherent risk. And earlier in this chapter we listed some of the accounting conventions which can differ across firms so that the affected ratios are not comparable. Now we consider three additional problems in using the industry data.

First, it is difficult to define an industry. Most definitions are based on the nature of the end product such as "furniture and fixtures" or "paper and allied products." The SIC code to the two-digit level of aggregation is widely accepted. However, many analysts would admit that very often a company does not "fit" well within the group because of unique product diversification, vertical or horizontal integration, and so on.

A second and related problem in using industry comparisons is the numerous possibilities for natural differences between firms within well-defined industry categories. For example, firms in the same industry may differ substantially in financial or operating factors, and in related ratios, for the following reasons:

1. Geographic separation, differences in price levels and costs of operations.
2. Different ownership or financial structure. For example, the levels of current assets may be significantly different for an independently run firm than for a subsidiary of a conglomerate firm.
3. Nonoperating factors in the balance sheet or income statement.
4. Different levels of capacity utilization.
5. Product diversification.
6. Age and productivity of assets.
7. Different customer mix, number of customers, and geographic dispersion including international clientele.

This is merely a partial listing. The auditor who has a good understanding of the client's business will be able to identify those unique aspects of the business which might distinguish it from others in the industry.

These potential intra-industry differences are reflected in intra-industry variability of ratios. For example, Trapnell found that many ratios did not consistently differentiate between two-digit, SIC-code industry groups; that is, there was approximately as much interindustry variability in ratios as there was intra-industry variability.[8] However, the best differentiating ratios were those related to certain of the asset accounts, such as the current ratio and the asset turnover ratio. In a related study, Gupta and Huefner had results consistent with the above.[9] The consequence of the high intra-industry variability is that an industry average ratio does not provide a very reliable target.

The comparison of firm to industry ratios is laden with the difficulties identified above. In many cases, the auditor will be satisfied that they are not too severe for the engagement at hand and that the tie-in to industry data is meaningful and useful. Exhibit 2 at the end of the chapter lists many sources of industry data which are available.

Industry Ratio Data for Analysis

Appendix G provides a detailed presentation of actual industry data for the 24 ratios in Table 3-2 plus the Altman Z-score. The ratios are shown for 40 important industry categories. The data is presented for both large and small firms, to facilitate a useful comparison of a given firm's data to the average for the industry. Additionally, the ratios are shown for both the upper and lower quartiles and for the median. The ratios were computed using the formulas presented in Table 3-2. Other specific information about the preparation and presentation of these data are included in the Appendix.

We recommend the use of the industry data in this appendix for comparing the *trend* of an entity's financial ratio to the trend of the industry ratio, rather than to compare the current year values only. This analysis approach avoids a number of the problems of using industry data noted earlier in this chapter and in Chapter 3.

§5.06 References

Beaver, Kettler & Scholes, *The Association between Market-Determined and Accounting-Determined Risk Measures,* Account Rev, Oct 1970, at 654-82.

L. Bernstein, *Financial Statement Analysis* (Irwin rev ed 1978).

Deakin, *Distributions of Financial Accounting Ratios: Some Empirical Evidence,* Account Rev, Jan 1979, at 90-96.

---

[8] J. Trapnell, An Empirical Study of the Descriptive Nature of Financial Ratios Relative to Industry Operating Characteristics (1977) (unpublished Doctoral Dissertation, University of Georgia.

[9] Gupta & Huefner, *A Cluster Analysis of Financial Ratios and Industry Characteristics,* J Account Res, Spring 1979, at 77-95.

Financial Ratio Analysis: An Historical Perspective (Arno J. Horrigan ed 1978).

J. Finnerty, *Corporate Financial Analysis* (McGraw Hill 1986).

G. Foster, *Financial Statement Analysis* (Prentice-Hall 1978).

Gibson & Boyer, *The Need for Disclosure of Uniform Financial Ratios,* J Accountancy, May 1980, at 78-84.

Gonedes, *Evidence on the Information Content of Accounting Numbers: Accounting-Based and Market-Based Estimates of Systematic Risk,* J Fin & Quantitative Analysis, June 1973, at 407-44.

Gupta & Huefner, *A Cluster Analysis of Financial Ratios and Industry Characteristics,* J Account Res, Spring 1972, at 77-95.

Lev & Sunder, *Methodological Issues in the Use of Financial Ratios,* J Account & Econ, 1979, at 187-210.

S. McMullen, *Financial Statements: Form, Analysis and Interpretation* (Irwin 7th ed 1979).

J. Siegel, *How to Analyze Businesses, Financial Statements, and the Quality of Earning* (Prentice-Hall 1982).

J. Trapnell, An Empirical Study of the Descriptive Nature of Financial Ratios Relative to Industry Operating Characteristics (1977) (unpublished Ph.D. thesis, University of Georgia, Athens).

Exhibit 2

Sources of Information on Industry Ratios

Professional and commercial sources

Dun and Bradstreet, Inc., Business Economics Division.

Key business ratios. Important operating and financial ratios in 71 manufacturing lines, 32 wholesale lines, and 22 retail lines and published in *Dun's Review* of modern industry. Five-year summaries are also published. The data are presented in three ranges: lower quartile, median, and upper quartile.

Cost-of-doing-business series. Typical operating ratios for 185 lines of business, showing national averages. They represent a percentage of business receipts reported by a representative sample of the total of all federal tax returns.

Moody's Investor Service.

Moody's manuals contain financial and operating ratios on individual companies covered.

National Cash Register Company.

Expenses in Retail Businesses. Biennial. Operating ratios for 36 lines of retail business, as taken from trade associations and other sources including many from *Barometer of Small Business.*

Robert Morris Associates.

Annual Statement Studies. Financial and operating ratios for about 300 lines of business—manufacturers, wholesalers, retailers, services, and contractors—based on information obtained from member banks of RMA. Data are broken down by company size. Part 4 gives "Additional Profit and Loss Data."

Standard & Poor's Corporation.

Industry surveys in two parts: (1) basic analysis and (2) current analysis; contain many industry and individual company ratios.

Almanac of Business and Industrial Financial Ratios by Leo Troy, Prentice-Hall, Inc., Englewood Cliffs, N.J.

A compilation of corporate performance ratios (operating and financial). The significance of these ratios is explained. All industries are covered in the study; each industry is subdivided by asset size.

The Federal Government

Small Business Administration.

Publications containing industry statistics:

Small Marketers Aids.
Small Business Management Series.
Business Service Bulletins.
U.S. Department of Commerce.
Census of Business—surveys wholesale trade and releases summary statistics; monthly wholesale trade report; ratios of operating expenses to sales.
U.S. Department of the Treasury.
Statistics of income, corporation income tax returns. Operating statistics based on income tax returns.
Federal Trade Commission.
Quarterly financial report for manufacturing, mining, and trade corporations. Contains operating ratios and balance sheet ratios as well as the balance sheet in ratio format.

Sources of Specific Industry Ratios

Federal Deposit Insurance Corporation *Bank Operating Statistics.* Annual.
Institute of Real Estate Management. Experience Exchange Committee. *A Statistical Compilation and Analysis of Actual Income and Expenses Experienced in Apartment, Condominium and Cooperative Building Operation.* Annual.
Discount Merchandiser. *The True Look of the Discount Industry.* June issue each year. Includes operating ratios.
Eli Lilly and Company. *The Lilly Digest.* Annual.
National Electrical Contractors Association. *Operation Overhead.* Annual.
National Farm & Power Equipment Dealers Association. *Cost of Doing Business Study.* Annual.
Journal of Commercial Bank Lending. "Analysis of Year End Composite Ratios of Instalment Sales Finance and Small Loan Companies."
Harris, Kerr, Forster & Company. *Trends in the Hotel-Motel Business.* Annual.
Ohio Lumber and Building Product Dealers Association. *Survey of Operating Profits.* Compiled by Battelle and Battelle. Annual.
American Meat Institute. *Financial Facts about the Meat Packing Industry.* Includes operating ratios.
Chase Manhattan Bank. *Financial Analysis of a Group of Petroleum Companies.* Annual.
National Office Products Association. *Survey of Operating Results of NOPA Dealers.* Annual.
American Paint and Wallcoverings Dealers. *Report on Annual Survey.*

EXHIBIT 2   127

Printing Industries of America. *Ratios for Use of Printing Management.* Annual.

Laventhol Krekstein Horwath & Horwath. *Restaurants, Country Clubs, City Clubs: Reports on Operations.* Annual.

National Association of Textile and Apparel Wholesalers. *Performance Analysis of NATAW Members.* Annual.

Bibliographies

Robert Morris Associates, *Sources of Composite Financial Data—A Bibliography,* 3d ed., N.Y., 1971, 28 pages. An annotated list of sources, with an index, by specific industry, at front.

Sanzo, Richard, *Ratio Analysis for Small Business,* 3d ed., U.S. Small Business Administration, Small Business Management Series, no. 20, 1970, 65 pages. "Sources of Ratio Studies," pp. 22-35, lists the industries covered by basic sources such as D&B, Robert Morris Associates. Also includes the names of trade associations which have published ratio studies. Published financial and operating ratios are also occasionally listed in the monthly *Marketing Information Guide.*

SOURCE: Adapted from L. Bernstein, *Financial Statement Analysis* 87-89 (Irwin rev ed 1983) (reprinted with permission).

The Reasonableness Test

6

§6.01   Introduction
§6.02   Reasonableness Test Methods
§6.03   Statistical Methods
§6.04   The Expected Value Method
§6.05   References

§6.01 Introduction

I went home, and to bed, three or four hours after midnight.
. . . An accidental sudden noise waked me about six in the morning, when I was surprised to find my room filled with light. . . .
Rubbing my eyes, I perceived the light came in at the windows.
I got up and looked out to see what might be the occasion of it,
when I saw the sun just rising above the horizon, from whence
he poured his rays plentifully into my chamber.

This event has given rise in my mind to several serious and important reflections. I considered that, if I had not been awakened
so early in the morning, I should have slept six hours longer by
the light of the sun, and in exchange have lived six hours the following night by candlelight; and, the latter being as much more
expensive light than the former, my love of economy induced me
to muster up what little arithmetic I was master of, and to make
some calculations, which I shall give you, after observing that
utility is in my opinion, the test of value. . . .

In the six months between the 20th of March and the 20th of
September, there are

128

Nights..183
Hours of each night in which we burn candles........................7
Multiplication gives for the total number of hours............1,281
These 1,281 hours multiplied by 100,000 the number of inhabi-
tants (of Paris) give 128,100,000
One hundred twenty-eight millions and one hundred thousand
hours, spent at Paris by candlelight, which, at half a pound of wax
and tallow per hour, gives the weight of.......................64,050,000
Sixty-four millions and fifty thousand of pounds, which, estimating the whole at the medium price of thirty sols the pound, makes
the sum of ninety-six millions and seventy-five thousand *livres*
tournois 96,075,000
An immense sum! that the city of Paris might save every year,
by the economy of using sunshine instead of candles.

Benjamin Franklin
"An Economical Project"
(apparently written Mar. 20, 1784)

Benjamin Franklin appears to have been one of the earliest advo-
cates of daylight saving time. His frugal disposition and keen intellect
which led to this advocacy are well illustrated in this series of multipli-
cations which projects immense savings for the city of Paris. These
computations are characteristic of what we describe in this chapter,
the reasonableness test. The reasonableness test is generally a very
simple computation or series of computations which develops an estimate of an amount through the use of relevant financial and operating
data. A good example is the estimation of bad debt expense from current sales and receivables data, or the estimation of payroll expense
from data about the number of employees, average wage rate, and time
worked.

Since the reasonableness test employs a limited amount of data and
simple computations, the resulting estimate is generally viewed as a
good approximation, but not as precise an estimate as would be obtained, say, from statistical methods. But, since the reasonableness test
requires far less auditor time, it may often be more cost-beneficial than
other estimation methods.

An important aspect of the use of a reasonableness test in audit planning is that it requires the auditor to consider all the financial and operating factors (independent variables) which are relevant for the
amount to be estimated (dependent variables). That is, to complete
a reasonableness test, the auditor must in effect develop a simple
model to explain changes in the dependent variable by analyzing
changes in related independent variables. We touched on this type of

modeling approach briefly in Chapter 4 in connection with trend analysis. However, the focus of Chapter 4 was changes over time, a time-series analysis using a time-series model. In contrast, we extend that idea in this chapter to the simple one-period model which the auditor can analyze with pencil and paper. The important thing here is that the reasonableness test requires the auditor to structure, or "model," the process of developing the desired estimate.

The benefits of modeling the estimation process are the greater knowledge acquired by the auditor and the greater precision of the estimate. Both benefits stem from the explicit recognition of the relevant independent variables and from the quantification of the relationships between these variables that is required to complete the reasonableness test. To illustrate, let us consider the hypothetical case of an auditor involved in planning year-end tests for payroll expense. The auditor performs trend analysis and observes a 9 to 10 per cent increase over the previous year. Having noted that this rate of increase is consistent with the approximately 10 per cent rate of inflation in the local economy, and with the 8 to 12 per cent average wage increases, the auditor gains confidence that a modest level of substantive testing is required. In contrast, if the auditor had taken a reasonableness test approach, he or she would have found (in this hypothetical case) that the company had had to interrupt production and lay off plant personnel for an entire month to repair a crucial piece of equipment. The cost of repairs was improperly charged to direct labor expense so that payroll expense is overstated and repairs expense is understated. The reasonableness test would have required an analysis of hours worked and in this way would have led the auditor to detect the accounting classification error.

The chapter is organized as follows: First, there is a discussion of the reasonableness test method for both the single- and the multiple-independent-variable cases. This includes illustrative applications for selected accounts. Second, there is a brief presentation of the manner in which a statistical approach or an expected value approach could be used to enhance the precision of the reasonableness test.

§6.02   Reasonableness Test Methods

The auditor performing a reasonableness test to analyze an account balance begins with a simple model of financial and operating factors affecting that account. Four different modeling approaches are possible, as illustrated in Table 6-1. Each of the four model types represents a different approach to the reasonableness test.

Table 6-1   Four Types of Models of the Account Balance

	Complexity of the Model	
What the Model Predicts (dependent variable)	One Independent Variable	Two or More Independent Variables
Current account balance	Type one	Type three
Change in account balance from prior year	Type two	Type four

The models differ according to what it is the auditor is predicting with the reasonableness test (the dependent variable is either the account balance or the change in the account balance) and according to the number of financial and operating factors (independent variables) the auditor plans to incorporate in the model. Assuming all the independent variables are relevant, the greater the number of independent variables, the more informative is the model and therefore the more precise its prediction. Of course, the multiple-variable model is also more complex and costly to apply than the single-variable model.

The auditor chooses also whether to apply a model which predicts the total current account balance, or the change in balance from the prior year. While the former is more common and perhaps more intuitively appealing, the latter may be more economical and effective in those situations in which the prior year's balance is audited. The reason for this is that, by considering only the change in the balance, the auditor is able to eliminate from the model all those independent variables which did not change from the prior year. These variables would therefore be irrelevant for the *change* model, whereas they would probably have to be included in the *current-balance* model. Thus, in this case, the change model is simpler, and more effective and economical.

One-Variable Models (type one and type two)

The most popular model for use in reasonableness tests appears to be the type one model. There are many examples of this approach in accounting and auditing. It is widely used as an estimating technique in a variety of contexts. For example, construction costs are often predicted on the basis of square feet of livable space. Also, factory overhead costs are often predicted as an amount per direct labor hour. And, revenues from hospital room charges for a given period can be estimated directly from room charge and occupancy data.

These simple estimates can be computed quite easily and are often reasonably accurate. Many times they are just as accurate as detailed methods that are more time-consuming and costly. It is often argued that the simple, one-variable models are as useful as the more complex models because those variables not included will generally have offsetting effects, so that on the average, the use of the single most important independent variable produces very good results. This is likely to be one of the reasons for the wide usage of the simple methods in practice.

The reader is referred back to those two sections of Chapter 5 which dealt with the use of ratios to analyze revenue and expense accounts, and to the use of common-size income statements. Both of these forms of analysis are closely related to the type one reasonableness test model. Both analyses use a simple relationship between accounts to predict an account balance. For example, a reasonableness test of the account *repairs and maintenance expense* could be done by examining the ratio of repairs and maintenance expense to the value of the related plant and equipment. Similarly, the ratio of a sales representative's commission expense to sales could be used to examine the reasonableness of this expense category.

In contrast to the above illustrations, reasonableness tests typically involve a selected operating datum as the independent variable— occupancy rate, production level, and the like. That is, the reasonableness test examines the correspondence that should exist between the operating and financial data. Quite naturally, there should be good correspondence between operating data and the "results of operations" portion of the financial data. In contrast, there is less reason to expect a relationship between operating levels and the levels of the "stock" balances of the financial statements—assets, liabilities, and equities. Thus, reasonableness tests are naturally more applicable for revenue and expense accounts, the financial record of results of operations.

For some organizations, virtually every revenue and expense account can be readily tied to an index of operating activity. For example, room charge revenue for hospitals and hotels should be easily correlated to occupancy rates. Revenue for freight haulers can be related to tons of material carried. Similarly, utilities expenses, fuel costs, and related production costs are easily estimated from data about production activity.

For other organizations, the direct correspondence between operating data and financial results may not exist, or reliable operating data may not be available. For example, sales levels for retailers often cannot be tied to a readily available, independent index of operating activity. This would probably be the case for a videotape and phonograph record retailer. A convenient predictor variable is not available in this case. Certain demographic and macroeconomic data may be useful in predicting broad movements of videotape and record sales, but not with the precision required by auditors. Thus, a reasonableness test approach is not applicable in this situation.

Because it is most common, the type one reasonableness test model has been the focus of our discussion to this point. The type two modeling approach is very similar. For example, the auditor examining hotel revenue may have good reason to assume that the occupancy rate for the current year is very nearly the same as for the prior years, but room charges have increased by an average of 10 per cent. Then, an appropriate reasonableness test would be to predict current year's revenue as 110 per cent of the prior-year (audited) amount.

Index Models

A very special and unique single-variable approach for the type one reasonableness test is the use of an index model.[1] Index models are useful particularly for large manufacturing companies, where a variety of different sizes of products of a similar design are made. For example, the manufacture of products such as furniture, steel and concrete pipes, electric motors, certain appliances, and fuel tanks represents a situation in which the index model could be applied. Basically, the index model is an exponential equation which predicts the cost of a given size of a product on the basis of the known size and cost of a product of similar design. Index models therefore can be used to test the reasonableness of inventory costs in cases in which production output varies in size but is similar in type. The index model is

$$C = C_r \left(\frac{Q_c}{Q_r} \right)^m$$

where C total cost sought for design size Q_c

C_r = known cost for a reference design size Q_r
Q_c = design size
Q_r = reference design size
m = correlating exponent, $0 \leq m \leq 1$ $m = 1.0$ means no economies of scale in production

---

[1] This section on index models is adapted from P. Ostwald, Cost Estimating for Engineering and Management 201-02 (Prentice Hall 1974). The index model is also sometimes called the "power law and sizing model."

The use of the model can be illustrated as follows. Suppose the auditee manufactures concrete tanks of similar design in many different sizes, lengths, and diameters. Assume the value of m = 0.6 for tanks ranging from 100 to 1000 cubic feet of capacity. The value for m may be known from engineering studies or analyses of past cost records. Assume also that it is known that a tank of 200 cubic feet has a cost of $2500, and assume that the auditor wants to assess the reasonableness of the cost of a batch of 600-cubic-foot tanks, as reported by the client. The 600-cubic-foot tanks are a new product for the firm, and the auditor is not familiar with the cost behavior of the larger tanks, so the index model analysis is desired. The estimated cost of each tank of the 600-cubic-foot size is

$$C = 2500\left(\frac{600}{200}\right)^{0.6} = \$2500 \times 1.933182 = \$4832.96$$

If the exponent m is reliable, then a good estimate of the larger tank is approximately $5000, as computed above. The size of the tank increases threefold, whereas the cost nearly doubles.

This illustration is for the model in the basic form, and it may require adjustment for price changes, if the price of the "reference" size is dated. Also, the determination of the exponent m should take into account any technological differences, batch size differences, or other factors which might impact the comparability of the costs for the two product sizes involved. Tables of values of m for a variety of products can be found in engineering reference books such as the text by Peters and Timmerhaus.[2]

Multiple-Independent-Variable Models

In many cases, the auditor may find that two or more independent variables are necessary to estimate the given account balance with acceptable precision. For example, consider again the case of estimating room charge revenue for a motel or hotel on the basis of occupancy and room charge data. This is the simple one-variable problem discussed earlier. If, however, the motel or hotel has a seasonal rate structure, then it will be necessary to add the seasonality dimension as a second independent variable. Now, the estimated revenue is computed for each rate season, and the seasonal figures are aggregated to obtain the desired estimate for the annual amount.

---

[2] M. Peters & K. Timmerhaus, Plant Design and Economics for Chemical Engineers (McGraw-Hill 2d ed 1968).

Two additional examples will further illustrate this multiple-variable approach. The first example involves the reasonableness test of the fuel expense for the auto and truck fleet of a large construction firm. This is an example of the type three model in that it involves the estimation of an account balance without the use of the prior year's balance. The example is outlined in worksheet form in Table 6-2. Two types of fuel, eleven types of vehicles with related fuel consumption measures, and usage figures for each vehicle type are incorporated in the analysis. Much of the information required for the analysis is readily available from the financial records (fuel cost per gallon, number of vehicles of each type). The fuel consumption data could be obtained by inquiry of management and corroborated by an outside source such as the local dealer for the vehicle. The usage data may be available in the client's operating reports or maintenance records. The hypothetical data given in Table 6-2 reflect the reasonable assumption that this type of data is available for some vehicles and not for others. Where the usage data are not available, the auditor must provide an estimate. This can be done by taking a sample of the vehicles of a given type, obtaining the records or data necessary to figure the usage for these vehicles, and then projecting the sample results to the total number of vehicles. Alternatively, the auditor can use rough estimation methods based on whatever relevant information is available. For example, a usage estimate could be based upon the known number of working days in the year together with some assumption of the radius (in miles) of the region in which the operations took place.

Once the relevant data are assembled, as in the hypothetical case just depicted, the estimate of aggregate fuel expense is easily derived. This can be compared with the recorded amount for reasonableness. If the difference is significant, the auditor, depending on the materiality of the amount, may choose to do further testing or propose an adjustment to fuel inventory and fuel expense. Since fuel inventory for a construction company may be in small amounts in many locations, an accurate year-end inventory measurement with acceptable cutoff may be impractical. In this situation both the client and the auditor may feel that a reasonableness test in the manner described is an appropriate approach for adjusting fuel inventory and fuel expense accounts for the current year-end statements. A similar case could be made for taking this approach in similar circumstances for the accounts, supplies inventory, and supplies expense.

A second example illustrates the type four model, in which the prior year's account balance is included in the model for estimating the current year's balance. The payroll expense account provides a useful illustration. The three steps of the analysis for a hypothetical case are

Table 6-2 Reasonableness Test Worksheet

Fuel Expense for Hypothetical Construction Company

No.	Vehicle	Fuel Consumption	Usage (and Data Source)	Gallons Used	Total Fuel Used	Fuel Cost
			Gas*			
59	Small autos	20 mpg	$21,000 \times 59 = 1,239,000$ miles (no client records; estimated mileage from samples of 10 autos)	61,950		
23	Large autos	10 mpg	$24,000 \times 23 = 552,000$ miles (no client records; estimated mileage from sample of 6 autos)	55,200		
44	Pickup trucks	8 mpg	836,241 miles (client records)	104,530		
36	Vans	7 mpg	333,036 miles (client records)	47,576	269,256	$282,719
			Diesel†			
6	Flatbed trucks	4 mpg	39,204 miles (client records)	9,801		
4	Dump trucks	3 mpg	29,280 miles (client records)	9,760		
2	Payloaders	3 gal/h	3152 hours (client records)	9,456		
3	Bulldozers	3 gal/h	$\frac{3152 \times 3}{2} = 4728$ hours (no records; assumed same as for payloader	14,184		
1	Gooseneck	2 gal/h	4095 (client records)	8,190		
2	Graders	2 gal/h	190 working days (client records) $190 \times 8 \times 2 = 3040$ hours	6,080		
2	Scrapers	2 gal/h	Assumed same as for grader	6,080	63,551	$ 62,280
			Estimated fuel expense			$344,999

*Cost = $1.05 per gallon.
†Cost = $0.98 per gallon.

shown in Table 6-3. The analysis begins with the prior-year amount. Then, the three elements involved in explaining a change in the balance over the current year are presented and analyzed. The three elements are (1) the wage rate, (2) the number of employees, and (3) the number of hours worked per employee. If the change in wage rate or the number of hours worked for the current year differs significantly for certain subgroups of employees, then these groups would be separately analyzed. However, often wage increases are across the board, and merit increases affect all employee groups, so that the use of a plantwide change in wage rate is often reasonable. Also, changes in the number of hours worked generally affect all employee groups, and the plantwide analysis is reasonable in this case.

In the hypothetical illustration, we have assumed that wages increased on the average by 8 per cent over the prior year and that the increase was effective near the middle of the year. Also, there was a loss of two full-year-equivalent personnel from the prior-year total of 151. Finally, the entire applicable work force worked the same number of normal hours as the prior year, but worked approximately 40 hours of overtime compared with none in the prior year.

As the third step of the worksheet shows, these three elements are combined using simple arithmetic to obtain an estimate for the current-year payroll expense. Notice that the wage rate factor (1.04) and

Table 6-3 Reasonableness Test Worksheet
Hypothetical Payroll Expense Account

1. Wage expense for the prior year (audited)	$2,962,430
2. Elements affecting change in wage expense (and data for current year)	
a. Increase (decrease) in average wage rate applicable to these personnel (8% increase effective midyear; net effect is 4% annual increase, or *104%*)	1.04
b. Increase (decrease) in the number of applicable personnel (loss of 4 of 151 positions, effective near the middle of the year)	
$$\frac{151 - (4 \times 1/2)}{151} = \frac{149}{151}$$	0.9868
c. Increase (decrease) in the number of hours worked for applicable personnel (additional 40 h/employee of overtime, early in the year)	
$(1/52)(1.5)$	0.02884
3. Estimated wage expense for current year	
$2,962,430\,[(1.04) \times (0.9868) + 0.02884]$	$3,125,695

the percentage change in number of personnel (.9868) are multiplicatively related, since they apply to the entire year. The effect of the change in the number of overtime hours, however, is additively related to the prior-year amount, since it occurred early in the year and thus was not affected by the other two elements. Our work with auditors performing analytical review tasks such as this shows that auditors often fail to assess correctly whether a relationship is multiplicative or additive, as in this example. The tendency appears to be to assume an additive relationship, even when it is not appropriate. An awareness of this bias should help auditors to mitigate its effect on their own judgments.

Another common practice we have observed among auditors is the extensive use of rounding of figures in reasonableness tests such as the above illustrations. The effect of this rounding is to reduce the precision of the prediction, since fewer significant digits are used. Auditors should be aware of this tendency toward rounding and understand its effect on the precision of their predictions.

Dependent Variables	Independent Variables
Sales or sales returns and allowances	Competition
	Interest rates
	Demographic trends
	Employment trends
	Economic indicators
	Advertising policies
	Pricing policies
Cost of sales	Inflation rate
	Fuel costs
	Labor rates
	Materials costs and availability
	Union contracts
	Production technology
	Personnel policies
	Employee benefit policies
	Location of facilities
General, selling, and administrative expenses	Employment and space rental contracts
	Number of sales personnel

To summarize, the reasonableness test approach can be characterized as the method which involves (1) identifying the relevant variables, (2) identifying the proper (multiplicative or additive) relationship between the variables, and (3) combining the variables to obtain an estimate of the current account balance. It follows that effective use of the model requires a good understanding of the operating environment of the client. This is necessary so that the relevant independent variables are properly identified. Also, it is important for the auditor to have the analytical ability to identify the correct form of the relationship between variables, whether multiplicative, additive, or some combination. This latter ability probably improves with audit experience, though many would also argue that some auditors are inherently better able to identify these relationships correctly than are others. Research from diverse areas of judgment investigation provides little guidance as to whether experience, ability, task context, or some other factor may be associated with the occurrence of these judgment errors. However, the research does consistently show that both expert and novice decision makers commonly make judgment mistakes of this type.

The examples we have shown are illustrative of the wide variety of contexts in which a reasonableness test approach can be useful. Because the approach typically models the relationship between financial results and operating data, the revenue and expense accounts will be naturally more amenable to the analysis. The table on the preceding page is offered as a partial listing for use in identifying the relevant independent variables when developing a reasonableness test.

§6.03   Statistical Methods

A way to enhance the precision of the reasonableness test approach is to apply statistical methods or probabilistic models. These methods add precision because they (1) quantify the uncertainty present in the estimation problems and (2) provide a means for evaluating the accuracy of the estimate.

The most appropriate statistical method in this context is regression analysis, which is described briefly in Chapter 11. The technical aspects of this method are presented in Appendix F. The application of regression analysis provides a more precise predictive model because it utilizes available data to produce a best-fitting linear model. The quantitative measure of predictive accuracy is the *standard error of the estimate,* which is provided with the regression results. It is a range around the predicted value wherein the auditor can be fairly confident the unknown "true" value will lie.

Regression can be used in either a time-series or cross-sectional model. In the time-series approach, the auditor collects data on the account balance and related operating data for the most recent 10 to 40 periods, usually months. The model which results from the data provides a prediction for the current balance based on the current operating data. As an example, the auditor could develop a time-series model for wage expense, using the independent variables identified in the example in the previous section.

> Wage expense = average hourly wage rate
> × average number of employees
> × average hours worked per employee

In symbols

$$W = WR \times E \times H$$

Note that this model is *not* linear since the independent variables are multiplied rather than added. Thus, a linear regression on these data would be inappropriate. Rather, the auditor would have to transform the data to an equivalent linear form. The logarithmic transform is most common; when applied to a multiplicative relationship, the resulting model is linear:

$$\log W = \log WR + \log E + \log H$$

The auditor transforms each data item by taking its logarithm (most computer-based statistical packages will do this automatically). The resulting equation is in log form, so that the desired estimate for wage expense is found by taking the antilog of the amount predicted by the equation.

The log transform is a convenient approach for dealing with nonlinear relationships in regression models. As noted before, the auditor must be alert to determine properly whether a multiplicative (nonlinear) or additive relationship applies for the model under analysis. Once this has been ascertained, it will be clear whether or not a log transform is necessary.

Another type of regression approach is to develop the model from cross-sectional data. For example, a regression equation to estimate sales revenue for different locations of a chain of auto repair shops would require a cross-sectional model. All the data would be obtained from the current period. The relevant independent variables might be staff size, inventory value, square feet of repair service area, and so on. In this case, the model is fitted from data across different stores in the chain, rather than across time, as for the wage expense example.

§6.04   The Expected Value Method

Alternatively, if time and resources are such that regression analysis is not cost-effective, the auditor can apply probability modeling to obtain a measure of the accuracy of the estimate from the model. The probability modeling approach centers on the use of subjectively assessed probabilities for the independent variables. The approach is simple to apply and requires little time. The probabilities reflect the auditor's knowledge of both the range within which the independent variable lies and a likelihood for where it is most likely to fall within that range, usually near the midpoint. Though there are many ways to obtain subjective probabilities, one of the most convenient is based on the beta probability distribution that is often used for network scheduling models. To use this method, the auditor simply estimates three values—the most likely value (M) for the independent variable, the smallest possible value (S) for the independent variable, and the largest possible value (L). Then, the best prediction for the variable (called the "expected value," or "EV") may be found by

$$EV = \frac{S + 4\,M + L}{6}$$

And, the measure of the accuracy of the prediction is inversely proportional to the statistical variance (VAR) of the probability distribution for the variable, which is given by

$$VAR = \frac{(L-S)^2}{6}$$

The square root of VAR is called the "standard deviation" of the probability distribution, and it is interpreted in the same manner as the "standard error of the estimate" in the regression context. That is, it gives a range (plus and minus) around the expected value such that the auditor can be fairly confident that the unknown true value of the distribution will lie in that range. See Chapter 11 and Appendix F for a more complete discussion of the proper interpretation of the standard error of the estimate.

As an example of this approach, consider again the wage expense case. And suppose the auditor is uncertain about the number of hours worked per employee (H) because of inadequate records or for other reasons. But the auditor is confident that the figure is between 35 and 45 hours per week and is most likely to be 38 hours per week. Then using our probability model, we can obtain the expected value and variance as follows:

$$EV_H = \frac{35 + (4)(38) + 45}{6} = 38.67 \text{ hours}$$

$$VAR_H = \frac{(45 - 35)^2}{6} = \frac{100}{6} = 16.67 \text{ hours}$$

This information can be used to evaluate the precision of the estimate for wage expense in the following manner. Suppose that, in addition to the above EV and VAR for the number of hours per employee (H), we know that the applicable average wage rate (WR) is \$8.50 per hour and that the number of employees (E) is 150. Then *weekly* wage expense is estimated as

Wage expense per week $= WR \times W \times E$
$= \$8.50 \times 38.67 \times 150$
$= \$49,304.25$
Annual wage expense $= \$49,304.25 \times 52$
$= \$2,563,821$

We now utilize the variance $(VAR = 16.67)$ to obtain the range around the estimated amount wherein we would expect the true value to lie. This range is approximately \$270,000 for the above data.[3] This interval is the computed standard deviation for wage expense and can be interpreted as a measure of the accuracy of the estimate. This clearly reflects a very imprecise estimate, as the interval is quite large relative to the estimated amount. The reason for this is the lack of precision in the estimate for the number of hours (H), which we have allowed to range from 35 to 45 hours, a very wide range in itself. A more precise estimate for H would have produced a correspondingly more precise estimate for the annual wage expense. For example, suppose that, as above, the auditor's best guess for the number of hours H was 38, but in contrast to the above, the auditor was confident that

---

[3] The precision interval is found by computing the standard deviation of wage expense as follows: $VAR_W = (WR \cdot E \cdot 52)^2 VAR_H$, and the standard deviation is $\sqrt{VAR_W}$. For $VAR_H = 16.67$ the standard deviation is \$270,695, and for $VAR_H = 2.67$ it is \$108,335. Note that while the standard deviation computed for this example can be interpreted as a measure of accuracy, as for the standard error of the estimate in the regression model, it does not provide a basis for constructing a symmetric precision interval around the estimate unless the underlying distribution is symmetric. When the smallest (S), largest (L) and midpoint (M) values for the distribution are such that M is equidistant from S and L, the distribution is symmetric and the precision interval is symmetric. When M is not equidistant from L and S, the distribution is not symmetric and, therefore, a symmetric precision interval cannot be constructed.

the number of hours would be between 38 and 42. Now, recomputing the expected value and variance

$$EV_H = \frac{38 + (38)(4) + 42}{6} = 38.67 \text{ hours}$$

$$VAR_H = \frac{(42 - 38)^2}{6} = \frac{16}{6} = 2.67 \text{ hours}$$

Notice that EV_H does not change, so the estimated annual wage expense will also remain the same as for the previous case, at \$2,563,821. But now the confidence range for the estimate is much smaller, at approximately \$108,000.

The above probability model is easy to use and interpret and does not require complex calculations. The auditor can use it as a shorthand, preliminary method to assess the precision of a given estimate. The regression method and more detailed analysis can provide a more complete evaluation of the precision of the estimate, if necessary.

§6.05   References

VI *The Complete Works of Benjamin Franklin* 277-83 (Putnam John Bigelow ed 1888).

P. Ostwald, *Cost Estimating for Engineering and Management* (Prentice-Hall 1974).

M. Peters, & K. Timmerhaus, *Plant Design and Economics for Chemical Engineers* (McGraw-Hill 2d ed 1968).

Using Analytical Procedures for Selected Accounts

7

§7.01   Introduction

This chapter ties together much of the material in various parts of the book. Whereas previous chapters have dealt primarily with the description of a variety of analytical procedures and selected illustrative applications, the objective of the present chapter is to present a somewhat comprehensive approach for selecting the extent and type of analytical procedures to apply when analyzing a given account. The material is presented in two steps. First, there is a general discussion which develops an approach for determining when and to what extent to apply a trend analysis, ratio analysis, or reasonableness test method when analyzing balance sheet accounts or revenue and expense accounts. The discussion, which is based in part on research results, shows that the potential effectiveness of each of the three methods differs somewhat in either context. While balance sheet accounts are best analyzed by ratio analysis, the revenue and expense accounts are best examined by either ratio analysis or a reasonableness test. Trend analysis is useful to a lesser degree in both cases. The arguments and research which support these generalizations are developed in this first section of the chapter.

Second, we present a suggested listing of analytical review methods for selected financial statement accounts, together with a brief explanation of the methods and their interpretation. The seven accounts included in this section are as follows:

1. Accounts receivable
2. Inventory
3. Property, plant, and equipment
4. Accounts payable, unrecorded liabilities, and other liabilities
5. Revenue accounts
6. Expense accounts
7. Prepaid expenses; accrued liabilities

The last three of these—revenue, expense, and prepaid expenses and accruals—are groups of accounts. These accounts are treated as groups for economy in presentation since the applicable methods are the same within each group. Some accounts are excluded from the presentation because they are generally not effectively analyzed by analytical methods. An account may not be amenable to analytical procedures for either of the following two reasons, or for a combination of the two:

1. The account balance is very much subject to management discretion and does not for this reason show a predictable relationship with other financial or operating data. The cash account, investments, long-term assets, and long-term liabilities are accounts which are of this nature.
2. The account is influenced by many complex factors which are not likely to remain constant over time. Tax expense is one such account.

The third and final section of the chapter deals with the situation in which analytical procedures are used to allocate audit effort within the context of a single account balance. For example, the audit of inventory for a chain of retail stores involves the determination of which subset of all retail outlets will be selected for inventory test procedures. This decision is based in part on the materiality of the inventory amount of each location and upon the auditor's evaluation of risk at each location. Analytical methods can be used to supplement this decision process by helping to determine which outlets should be examined, using as a basis for the decision any unusual relationships of financial and operating data for the outlet. Four of these methods are described in this final section of the chapter.

§7.02   A General Approach for Using Analytical Procedures

To develop a general approach, or strategy, for using analytical procedures, we consider the issues of the proper timing, extent, and nature of analytical procedures for both balance sheet and income statement accounts.

Timing of Analytical Procedures

Analytical procedures are applicable at three phases of the audit engagement—planning, field work, and final review. Also, it is required at the planning and review phases. Should there be differences regarding which of the three methods—ratio, trend, or reasonableness test—are applicable at each phase? Probably there is no difference, since each of the methods is easy to apply and each generally requires a limited amount of data and computation. Also, the objective for each of the three phases is relevant for each balance sheet and income statement account. Thus, the auditor will find each method to be applicable at each phase and for each account.

One exception to this might be that a reasonableness test would be infeasible at the planning phase because, at this early point in the engagement, certain of the relevant operating data may not be available to the auditor. Also, it is likely that in the final review phases the reviewing auditor will principally use the less quantitative of the methods, ratio and trend analysis, to get a quick "over the top" look at the reasonableness of the statements. Apart from these exceptions, it seems that timing is not an important factor in developing a strategy for choosing an effective analytical procedures approach for a given account.

Extent of Analytical Procedures

Again, since each of the three types of analytical methods generally requires little time to perform, the issue of "extent of testing" is not really applicable to analytical procedures themselves. Rather, the issue of the extent of testing revolves around how much evidence is obtained through analytical procedures to reduce the extent of subsequent substantive testing. This is the "work-reducing" role of analytical procedures. In determining the extent to which subsequent testing can or cannot be reduced, the auditor considers five important aspects of the

analytical method, the account under analysis and the results of applying the method:

1. *Detail of Analysis.* The auditor considers the level of detail for the
    account or item under analysis.

2. *Risk.* The auditor evaluates the potential for material error to
    occur in the account and not be detected by existing controls.

3. *Materiality.* The auditor assesses the impact on the financial state-
    ments taken as a whole if the account balance is substantially mis-
    stated. This is the concept of account materiality.

4. *Precision.* The auditor evaluates the precision associated with the
    use of the analytical method for the account. That is, how much
    confidence can the auditor have in the projections and results
    of the method? For example, the gross margin percentage is
    often considered a relatively precise form of analytical procedure
    since the cost-of-sales/sales relationship is generally a very sta-
    ble, predictable relationship. On the other hand, the ratio of
    maintenance expense to total sales is generally less stable and
    predictable, and thus in our terms, it provides less precision.

5. *Findings.* If the findings of analytical procedures indicate no un-
    usual or unexpected relationships for the account, then the audi-
    tor may be able to reduce the scope of subsequent substantive
    testing if he or she is satisfied as to risk, materiality, and precision
    for the account.

The auditor considers all five of these factors in choosing the scope
of subsequent testing. At one extreme, if risk and materiality are low,
the analysis is at a detail level and precision is high, and if the findings
show nothing unexpected, then this evidence argues for the auditor
to reduce the scope of subsequent tests. The extent of the reduction
should vary proportionately to the degree that the five factors indicate
the absence of material error. Alternatively, if all five factors are unfavorable, then the auditor may consider increasing the scope of substantive testing beyond the current plan. There is not now a
mathematical formula which relates the four factors to a precise
amount or percentage of reduction (or increase) in scope; this is left
to the auditor's judgment. What is important is that the auditor give
sufficient consideration to each factor.

Of the five factors, detail level, risk, materiality, and findings relate
directly to the account or item being examined, whereas precision is
affected both by the nature of the analytical method and by the account
under examination. That is, certain methods are more precise than

others, and some accounts are more easily analyzed than others, thereby leading to more precise results. Examples of relatively simple and relatively complex accounts were given directly above. Also, the reader may refer again to the section of Chapter 4 which deals with the evaluation of prediction error. Here there is a discussion of the nature of the confidence interval around the prediction, that is, the potential for error associated with different methods. For example, because of the precision derived from statistical methods, the use of regression-based analytical methods is generally more precise than other methods. Also, a reasonableness test may be more precise than other methods, since it can capture the relationship between operating and financial data and thereby explain a greater portion of the behavior of the account than would be obtained, say, from a simple trend analysis.

One final comment about the five factors. They are to be interpreted as independent elements of the decision problem; that is, the degree or level for any one of the factors should not influence the evaluation of any other factor. For example, the fact that the findings were unfavorable (detected unexpected relationships) should not influence the auditor's evaluation of the precision associated with the analytical procedure. If it does, the auditor's decision is improperly biased. This point should be noted carefully, because we have observed in our research a tendency for auditors to perceive incorrectly that certain of these factors are not independent.

Nature of Analytical Procedures

In developing a strategy for using analytical procedures, the auditor considers three available methods—trend analysis, ratio analysis, and the reasonableness test. Choosing from among these methods depends in part on the desired precision, as noted above. Also, certain methods are generally more effective for certain accounts, as summarized in Table 7-1. Three important patterns emerge from this table. The first is that analytical procedures tend to be more useful (effective and precise) for the income statement accounts than for the balance sheet accounts. The reason for this is that the income statement accounts reflect "flows" (receipts, purchases, disbursements), whereas the balance sheet accounts represent "stocks" which are the net effect of one or more different flows. Thus, the balance sheet accounts are inherently more complex and therefore less easily analyzed by simple analytical techniques. Kaplan has studied the time-series behavior of balance sheet and income statement accounts and found the balance sheet accounts to be more difficult to "model," or predict.[1] The best models of the balance sheet accounts were those that attempted to capture the flows in the accounts, as you would expect, but even these more complex models were inferior in predictive ability to those for the income statement accounts. The auditor can infer from this that analytical applications for the balance sheet accounts may not be as effective and precise as desired.

Table 7-1   Usage of Analytical Methods

	Method		
Type of Account	Trend Analysis	Ratio Analysis	Modeling
Balance sheet account	Of limited usefulness*	Useful	Of limited usefulness
Revenue and expense account	Useful	Very useful	Very useful

*The term "useful" is meant to indicate the relative cost-benefit and precision of the method.

A second pattern that emerges from Table 7-1 is that the income statement accounts are most effectively analyzed by ratio analysis and reasonableness tests. Here, ratio analysis refers to the ratio of a revenue or expense account to (1) an asset or liability account, (2) another expense account, or (3) total sales. The last ratio is commonly called the "common-size" income statement. The reason ratio analysis and reasonableness tests should be more effective and precise than trend analysis is that they are more likely to capture the variations in operating activity (the flows) which influence these account balances. In this sense, ratio analysis and reasonableness tests are more "informative." Trend analysis, in contrast, only captures the change from the prior year, and this change is made up of the net effect of many different factors, or flows.

The third and final pattern seen in Table 7-1 is that, when one is analyzing balance sheet accounts, ratio analysis is preferred. The reason is based partly on the observed success in the practical use of turnover ratios. Also, because balance sheet accounts reflect stocks rather than flows, the otherwise strong reasonableness test method is inappropriate, since it captures operating (flow) relationships.

These three patterns are reasonably descriptive of the overall ap-

---

[1] R. Kaplan, Developing a Financial Planning Model for an Analytic Review: A Feasibility Study, Symposium on Auditing Research III, University of Illinois, Urbana (1979).

proach auditors appear to be using, so far as is indicated by our limited survey of audit practice. The one exception is that auditors in practice tend to use trend analysis somewhat more extensively than is suggested by our analysis above. Other results of our survey are that, as you might expect, the extent, timing, and nature of the usage of analytical review do not differ significantly for audits in the range of 500 to 2500 budgeted hours. For the largest engagements (2500 hours and larger), there was a greater tendency to use specialized analytical review methods in certain areas, especially inventory, but overall the pattern was one in which the usage of analytical procedures appeared not to be influenced by engagement size. Also, as expected, there were no differences in usage that could be explained by either the ownership of the client (private or public) or the geographic location of the client.

§7.03 Suggested Analytical Procedures for Selected Accounts

The objective to this point in the chapter has been to help the auditor develop an effective overall approach for using analytical procedures. We now show a suggested list of specific procedures to use in applying this overall approach for each of seven selected accounts— accounts receivable, inventory, long-term assets and depreciation, accounts payable and other liabilities, revenue accounts, expense accounts, prepaid expenses and accrued liabilities.

In using the suggested lists, the auditor should keep in mind the overall strategy plus the five following matters:

1. What is the audit objective for analytical procedures? Is the audit question the completeness, existence, ownership, collectibility, valuation, cutoff, or proper classification for the account under analysis? Stating an objective is very important. We have found that there is a tendency for auditors to perform unnecessary analytical procedures, in part because it is viewed as an inexpensive audit procedure. If the auditor cannot state a specific objective for the use of analytical procedures, then it probably is not worthwhile.

2. One method which is useful for identifying the potential for material error is simply to review the adjustment summary from the prior year's working papers. An adjustment in the prior year is a useful signal of the likelihood of need for an adjustment in the current year.

3. Many of the "indicators" of risk which were identified in Chapter

3 should be kept in mind as the auditor approaches a specific audit area. For example, turnover of key personnel and other operating problems should influence the potential for accounting error. This and item 2 above are reminders that an analytical procedure is only one of the sources of information the auditor can use to detect areas with high potential for material misstatement.

4. Whenever possible, the analytical results should be summarized for each account and maintained on a permanent working paper. This will facilitate the auditor's comparison of ratios and other data with data of prior years.

5. Whenever feasible, analytical procedures should be performed on a divisional or product line level so as to facilitate the detection of unusual and unexpected relationships.

Accounts Receivable

As we will see, most analytical procedures for accounts receivable address the audit objective of assessing collectibility of accounts receivable. The procedures also provide some evidence for evaluating completeness and existence. The listing below is intended to be comprehensive; thus, the auditor may choose to apply only a portion of these for any given audit engagement. The relevance of each will vary with the circumstances.

The procedures are listed in five groups which address four different audit issues and one "other" category.

1. *Collectibility of receivables*
   a. Receivables turnover, the ratio of credit sales to average net receivables
   b. Average balance per customer
   c. Ratio of accounts receivable to current assets
   d. Notes receivable to accounts receivable
   e. Renewed notes receivable to notes receivable
   f. Aging schedule of accounts receivable
2. *Provision for doubtful accounts*
   a. Ratio of provision for doubtful accounts to credit sales
3. *Discount policy*
   a. Ratio of customer discounts to credit sales
4. *Special problems*
   a. Ratio of largest receivable account balance to total receivables

b.   Analysis of receivables for related parties

c.   Analysis of any significant year-end fluctuations in credit sales

5.   *Other*

a.   Roll-forward of beginning balance *plus* credit sales *less* cash receipts to estimate the ending balance of accounts receivable

The use and interpretation of these procedures need little explanation. Most of them are commonly used in auditing practice. All the procedures emphasizing ratios are described briefly in Chapter 5. Chapter 5 also has a useful discussion of the problems and limitations involved in ratio analysis.

Table 7-2 illustrates a worksheet that can be used to summarize the information derived from applying the procedures in a hypothetical case. The worksheet would become a part of the permanent work papers for the audit engagement in order to facilitate year-to-year comparisons of the ratios and results of procedures. Significant trends and year-to-year changes would be easily detected in this manner. Also, to be most useful, the worksheet should be prepared for each major distinguishable operating segment of the auditee, since the relationships analyzed by these ratios and other procedures are likely to differ across segments.

The last three procedures listed above will generally require some working paper support which would include the relevant calculations, the auditor's explanation of the source and credibility of the data, and the auditor's conclusion for the analysis. The conclusion is brought forward to the permanent worksheet, and a working paper (W/P) reference is made for the detailed analysis. Note that the permanent worksheet also contains space for the auditor to show any other significant factors which are important in evaluating the potential for material error in the account, such as the turnover of key personnel in the receivables area.

Analyzing the Receivables Turnover Ratio

In this section we present some useful ideas and suggestions for properly interpreting the accounts receivable turnover ratio, which is one of the focal points of the use of analytical procedures in examining the receivables account. A significant change in this ratio, or a significant difference from an industry average could signal a simple accounting error, a potential fraud, or simply a very unusual operating condition. The suggestions listed below are provided to help you determine the likely explanation for a significant change in the ratio, up or down, and the most desirable course of action and/or investigation.

Table 7-2   Accounts Receivable—Hypothetical Analytical Procedures Worksheet

Analytical Procedure	1985	1986	1987	1988
Part 1: Collectibility of Receivables				
Turnover ratio	10.8	11.6	9.9	10.5
Average balance per customer	$252	$310	$288	$301
Ratio of accounts receivable to current assets	62%	58%	60%	65%
Notes receivable to accounts receivable	15%	12%	14%	16%
Renewed notes receivable to notes receivable	0%	15%	18%	9%
Aging, %				
0–30 days	63	59	60	54
30–60 days	15	10	16	18
60–90 days	11	16	15	14
Over 90 days	11	15	9	14
Part 2: Provision for Doubtful Accounts				
Ratio of provision for doubtful accounts to credit sales	2.5%	3.1%	2.4%	2.2%
Basis for provision	Specific + 2% of credit sales	Specific + 2% of credit sales	Specific + 2% of credit sales	Specific + 2% of credit sales
Part 3: Discount Policy				
Ratio of customer discounts to credit sales	0.8%	1.1%	0.5%	0.4%
Credit terms	2%/10; net 30	2%/10; net 30	2%/10; net 30	2%/10; net 30

Analytical Procedure	1985	1986	1987	1988
Part 4: Special Problems				
Ratio of largest receivable account balance to total receivables	2.1%	5.4%	3.6%	4.8%
Analysis of receivables for related parties	OK Not OK W/P ___	OK Not OK W/P ___	OK Not OK W/P ___	OK Not OK W/P ___
Analysis of any significant year-end fluctuations in credit sales	OK Not OK W/P ___	OK Not OK W/P ___	OK Not OK W/P ___	OK Not OK W/P ___
Part 5: Other				
Roll-forward of beginning balance *plus* credit sales *less* cash receipts (should approximately equal ending balance)	OK Not OK W/P ___	OK Not OK W/P ___	OK Not OK W/P ___	OK Not OK W/P ___
A material adjustment in the account this year?	Yes No W/P ___	Yes No W/P ___	Yes No W/P ___	Yes No W/P ___
Other significant factors, such as turnover of key personnel?	Yes No W/P ___	Yes No W/P ___	Yes No W/P ___	Yes No W/P ___

Possible explanations for a significant *decline* in the ratio:

1. Excessive uncollectible receivables
2. Fictitious credit sales
3. Improper cutoff—cash sales are understated, and/or credit sales are overstated
4. Collections not recorded—possible lapping of receivables
5. Poor management of accounts receivable; poor credit policy, or the policy is implemented poorly
6. Sales are recognized improperly, for example, after shipment, but before the customer has promised to pay, leading to an excess of uncollectible accounts
7. Change in credit policy

Possible explanations for a significant *increase* in the ratio:

1. Good receivables management
2. Unreported credit sales
3. Failure or delay in billing shipments to customers, that is, there is a lag between the recording of a sale and the recognition of a receivable
4. Cutoff error—cash sales are overstated and/or credit sales are understated
5. Cash sales are overstated
6. A significant amount of receivables has been written off as uncollectible—could mean poor credit policy in the past, or fraud to cover up fictitious credit sales
7. Improper use of credit memos, with the same interpretation as above
8. Change in credit policy

Inventory

As for accounts receivable, analytical procedures are useful for achieving certain audit objectives when examining inventory, but not useful for other objectives. We present a suggested listing of procedures for each audit objective in examining inventory, and we take a worksheet approach to aggregating the information, very much as was done for receivables.

Analytical procedures' principal contribution is to assist the auditor in testing inventory pricing, and in efforts to detect misclassification errors arising from improper treatment of overhead. The latter might occur from improperly including a cost (maintenance expense, employee travel, etc.) in overhead.

A secondary contribution of analytical procedures is to examine for obsolete inventory, improper handling of inventory shrinkage, and improper cutoff. Analytical procedures can contribute little, unfortunately, to the audit objectives of examining existence and ownership. These objectives are achieved by other substantive procedures.

The analytical procedures recommended for inventory are as follows, listed by audit objective:

1. *Pricing, Obsolescence, and Shrinkage*

    a. Turnover ratio, the ratio of cost of sales to average inventory.

    b. Gross profit percentage.

    c. Raw materials turnover, the ratio of raw materials issued to production versus the average raw materials inventory.

    d. Shrinkage ratio, the ratio of inventory write-downs to total inventory.

    e. Analysis of standard cost budget variances; review of standard costs for reasonableness.

    f. Reasonableness test using average prices and units on hand to estimate the current inventory value.

2. *Misclassification and Cutoff*

    a. Comparison of the ending balance of products for sale to budgeted sales.

    b. Comparison of the ending balance of raw materials to budgeted usage.

    c. Examination of the relationship between materials, labor, and overhead to total product cost.

3. *Other*

    a. Inspection for unusually large purchases near year-end.

    b. Roll-forward of beginning balance *plus* purchases *less* cost of sales. Should approximately equal ending balance.

The above procedures should be completed for each major group of related products, or on a product line basis, if feasible. Notice that some of the procedures apply to materials inventory as well as to the inventory of products for sale. The use and interpretation of these procedures are well known. For example, an unexpectedly low turnover ratio indicates a potential for a significant amount of obsolete inventory or overstated valuation. Chapter 5 has a discussion of some problems and limitations in using many of these procedures.

Table 7-3 illustrates a worksheet approach for analytical review of inventory based upon the above procedures. It is a permanent worksheet so that significant trends and changes over the years can be more readily detected. Also, some of the procedures require additional working paper support to document more extensive analysis. For example, a schedule of purchases near year-end can be used to identify any unusually large purchases which might indicate an attempt to artificially improve the financial statements.

Analyzing the Inventory Turnover Ratio

As above for the analysis of the receivables account, we view the inventory turnover ratio as a focal point of the analysis of the inventory account. The following provides some suggestions and ideas for interpreting a significant change, up or down, in the ratio.

Possible Explanations for a significant *decline* in the ratio:

1. Excessive obsolete or unsalable inventory
2. Nonexistent (though recorded) inventory, due to poor test counts, fraud, or other means
3. Overvalued inventory due to improper pricing, fraud, or other means
4. Poor inventory management
5. Change in inventory management policy

Possible Explanations for a significant *increase* in the ratio:

1. Good inventory management
2. Change in inventory management policy
3. Unrecorded inventory due to poor test counts or other means
4. Excessive write-down of inventory to conceal poor inventory policies or theft
5. Undervalued inventory due to pricing errors or some other cause

Property, Plant, and Equipment

Because of relatively infrequent transactions in this account, it is often most cost-effective to audit it by detail methods. However, analytical procedures can be useful for two audit objectives for this account. One objective is to test the accuracy of the allowance for depreciation and related current expense. This can be done by a rea-

Table 7-3   Inventory—Hypothetical Analytical Procedures Worksheet

Analytical Procedure	Product A				Product B			
	1985	1986	1987	1988	1985	1986	1987	1988
Part 1: Pricing, Obsolescence, Shrinkage								
Turnover ratio	9.2	9.6	9.5	10.1	8.6	8.1	8.0	7.5
Gross profit percentage	24.2	24.9	26.1	25.8	19.1	18.1	18.8	19.2
Raw materials turnover	5.9	6.5	4.8	6.0	8.8	6.0	6.5	6.2
Shrinkage rate, ratio of write-downs to total inventory	0.021	0.035	0.028	0.022	0.061	0.045	0.021	0.035
Analysis of standard cost budget variances; review of standard costs for reasonableness	N/A OK Not OK W/P ___	N/A OK Not OK W/P ___	N/A OK Not OK W/P ___	N/A OK Not OK W/P ___	N/A OK Not OK W/P ___	N/A OK Not OK W/P ___	N/A OK Not OK W/P ___	N/A OK Not OK W/P ___
Reasonableness test using average prices and units on hand to estimate current inventory value	OK Not OK W/P ___	OK Not OK W/P ___	OK Not OK W/P ___	OK Not OK W/P ___	OK Not OK W/P ___	OK Not OK W/P ___	OK Not OK W/P ___	OK Not OK W/P ___
Part 2: Misclassification, Cutoff								
Comparison of the ending balance in products for sale to budgeted sales	OK Not OK W/P ___	OK Not OK W/P ___	OK Not OK W/P ___	OK Not OK W/P ___	OK Not OK W/P ___	OK Not OK W/P ___	OK Not OK W/P ___	OK Not OK W/P ___
Comparison of the ending balance of raw materials to budgeted usage	OK Not OK W/P ___	OK Not OK W/P ___	OK Not OK W/P ___	OK Not OK W/P ___	OK Not OK W/P ___	OK Not OK W/P ___	OK Not OK W/P ___	OK Not OK W/P ___

Part 2: Misclassification, Cutoff

Analytical Procedure	Product A				Product B			
	1985	1986	1987	1988	1985	1986	1987	1988
Components of cost, %								
Materials	24.2	23.8	25.1	24.8	16.2	18.3	19.2	18.8
Labor	48.6	46.9	49.2	47.1	55.1	50.6	51.5	50.8
Overhead	27.2	29.3	25.7	28.1	28.7	31.1	29.3	30.4

Part 3: Other

Analytical Procedure	Product A				Product B			
	1985	1986	1987	1988	1985	1986	1987	1988
Inspection for unusually large purchases near year-end	OK Not OK W/P ___	OK Not OK W/P ___	OK Not OK W/P ___	OK Not OK W/P ___	OK Not OK W/P ___	OK Not OK W/P ___	OK Not OK W/P ___	OK Not OK W/P ___
Roll-forward of beginning balance *plus* purchases *less* cost of sales (should approximately equal the ending balance)	OK Not OK W/P ___	OK Not OK W/P ___	OK Not OK W/P ___	OK Not OK W/P ___	OK Not OK W/P ___	OK Not OK W/P ___	OK Not OK W/P ___	OK Not OK W/P ___
A material adjustment in the account this year	Yes No W/P ___	Yes No W/P ___	Yes No W/P ___	Yes No W/P ___	Yes No W/P ___	Yes No W/P ___	Yes No W/P ___	Yes No W/P ___
Other significant factors, such as turnover of key personnel?	Yes No W/P ___	Yes No W/P ___	Yes No W/P ___	Yes No W/P ___	Yes No W/P ___	Yes No W/P ___	Yes No W/P ___	Yes No W/P ___

SOURCE: Adapted from Blocher, *Approaching Analytical Review*, CPA J, Mar 1983; reprinted with permission of *CPA Journal*, copyright 1983, New York State Society of Certified Public Accountants.

sonableness test in which assets are grouped into reasonably homogeneous groups for lives and depreciation methods. Depreciation is then computed for each asset group. Using this approach, the auditor can easily approximate the correct amounts for the allowance and expense accounts.

A second objective is to examine the utilization of assets in order to evaluate the potential need for writing down the value of underutilized assets. If certain assets will be idled indefinitely, then they should be written off. The ratio of net property plant and equipment to sales can provide a useful measure of asset utilization for this purpose.

Accounts Payable, Unrecorded Liabilities, and Other Liabilities

The principal audit objective for these balance sheet accounts is to evaluate the completeness of the client's disclosure. Detail test procedures, including the analysis of payments after year-end, are the most useful for this purpose. However, analytical procedures can be used to supplement the detail procedures by indicating the extent of the pressures on management to understate liabilities to creditors and others. A good measure of the magnitude of these pressures is the current cash needs of the company. Three ratios, which are explained in Chapter 5, are well suited for identifying severe cash needs:

$$\text{Acid-test ratio} = \frac{\text{cash + marketable securities + receivables}}{\text{current liabilities}}$$

$$\text{Defensive interval} = \frac{\text{cash + short-term marketable securities}}{\text{estimated daily cash operating expenditures}}$$
$$\text{(excludes depreciation)}$$

$$\text{Payables turnover} = \frac{\text{accounts payable}}{\text{total disbursements}}$$

A significant unfavorable trend in any of these ratios could be an indication of critical cash need.

A second objective in this area is to evaluate the reasonableness of contingent liabilities. When the contingency is due to pending legal matters, the amount of the contingent liability is either well known or best assessed by legal opinion. So the auditor seeks legal advice on these matters. For other types of contingencies, such as one due to product warranties, the assessment of a reasonable contingency may be based on legal knowledge combined with the use of detailed analytical procedures. For example, product warranty costs may be a well-known proportion of total sales, adjusted for geographic location of sales and other factors. In this case, a careful reasonableness test should be appropriate, or a recomputation of the client's figures, as is done in some cases for the allowance for doubtful accounts.

Revenue

Analytical procedures can serve to address two of the audit objectives involved in the examination of revenue. The first is the test of the validity of the reported sales. Does the given amount represent legitimate sales for the accounting period? A second objective is to test for unrecorded sales. Unrecorded sales may occur if management wishes to lower tax liability, to smooth sales figures over different accounting periods, or the like.

The examination of the validity of sales is tested in part by procedures applied to other accounts, particularly accounts receivable and inventory. Thus, an unusual relationship detected in the examination of inventory or receivables may reflect an accounting problem for the reported sales figure as well. For example, unrecorded sales could be reflected in unusually high inventory shrinkage figures or an unusually low receivables turnover ratio. Because of these interrelationships, the auditor may wish to review sales at or about the same time that receivables and inventory are reviewed. Three procedures are appropriate for an examination of the validity of sales:

1. *Examination of gross profit percentage.* This ratio is compared with that of recent years for each major product line or segment. Unexplained large differences could be an indication of unreported or nonexistent sales.

2. *Comparison of reported sales to budget.* If available, a sales budget provides a valuable benchmark for evaluating actual sales performance. For the comparison to be most useful, the auditor must examine the reasonableness of the budget through knowledge of the company and its current market environment.

3. *Reasonableness test of sales.* The reasonableness test for sales resembles the roll-forward of finished goods inventory noted earlier for examining the reasonableness of the ending inventory balance. The auditor simply takes the units in beginning inventory of goods for sales, plus units completed in the current period, less ending inventory in units, to approximate the number of units sold this period. The production and sales units figures may be obtained from operations data and shipping documents, if not available with the financial records.

The examination for unrecorded sales would use the same three procedures. However, unrecorded sales are difficult to detect by the use of analytical procedures, since none of the financial records may be affected. For this reason, the first two procedures above will probably not be as useful as the third, the reasonableness test, as it requires use of operating data which are more likely to show in some way the effect of unrecorded sales.

Two additional procedures may be useful in the application of analytical procedures to the examination of revenue:

1. Computation of the ratio of sales returns and allowances to sales. An unexpected change in this ratio from the prior period may indicate an accounting error in the treatment of this account.

2. Reasonableness test of investment income. The income from investments can most often be predicted quite easily and accurately from information about the invested amount and rate of return.

Expenses

The principal objective for the use of analytical procedures in examining the expense accounts is to evaluate whether each account is completely and properly stated. A preliminary approach to accomplish this would be to perform a trend analysis to isolate those accounts with unusual changes. The trend analysis is easy to apply and will be effective when all expense accounts are similarly affected by the factor or factors causing all the accounts to change. A significant problem in this regard is that expense accounts differ from one another in the proportion of "fixed" and "variable" cost components for the expense. For example, rent expense may be entirely fixed, whereas selling expense, when based primarily on commissions, would be largely variable in nature. This is a problem when applying trend analysis because a change in operating level will have a proportional change on variable expenses, but no change on fixed expenses. The implication of this for the auditor is that the balance changes derived from trend analysis must be interpreted with an understanding of the nature of the expense under examination. Is it largely variable or fixed? And, should it have changed or not?

One way to avoid the above difficulty is to use a ratio analysis or reasonableness test approach for the review of the expense accounts. A suggested list of three types of ratio analysis and a variety of reasonableness test examples is given below:

1. *Ratio of expense account to related asset account*
   a. Interest expense to debt

    b. Depreciation expense to gross assets subject to depreciation

    c. Bad debt expense to the allowance for bad debts

    d. Repair and maintenance expense to related property, plant, and equipment accounts

    e. Insurance expense to inventory plus property, plant, and equipment

2.   *Ratio of expense account to related expense account*

    a. Payroll taxes to payroll expense

    b. Employee benefit expense to payroll expense

3.   *Common-size income statement*

    a. The ratio of each expense account to total sales. This type of ratio analysis, common-size income statements, is virtually equivalent to trend analysis, and it suffers from the same difficulty with respect to differences in the mix of variable and fixed costs across expense accounts. Thus, its use is subject to the interpretation problem noted above. The other two forms of ratio analysis are not subject to this problem and thus can be interpreted directly and easily.

4.   *Reasonableness test.* Many expense accounts are easily estimated from one or a few items of relevant operating data. Illustrations of this method for fuel expense and for payroll expense were given in Chapter 6. Additional applications are:

    a. Depreciation expense, estimated from data for asset lives and depreciation methods, for homogeneous asset subgroups

    b. Maintenance expense, estimated from floor space, direct labor hours, machine hours, and related operating data

    c. Interest expense, estimated from relevant rates and debt amounts

    d. Utilities expense, estimated from capacity utilization data, labor hours, possibly seasonally adjusted

    e. Supplies expense, estimated from labor hours, machine hours, and related operating data

Prepaid Expenses and Accrued Liabilities

Both these types of accounts represent the effect of year-end adjustments to achieve statements on the accrual basis of accounting. Thus, the audit objective is to see that the adjustments are complete and proper. Generally, the best approach for evaluating the accounts would be to employ a reasonableness test based upon relevant financial and operating data. This would involve approximating the amount of the related expense per week or month and then projecting this to the period necessary for the accrual. In some cases, the client's computation to arrive at the accrual may be simple enough that a full recomputation by the auditor may be the cost-effective approach. On the other hand, when the account balance comprises many items, as in the case of several different insurance policies—all prepaid with different premiums and periods of coverage—then a reasonableness test might be more appropriate. The auditor could estimate the premium per week for all policies and use approximated average accrual periods to compute an accrual estimate.

Similar methods would apply for the analyses of accrued liabilities. Recomputation or a reasonableness test is recommended, depending on the complexity of the account balance.

§7.04   The Multiple Location Problem

Up to this point in the chapter, we have been concerned with the use of analytical procedures for account balances—to direct attention to those with a high potential for material misstatement or to provide evidence as a basis for reducing the scope of detail tests when the potential for misstatement appears to be low. Now, we turn our attention to a special case of the attention-directing role of analytical procedures which is used to *allocate* a given scope of audit effort rather than to *reduce or increase* scope, as we have done up to now.[2] This use of analytical procedures applies in those situations in which the object of audit concern (say, inventory) is dispersed over two or more locations. Thus, it is called the "multiple location problem." A common example is the retailing company with many retail outlets. The audit question is which of the outlets should be examined, since it is not feasible or necessary to examine them all. We discuss here four approaches to resolving the question. The four are presented in increasing order of complexity, required expertise, and precision. The more precise methods will tend to be cost-beneficial on only the largest engagements, owing to their complexity. The simpler methods should be useful in a wider range of applications. All methods involve in some way the evaluation and

---

[2] The term "allocate audit effort" can be considered quite broadly. It can refer to defining (1) which subset of a set of outlets will be examined, or (2) how much time to spend on each outlet, if all outlets are examined, or (3) which outlet to examine first, second, third, and so on. Typically, the audit decision is of the nature of (1) above, but the methods described for multiple location problems are applicable to each of the three forms of allocation.

weighting of risk and materiality across all outlets. In describing each method, we will assume that we are analyzing the case of multiple retail outlets and that our objective is to allocate audit effort to inventory across outlets. Some outlets will be audited and others not.

The Direct Assessment Method

The first, and simplest, of the methods is that whereby the auditor makes a direct assessment of the risk associated with each outlet, and in this way derives a ranking of risk for the outlets. This ranking is used together with a measure of materiality of each outlet (this can be simply the dollar value of inventory at each outlet) to derive a ranking of a risk-weighted materiality measure for all outlets. This is illustrated in the hypothetical case shown in column 3 of Table 7-4.

The risk-weighted materiality measure can be used directly to determine which outlets to examine. For example, if audit scope calls for examining two outlets, then outlets A and B would be chosen, since they have the highest values. If a third outlet is to be included, then outlet C would be chosen. Notice that the choice of outlets is different when using risk alone (column 1), materiality alone (column 2), or the risk-weighted materiality (column 3). Using column 3 is preferred, since it incorporates both risk and materiality.

The Indirect Assessment Method

The indirect assessment method differs from the above in that the auditor directly assesses various *components* of risk and then aggregates these components to produce an indirect, overall risk assessment. This method is described in detail in Patton et al.[3] The approach of Patton and his coworkers employs what is called the "analytical hierarchy method" to derive and combine the various attributes of overall risk. The method is somewhat complex. A simplified version of it is illustrated in Table 7-5. For simplicity, assume that the overall risk associated with an outlet comprises two major components—the quality of controls to safeguard inventory (control of inventory shrinkage) and the quality of internal control systems for cash receipts (prevention of unrecorded or misrecorded sales). The auditor makes a direct assessment of each component of risk in the same manner as used in the direct method. Then, a subjective relative weight is assigned to each of the two risk components to indicate the relative contribution of each to overall risk.

---

[3] J. Patton, J. Evans, & B. Lewis, A Framework for Evaluating Internal Audit Risk (Institute of Internal Auditors Research Report 1982).

Table 7-4   The Multiple Location Problem—Direct Assessment Method

Outlet	Risk Assessed by Auditor* (1)	Materiality, Inventory Value, $ (2)	Risk-Weighted Materiality, $† (3)
A	2	550,000	1,100,000
B	4	160,000	640,000
C	3	150,000	450,000
D	1	435,000	435,000

*The risk measure is assessed by the auditor on a scale of 1 (lowest risk) to 7 (highest risk). The assessment is based upon the auditor's judgment, supported by knowledge of the personnel and quality of control systems in place at each outlet.

†(3) = (1) × (2).

If, for example, safeguard controls are twice as important as cash receipt controls, then the relative weights could be 2.0 and 1.0, respectively. Note that the amount of the weights is not important in itself; what is important is the relative values between weights, so that risk weights of 4.0 and 2.0 (for safeguard and cash controls, respectively) would produce results identical to the case in which the risk weights are 2.0 and 1.0. That is, the ranking of overall risk would not be different.

The results of the indirect assessment method are shown in column 3 of Table 7-5. The overall risk-weighted materiality rankings indicate that outlet A should be investigated first and that B and D are of second priority. Alternatively, more time needs to be spent on outlet A,

Table 7-5   The Multiple Location Problem—Indirect Assessment Method

Outlet	Auditor's Assessment, Each Component of Risk* Safeguard Controls†	Cash Receipts Controls‡	Overall Risk Assessment (1)	Materiality, Inventory Value, $ (2)	Risk-Weighted Materiality, $§ (3)
A	2	3	(2 × 2) + (3 × 1) = 7	550,000	3,850,000
B	5	2	(5 × 2) + (2 × 1) = 12	160,000	1,920,000
C	1	6	(1 × 2) + (6 × 1) = 8	150,000	1,200,000
D	1	2	(1 × 2) + (2 × 1) = 4	435,000	1,740,000

*The risk measure is assessed by the auditor on a scale of 1 (lowest risk) to 7 (highest risk).
†Relative weight = 2.0.
‡Relative weight = 1.0
§(3) = (1) × (2).

and correspondingly less time on B and D. Outlet C should get the least attention.

Statistical Risk Assessment

The statistical approach is comparable to what was described in Chapter 4 as the use of regression analysis to identify accounts with unexpected fluctuations. In the multiple location problem, the regression model is used to identify outlets with unexpected fluctuations or relationships.[4] The regression model is fitted from cross-sectional data from one point in time for all outlets. This means that there should be at least 10 to 12, and, ideally, 30 or more, outlets used to fit the regression to achieve an acceptably low level of sampling error. The dependent variable in the regression might be cost of sales, with the geographic area of the outlet, the size (floor space) of the outlet, and certain other attributes of the outlet (age, configuration, etc.) as independent variables. Another possible dependent variable is net sales, with similar independent variables. John Neter reports a case study in which a cross-sectional regression of this type was employed for the multiple location problem.[5] His results are very interesting. The regression models have good predictive power, even though data for some key independent variables were unavailable.[6] The evidence appears to be that the regression approach is very useful to the auditor in applications such as these.

Sequential Probability Ratio Method

Godfrey and Andrews have adapted the sequential probability ratio method for the multiple location audit problem.[7] The method employs the precision of mathematical statistics to obtain a minimum cost allocation of sampling effort. The method is somewhat complex, but can be facilitated by interactive computer programming, as the authors indicate.

---

[4] In the regression approach, an unusual outlet is identified by a large residual term for that outlet. The residual is the difference between the predicted value for the outlet and the actual value. This is explained more fully in **ch 11** and in **app F.**

[5] J. Neter, Two Case Studies for Use of Regression for Analytic Review, Symposium on Auditing Research IV, University of Illinois, Urbana (1980).

[6] The predictive ability of the models, as measured by the coefficient of determination, was greater than 90 per cent for five of the seven models; the other two had coefficients of 76 per cent and 80 per cent.

[7] J. Godfrey & R. Andrews, Testing Compliance at Multiple Sites: A Sequential Probability Ratio Model (May 1980) (Graduate School of Business, University of Michigan).

§7.05 References

J. Godfrey & R. Andrews, Testing Compliance at Multiple Sites: A Sequential Probability Ratio Model (May 1980) (Graduate School of Business Administration, University of Michigan, Ann Arbor).

R. Kaplan, Developing a Financial Planning Model for an Analytic Review: A Replication (June 1979a) (GSIA Working Paper 74-78-79, Carnegie-Mellon University, Pittsburgh).

R. Kaplan, Developing a Financial Planning Model for an Analytic Review: A Feasibility Study, Symposium on Auditing Research III, University of Illinois, Urbana (1979b).

R. Kaplan, A Financial Planning Model for an Analytic Review: The Case of a Savings and Loan Association (July 1980) (GSIA Working Paper 84-79-80, Carnegie-Mellon University, Pittsburgh).

J. Neter, Two Case Studies for Use of Regression for Analytic Review, Symposium on Auditing Research IV, University of Illinois, Urbana (1980).

J. Patton, J. Evans, III, & B. Lewis, *A Framework for Evaluating Internal Audit Risk* 25 (Institute of Internal Auditors Research Report 1982).

Analytical Procedures at the Completion of the Audit

8

§8.01   Introduction

"The three princes of Serendip . . . were always making discoveries, by accidents and sagacity, of things they were not in quest of."

Horace Walpole
"The Three Princes of Serendip,"
January 1754
(in coining the term "serendipity")

The quality of serendipity is a good notion to begin this chapter on the final review phase for the audit engagement. Essentially, the reviewing audit partner applies "sagacity" to the review of the completed financial statements, to obtain additional assurance as to the reasonableness of the financial statements. The auditor at times and in a serendipitous fashion discovers unusual or unexpected relationships in the audited data which lead to further audit work to uncover accounting errors in the statements. Walpole's use of the term "sagacity" seems to fit here; it can be defined as a "discriminative intelligence," or an "acute, practical judgment," which leads to the serendipitous discovery.

Apart from the above, it is difficult to define that relatively specialized skill which the reviewing auditor applies in this final phase to detect problems not identified earlier in the planning and field work phases of the audit. The skill, it is argued, comes from in-depth knowledge of the client's business and accounting policies and procedures, which is derived in turn from extensive knowledge and experience in auditing.

Also, some argue that certain auditors are inherently better able to detect problems in this manner than are other auditors. The critical factors and relationships which identify the potential for material misstatement are more "transparent" for these auditors. However, no research we are aware of has been undertaken to determine if these experts exist, or what proportion of practicing auditors might be qualified as analytical experts in some way. Additionally, none of the existing research has results which would be consistent with the hypothesis that some significant subpopulation of all auditors has these expert skills. The matter needs investigation, but at this point it seems unlikely we will find that a significant portion of auditors have substantially better analytical skills than others. Some suggestions for how firms or individual auditors can improve their skills are given in Chapter 9.

Now, we consider an approach and a set of procedures that the auditor can employ in the final review phase. Since the approach consists of a sequence of somewhat interdependent elements, we present it in the form of five steps.

§8.02   Step One

The auditor reviews the trend analysis on the working trial balance accounts, after correction for any adjustments and reclassifications. This will require recomputation of the amount and percentage trend used in planning, for the corrected amounts. Also, the auditor reviews the analytical procedures worksheets for inventory and accounts receivable, as illustrated in Chapter 7. Again, the figures in these worksheets are corrected for adjustments and reclassifications.

The auditor gives special attention to inventory and receivables, since they are generally the most critical audit areas. If any other audit area is critical for the engagement (say, transactions with related parties for some companies), then there should be a review of the planning phase analytical procedures in that area as well. Thus, the focus of the review is on the critical audit areas, with a brief review of the trend analysis for all accounts also being conducted.

The benefit of this overall review at the final stage is that sometimes a quick overview of all audit areas will uncover a potential problem when a detailed analysis in each area, taken one at a time, will not reveal the problem. Thus, something which might have been missed by a careful application of analytical procedures and detail tests in a given area might be identified when the results of the analytical procedures for all accounts are considered together, at one time. To accomplish this, the final review must be employed carefully, with sufficient quiet, reflective time for a thorough evaluation.

§8.03   Step Two

The reviewing auditor should summarize all unexpected audit findings and try to tie them together. A review of the adjustment summary and memos of work done is useful at this point. Is there a pattern which leads to a significant audit concern not previously identified and addressed in the field work? For example, taken as a whole, the audit findings may reflect a comprehensive strategy to lower the "quality" of earnings or the reported financial position through accounting and operating policies which tend to overstate assets and revenues and understate expenses and liabilities. To illustrate, the client may be putting off necessary maintenance and repairs, taking a very optimistic position on the collection rate for receivables, and experiencing an increase in the payables to disbursements ratio. Individually, the items would not be a concern, but in the aggregate they may be.

An important overall concern in this second step is for the reviewing auditor to be conscious of the *qualitative* rather than the quantitative value of the evidence. Because of checklists and other formal procedures, the quantity of evidence is likely to be complete, but it may be lacking in quality because of the inexperience of the staff assigned to the engagement. For example, the reviewing auditor should address the credibility of the data. To what extent does it rely on unsupported assertions of management, or upon data which have not been independently verified? This is particularly important when evaluating the results of analytical procedures which may rely in part on unsupported assertions or data. We are aware of at least one case in which an auditor was misled on the results of an analytical review because of reliance on incorrect operating data which later became the focus of litigation against the auditor.

§8.04 Step Three

The auditor should reevaluate the going-concern status of the client, if appropriate, using the methods described in Chapter 3. The elements of operating risk and financial risk are particularly relevant at this time. The reviewing auditor can analyze certain financial ratios as indicators of financial distress and apply some of the financial distress models described in Chapter 3. See especially Tables 3-1 and 3-3.

Also, operating risk can be reevaluated by reference to the relevant indicators set forth in Chapter 3. In this regard, the auditor should try to anticipate potential significant events in the coming year which might have a substantial effect on financial position. Are all contingencies addressed and disclosed in the present draft of the statements and auditor's report? What regional economic trends, if any, are likely to affect the company in the coming year? Also, to what extent has management developed plans and procedures for dealing with contingencies? The existence of well-developed contingency plans is an offset to the degree of financial risk associated with the contingency.

§8.05 Step Four

The auditor should in addition reassess the management integrity issue, as described in Chapter 3. Has anything developed during the audit which should cause the auditor to question management's intentions? Is there evidence that management has tried to mislead the auditor on any matter? Further, are there reasons which would likely create a motivation for management to misrepresent the financial statements? Incentive-based executive compensation schemes, competition for promotion, personal financial distress, and related factors may have an impact on the motivations underlying management integrity on accounting matters.

§8.06 Step Five

The final step we suggest is to seek assistance of others with expertise in the client's industry and accounting systems. The objective of seeking assistance is primarily to improve the assessment of inherent risk and the related going-concern question, as noted above. The most convenient source for this would be others within the auditor's own firm who have the necessary expertise. Other sources include professional industry analysts, other financial analysts, local banking professionals, and industry publications. Useful references for this purpose include those noted in Chapter 3, plus *Standard and Poor's Industry Surveys,* and the industry data presented in Appendix G.

Guidance for Using Analytical Procedures

9

§9.01   Introduction

This chapter sets forth our ideas and suggestions for enhancing the planning and usage of analytical procedures. The chapter serves as a guide for the auditor to develop a strategy for planning and using analytical procedures more effectively.

The strategy is a framework of concepts and knowledge which the auditor can apply to a given audit situation to answer certain basic questions about analytical procedures: *when* to employ them, *how* to employ them, and so on. In this manner, usage of analytical procedures should be enhanced:

1. The audit objective of analytical procedures will be more clear; the findings of analytical procedures will be better integrated into other audit work.

2. Documentation of analytical procedures will be improved

3. There will be less tendency to use analytical procedures for no apparent purpose.

4. There will be increased usage of analytical procedures to reduce the scope of tests of details; by clarifying when and to what extent this role of analytical procedures applies, the framework will facilitate usage for this purpose.

5. There will be increased consensus among auditors in planning and usage of analytical procedures.

The chapter is organized as follows. There are two major objectives for the chapter. The first is to address the question "When does the auditor use and rely upon analytical procedures?" A guidance worksheet is developed for facilitating the auditor's consideration of this question, using the decision flowchart format. The guidance worksheet analyzes the question by identifying the five elements of the question and then formalizing the relationships between these elements.

The second objective of the chapter is to address the question "How does the auditor use analytical procedures most effectively?" Once the auditor has chosen to use analytical procedures, the question remains as to which analytical procedure to apply and how to evaluate the results properly. This set of questions is addressed in two ways. First, there is a discussion of each of four analytical methods an auditor might employ. The discussion looks at the nature of each method to determine the required data and auditor expertise and uses this basis for determining what sorts of aids and guidance to give the auditor for the performance of each method. Second, there is a brief summary of the specific suggestions made in Chapters 3 through 6 regarding the proper use of trend analysis, ratio analysis, and reasonableness tests.

§9.02   When Does the Auditor Use and Rely Upon Analytical Procedures?

There are five elements to the question of when to use and rely upon analytical procedures. We discuss each element and incorporate it in a guidance worksheet. The five elements are (1) timing of analytical procedures, (2) the audit exposure associated with the account, (3) the objective of the use of analytical procedures, either attention-directing or detail test-reducing, (4) the findings of the use of analytical procedures, either an unexpected or an expected result; and (5) the precision of the procedure. Each element is described briefly below.

Timing

Analytical procedures are usefully employed at the planning, field work, and final review phases of the audit engagement. They can also be used as a compensating test when the system of internal controls does not justify full reliance because of inadequate controls or compliance. The "compensating" analytical procedures can be used to justify a higher level of reliance when no unusual relationships or other signs of potential material error are identified by the review.

Exposure

Exposure is the audit significance of the account as measured by the combination of (1) the materiality of the account balance and (2) the audit risk for material misstatement in the account. The latter is determined from an evaluation of inherent risk and of the internal control risk for the account. What are the odds that a material error will occur in the account and not be detected by management's system of internal controls? These odds are the audit risk for the account. Exposure is greatest when the account is material in amount and audit risk is high. It is least when both materiality and risk are low.

Objective of the Use of Analytical Procedures

The objective of the use of analytical procedures is either to direct the auditor's attention to an account, item, or element of the financial statements where there is significant potential for misstatement, or to serve as a basis for reducing the scope of other tests. The priority placed on either of these two objectives depends in part on the evaluation of exposure. When exposure is high, the attention-directing objective is primary. But, when exposure is moderate or low, the test-reducing objective becomes primary. The primary and secondary objectives are illustrated by solid and dotted lines, respectively, in Figure 9-1.

Findings of the Use of Analytical Procedures

Another important element of using analytical procedures effectively is the ability to interpret the findings properly. When do the trend, ratio, or reasonableness test findings indicate an unusual relationship, a sign of a potential material misstatement? In practice, the auditor determines a threshold for the amount or percentage change or difference such that any change or difference greater than the threshold is considered unusual and further investigation is indicated. The choice of a threshold is a matter of judgment, and it is known to differ among industries and among clients of different sizes. A common rule is to

Figure 9-1 Guidance worksheet to determine when to use and rely upon analytical procedures.

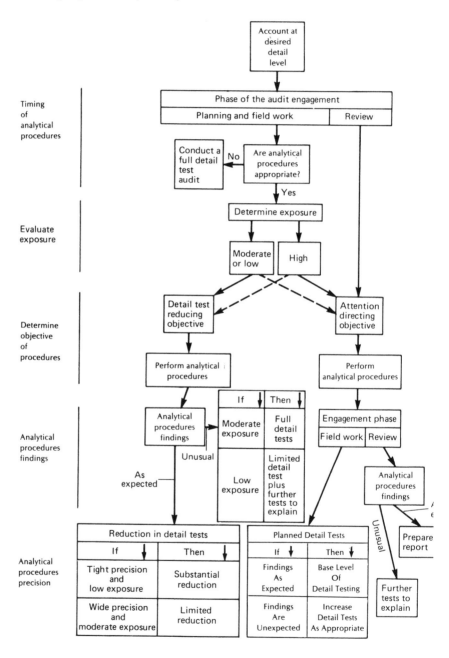

use a threshold of 5 to 10 per cent of net income, though rules based on assets or revenues are also in use.

Precision

Precision in the context of analytical procedures refers to the degree of confidence the auditor has in the prediction from the use of analytical procedures. Precision is influenced by the nature of the account, the nature of the analytical procedure, and the accuracy of the data required by the analytical procedure. In the first place, some accounts are simply more predictable than others. Depreciation expense is more predictable than maintenance expense, for example. Similarly, interest income is usually among the most easily predicted accounts.[1] A common aspect of the more predictable accounts is that at most one or two causal factors are involved in explaining the change in the balance over time. In the case of interest expense, for example, outstanding debt, period, and the relevant rate of interest are all that are necessary to explain interest expense fully. The more predictable an account is, the more precise is the analytical procedure applied to it.

A second component of precision is the nature of the procedure applied. Regression analysis is generally regarded as among the most precise of the procedures, since it employs a best-fitting linear statistical method. Apart from this, it is difficult to generalize about the relative precision of the ratio, trend, and reasonableness test procedures. However, it can be argued that the reasonableness test is more precise than the others because it involves a formal modeling process based on operating data and other external data. In a similar vein, ratio analysis can be considered superior to a simple two-period trend analysis in that the ratio should capture some stable relationship between accounts, whereas many factors are involved in the one-period change in the balance. Also, an average of two or more predictions from different methods is often more accurate than a single prediction. By applying considerations such as these, the auditor must assess the relative precision of the procedure or procedures being employed.

The final component of precision is the degree of accuracy of the data used in the analytical procedure. This applies particularly to the reasonableness test or regression analysis, which require operating

---

[1] We are using the term "predictable" in the "ex post" sense; that is, we are interested in the ability to predict, after the close of the account period, what the account balance *should* be, as in the typical audit context. The ability to predict the account balance at some future time is a far different matter and is not directly relevant for the auditor's use of analytical procedures.

data and external data. If the data are of limited or unknown accuracy, the precision of the procedure is adversely affected.

The Guidance Worksheet

The guidance worksheet, Figure 9-1, ties all five elements together to develop a framework for choosing when to use and rely on analytical procedures. The worksheet is most easily used from top to bottom, beginning with the account under examination. At an early point in the decision flow the auditor must decide, "Is the use of analytical procedures appropriate?" The point of this question is to eliminate such accounts as cash and the capital accounts which are most conveniently and effectively tested by detail methods. The worksheet continues from this point to show how the auditor can choose the appropriate level of detail testing under various combinations of the five key elements.

§9.03 How to Use Analytical Procedures— Developing an Approach

It is more difficult to address the question of which analytical procedure to choose and how to apply it than it is to identify the key elements in determining when to use analytical procedures, as we have done above. The "how" question is more difficult because a variety of procedures can be equally appropriate for a given situation. As a result, the auditor often completes two, three, or more analytical procedures at the same time, as illustrated in the accounts receivable and inventory worksheets in Chapter 7.

For this reason, we have chosen to analyze the "how" question by studying the nature of four types of analytical methods which can be used. Three of the four are trend analysis, ratio analysis, and the reasonableness test, as described in Chapters 4, 5, and 6. The fourth, inherent risk analysis, is a term to summarize the variety of methods described in Chapter 3. A key aspect of inherent risk analysis is that the methods involve the application of accounting and business knowledge, often in a nonquantitative manner, to analyze the potential for material misstatement. In contrast, ratio, trend, and reasonableness tests are based on quantitative procedures.

Table 9-1 follows directly from this set of distinctions. It shows the extent to which judgment in applying the various analytical methods is, or can be, aided by computational analysis, and, in cases involving computational analysis, whether regression analysis is used. It also shows the nature of auditor judgment when using each method, on a scale from "most subjective" to "most objective."

When one is considering methods that involve computational analysis (columns 2 and 3), it is important to know how the threshold is determined. The threshold is the cutoff point used when applying the method that establishes whether a given amount or per cent deviation is unusual or not.

Since most types of inherent risk analysis used in auditing are not computational, they do not involve a threshold. However, ratio analysis is computational, requiring judgment concerning the threshold for a significant deviation. Trend analysis and reasonableness tests are also computational and usually involve a threshold determined judgmentally. Moreover, these last two methods can be augmented by a regression analysis which provides a statistically determined threshold, the standard error of the estimate.

For purposes of developing a framework of guidance that will help the auditor answer the "how" question, we consider the three columns in Table 9-1 to represent three different "approaches" to analytical review which differ on a subjective-objective dimension as indicated.

The differences between approaches can be directly related to differences in the nature of the required guidance and support to be

Table 9-1   The Nature and Extent of Judgment When Using Analytical Procedures

	Three Approaches		
		Aided by Computational Analysis	
Analytical Method	Unaided by Computational Analysis (1)	Estimation of Thresholds Judgmentally (2)	Estimation of Thresholds by Regression Analysis (3)
1. Inherent risk analysis	X	X	
2. Ratio analysis		X	
3. Trend analysis		X	X
4. Reasonableness tests		X	X
Subjectivity versus objectivity level of the method	Most subjective (uses knowledge and experience only)	Most objective (uses structured mathematical methods)	

SOURCE: Adapted from Blocher, *Approaching Analytical Review*, CPA J, Mar 1983; reprinted with permission of *CPA Journal*, copyright 1983, New York State Society of Certified Public Accountants.

given to the auditor.[2] For example, since approach 1 encompasses a broad range of methods which require a substantial amount of accounting and business knowledge, it follows that major concerns are:

1. The *consensus* among auditors concerning how this approach is applied
2. The *consistency* with which any given auditor applies the approach over time
3. The *completeness* and thoroughness with which the approach is applied

The choice of an appropriate form of guidance for auditors when using approach 1 should address these three concerns. For example, one could attend to the objectives of consensus and consistency by requiring the auditor to use a list of suggested analyses that are commonly used in effective risk analysis. The listing would primarily serve as a reminder of possible analyses rather than as a device to restrict the auditor's judgment in a predetermined manner, since the auditor in the field is best able to choose the form of analysis for a particular engagement. Also, the guidance objective of completeness could be addressed by making training materials and relevant databases readily available in a very easy-to-use form. This discussion is summarized in Table 9-2.

In approach 2 the guidance objectives of consensus and consistency still apply, but the objective of completeness is less relevant, since the methods applied are more well defined. Thus, experience and training are relatively less important. However, approach 2 often involves lengthy, tedious calculations, such as those necessary for a trend analysis of the working trial balance accounts. Thus, a relevant objective here is to reduce the amount of arithmetic required of the auditor. In consideration of these objectives, support for approach 2 might include the following:

1. Computer-assisted preparation of "exception schedules" which highlight significant deviations from expected trends and ratios.

---

[2] Libby, Accounting and Human Information Processing (Prentice Hall 1981) surveys the research which has been done to investigate the effectiveness of various forms of guidance. Relatively little research of this type has been done in an accounting or auditing context. Important papers on the topic in the psychological literature are those by Hogarth & Makridakis, *The Value of Decision Making in a Complex Environment: An Experimental Approach*, Mgmt Sci, Jan 1981, at 93-107 and Einhorn, *Expert Judgment and Mechanical Combination*, Organizational Behavioral and Human Performance, Feb 1972, at 86-106.

Table 9-2   Requirements, Objectives, and Suggested Support Aids for Each Analytical Approach

	Three Approaches		
	Unaided by Computational Analysis (1)	Aided by Computational Analysis	
		Estimation of Thresholds Judgmentally (2)	Estimation of Thresholds by Regression Analysis (3)
		Requirements	
Knowledge	A substantial amount of knowledge about (1) the client's organization and business and (2) the financial and operating relationships of the client.	Same as for (1), plus knowledge of how to apply the chosen method properly.	An understanding of regression analysis: 1. How to apply it properly. 2. How to interpret the results.
Data	1. Client financial and operating data. 2. Other client data: correspondence, minutes of meetings, and so on.	Client financial and operating data.	1. Reliable time-series data for the account being analyzed. 2. Reliable operating and financial data for the account being analyzed.
Computation	Typically negligible.	Tedious; sometimes voluminous; arithmetically simple.	Done by a computer program.
		Objectives	
	1. Consensus. 2. Consistency. 3. Completeness.	1. Consensus. 2. Consistency. 3. Removal of the burden of tedious computations.	1. Proper application of the model and interpretation of the model's results. 2. Use of accurate and comparable data.

Three Approaches

Unaided by Computational Analysis (1)	Aided by Computational Analysis	
	Estimation of Thresholds Judgmentally (2)	Estimation of Thresholds by Regression Analysis (3)
	Aids	
1. A listing of risk analyses. The auditor should provide responses explaining (a) which measures the auditor feels are appropriate, (b) the work done, and (c) the auditor's conclusion. 2. Easy access to training materials and databases.	1. Computer-assisted preparation of exception schedules, given the auditor's desired threshold. 2. Computer-assisted sensitivity analyses and "what if" analyses. 3. Computer-stored databases of client and industry data. 4. Guidance for deciding when a fluctuation or deviation from the expected value is significant, and the nature of further audit work, it any.	1. An interactive computer program for solving the mathematics of regression. 2. In connection with the computer program, a set of questions to test the program user's proper understanding of the program and proper interpretation of the results. 3. Guidance for evaluating the accuracy and comparability of the operating data. 4. Accurate industry and economic data.

SOURCE: Adapted from Blocher, *Approaching Analytical Review*, CPA J., Mar 1983. Reprinted with permission of *CPA Journal*, copyright 1983, New York State Society of Certified Public Accountants.

2. Computer-assisted sensitivity analyses and "what if" analyses. For example, a "what if" analysis could be used to show the effect on the client's current ratio if a certain contingent liability is realized shortly after the report date.

3. Computer-based client and industry data, to facilitate various analyses.

4. Guidance for deciding when a fluctuation or deviation from the expected value is significant and what adjustments to audit scope are necessary in this event.

When one is considering guidance for approach 3, the issues of consensus and consistency are not important because they are provided by the structure involved in applying the regression model. However, there are two new objectives:

1. The regression analysis must be done properly, and the results must be interpreted properly.

2. The auditor must be satisfied that the data used to fit the regression model are both accurate and comparable across different time periods.

These objectives can be achieved by providing an interactive computer program to solve the regression model. The computer can also be used to present the results in a manner designed to facilitate proper interpretation. For example, a set of questions could be used. The auditor would have to answer the questions correctly to receive the final regression results. Alternatively, the regression results could include a diagnostic report, in simple language, which would advise the auditor of problems such as an ill-defined model and the implication of those problems for interpreting the results.

§9.04 Using Analytical Procedures—Summary Notes

The objective of this final portion of the chapter is to summarize relevant aspects of Chapters 3 through 6 which bear upon the effective use of trend analysis, ratio analysis, and the reasonableness test. The reader should refer to these previous chapters for a more thorough treatment of these points.

Trend Analysis

Our survey of research into the judgments of auditors and others, in contexts related to the trend analysis task, has identified six concerns that the auditor should be alert to when performing a trend analysis task and interpreting its results. A useful broad survey of this research is given by Hogarth and Makridakis and by Libby.[3]

1. The confirmation bias. Decision makers in a wide variety of decision contexts have shown a bias favoring the apparent hypothesis. There is a tendency not to seek out disconfirming evidence, nor to search for alternate explanations for what appears to be an obvious interpretation of results. For example, an auditor might be inclined to accept the generic explanation of "inflation" to explain rising costs, when a closer examination of operating data might show that costs in fact should have declined.

   Auditors should be conscious of this pervasive judgment bias. One way to respond to it is to use a *causal reasoning* approach in analytical review. By this approach, the auditor predicts what the balance or relationship should have been for the current year, using as a basis for the prediction operating and external data, and then compares the predicted and reported amounts for reasonableness. In contrast, auditors have often taken a *diagnostic* approach wherein the current balances are reviewed for reasonableness, with no explicit prediction involved. This latter approach causes the auditor to be more prone to the confirmation bias, since it does not require an assessment of relevant operating and external data.

2. Studies have shown that auditors and others tend to overestimate the degree of trend to a series of numbers. Their "intuitive" predictions are biased too high.

3. Studies have shown that auditors and others tend to underestimate the degree of variability in a series of numbers. As a result, they are overconfident as to the accuracy of their predictions.

4. Simple quantitative prediction models tend to outperform unaided human decision makers, a fact which is consistent with items 2 and 3. This suggests that auditors should be cautioned about using a strictly intuitive approach to prediction; some of the simple quantitative trend analysis methods shown in Chapter 4 should be used as well.

---

[3] Hogarth & Makridakis, *The Value of Decision Making in a Complex Environment: An Experimental Approach,* Mgmt Sci, Jan 1981, at 93-107; and R. Libby, Accounting and Human Information Processing: Theory and Application (Prentice Hall 1981).

5. The simple quantitative models discussed in item 4 have been found to be as accurate as or better than more complex models in a wide variety of contexts. This suggests that one or a few independent variables will be sufficient for many of the prediction models the auditor will need.

6. Our research results indicate that auditors tend to base their judgments about whether or not a given change in an account balance is significantly unusual upon the amount of the change rather than upon the per cent change from the prior year. This means that auditors will potentially underweight the significance of deviations in small accounts.

Ratio Analysis

The discussion in Chapter 5 includes the three assumptions and limitations involved in using ratio analysis:

1. When comparing the ratio with either a prior year's ratio or an industry average, the auditor should ensure that the comparison is appropriate. There are two reasons why the ratios may not be comparable. First, two ratios being compared may have been computed differently. Second, there may be differences in the accounting policies and conventions used to prepare the account balances in the ratios. For example, inventory turnover ratios may differ because of differences in accounting methods for inventory—LIFO or FIFO, the cost accounting method (including the treatment of overhead), and the treatment of obsolete or damaged inventory.

2. For a ratio comparison to be meaningful, the relationship between the numerator (y) and the denominator (x) must be strictly *linear;* that is, a given change in the denominator must produce a predictable amount of change in the numerator. Also, the relationship between the numerator and denominator must be strictly variable; that is, the intercept term "a" in the linear model relating the two must be equal to zero. In symbols, $y = a + bx$ becomes $y = bx$, and the ratio $b = y/x$ reflects the assumed strictly linear, strictly variable relationship between x and y.

    The strict variability assumption is often violated by ratios of certain expense accounts to total sales or total expenses. Whenever an expense has a fixed-cost component, the ratio does not reflect a strictly variable relationship.

    The assumption of a strictly linear relationship is sometimes inappropriate as well. For example, when the economic order quantity (EOQ) formula is used to determine inventory levels, the inventory turnover ratio is nonlinear. The reason for this is that the EOQ formula prescribes a relationship between the level of inventory and the *square root* of sales, and thus the ratio is not linear.

3. A variety of operating and financing differences between firms can cause ratios to be noncomparable. Differences in such factors as production technologies, capacity utilization, geographic location, financial leverage, and growth rate would cause a firm's ratios to be noncomparable with those of other firms.

Reasonableness Tests

It is difficult to generalize about the potential problems in using the reasonableness test method, since the exact form of the reasonableness test will differ substantially in different applications. However, two general observations should be useful to the auditor. First, our work with auditors indicates that many auditors always assume a linear, additive relationship between variables, though in some cases a nonlinear or multiplicative relationship is involved. For example, total payroll expenses can be predicted by multiplying wage rate, hours worked, and number of employees. Many auditors have mistakenly modeled these variables in an additive form.

Second, when one is using a reasonableness test, it is important to identify *all* the variables which are relevant for predicting the account balance. Failure to identify a complete model will result in relatively inaccurate predictions and overconfidence in the precision of the predictions.

Exhibit 3 illustrates a guidance form which can be used to facilitate proper application of the reasonableness test in analyzing payroll expense. Similar guidance forms could be developed for such accounts as maintenance expense, utilities and fuel expense, depreciation expense, and so on.

§9.05 References

Blocher, *Approaching Analytical Review,* CPA J, Mar 1983, at 24-32.

Blocher & Luzi, *Guidance Effects on Analytical Review Decisions,* Advances in Accounting, Fall 1987, at 201-13.

Einhorn, *Expert Judgment and Mechanical Combination,* Organizational Behavior and Human Performance, Feb 1972, at 86-106.

Hogarth & Makridakis, *The Value of Decision Making in a Complex Environment: An Experimental Approach,* Management Sci, Jan 1981, at 93-107.

R. Libby, *Accounting and Human Information Processing: Theory and Application* (Prentice-Hall 1981).

Exhibit 3
Illustrative Reasonableness Test
Guidance for Payroll Expense

1. **Objectives**

   a. To analyze the relationships between relevant financial, operating, and economic data to aid the auditor in making an independent prediction of the payroll account.

   b. To use the predicted payroll expense balance in making an assessment as to the possibility of a material error in the unaudited payroll expense account.

2. **Problem Identification**

   a. Obtain the prior year's audited account balance and this year's unaudited account balance.

   b. Calculate the difference between these account balances. Is this difference in line with the financial, operating, and economic factors related to this account?

3. **Model Development and Prediction for Payroll Expense.** (The analysis that follows is designed to assess the potential that an error exists that could materially affect the financial statements. Note that the above comparison of current and prior year's balances, alone, is not sufficient because of financial, operating, and economic changes between years. Thus, the analysis requires the prediction of the current balance using relevant financial, operating, and economic information.)

   a. Model
   Factors to consider when analyzing the relationships affecting payroll expense:
   • Wage rates
   • Idle time
   • Overtime
   • Number of employees
   • Other factors relevant to this account balance:

   _____

   _____

   The *type* of predictive relationship (model) applicable to this case is:
   Predicted expense = prior-year audited expense × a predicted per cent adjustment for the effect of any changes in the above factors for the year.

188

EXHIBIT 3   189

Using the above general information and the specific facts of the audit, write out the predictive relationship you will use for this audit to predict payroll expense:

Payroll Expense = _____

_____

_____

_____

b. Acceptance Criteria

Select acceptance criteria that will indicate a possibility of material error in the payroll expense account when compared with the difference (or per cent/relationship) between the current-year unaudited payroll expense and the predicted balance in the payroll expense account.

c. Prediction

(1) Obtain the required information:
- Prior-year audited
   payroll expense   _____
- Wage rates   _____
- Idle time   _____
- Overtime   _____
- Number of employees   _____
- Other information: _____

_____

(2) Compute the predicted account balance using the model in **3.a.** and the data immediately preceding:

_____

_____

_____

_____

Predicted account balance $ _____

4. Decision Analysis

a. Calculate a "predicted difference" by subtracting the predicted account balance from the current unaudited account balance.

b. Compare the predicted difference with the difference criteria for acceptance in **3.b.**

c. On the basis of this comparison, determine the nature and extent of any further audit work needed.

SOURCE: Adapted from Blocher & Luzi, *Guidance Effects on Analytical Review Decisions,* Advances in Accounting, Fall 1987.

Analytical Procedures and the Computer

10

§10.01   Introduction

The use of the microcomputer in audit practice has increased dramatically since the first edition of this book, and the commonly cited projections suggest an increasing rate of acceptance of these computers within CPA firms in the coming years. The use of the microcomputer has been motivated by significant applications in the planning and field work phases of the audit—data manipulation and analysis, word processing, and automated working papers and reports. One of the more prominent uses of the microcomputer for analysis has been analytical procedures. The microcomputer systems have been used to facilitate the computation and presentation of ratios and projections used in analytical procedures. The speed and accuracy of the computer have been used to replace the pencil-pushing aspect of analytical procedures and to produce reports which are readable, consistent, and prompt.

This chapter describes three broad types of microcomputer software which are being used to facilitate analytical procedures:

1. Database systems such as DBASE III

2. Spreadsheet systems such as Lotus 1-2-3

3. Audit working paper systems such as FAST! (Financial Audit Systems, Raleigh, NC) or BASIC FINANCIAL STATEMENTS (Peat Marwick Main and Co) or AUTOMATED TRIAL BALANCE (AICPA)

Other, more specialized types of microcomputer software systems which are relevant for analytical procedures include software for regression analysis and expert systems. The regression analysis software is discussed in Chapter 11, and the area of expert systems and specific applications for the microcomputer are presented and discussed in Chapter 12. Before discussing these systems, we present a general introduction to the use of the microcomputer in auditing.

§10.02   Microcomputer Audit Applications

The American Institute of CPAs has recently prepared an Auditing Procedure Study which describes potential uses of microcomputers by auditors.[1] This guide is a useful resource for information about the different uses of the microcomputer and the criteria an auditor should use in selecting software. The guide notes a wide variety of significant uses for the microcomputer in auditing. Each of these areas of audit application is discussed below.

Audit Procedures and the Audit Process

Micro-based software systems have been developed to automate a number of the elements of the audit process and to automate specific audit procedures.

Audit Working Papers. Perhaps the single most important use of the microcomputer is in providing an "automated working paper." This software in effect replaces a pencil-and-paper worksheet with one in electronic media. For example, the working trial balance is a working paper which is tedious to prepare and maintain, as adjustments and corrections are made throughout the audit, especially when there are

---

[1] American Institute of CPAs, Auditors' Use of Microcomputers, (1986).

Microcomputer Audit Applications

- Audit Procedures/Process
  Audit Working Papers
  Graphics Reports
  Confirmation Control
  Statistical Sampling
  Analytical Review
  Engagement Time Control
  Audit Planning
- Write Up
- Word Processing
- Office Administration
- Communication
- Training
- Decision Support

a large number of corrections and adjustments just prior to the report date. The working paper software, by automating the trial balance, allows the auditor to quickly and accurately maintain the working trial balance. The same is true of other working papers which are tedious and require a good bit of pencil pushing, such as those needed for consolidations.

Reports. Micro-based software can be used to prepare quickly, neatly, and accurately various reports and schedules required during the audit. The systems are especially useful for reports that are derived from the working trial balance, such as the financial statements, tax returns and related supporting schedules. The systems can be "programmed" to tie the appropriate working trial balance accounts to the proper lines on the financial statements and tax returns, so that in effect, not only is the working trial balance "automated," but the financial statements and tax returns are also "automatic."

Graphics. An additional feature of some of the audit software systems is the opportunity to present data in graphic format. Though this tool probably does not enhance audit decision making, it may be useful for presentations to clients and others.

Confirmation Control. Another set of working papers which is quite tedious relates to confirmation control. Some software systems offer a module which replaces this pencil pushing with electronic media. These systems are very much like word processors, in that no analysis is done, but simply, the pencil-and-paper worksheet is replaced with an electronic one. The advantages of this type of system, then, are the same as for any word processing type of system—speed, neatness, and consistency. One point requires clarification with respect to these systems, however. These systems do *not* have the ability to *select* confirmations and *print* confirmation requests. The reason is that the microcomputer systems do not have access to detailed account data, which would be necessary for this type of application. The microcomputer systems have limited data storage, and detailed account data or transactional data are not typically stored in these systems. Thus, only mainframe type audit software is designed to perform the select and print functions noted above. This is a limitation of the micro-based systems, which we will discuss further in the next section. The real contribution of the confirmation control systems for the microcomputer, then, is to replace the workpaper which tallies the results of the confirmation procedure.

Statistical Sampling. Relatively few software systems now available to auditors offer this feature, in part because the micro-based systems do not have access to the requisite detailed transactional data, as noted above for confirmation control. The sampling systems which are available perform two functions. One, they replace the pencil-and-paper worksheets as do the confirmation control systems described above, and thus perform a word processing role. Two, the systems often perform some analysis functions, such as to compute the required statistical sample size, to generate a series of random numbers, and to perform a statistical evaluation of the sample results. These three analysis functions are usually taken from statistical sampling tables such as those provided in the AICPA audit sampling guides, and other sources for statistical sampling applications. That is, the sampling tables are integrated into the software as "look-up tables" which are accessed by the user when he or she specifies the parameters of the sampling application (desired risk level, planned tolerable error, and population characteristics).

Note that these systems are not able to access transactional data, so that they do not actually select a sample. Rather, they replace the working paper in which the auditor tallies the results of the sampling application, and they provide the three analysis functions noted above.

Note also that the variables sampling technique preferred by many auditors, the Probability-Proportional-to-Size (PPS) method, requires a sample selection approach different from that based on a list of random numbers only. This technique in fact requires access to transactional data as part of the sample selection process.[2] Thus, PPS sampling cannot be implemented easily on microcomputer systems, and the sampling software products which are widely available tend to be attributes applications, rather than variables applications. This presents another limitation of the microcomputer-based systems for audit sampling applications.

Analytical Procedures. Coming close behind the "automated working paper" application for micro-based systems in terms of popularity is the use of these systems for analytical procedures. The systems are used to prepare reports showing calculated ratios, trends, and projections as well as common size statements, and other related analyses. These reports are particularly convenient to present for the "working paper" systems, since the working trial balance is automated in these systems, and these reports are programmed to derive directly from the working trial balance. The remainder of this chapter will present an overview and some detailed illustrations of these types of systems.

Engagement Time Control. Perhaps the third most popular application, behind the working paper application and analytical procedures, is the use of the microcomputer to replace the engagement time control worksheet. Again, as for the confirmation control and statistical sampling applications, these systems perform primarily a word processing function, to replace the pencil-and-paper worksheet with an "automated" one. The advantages are those for word processing, as noted above, consistency, neatness, and speed.

Audit Planning. Interpreted broadly, audit planning includes the applications of analytical procedures and engagement time control described above. Additionally, expert systems applications are available on the microcomputer for risk analysis and for evaluating the going-concern issue for an engagement. These are described in Chapter 12. Moreover, the American Institute of CPAs has recently introduced a micro-based system for planning called the "Audit Program Generator." Essentially a database system, this system allows the user to design an audit program by selecting steps from a database of audit programs contained in the AICPA's *Audit and Accounting Manual,* §5400. The database, then, is a library of audit programs from which the auditor can select to design the program suitable for a particular engagement.

---

[2] Good references for an introduction to PPS Sampling include books by A. Bailey, Statistical Auditing (Harcourt, Brace, Jovanovich 1981) and D. Guy Introduction to Statistical Sampling in Auditing (Wiley 1981).

Write-Up Systems

Though not an audit function, the use of write-up systems is a common application for microcomputers. The audit implications of the use of a write-up system by the client or accounting service is that the auditor can use "linking" software to pull data directly from these systems into the audit system. This is a very important benefit, as it avoids the time-consuming and error-prone nature of direct keyboard data entry.

Word Processing

The use of the microcomputer to replace the common typewriter is perhaps the single most significant effect of growth in the use of microcomputers. This is true of audit firms as well as other business and professional users. Memos, reports, and financial statements can be prepared more quickly and easily with these systems. Also, some of the audit systems produce report files which can be read by word processing systems, thus making it possible for the auditor to integrate auditing and word processing system applications.

Office Administration

While this is one of the least common applications of the microcomputer in audit practice, the potential applications are meaningful and significant. Here it is possible for the firm to use scheduling software (many systems are now available), planning and organizing software (such as THINKTANK by Living Videotext, Inc.), and database programs to manage client data, mailing lists, and technical references.

Communication

At this time there is relatively little use of communication software in audit practice, though it is clear that there are important potential applications, such as the communication of working papers from the field to the firm's office for review. Also, working papers and other documents can be communicated via a microcomputer and modem to training sites, other firm offices, or residences when desirable.

Training

Microcomputers are quite naturally used in training auditors to properly use certain software systems. However, an additional training use of microcomputers is for drill and reinforcement of concepts and techniques normally taught in a paper-and-pencil fashion. For example, some firms have developed micro-based training materials for such topics as audit planning and internal control review. The advantage of these training tools is that they are consistent, they can be used at virtually any time and place, and they can be designed to be very pedagogically effective. Microcomputer courseware development is perhaps one of the most promising new areas for application of microcomputer technology.

Decision Support

The use of micro-based systems to facilitate human judgment in the form of expert systems is an important application area. Most of the large audit firms have a significant commitment to the development of these systems to enhance the quality and competitiveness of their practice. Expert systems applications are covered in Chapter 12.

Writing in *The Practical Accountant,* Holley and Chester (1987) show survey results which describe the types of software products being used in audit firms, and the most popular products in each category. This article provides a useful perspective for considering the potential for application of the microcomputer in audit practice.

§10.03   Mainframe and Micro-Based Systems Contrasted

To clarify the role of the microcomputer in auditing generally and in analytical procedures particularly, this brief section contrasts the nature of the applications of the two types of systems. This contrast is outlined here, and a more detailed presentation is given in Figure 10-1.

This outline shows the four broad areas of application for audit software, whether it be mainframe or micro-based. We start with a discussion of the database type applications. For this discussion, we define a database as a set of financial or operating data of interest to the auditor that is organized by "record" and "field." A record is used to index the database; for example, in a payroll database, each employee's data represents a record. There would be as many records in the database as there are employees. "Fields" are used to describe certain characteristics of each record that are of interest to the user. For example, the fields in a payroll database would ordinarily include the employee's name, address, employee number, pay rate, and so on.

Database management applications include those in which the objective is to manipulate a database to derive audit relevant information by methods such as sorting the database, selecting records by certain criteria, combining records or fields of the database, or generating new fields by mathematical operations on existing fields, among others. Good examples of database applications in auditing include selecting

Fuctions of Computer Audit Software

- Database Operations
  Combine, Aggregate,
  Summarize, Sort,
  Select, Generate
  [Listing of Large Accounts, Aging
  Receivables, Select Confirmations,
  Select a Sample]
- Tests
  Test EDP Controls,
  Recalculation,
  Reconciliation
- Analyses
  Financial Ratios,
  Trends, Risk Analysis
- Reports
  Financial Statements,
  Various Schedules

confirmations, selecting samples, preparing an aging of receivables, and selecting large accounts or transactions for further investigation.

The second category of applications, "tests," includes a wide range of functions in which the computer reprocesses transactions to check for arithmetic errors, reconciles the handling of transactions to the related accounts, or tests the effectiveness of a software system's programmed controls. Programmed controls refer to the controls designed to replace the human element. They are able to detect unusual amounts or relationships. For example, a programmed control could be designed to detect payroll errors by printing on an error list all payroll amounts over a certain limit, or all employees with more than a certain number of hours. Programmed controls are also used to edit input data or to validate the correctness of an employee number or the correct relationship between an employee number and the related department number, for example.

The third category of applications, analyses, includes schedules and work papers prepared directly from the financial and operating data in the system. The best examples here are analytical procedures, in which financial ratios, common-size statements, trend analysis, and reasonableness tests are prepared from the working trial balance and a small amount of operating data entered by the auditor. Other examples include financial projections, pro forma financial statements, inventory price tests, and analyses of contingent liabilities and reserves.

The fourth and final category of application is reports such as the financial statements, schedules listing items of audit interest such as significant customers or significant vendors, related parties, purchase commitments, and so on.

§10.04 Specific Mainframe and Micro-Based Applications

In this section, we discuss the extent to which each of the four categories of computer-based applications described in the previous section can be achieved by a mainframe software system such as many of the largest audit firms have developed, or by a micro-based software system which has been developed by some of the large firms and is also available from various software vendors.

The discussion in this section is outlined in Panel A of Figure 10-1. Note that all four categories of applications can be achieved with a mainframe type of system. The reason for this is that this type of system has access to detailed account data and transactional data. This means that these systems can perform any kind of test or analysis that is possible with the given database. In contrast, all of the commonly cited micro-based systems operate on data at an aggregate level, and detailed account data and transactional data are often not available to these systems. The storage and processing speed of the microcomputer is somewhat limited in contrast to the mainframe computer, so that the micro-based systems are designed to operate in a smaller and simpler database environment. The effect is that the micro-based systems are limited in the types of database functions that can be performed. For example, these systems are usually not able to select a sample or to select confirmations. However, they do provide a convenient means to record and summarize the results of the sampling or confirmation procedures, as noted in the previous section.

As Figure 10-1 shows, the micro-computer system is often not able to perform the "test" category of applications—tests of EDP controls, recalculation and reconciliation tests—since these are all at the detailed level. On the other hand, since many audit-relevant analyses such as analytical review are done at a relatively aggregate level, these analyses can be performed on either the micro-based or mainframe type of system. Finally, the fourth category, producing audit-relevant reports, is a function that the micro-based software can perform with some limitations. Again, the limitation is based on the fact that the detailed level data is not available in the micro-based system, so that the

Figure 10-1   Capabilities of Different Types of Audit Software

Functions of Computer Audit Software	Panel A Software Capability		Panel B Microcomputer Software Capability	
	Micro- Computer	Mainframe Computer	Spreadsheet	Database
● Database Operations	Limited	Yes	Limited, -Storage -Account Level	Limited -Account Level
● Tests Test EDP Controls, Recalculation, Reconciliation	No	Yes	No	No
● Analyses Financial Ratios, Trends, Risk Analysis	Yes	Yes	Yes	Yes
● Reports Financial Statements, Various Schedules	Yes, Some Limitations	Yes	Yes, Some Limitations	Yes, Some Limitations

reports which can be prepared must be derived from aggregate data. For example, the micro-based system can be used to produce financial statements from the working trial balance.

In summary, the micro-based software has certain limitations related to the limited storage capacity and processing speed of the smaller computers. The primary applications for the micro-based systems turn out to be those associated with analyses and with producing reports from aggregate level data. As technology changes, it is likely that the smaller computers will be able to store larger amounts of data and to process this data much faster. As these developments take place, the distinction between the mainframe computer and the microcomputer will begin to fade away, and we will see micro-based systems being designed to achieve a broader scope of audit functions, as the mainframe systems can now achieve.

§10.05   Microcomputer Spreadsheet Systems and Database Systems Contrasted

There are two conventional designs for audit software available at this time. One type of software is designed around a spreadsheet system, such as a LOTUS 1-2-3 system. These software systems utilize the speed, familiarity, and flexibility of the spreadsheet as a base to produce audit systems which run together with the spreadsheet system. The systems are fast and flexible, in part because all the data in the spreadsheet are in RAM storage, that is, the user has immediate access to any data in the spreadsheet. Also, an advantage of the spreadsheet approach is that spreadsheet programming is familiar to many auditors, whereas database programming is not.

A significant weakness of the spreadsheet type system, however, is the lack of convenient file handling and simple storage of relatively large databases. The systems are limited by the amount of data that can be stored in a spreadsheet. The maximum size of a spreadsheet depends on the RAM storage of the microcomputer. Software tools are available to "compress" spreadsheets, and a large database can be broken down into two or more logically related spreadsheets, but the ease and simplicity of use decreases when this becomes necessary.

In contrast to the spreadsheet systems, database systems are designed to handle files conveniently and to deal effectively with large volumes of data. This is possible because in the database system, not all the data is "live," but, instead, the system is programmed to "call" just the data it needs for a certain operation. Thus, the database system can be somewhat slower because it may be opening and closing a number of files repeatedly through the execution of a given audit application. However, for very small database applications, where extensive file handling is not necessary, the speed of the two types of systems is likely to be very similar. Most importantly, the size of the database is no longer limited by the RAM storage capacity of the computer, but the disk storage capacity, and many hard disk type computers have 10 or 20 megabytes of disk storage, or more. Also, an advantage of the database language approach is the relative ease to the user of adding records to the database, of modifying the database, and of getting reports from it. From a user's viewpoint, it is a simpler system than most spreadsheet systems. In summary, the relative effectiveness of the two types of systems depends primarily on the size and complexity of the application, with the smaller and simpler applications favoring the spreadsheet approach, and the larger and more complex applications favoring the database approach. Panel B of Figure 10-1 summarizes the above discussion. Note that the major difference between the two types of systems is the database operations—while the database systems are limited to account level detail, the spreadsheet systems are limited in addition to less storage capacity relative to the database systems.

The following sections show examples of each type of system:

Database system
Spreadsheet system
Working paper system

The third type of system, the "working paper system," is an audit system designed to automate routine pencil-pushing tasks, such as maintaining the working trial balance. These systems are most often programmed in a database language. Thus, to contrast §§1 and 3 above, the discussion in §1 is intended to describe simple, single-purpose database applications which auditors can perform if they are able to use a database language such as DBASEIII, FOXBASE, or KNOWLEDGEMAN. In this case, the auditor is both designer and user of the system. In contrast, the working paper systems are written in a language such as DBASEIII or FOXBASE, and they are quite a bit more complex, having been designed to achieve a relatively broad set of audit objectives. In summary, all three types of systems represent potential significant benefits to the auditor in certain applications. In the following sections, we describe representative analytical review applications for each type of system. It will become apparent that each type of system is best suited for a certain type of application.

§10.06 Database Applications

In this section, we present some of the audit applications of the microcomputer using generalized database software. Database software systems are widely used in accounting to achieve a variety of applications, from a simple system to manage a mailing list to complex general ledger and auditing systems.

In this section, we provide illustrations of database applications in the three audit areas—receivables, inventory, and payroll. These three audit areas were chosen because auditors frequently apply analytical procedures in these areas. Also, receivables and inventory are commonly considered to be critical audit areas, while payroll is an area that can sometimes be tested by a purely analytical approach, with little or no reliance on detail test procedures. Thus, these three areas represent very important application areas for analytical procedures.

Each of the applications presented below presumes a relatively small database with a relatively simple file structure, say, one with a few hundred to a few thousand records, and no more than eight to ten fields per record. Database applications could be run for these databases on most microcomputers, with readily available software. The AICPA guide on computer-assisted auditing (AICPA, 1979) is also a useful resource for examples of these applications.[3] (See especially Appendix A of this guide.)

Database Applications in Accounts Receivable

The following outlines a number of possible applications in accounts receivable, by category.

1. *Database Operations*
   - Select and list accounts having a balance over a certain amount
   - Select and list all accounts with a credit balance
   - Select and list all accounts with a balance greater than a given percentage of the total for all accounts
   - Select and list all accounts with a volume of invoices untypical relative to the prior period (presumes prior year data is included in the database)
   - Select and list all balances which have increased by greater than a given dollar amount and/or percentage from the prior year
   - Select and list all *new* accounts over a given dollar amount
   - Select and list all accounts with no payments in a given number of days
   - Sort accounts by credit code
   - Select and list accounts by credit code
   - Select and list all accounts which were reduced or written off by more than a given amount
   - Select and list all accounts with an unusual pattern of refunds, debit memos, etc., based upon predetermined criteria for "unusual patterns"
   - Select and list accounts with past due balances over a given amount
   - Select balances for confirmation and print related confirmation requests
   - Sort the accounts by account number
   - Sort the accounts by balance amount
   - Summarize the accounts by customer class, location, or credit code

---

[3] American Institute of CPAs, Computer-Assisted Audit Techniques (1979).

2. *Tests*

- Check for valid account numbers by comparison to a look-up table of authorized account numbers or by use of a self-checking number approach
- Compare credit limit to the current balance for each account
- Using transaction data and interim account balances, update these balances and compare to the year-end balances
- Compare cash receipts after year-end to invoices at the balance sheet date

3. *Analyses*

- Compute a relevant set of ratios, such as the turnover ratio, the average balance per customer, the ratio of accounts receivable to current assets, the ratio of bad debt expense to accounts receivable, and so on.

4. *Reports*

- Perform an aging of receivables

Database Applications in Inventory

1. *Database Operations*

- Select a sample for inventory test counts
- Select a sample for inventory price tests
- List all items not sold in the last given number of days, to examine for obsolete items
- Summarize inventory data by location, product line, or inventory class

2. *Tests*

- Compare data in the inventory and sales transactions databases to assess the reasonableness of the amount on hand, and to examine for obsolete and slow moving items
- Test for clerical accuracy of totals and extensions
- Compare on-hand quantity to reorder quantity to examine for obsolete items
- Compare on-hand quantity to sales forecast data as a test of the reasonableness of the on-hand quantity and as a test for obsolescence
- Test for valid inventory part numbers by reference to a look-up table of authorized numbers or the use of a self-checking digit approach

- Test for duplicate part numbers

3. *Analyses*
   - Test for reasonableness of unit costs by
     Comparison to prior years
     Comparison to a look-up table of authorized prices
   - Compute relevant ratios by inventory class, product line, or location
     Inventory turnover
     Ratio of write-downs to inventory amount
     Percentage components of unit cost—labor, materials, and overhead
   - Calculate gross profit by product line
   - For LIFO inventories,
     Calculate the base and current year extensions
     Summarize and compute current year index
     Compare base year and current year prices
     Compute the LIFO value for each LIFO pool

4. *Reports*
   - List unusual increases in
     Unit costs
     Cost mix of labor, materials, and overhead
     Quantity on hand
     Spoilage, loss, and waste

Database Applications for Payroll

1. *Database Operations*
   - Select and list employees with gross pay in excess of a given amount
   - Select and list employees with regular or overtime pay in excess of a given number of hours
   - Summarize employees by department
   - Sort employees by date of hire
   - Select a sample for detail test work

2. *Tests*
   - Test for duplicate employees

- Test for invalid employees using reference to a look-up table of authorized employees or using a self-checking digit approach
- Compare job classification and wage rate for reasonableness
- Merge the payroll master database and the payroll transactions database and test for:

  Differences in number of exemptions

  Maximum FICA earnings exceeded

  Differences in wage rates

  Effective removal of terminated employees
- Recalculate all extensions

3. *Analyses*
   - Prepare ratios for analysis and interpretation:

     Average payroll expense per employee

     Employee benefits expense to payroll expense

     Payroll tax to payroll expense

     Commissions expense to sales

4. *Reports*
   - Summarize payroll by the respective general ledger account for reconciliation to the general ledger

§10.07   Spreadsheet Applications

In this section, we present applications of microcomputer spreadsheet software for analytical procedures. The applications are presented on the LOTUS 1-2-3 software, though any equivalent spreadsheet system will produce comparable results. The illustrative applications include examples in each of the three areas:

- Trend analysis
- Ratio analysis
- Reasonableness testing

Trend Analysis Spreadsheets

An example of a trend analysis spreadsheet is illustrated in Figures 10-2 through 10-4. Figure 10-2 shows the menu screen for the spreadsheet. This is the screen at the "Home" position of the spreadsheet, which the user enters when the spreadsheet file is opened for the first time in a given analysis session. The purpose of this screen is to organize the contents of the spreadsheet and to give the user a table of contents for the spreadsheet. Thus, during any analysis session, the user can enter "Home" and come to the menu screen to select another option. The menu options are supported by spreadsheet macros, so that the user need only press the "ALT" key and the option code to arrive at the location of the desired option on the spreadsheet.

The first option on the menu screen, the working trial balance, is the basic database for the spreadsheet. It is shown in Figure 10-3. This data is entered by the user, or imported from another spreadsheet file, or extracted from a DBF file. The spreadsheet is constructed so that it can be easily updated for new accounts or for a new year.

The output of the spreadsheet, the trend analysis report, is shown in Figure 10-4. This is the report which is produced under option "D" on the menu screen, which produces a trend analysis for both amounts and percentages. Reports for amount changes or percentage changes only are also available, but are not shown. These reports articulate with the data in the working trial balance, and are produced by formulas in each cell. Overall, the design of this spreadsheet requires only basic knowledge of the spreadsheet commands concerning labels, formulas, and macros.

The spreadsheet can be used as an "automatic" trend analysis, to produce trend analysis reports neatly and consistently from trial balance data. The spreadsheet can be modified to add columns for adjustments to the trial balance, so that the trend analysis can be presented for either the unadjusted or the adjusted balances. Additionally, a major benefit is that the spreadsheet can be saved and used again in the following year's engagement by simply inserting the current year's data.

A special enhancement of the trend analysis spreadsheet is available as menu selection "E," Prediction Model Analysis, and is shown in Fig-

Figure 10-2   Menu Screen for Trend Analysis Spreadsheet

1987 ED BLOCHER   **Trend Analysis**

Enter "ALT" and Code Below to View Reports

Code	Report
A	Working Trial Balance
B	Amounts
C	Percentages
D	Amounts and Percentages
E	Prediction Model Analysis

Figure 10-3 Working Trial Balance for Trend Analysis
Spreadsheet

Clarion Company
Working Trial Balance
12/31-

Account Name	1984	1985	1986	1987	1988
Cash	10234	15283	11879	24198	12840
Accounts Receivable	1123893	1133429	1202283	1223765	1302178
Prepaid Expenses	890	364	712	1109	856
Raw Materials Inventory	11903	12850	15034	12785	18934
Supplies Inventory	434	782	401	749	334
Product Inventory	425687	493956	515535	603668	635476
Furniture and Equipment	67234	89476	118902	128974	130683
Plant and Equipment	625390	698903	709945	715038	755492
Accumulated DEPR-F&E	− 7203	− 8205	− 9481	− 10493	− 11593
Accumulated DEPR-P&E	− 100235	− 113894	− 134875	− 156304	− 178362
Accounts Payable	− 145023	− 112074	− 105923	− 111113	− 163023
FICA Tax Payable	− 12945	− 15934	− 7034	− 23045	− 15893
Federal Tax Payable	− 13045	− 4056	− 13667	− 18339	− 19304
State Tax Payable	− 1192	− 1903	− 1293	− 1445	− 1500
Notes Payable	− 650000	− 750000	− 795000	− 795000	− 805000
Capital Stock Class A	− 1100000	− 1125000	− 1150000	− 1150000	− 1150000
Capital Stock Class B	− 55000	− 100000	− 100000	− 100000	− 100000
Retained Earnings	− 116191	− 181022	− 213977	− 257418	− 344547
Sales	− 3254783	− 3798453	− 3688364	− 4325874	− 4023957
Returns and Allowances	37157	84035	97465	76394	55398
Cost of Goods Sold	2562247	3108381	2937507	3493950	3184670
Admin Salaries	287394	293910	287961	301244	303874
Rent	16000	16000	17500	17500	20000
Office Supplies	3901	4593	6521	3498	4472
Telephone	8421	9823	10234	11543	14326
Office Utilities	1254	1432	1672	1983	1843
Advertising	89273	83674	95283	112394	167234
Insurance	12456	13748	14123	14783	14927
Professional Fees	892	1025	1183	1845	1562
Depreciation F&E	3374	3945	4294	4521	4983
Depreciation P&E	34528	38729	41837	42947	44983
Interest Expense	66723	78192	80193	83042	82939
Tax Expense	32485	12084	21958	35893	25439
Misc Expenses	33847	15927	27192	37208	29736
Balance	0	0	0	0	0

Figure 10-4   Trend Analysis Spreadsheet Report

Trend Analysis

	1984 Amount	−1985 Percent	1985 Amount	−1986 Percent	1986 Amount	−1987 Percent	1987 Amount	−1988 Percent
Cash	5049	33	−3404	−29	12319	51	−11358	−88
Accounts Receivable	9536	1	68854	6	21482	2	78413	6
Prepaid Expenses	−526	−145	348	49	397	36	−253	−30
Raw Materials Inventory	947	7	2184	15	−2249	−18	6149	32
Supplies Inventory	349	45	−381	−95	348	46	−415	−124
Product Inventory	68269	14	21579	4	88133	15	31808	5
Furniture and Equipment	22242	25	29426	25	10072	8	1709	1
Plant and Equipment	73513	11	11042	2	5093	1	40454	5
Accumulated DEPR-F&E	−1002	12	−1276	13	−1012	10	−1100	9
Accumulated DEPR-P&E	−13659	12	−20981	16	−21429	14	−22058	12
Accounts Payable	32949	−29	6151	−6	−5190	5	−51910	32
FICA Tax Payable	−2989	19	8900	−127	−16011	69	7152	−45
Federal Tax Payable	8989	−222	−9611	70	−4672	25	−965	5
State Tax Payable	−711	37	610	−47	−152	11	−55	4
Notes Payable	−100000	13	−45000	6	0	0	−10000	1
Capital Stock Class A	−25000	2	−25000	2	0	0	0	0
Capital Stock Class B	−45000	45	0	0	0	0	0	0
Retained Earnings	−64831	36	−32955	15	−43441	17	−87129	25
Sales	−543670	14	110089	−3	−637510	15	301917	−8
Returns and Allowances	46878	56	13430	14	−21071	−28	−20996	−38
Cost of Goods Sold	546134	18	−170874	−6	556443	16	−309280	−10
Admin Salaries	6516	2	−5949	−2	13283	4	2630	1
Rent	0	0	1500	9	0	0	2500	13
Office Supplies	692	15	1928	30	−3023	−86	974	22
Telephone	1402	14	411	4	1309	11	2783	19
Office Utilities	178	12	240	14	311	16	−140	−8
Advertising	−5599	−7	11609	12	17111	15	54840	33
Insurance	1292	9	375	3	660	4	144	1
Professional Fees	133	13	158	13	662	36	−283	−18
Depreciation F&E	571	14	349	8	227	5	462	9
Depreciation P&E	4201	11	3108	7	1110	3	2036	5
Interest Expense	11469	15	2001	2	2849	3	−103	0
Tax Expense	−20401	−169	9874	45	13935	39	−10454	−41
Misc Expense	−17920	−113	11265	41	10016	27	−7472	−25

ure 10-5. This analysis takes any trial balance account chosen by the user and prepares a prediction of the balance for the current year, based upon the prior years' data. The unique aspect of the analysis is that the predictions are prepared for each of seven models, as described in Chapter 4. Also, an average error amount is computed for each model, based upon the model's accuracy in predicting this account in prior years. This gives the auditor a means to evaluate the usefulness of each of the seven models for predicting the account under analysis. The best model for predicting one account may not be the best model for another account because of differences in the time-series properties of the different accounts. Thus, this spreadsheet gives the auditor a means to choose a prediction model best suited for the account under analysis.

As indicated in Chapter 4, the prediction model approach is a superior method for employing analytical procedures, in that it explicitly includes the prediction step of the analysis. The appropriate comparison is between the amount that is expected or predicted for the current year and the current year amount. As noted in Chapter 4, a simple comparison of the current year to the prior year embodies the assumption, which may be faulty, that the best prediction of the current year's balance is the prior year's balance. In contrast, the prediction model approach (models 2 through 7) takes into account the time-series properties of the account for all prior years.

Ratio Analysis Spreadsheets

An example of a ratio analysis spreadsheet is illustrated in Figures 10-6 through 10-8. As for the trend analysis spreadsheet, this one is designed with a menu structure at the "Home" position of the spreadsheet. Also, it includes a basic database for the ratio analysis, which is simply the working trial balance plus a selected set of additional operating and industry data. The menu and working trial balance screens of this spreadsheet are very similar to those for the trend analysis spreadsheet shown in Figures 10-2 and 10-3, and they are not shown here.

The ratio analysis report group includes two major reports. The first is a common-size statement which is shown in Figure 10-6. This is a common-size analysis of the working trial balance. The spreadsheet could also be extended to produce simple financial statements from this data, and to present common-size analysis of the balance sheet and income statement. Additionally, the analysis could be performed

Figure 10-5   Prediction Model Analysis

Prediction Model Analysis
Supplies Inventory

Model	Average Error	Predicted Balance 1988	Actual Balance 1988	Actual— Predicted 1988
1. This Year Equals Last	359	749	334	−415
2. Year to Year Change	547	854	334	−520
3. Weighted Yearly Change	746	1379	334	−1045
4. Two Year Cycle	365	733	334	−399
5. Smoothed, To Distant Years	3	863	334	−529
6. Smoothed, Unweighted	165	948	334	−614
7. Smoothed, To Recent Years	392	1140	334	−806

for expense accounts only, as a way of targeting unusual changes in expense account relationships.

The second major element of the spreadsheet is the report of calculated ratios in each of the three principal categories:

- Operating ratios, including profitability and activity ratios
- Liquidity ratios, including short term liquidity and turnover ratios
- Leverage ratios, including debt coverage and capital structure ratios.

These categories of ratios and the proper interpretation of each are presented in Chapter 5. The spreadsheet report is shown in Figure 10-7.

As for the trend analysis spreadsheet, these two reports of the ratio analysis spreadsheet are produced by formulas in the related cells which articulate with the working trial balance database. These ratios are grouped on screens so that the user simply presses the page-up or page-down key to select the ratio category desired. Since the working trial balance is common to both spreadsheets, it would be convenient to combine the two spreadsheets into one, for a combined trend and ratio analysis of the client.

Spreadsheet software commonly includes graphics capability, and the ratio analysis or trend analysis spreadsheets would be natural applications for this capability. As an example, a graph taken from the liquidity ratio portion of the ratio analysis spreadsheet is shown in Figure 10-8. The use of graphics aids such as this can facilitate demonstrations and discussions with the client and can enhance the visual quality of reports to the client.

Reasonableness Testing Spreadsheets

The reasonableness testing approach to analytical procedures is discussed in Chapter 6. It is a strong analytical procedures approach because it explicitly models the account under analysis, and because it usually brings in operating data and thereby ties the operating facts and financial results together in a way that other analytical procedures cannot.

Two examples of reasonableness tests using spreadsheets are shown in Figures 10-9 and 10-10. These are simply two of a long list of possible examples which would include payroll expense (as analyzed in Chapter 6) and the other expense accounts. Figure 10-9 illustrates a reasonableness test of fuel expense for a construction contractor who has a fleet of trucks and various types of construction equipment. The

Figure 10-6   Common-Size Statements

Clarion Company
Working Trial Balance — 12/31
Common Size Statements

Account Name	1984	1985	1986	1987	1988
Cash	0.5	0.7	0.5	1	0.5
Accounts Receivable	52.1	48.8	49.5	48.1	48.8
Prepaid Expenses	0	0	0	0	0
Raw Materials Inventory	0.6	0.6	0.6	0.5	0.7
Supplies Inventory	0	0	0	0	0
Product Inventory	19.7	21.3	21.2	23.7	23.8
Furniture and Equipment	3.1	3.9	4.9	5.1	4.9
Plant and Equipment	29	30.1	29.2	28.1	28.3
Accumulated DEPR-F&E	−0.3	−0.4	−0.4	−0.4	−0.4
Accumulated DEPR-P&E	−4.6	−4.9	−5.5	−6.1	−6.7
Accounts Payable	−6.7	−4.8	−4.4	−4.4	−6.1
FICA Tax Payable	−0.6	−0.7	−0.3	−0.9	−0.6
Federal Tax Payable	−0.6	−0.2	−0.6	−0.7	−0.7
State Tax Payable	−0.1	−0.1	−0.1	−0.1	−0.1
Notes Payable	−30.1	−32.3	−32.7	−31.3	−30.2
Capital Stock Class A	−51	−48.4	−47.3	−45.2	−43.1
Capital Stock Class B	−2.5	−4.3	−4.1	−3.9	−3.7
Retained Earnings	−5.4	−7.8	−8.8	−10.1	−12.9
Sales	98.9	97.8	97.4	98.3	98.6
Returns and Allowances	−1.1	−2.2	−2.6	−1.7	−1.4
Cost of Goods Sold	−77.8	−80.1	−77.6	−79.4	−78.1
Admin Salaries	−8.7	−7.6	−7.6	−6.8	−7.4
Rent	−0.5	−0.4	−0.5	−0.4	−0.5
Office Supplies	−0.1	−0.1	−0.2	−0.1	−0.1
Telephone	−0.3	−0.3	−0.3	−0.3	−0.4
Office Utilities	0	0	0	0	0
Advertising	−2.7	−2.2	−2.5	−2.6	−4.1
Insurance	−0.4	−0.4	−0.4	−0.3	−0.4
Professional Fees	0	0	0	0	0
Depreciation F&E	−0.1	−0.1	−0.1	−0.1	−0.1
Depreciation P&E	−1	−1	−1.1	−1	−1.1
Interest Expense	−2	−2	−2.1	−1.9	−2
Tax Expense	−1	−0.5	−0.8	−1.1	−0.9
Misc Expense	−1	−0.4	−0.7	−0.8	−0.7

Figure 10-7   Ratio Analysis

Ratio Type	1984	1985	1986	1987	1988
Operating Ratios					
Return on Sales	0.02	0.01	0.01	0.02	0.02
Return on Total Assets	0.03	0.01	0.02	0.04	0.03
Return on Equity	0.05	0.02	0.03	0.06	0.04
Change in Net Income		−0.49	0.32	1.01	−0.22
Change in Net Sales		0.15	−0.03	0.18	−0.07
Net Sales to Total Assets	1.49	1.60	1.48	1.67	1.49
Liquidity Ratios	**1984**	**1985**	**1986**	**1987**	**1988**
Current Ratio	9.13	12.37	13.65	12.12	9.87
Quick Ratio	6.59	8.57	9.49	8.11	6.58
Working Capital/Total Assets	0.65	0.66	0.67	0.67	0.66
Working Capital Turnover	2.30	2.54	2.29	2.55	2.28
Accounts Receivable Turnover	2.86	3.29	3.07	3.50	3.14
Inventory Turnover	6.02	6.76	5.82	6.24	5.14
Leverage Ratios	**1984**	**1985**	**1986**	**1987**	**1988**
Long Term Debt to Equity	0.49	0.47	0.51	0.51	0.49
Total Debt to Equity	0.62	0.59	0.60	0.60	0.58
Cash Flow to Total Debt	0.12	0.09	0.10	0.14	0.12
Total Debt to Total Assets	0.38	0.39	0.39	0.38	0.39

costs of gas and diesel fuel are indicated in a separate cell and used in formulas throughout the spreadsheet, so that changes in fuel cost can easily and quickly be reflected in the spreadsheet. In this form, the spreadsheet can be used on a monthly or annual basis to test the reasonableness of the expense for that period. The user simply enters the current fuel cost data and the hours or mileage usage figures for the vehicles and equipment, and the fuel usage and related cost numbers are produced automatically by the spreadsheet.

This spreadsheet can also be used by the auditor to provide a service to the client. It can be used to show the client the implications of expected trends in fuel costs on total expected fuel costs, or to estimate the impact on total expected fuel costs of the replacement or addition of equipment or vehicles.

Figure 10-10 shows an example spreadsheet which performs a reasonableness test of interest expense. The interest rate for each loan

Figure 10-8 Using Spreadsheet Graphics

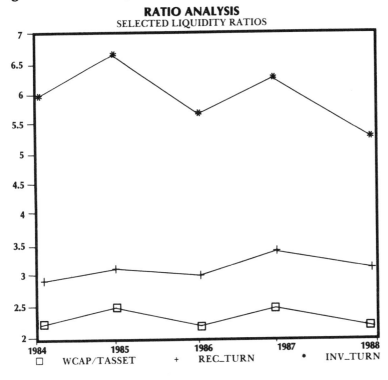

RATIO ANALYSIS
SELECTED LIQUIDITY RATIOS

□ WCAP/TASSET   + REC_TURN   * INV_TURN

Figure 10-9 Fuel Expense Reasonableness Test Spreadsheet

1987 Ed Blocher   **Fuel Expense Reasonableness Test**

Fuel Type, Gas = 1   Fuel Cost Per Gallon, Diesel: 1.15
            Diesel = 0   Gas: 1.04

Vehicle Type	Fuel Type	No of Veh	Miles/ Gallon	Gallons/ Hour	Avg Usage Per Veh	Gallons Used	Total Fuel Cost
Small Auto	1	59	20		21000	61950	64428
Large Auto	1	23	10		24000	55200	57408
Pickup Truck	1	44	8		19000	104500	108680
Vans	1	36	7		9000	46286	48137
Flatbed Truck	0	6	4		6500	9750	11213
Dump Truck	0	4	3		7000	9333	10733
Payloader	0	2		3	1500	9000	10350
Bulldozer	0	3		3	1500	13500	15525
Gooseneck Trlr	0	1		2	1600	3200	3680
Grader	0	2		2	3000	12000	13800
Scraper	0	2		2	3000	12000	13800

357754

is placed in a separate cell and used in the related formulas elsewhere in the spreadsheet for convenience of changing these rates at a later time. Also, the computational sequence and functions used in the spreadsheet system allow the user to enter the amount of the loan only once if it does not change during the year, as for loan type 2 or 4. If the loan balance does change during the year, then the actual balance for each month must be entered, as for loan type 1 or 3. The spreadsheet then shows the estimated total interest expense for each loan and the total interest expense, as a basis for comparison to reported amounts for reasonableness. By design, the spreadsheet can easily be modified for changes in rates, balances, or the addition or deletion of loans. Thus, it is a tool which can be used again for subsequent years or other audit engagements.

§10.08   Working Paper Software Applications

In contrast to the relatively simple, single-purpose database applications noted above, micro-based working paper software is designed to achieve an integrated set of database functions from a single system. These systems are used to prepare working papers, special reports and schedules, the financial statements, tax returns, and other related func-

Figure 10-10   Interest Expense Reasonableness Test Spreadsheet

1987 Ed Blocher   **Interest Expense Reasonableness Test**

Month	Type 1 Rate = 11.5 Ending Balance	Type 2 Rate = 10.5 Ending Balance	Type 3 Rate = 12 Ending Balance	Type 4 Rate = 11.7 Ending Balance
January	49000	335000	65000	1200000
February	34500		65000	
March	23000		65000	
April	0		65000	
May	12500		30000	
June	34000		30000	
July	88750		30000	
August	98000		30000	
September	115000		30000	
October	12000		30000	
November	0		30000	
December	0		30000	
Int Exp	4473.020	35175	5000	140400
Tot Exp	185048.0			

tions. They are a powerful tool for automating many of the pencil-pushing tasks of the audit. In this section, we review some of the analytical procedures these systems can perform. Recall as explained above that these systems work from a microcomputer database, and, as such, they typically are limited to the third and fourth functions of audit systems (see "Functions of Computer Audit Software" in **§10.03**)—special analyses and reports.

Most of the largest audit firms have developed or acquired working-paper software of the type described above. Also, the AICPA has recently introduced a workingpaper system, called ATB, the "Accountant's Trial Balance." The system we use for illustration is called FAST! which is the most popular of systems currently available from software vendors.[4]

The systems focus on the working trial balance as the basic database of the system. The individual accounts can be grouped into logically related groups, or lead schedules. The reports of this system which relate to analytical review are shown in Figures 10-11 through 10-14. Figure 10-11 shows an example of a simple trend analysis of the working trial balance, performed at the lead schedule level. It is also typically possible to obtain this report at the detail account level. Figure 10-12 is best interpreted as an exception report—it is a trend analysis of the accounts which shows only those accounts which have changed from the prior year by more than a threshold criterion which is specified by the user. In the case of this report, the critera were changes exceeding both $10,000 and 15% from the prior year.

The common-size statement analysis, shown in Figure 10-13, shows the analysis of the working trial balance at the lead schedule level. Figure 10-14 shows a ratio analysis of the data in the system. Many systems include graphics support, so that the reports shown above can be enhanced.

§10.09 References

American Institute of CPAs, Auditors' Use of Microcomputers, An Auditing Procedure Study (1986).

American Institute of CPAs, Computer-Assisted Audit Techniques, An Audit and Accounting Guide (1979).

American Institute of CPAs, Audit Program Generator (1987).

---

[4] See the survey results presented by Holley & Chester, *Survey of Microcomputer Use in Public Accounting Firms*, Prac Account, May 1987, at 83-86), and *AICPA 1985 EDP Survey: Software*, J Accountancy, Nov 1987, at 128-32.

Figure 10-11   Trend Analysis—Working Paper Software

Report Date: 03/10/86   **Example Client Company**   Page 1
Prepared By: **December 31, 1985**
Financial Audit Systems   **Account Balance Comparison (Lead Schedule)**
INDEX: 0400   TYPE: X   **General and Administrative Expenses**

Account	Description	Prior Year Balance	Current Year Adj. Balance	Difference	Percent Change
501	Accounting Fees	5,000.00	6,000.00	1,000.00	20.00%
503	Amortization	482.00	482.00	0.00	0.00%
504	Automobile Expense	3,822.65	6,547.35	2,724.70	71.28%
508	Bad Debt Expense	26.66	253.95	227.29	852.55%
512	Contributions	400.00	350.00	−50.00	−12.50%
514	Depreciation Expense	2,388.62	5,198.00	2,809.38	117.62%
519	Franchise Fees	10,000.00	22,300.00	12,300.00	123.00%
520	Insurance - Employees	1,200.00	1,500.00	300.00	25.00%
524	Insurance - Property	1,500.00	2,354.00	854.00	56.93%
526	Interest Expense	1,439.23	7,612.00	6,172.77	428.89%
530	Licenses and Fees	200.00	450.00	250.00	125.00%
534	Maintenance and Repairs	3,847.04	2,465.40	−1,381.64	−35.91%
536	Miscellaneous Expense	2,873.12	1,425.00	−1,448.12	−50.40%
540	Office Expense	729.21	578.45	−150.76	−20.67%
550	Rent Expense	12,000.00	15,000.00	3,000.00	25.00%
560	Salaries - Officers	80,000.00	120,000.00	40,000.00	50.00%
562	Salaries and Wages - Other	64,039.00	78,534.00	14,495.00	22.63%
564	Supplies Expense	746.98	985.80	238.82	31.97%
570	Taxes - Payroll	10,317.45	14,325.76	4,008.31	38.85%
572	Taxes - Property	2,634.00	3,645.20	1,011.20	38.39%
	Total	203,645.96	290,006.91	86,360.95	42.41%

A. Bailey, Jr, *Statistical Auditing* (Harcourt, Brace, Jovanovich 1981).

D. Guy, *An Introduction to Statistical Sampling in Auditing* (Wiley 1981).

Holley & Chester, *Survey of Microcomputer Use in Public Accounting Firms,* Prac Account, May 1987, at 83-86.

Figure 10-12   Report of Accounts with Significant Changes—Working Paper Software

Report Date: 03/07/86   **Example Client Company**   ****Materiality Levels**** Page 1
Prepared By: **December 31, 1985**   Dollars -   10,000.00
Financial Audit Systems   **Material Variance Report**   Percent -   15.00%

WP	Acct No	Account Description	Prior Year Balance	Current Year Adj. Balance	Difference	Percent Change
F	130	Inventories	172,345.51	253.643.54	81,298.03	47.17%
M	151	Furniture and Fixtures	19,000.00	31,425.85	12,425.85	65.39%
M	155	Equipment	142,732.50	207,868.92	65,136.42	45.63%
M	157	Leasehold Improvements	65,291.25	101,804.52	36,513.27	55.92%
0100	301	Sales - Module A	− 289,701.90	− 435,212.00	145,510.10	50.22%
0100	302	Sales - Module B	− 122,934.32	− 243,875.00	120,940.68	98.37%
0100	303	Sales - Module C	− 2,439.19	− 53,623.00	51,183.81	2098.39%
0100	304	Sales - Module D	− 46,192.73	− 75,843.25	29,650.52	64.18%
0100	305	Sales - Module E	− 5,244.11	− 16.234.95	10,990,84	209.58%
0200	405	Purchases	85,008.91	234,537.62	149,528.71	175.89%
0200	407	Subcontract Labor Cost	43,978.89	63,714.12	19,735.23	44.87%
0200	408	Miscellaneous Supplies	17,776.18	36,721.23	18,945.05	106.57%
0200	409	Ending Inventory	− 172,345.51	− 253,643.54	− 81,298.03	− 47.17%
0400	519	Franchise Fees	10,000.00	22,300.00	12,300.00	123.00%
0400	560	Salaries - Officers	80,000.00	120,000.00	40,000.00	50.00%
0400	562	Salaries and Wages - Other	64,039.00	78,534.00	14,495.00	22.63%
0800	650	Federal Income Tax Expense	22,731.00	56,341.00	33,610.00	147.85%

17 Accounts met the specified variances

Figure 10-13   Common-Size Statement—Working Paper Software

Report Date: 03/12/86   **Example Client Company**   Page 1
Prepared By: **Five Year Vertical Fluctuation Analysis**
Financial Audit Systems   **December 31, 1985**

	Lead Schedule Description	Period-5	Period-4	Period-3	Prior	Current
Assets						
A	Cash	2.58%	3.34%	4.65%	3.05%	3.27%
B	Securities and Other Negotiable Assets	0.58%	0.74%	0.58%	0.00%	0.00%
C	Accounts Receivable - Trade	37.01%	33.22%	33.06%	44.94%	37.24%
D	Accounts Receivable - Intercompany	0.00%	0.71%	0.40%	0.00%	0.00%
E	Other Receivables	0.02%	0.00%	0.00%	0.06%	0.02%
F	Inventories	26.91%	20.18%	12.14%	24.19%	27.20%
G	Prepaid Assets	0.01%	0.02%	0.24%	0.14%	0.01%
M	Property and Equipment	36.19%	46.74%	54.71%	31.87%	36.57%
N	Accumulated Depreciation	− 4.35%	− 6.30%	− 8.20%	− 5.66%	− 5.38%
P	Advances to Subsidiaries	0.00%	1.03%	1.81%	0.00%	0.00%
S	Goodwill	0.00%	0.00%	0.00%	1.05%	0.80%
T	Other Intangible Assets	0.27%	0.34%	0.60%	0.35%	0.27%
Total Assets		100.00%	100.00%	100.00%	100.00%	100.00%

Figure 10-14   Ratio Analysis—Working Paper Software

Report Date: 03/10/86   **Example Client Company**   Page 1
Prepared By: **December 31, 1985**
Financial Audit Systems   **Analytical Review Financial Ratios**

Description	Prior Year	Current Year	Percentage Change
Short-Term Liquidity Ratios:			
Acid Test Ratio	16.445	5.190	− 68.43%
Current Ratio	24.774	8.675	− 64.98%
Days Sales in Receivables	251.400	154.944	− 38.36%
Inventory Turnover	1.002	1.191	18.86%
Working Capital to Total Assets	0.695	0.599	− 13.81%
Movement of Current Assets:			
Average Days to Collect	235.580	144.492	− 38.66%
Average Days to Sell	364.207	306.467	− 15.85%
Operating Cycle	605.051	455.418	− 24.73%
Receivable Turnover	1.516	2.450	61.60%
Capital Structure & Long-Term Solvency:			
Creditors' Equity to Total Assets	0.039	0.086	120.51%
Debt to Equity	0.040	0.095	137.50%
Fixed Assets to L-T Liabilities	27.867	37.246	33.65%
Fixed Assets to Equity	0.273	0.341	24.90%
Long Term Debt to Equity	0.010	0.009	− 9.99%
Times Interest Earned	63.535	36.075	− 43.21%
Return on Investment:			
Return on Equity Capital	9.907%	22.737%	129.50%
Return on Total Assets	9.556%	21.890%	129.07%
Operating Performance Ratios:			
Gross Profit Margin	65.507%	69.479%	6.06%
Net Income to Sales	13.896%	21.021%	51.27%
Operating Profit to Sales	19.123%	32.123%	67.98%
Pretax Income to Sales	19.123%	32.123%	67.98%
Asset Utilization Ratios:			
Sales to Inventories	2.731	3.277	19.99%
Sales to Accounts Receivable	1.468	2.392	62.94%
Sales to Cash	21.692	27.271	25.71%
Sales to Fixed Assets	2.521	2.857	13.32%
Sales to Other Assets	47.065	83.115	76.59%
Sales to Total Assets	0.661	0.891	34.79%
Sales to Working Capital	0.951	1.487	56.36%

Description	Prior Year	Current Year	Percentage Change
Market Measures:			
Dividend Payout Ratio	57.340%	42.927%	−25.13%
Dividend Yield	10.000%	8.333%	−16.66%
Price Earnings Ratio	5.734	5.151	−10.16%
Ongoing Concern:			
Altman Z Score	18.812	10.059	−44.15%

Use of Regression Analysis as an Analytical Procedure

11

§11.01 Introduction

The objective of this chapter is to provide a nontechnical introduction to the use of regression analysis in analytical procedures. The need to consider regression analysis derives from its growing use within the accounting profession. Regression analysis is seeing wider use in large accounting firms in auditing and management services, and a common application area is in analytical procedures.

This chapter is written for anyone with an interest in analytical procedures, and it does not require a background in statistics. Appendix F contains the more technical details of regression analysis, and readers with that interest are referred there. A complete discussion of the statistical and auditing issues related to the use of regression analysis is beyond the scope of this book. Our intent is that this chapter will provide an elementary understanding of the application of regression analysis in analytical procedures—when and how it can be employed. Thus, this chapter has distinctly a *user's* perspective.

In harmony with the user's perspective, there is a presentation later in the chapter of how the regression analysis can be used and how the proper interpretation of regression analysis can be facilitated with commercially available software. The software product ANSWERS is featured, as it is the first regression analysis software designed for and widely available to auditors.[1]

The chapter is divided into four parts. The first part provides an introduction to the modeling approach which underlies any regression application. The second part provides a definition of regression analysis and explains when it should and should not be used. The third part explains and illustrates how to evaluate a regression model, and the fourth and final part illustrates actual applications of regression analysis.

§11.02   The Modeling Approach to Analytical Procedures

Recall from Chapter 2, when we defined analytical procedures, it was explained how the modeling approach to analysis is at the heart of any use of analytical procedures. You may want to refer back briefly to the first several pages of Chapter 2, which deal with the modeling approach, before going on. Note especially the second prediction task in Figure 2-5. Remember how difficult it was to predict very accurately the eighth number in these series, especially when the series were more variable, that is, the numbers jumped around more? The results of several studies show that most people have a difficult time predicting highly variable series, and they have certain prediction biases. In particular, many people will tend to underestimate a trend when it is present, and they will also tend to see a trend even when it is not there. That is, they seem to expect to see a very modest trend to the data.

---

[1] ANSWERS is a product of Financial Audit Systems, Raleigh, North Carolina (1986).

This leads to prediction errors and biases, and the results of the studies are sufficiently consistent that unaided predictions should be used carefully. The motivation for the use of regression analysis, then, is to provide a way to obtain mathematically precise predictions and thereby avoid the prediction biases and errors noted above.

Using the Modeling Approach

We now discuss what the modeling approach is all about, beginning with some of the necessary vocabulary. First, the *projected variable* is the amount to be predicted, for example, sales commissions. Sometimes the term *dependent variable* is used instead of projected variable, but we prefer the latter term, as it is more descriptive of the nature and quality of this type of variable. Second, the *predictor variable* is any financial data, operating data, or data external to the firm which can be used to help predict the projected variable. For example, sales can be used to help in the prediction of sales commissions. Often this type of variable is called an *independent variable,* but again we prefer the more intuitive term of predictor variable.

Third, a *model* is a specific framework or structure for defining the relationship between or among variables. Typically, the model presents the projected variable on the left and the predictor variables(s) on the right, stating simply but formally the expectation that the projected variable will behave in a way that can be predicted by knowing how the predictors are behaving or changing. To be more specific, a model states that the value of the projected variable can be predicted as the sum of two quantities: (a) a calculated amount equal to some quantity times the value of the related predictor variable(s), and (b) a constant amount which is necessary to "calibrate" the relationship between the predictor variable(s) and the projected variable. Thus, a simple model could be written as follows:

> THE VALUE OF THE PROJECTED VARIABLE EQUALS A CONSTANT AMOUNT PLUS A CALCULATION DERIVED FROM THE PREDICTOR VARIABLE (S)

An illustration of a specific model is as follows:

> Sales commissions = a constant amount + (some quantity) $\times$ (sales)

We will see later that in regression analysis the *constant amount* is called the *intercept* and the *some quantity* is the *coefficient* of the predictor variable.

Now let us consider further how variables are put together in models. For any pair of projected and predictor variables, a number of possible different relationships are possible between the variables in the pair. For example, the variables may move in the same direction (e.g., sales commissions and sales) or in opposite directions (interest rates and sales). Variables which move in the same direction are said to be *positively related,* whereas those which move in the opposite direction are said to be *negatively related.* Regression analysis can handle both types of relationships, and, when two or more predictors are included in a regression model, there is a mix of both positively and negatively related variables. As will be seen in the illustrations of regression applications, variables with a positive relationship will have a positive sign in the regression analysis, while variables which are negatively related will have a negative sign for the coefficient of that predictor in the regression analysis. It is important for the auditor to consider the nature of these relationships both in the design of the model (i.e., the choice of predictor variables) and in the interpretation of the results. The auditor should question the reliability of any regression application in which the observed signs on the regression coefficients do not conform to the expected direction, as determined when the application was designed.

Another word for *relationship between variables,* as discussed above, is *correlation.* Two variables are said to be correlated if there is a positive or negative relationship between them. The degree of correlation is measured by the *correlation coefficient,* which is sometimes represented by the letter r. Figures 11-1 and 11-2 show examples of positive and negative correlation, respectively.

In modeling, it is important to understand two concepts, model completeness, and the nature of the relationship between the predictor and projected variable. Completeness means that all relevant predictor variables are included and all irrelevant variables are excluded. A variable is relevant if it can help to predict the projected variable. For example, sales is a relevant predictor for sales commissions, as these two variables are logically related. However, the number of windows in the plant is not likely to have any relationship to sales commissions, so it is irrelevant and should be excluded. The more complete the model, the more precise it is, and therefore the more precise and accurate the predictions will be.

Concerning the nature of the relationship between the projected and predictor variables, it is important for the auditor to know that sometimes the relationship between the variables is simple, and we call it an *additive* model. For example, total expense is best predicted as the total of all the expense accounts. Other times, the relationship is

Figure 11-1   Positive Correlation

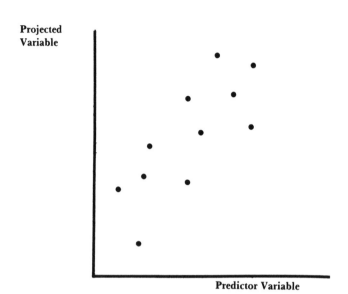

Figure 11-2   Negative Correlation

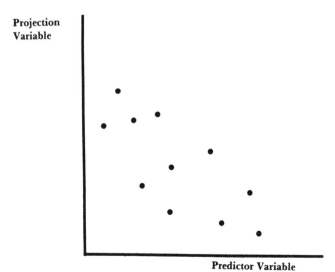

complex, and most often this means that it is *multiplicative*. For example, payroll expense is best predicted as the *product* of the following predictor variables: hours worked, wage rates, and number of employees. As another example, the same would be true for the variables and relationships underlying the prediction of interest expense. Sometimes the relationship between the predicted and predictor variables is unknown. In this case, it is best to assume the relationships are additive and to allow the regression model to find the best possible fit.

In summary, the modeling approach is a very crucial aspect of analytical procedures, and it is the first step in the application of regression analysis. Regression analysis simply takes the modeling approach to a logical higher level—to find the best-fitting model which will provide more accurate predictions. In the following section, we consider regression analysis and its uses.

§11.03   What is Regression Analysis?

Regression analysis is a mathematical technique for obtaining a precise prediction model which can be used for predicting financial and operating data. For example, it can be used to project sales, specific expense accounts, or any other item of financial or operating data. The predictions can be used as a basis for preparing budgets, analyzing financial statements, or reviewing or auditing the account balance.

Regression provides a mathematically precise prediction model (called the *regression equation* or *regression model*) by defining and measuring the relationship between any two or more variables. It examines a number of observations (time periods, locations, etc.) of each variable and statistically identifies a line which best fits through all these observations. It is one of the most precise and reliable prediction techniques available, and it is being used increasingly by auditors because of its precision. Regression uses both current period and historical interrelationships to develop a model for precisely estimating balances. In addition, it provides objective measures of the precision and accuracy of the resulting projections, giving the user guidance as to how much reliance, if any, can be placed on the results.

Regression analysis is a statistical method for finding the most accurate line through a set of data points The resulting regression line is represented by the following model or equation:

$$y = a + (bx) + E$$

In this equation, y represents the account balance or item being predicted, which we call the projected variable. The value of y is being projected based on its relationship with x, the predictor variable. The amount a (called the *intercept*) is a fixed level of y, which does not change as x changes. The amount b is the amount of change in y for a unit change in x. E is the error term, the amount of difference between each data point and the value predicted by the regression equation for that point. Often, this error term is called the *residual.*

Example

As an example, suppose you wish to predict the amount of supplies expense for the coming month at a given plant location, and you know that supplies expense is influenced by the production level. Further, you know the expected production level for the coming month, and you know the production levels for the three prior months and the related supplies expense for each of those months.

Month	Supplies Expense	Production Level
1	$120	50 units
2	$180	100 units
3	$195	150 units
4	?	200 units (est)

The objective of the analysis in this simple illustration is to predict supplies expense in month 4. Only three data points are being used in the illustration for convenience and clarity. An actual regression application would require many more data points for a precise projection.

Regression analysis finds the most accurate line through the data by determining the unique line which minimizes the sum of the *squared errors,* that is, the sum of the squared differences (the "E" values) between each data point and the regression line. Figure 11-3 plots the above data and shows the regression line which is obtained from these values:

$$y = 90 + .75X$$

Using this equation and the estimated production level (x) of 200,000 units, projected supplies expense is $240,000.

Up to this point, the regression application has included only one predictor variable. This is called *simple regression.* When two or more predictor variables are involved, it is called *multiple regression.* The discussion below is equally applicable to both simple and multiple regression.

Figure 11-3   Example Regression Model

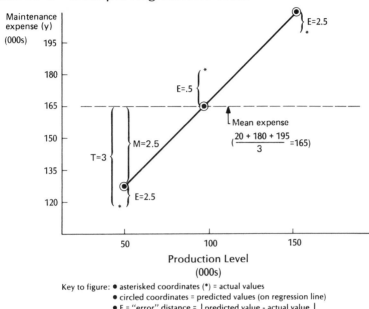

Key to figure: ● asterisked coordinates (*) = actual values
● circled coordinates = predicted values (on regression line)
● E = "error" distance = | predicted value - actual value |

§11.04   What to Use Regression For—Two Types of Regression

When considering the use of regression, it is important to understand the two most common applications. They are account-time analysis and multiple-location analysis.

Account-Time Analysis

Account-time analysis is used to project an account balance or item, using that account's relationship to other items of financial or operating data or data outside the firm, for several (usually 24-36) prior periods. This type of regression is often called the *time-series* regression, to indicate that it is based on several time periods of data. For example, projecting monthly sales for the coming year based upon monthly sales figures (the projected variable in this case) and other financial and operating data (the predictor variables) for the prior three years is an account-time type of analysis. Account-time analysis can be done in two different formats:

Type One: Reasonableness Testing. This format is used for comparing reported amounts to projected amounts as a reasonableness test of the accuracy of the reported amounts. The reported amount may be account balances for each month (or quarter) of the current year, or forecasted account balances for each month (or quarter) of the coming year. In the former case, the auditor is evaluating the reasonableness of previously recorded amounts, and in the latter, the auditor is evaluating the reasonableness of forecasted amounts. Type one format is typically used for an audit or review purpose to assess the reasonableness of current period data.

Type Two: Forecasting. This format is used for obtaining projections of account balances for months (or quarters) into the future. In this case, the auditor is interested only in obtaining the projections, rather than comparing the projections to reported amounts. The best example of this type of analysis is the projection of monthly sales for the coming year. This format is most often used in client advisory services, such as preparing forecasts and budgets.

A common element of both types of account-time models is the distinction between the *base period* and the *projection period.* The base period is the period for which the data is used to calculate the regression model, whereas the projection period is the period for which the projections are obtained from the model.

In the case of the Type One format, the base period includes 24 or more months (eight or more quarters) prior to the current year, while the months (or quarters) of the current year constitute the projection period. Since regression analysis may be used at an interim date in the current year, the projection period may contain fewer than twelve months (or four quarters). For example, if you are using Type One analysis in October for a company with a December 31 year end, there will be nine months, or three quarters, in the projection period.

In the case of the Type Two format, the base period includes all available data. The projection period is the period for which you want to obtain forecasted values—up to twelve months, or four quarters, of projected amounts.

The difference between base period and projection period, for each type of model, is illustrated in Figure 11-4. Note that data for the predictor variables is needed only for current and prior years when using the Type One model. However, data for the next (future) year also is needed for the Type Two model. The reason for this is apparent in studying the regression equation: future values of the predictor variables are necessary to predict future values of the projected variable.

The single most common audit application of account-time analysis is the reasonableness test of monthly sales data. Other uses include

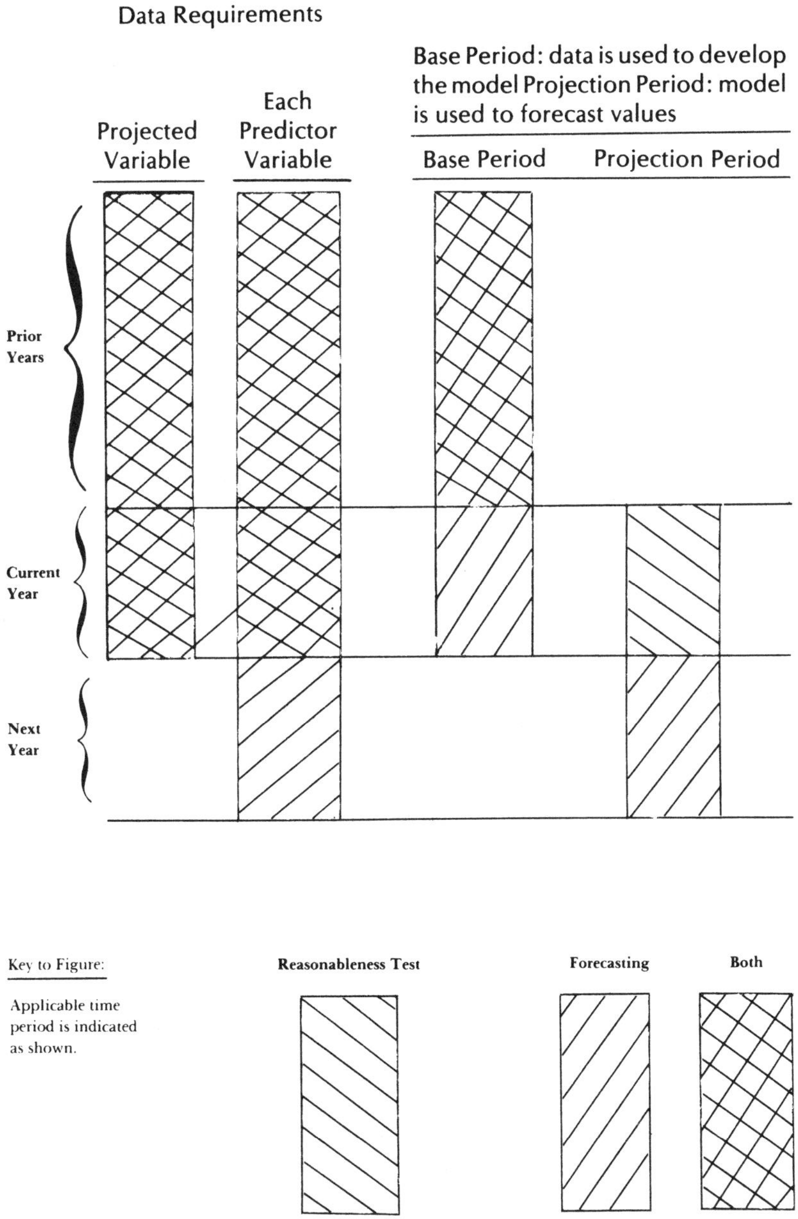

Figure 11-4 Data Requirements, Base Periods, and Projection Periods for Account Time Models

tests of selected expense accounts, such as payroll expense, maintenance expense or utility expense, and tests of selected operating data, such as production levels or overtime hours.

Multiple-Location Analysis

The second type of regression is called multiple-location analysis. It is used to analyze data from a number of different locations or subunits of a company when all the data come from a single time period. Multiple-location analysis is also referred to as *cross-sectional* analysis, which indicates that a cross section of data is analyzed within a single time period.

An example of a multiple-location analysis application is the analysis of inventory at each branch location of a retail company. The analysis might project the inventory balance at each location, using store size, regional economic data, type of store location, and related data as the predictor variables. The resulting regression model would project the inventory balance at each location, given the average relationships observed for all locations. The projected balance would be compared to the actual balances for reasonableness. A significant difference at any location might require further investigation.

Note that a *location* can be any entity, account, or item within a given period. For example, the projected variable in a multiple-location analysis could be:

- •Salesforce expenses
- •Productivity of employees or work stations
- •Repair expenses for machines
- •Downtime for different machines
- •Energy costs at different locations
- •Sales at different locations, or by individual salespersons
- •Retail store inventories

Figure 11-5 demonstrates graphically how multiple-location analysis and account-time analysis differ.

§11.05   When to Use Regression Analysis

The overriding concern when determining whether or not to use regression analysis is the cost/benefit of the application. Does the increase in predictive precision, obtained by using regression rather than another prediction approach, justify the additional costs and time required to perform the analysis and interpret the results? Another concern is whether or not the auditor is able to build a reasonably valid

Figure 11-5 Account-Time Analysis and Multiple-Location Analysis

Location	1983	1984	1985	1986	1987	1988
A	16,243	17,801	16,989	18,256	19,216	20,176
B	8,403	8,969	9,214	9,868	10,404	11,688
C	105,616	119,211	161,406	299,014	314,640	356,412
D	15,433	16,818	16,409	17,998	18,243	18,966
E	42,311	43,688	46,411	52,919	54,807	55,663
F	99,417	101,736	105,409	118,344	121,696	125,105
G Account Time Analysis -Location G	16,432	17,519	17,875	18,431	19,261	20,544
						Multiple Location Analysis - 1988

model. The auditor must be able to identify the relevant predictor variables and obtain the data that is necessary to build the model, and the data must be reasonably accurate. The positive and negative aspects of a regression application in auditing are discussed below.

Positive aspects of Regression are that it provides improved precision and reliability, which leads to better projections, due to the mathematical precision of least squares regression. Precision refers to the accuracy of the predictions of the model, whereas reliability refers to the completeness and correctness of the design of the model. These two terms are explained in greater detail later in this chapter. Regression also provides objective measures of the precision and reliability of the prediction model, measures which are seldom available in other methods of analysis. These objective measures are clear indications of the predictive ability of the model, and therefore provide a clear basis for determining the level of reliance to be placed on the results. The availability of quantitative, objective measures of the precision and reliability of the model allow for reliance on the model and its predictions. Regression provides a better understanding of client operations and financial/operating relationships, and also produces results which are consistent and easily interpreted and communicated. Regression applications follow predetermined rules of logic and interpretation which others can easily and quickly understand, even though they may not be familiar with the specific regression application or regression methodology.

A negative aspect of regression is that it creates some new costs. It is not as intuitive and easy to understand or explain as other techniques, and it may take some special training efforts for an auditor to develop a "critical mass" of regression expertise. Alternatively, the firm could use a "regression specialist" approach, as many firms have done for the areas of statistical sampling or evaluation of computer-based controls. The cost of obtaining data that is not currently accumulated or used for other purposes, such as operating and environmental data, is an expense of regression analysis. The cost of evaluating the accuracy and reliability of this data must also be included. Also to be considered is the cost associated with developing an understanding of the statistical assumptions required by regression analysis so that the auditor can apply and interpret it properly.

§11.06   When Not to Use Regression Analysis

In considering when regression analysis *is* appropriate, it is helpful to understand those situations in which regression analysis might *not* be appropriate.

Regression is not appropriate when a high degree of precision and reliability is not required for the analysis, for example, when an auditor is analyzing an account or item for which the dollar amount is immaterial in relation to the scope of the overall analysis. This will likely be the case for smaller expense accounts and smaller branch locations. It also should not be used when reasonably accurate data for the projected and predictor variables is not available. If the projected and/or the predictor variables cannot be measured accurately, other forms of analysis will be more appropriate.

The cost of obtaining the necessary data for a regression analysis might be too high. It might be more cost-effective to use other investigative procedures, as suggested above. The cost of obtaining data must include the costs of performing the necessary testing and reviewing to determine that the data is sufficiently accurate.

Regression should not be used when there is a lack of knowledge of the relevant predictors. If the auditor is unable to determine with reasonable certainty which predictor variables are relevant for estimating the projected variable, then regression would probably not be appropriate. The auditor should not employ regression unless there is a good reason to expect that the predictor and projected variables are related in some way.

Also, regression is not appropriate when the account or item can be predicted by a simple algebraic calculation rather than by regression analysis. Regression is appropriate for those cases in which the auditor wants to predict a particular variable, and there are certain predictor variables which are closely related to the projected variable, but the auditor *cannot* describe a unique mathematical relationship between the variables. For example, if the auditor wanted to predict gross margin as the projected variable, using sales and cost of sales as the two predictor variables, it would be most appropriate to use a mathematical equation to do this:

$$\text{gross margin} = \text{sales less cost of sales}$$

In this case, the variables have a clear and unique mathematical relationship, and regression cannot improve on this. Regression would only provide an indication of the degree of error in the measurement of the variables, and would not add any knowledge about how the variables are related.

A similar case would be the use of regression analysis to predict payroll expense using the number of employees, the average wage rate, and the average number of hours worked as predictor variables. There is a clear, mathematical relationship among these variables, and regression is not appropriate.

The correct application for regression is when the predictor and projected variable are related, but the auditor cannot specify the relationship in clear and unique mathematical terms. For example, the auditor may wish to predict sales of retail stores based on certain operating data, local economic data, and descriptors of the nature of each store and its location. These predictor variables have a logical relationship to the projected variable, sales, but there is no clear mathematical relationship among them.

Regression should not be used when there is a lack of knowledge about how to properly interpret the results of the regression analysis. The auditor should understand the limitations of the analysis and how to use the account-time or multi-location results.

§11.07 Developing a Regression Model

Development of a regression model is the most crucial of the three steps in a proper audit application of regression. The three steps are development of the model and acquisition of the data, performing the calculations and statistical checks, and interpreting the results of the model properly. The second step, involving calculations and checks, is not a significant concern, as this step can be easily automated. Proper interpretation of the results, step three, can be achieved by close attention to a relatively brief set of rules which are set forth later in this chapter. However, a poorly designed model will have inherently limited predictive power. Moreover, the design issue can be addressed only *by the auditor.* Software packages can detect many of the aspects of a poorly designed model, but only the auditor can design a proper model.

The design issue has five major elements:
1.   Determination of the projected variable
2.   Consideration of different types of predictor variables
3.   Consideration of data accuracy
4.   Consideration of possible missing data
5.   Choice of predictor variables for the model
Each of these elements is discussed below.

Determination of the Projected Variable

The choice of the projected variable is determined by the nature and objective of the audit application. For example, if the objective of the application is to review sales for possible misstatement, then the proper choice for the dependent variable is monthly or quarterly sales. Similarly, if the audit objective is to select branch retail locations for detail inventory tests, then a multiple-location analysis using inventory, inventory turnover, or inventory spoilage as a projected variable would be a reasonable choice.

Types of Predictor Variables

There are two possible types of predictor variables for a regression analysis. One type is called *interval* data which uses variables that can take on any numerical value, including integer and decimal figures. Most items of financial, operating, and economic data are interval type variables. Interval data is sometimes referred to as *real* data, or *real* variables. The projected variable is always an interval type variable in a regression application, whereas the predictor variables can either be interval or categorical.

The other possible type of variable is called a *categorical* variable. A variable having categorical data can take on only a small number of different values. A common use of a categorical variable is to indicate the effect on the projected variable of the presence (or absence) of a given condition. For example, in analyzing the different store locations in a retail chain, a categorical variable could be used to indicate whether the store location was in a shopping mall. In this case, the value of the categorical variable might be *zero* for each store located in a shopping mall and *one* for each store not in a shopping mall.

A categorical variable could also be used to indicate whether the store had an auto service department. Again, stores with an auto department might be indicated by *zero* and those without auto departments by a *one*. Similarly, in an account-time type of analysis, a categorical variable could be used to indicate a month or range of months which have significantly different operating facts than for the remainder of the period.

In addition to these two main types of data, there are possible *data transforms* which are used to adjust the data for special considerations, such as a lag relationship, seasonality, or trend. If these factors are present in the data, the predictions of the model will be unreliable unless they are taken into account in the development and design of the model.

Lag Variables are used in the account-time analysis when a given predictor has a lag relationship to the projected variable. For example, the consumer price index, as a predictor variable, may have a lag relationship to sales as the projected variable. A significant change in the consumer price index does not affect sales until sometime later.

Deseasonalization is used in the account-time analysis when there is a significant seasonality present in the data. This would often be the case for sales and related operating data. This process smooths the seasonal peaks and lows to produce a more precise regression calculation. The results are then reseasonalized to provide projections and reports.

A Trend Variable is a sequence of integer numbers. It is used to detrend a series of data in an account-time analysis to produce a more precise regression model. This variable allows the regression to account for a consistent increasing or decreasing trend as a function of time, as well as a function of interrelationships with other variables.

The effect of seasonality and trend, when not recognized, is that the model will be unreliable. The predictions of the model will be relatively inaccurate, and the measures of reliability and precision might be significantly misstated.

Data Accuracy

Perhaps the auditor's greatest concern during the design phase is to gain some assurance that the data is accurate. Any model is useful only if the data which was used to build it is reliable. The auditor should evaluate the accuracy of the data for each variable used in the regression. He or she must consider such things as whether there are errors or omissions in accruals or other types of cutoff errors or whether there have been significant technological changes or changes in operations (i.e., new products or production methods) which could affect the interrelationships. Such a change could cause a significant shift in the slope of the regression line. A categorical variable could be used to recognize the change. Obvious clerical errors in the data must, of course, also be considered. Another item of concern is whether the data is truly representative of the period being analyzed. Does the data contain periods or locations which do not conform to the normal relationship between the projected and predictor variables? Also to be considered is whether the data is measured in constant prices. This may be particularly important if more than three years of data is being used. The auditor also needs to know whether there are "passed" adjusting journal entries for some of the periods or locations in the data base and consider the need to record these adjustments before calculating the regression model. It is necessary as well to avoid excessive rounding of figures when using regression analysis. Rounding of figures has the effect of reducing the precision and reliability of the model.

Always edit the data to assure that it has been entered correctly. A good approach is to review the just-entered data for unusual data points. Any points that look out of line relative to the others should be checked for accuracy and for representativeness. The inclusion of an unusual data point in a regression analysis can bias the results and reduce the precision of the model significantly. These unusual data points are sometimes referred to as *outliers*. Study the distribution of the data points to determine if they are fairly evenly distributed over the entire range of the variables. For example, a given set of data may actually appear to be two separate sets of data when examined this way. Instead of one regression line for the entire set of data, it may be more appropriate to have two or more different regression lines through the various subsets of the data. This approach is most appropriate when the data is in two or more clusters, rather than evenly distributed over the entire range of each of the variables. It is also important to use homogeneous units of measure. For example, the auditor should make sure that either all of the data is in 000s, or alternatively that none of the data is in 000s. Recall also that rounding is to be avoided.

It is not necessary that all errors be removed from the data input, because it is not practical to remove all the small errors. However, the auditor's evaluation should be sufficient to determine whether or not there are significant deficiencies or errors in the data.

Missing Data

Sometimes it is not possible to obtain one or more of the data points for a variable. For example, the auditor may have floor space available as a variable for all store locations except one. In situations like this, it is useful to consider estimating the data point and including the estimated value, dropping the *variable* for account-time models if it is not the projected variable or a key predictor variable, or dropping the *location* for multiple-location models and analyze this location apart from the regression analysis.

Choosing Predictor Variables

In choosing the predictor for a given projected variable, the auditor must consider whether there is a logical relationship between this predictor and the projected variable and whether all possible predictor variables have been considered (i.e., whether the model is complete).

To help in determining if there are any omitted predictor variables, the auditor might also consider what variables might have an effect on the projected variable in some way. For example, in predicting sales for a retail store, the factors which could affect sales at each store— local economic data, age and condition of the store, etc., might be listed. Also, what variables might vary systematically with the projected variable might be considered. For example, the sales of retail store locations might be expected to vary directly with the square feet of floor space, with the number of salespersons, and so on.

The auditor might also question whether there is a clear mathematical relationship among the predictor variables(s) and the projected variable. If so, regression analysis is probably not appropriate, and simple computations would make more sense. Another consideration is whether the necessary data is available for the predictor variables and if it is, whether it is reasonably accurate. Also to be considered is whether the predictor variables should be classified as interval or categorical or adjusted to reflect a lag relationship. What does the variable add *above* that of other variables already in the model?

In choosing the predictor variables, the auditor does not need to look for a long list of variables, but a list of about two to five variables which are the best of the possible predictors. Five or fewer variables are often best for regression applications involving financial and operating data, since much of the relevant data for a given projected variable will be "telling the same story." In other words, the variables simply duplicate each other in the model.

Also, in choosing predictor variables, the auditor should try to use variables taken from different types of data, such as financial data (e.g., account balances), operating data (e.g., unit sales), economic data (e.g., regional unemployment figures), and environmental data (e.g., urban or rural location). This approach can help to produce a more complete model.

The economic and environmental data are sometimes called *external* variables, since they are produced outside the firm. An important concern regarding external variables is the timeliness and accuracy of the data. Some sources are more timely and reliable than others. The auditor should consider especially the data's reliability before employing it in a model.

Some of the best models contain one or two predictors selected from several different types of data. Figure 11-6 shows example predictors for some of the more common projected variables.

As an example of how predictors might be chosen, consider the case of a multiple-location analysis application with payroll expense at various plant locations as the projected variable. Logical predictor variables might include:

- Total expense
- Cost of goods manufactured
- Production units
- Hours worked
- A categorical variable for any significant work stoppage or change in labor mix

§11.08   Evaluating a Regression Model

Measures of Precision and Reliability

A key feature of the use of regression analysis is that it provides objective measures of its own precision and reliability. It is one of the few prediction models to do this. The nonstatistical prediction models which are alternatives to regression analysis (as described in Chapter 4) can only be evaluated on their past performance in a given application. In contrast, each time a regression model is developed, specific measures of its performance (i.e., precision and reliability) are produced, so that the user can assess the usability of the model *before the first prediction is made.* This provides a significant advantage for the regression approach, and a strong motivation for the auditor to consider its use, when the application satisfies the cost/benefit considerations noted above.

Figure 11-6 Example Predictors for Common Projected Variables

Example Projected Variable	Financial Data	Operating Data	Economic Indicators	Other
1 Sales—account-time analysis	1. Cost of sales 2. Selling expense 3. Advertising expense	1. Units shipped 2. Number of salespeople	1. price level index 2. Index of local economic growth	1. Trend variable 2. Categorical variable for differences in marketing effort
2 Sales—multiple location analysis	1. Cost of sales 2. Selling expense	1. Size of store 2. Store type 3. Store hour open 4. No. of salepeople	1. Price level index 2. Index of local economic growth	1. Categorical variable for difference in marketing effort
3 Inventory—multiple location analysis	1. Sales	1. Size of store 2. Store type	1. Price level index 2. Index of local economic growth	1. Categorical variable for difference in management policy
4. Accounts receivable-multiple location analysis	1. Sales 2. Categ. var. for differences to credit sales	1. Store type 2. Index of local in product mix	1. Interest rates 2. Index of local economic growth	1. Categorical variable for difference in credit/collection policy
5 Payroll expense—multiple location analysis	1. Total expenses 2. Sales or cost of goods manufactured	1. Hours worked 2. Categ. var. for difference in labor mix 3. Production level		1. Categorical variable to indicate sig. work stoppage or wage rate difference

Example Projected Variable	Financial Data	Operating Data	Economic Indicators	Other
6 Payroll expense—account-time analysis	1. Total expenses 2. Sales or cost of goods 3. Production level	1. Hours worked 2. Categ. var. for changes in labor mix		1. Trend Variable 2. Categorical variable for sig. work stoppage or pay rate change
7 Utilities expense—account-time analysis	1. Sales or cost of goods manufactured 2. Production level	1. Average daily temp 2. Categ. var. for plant additions		1. Categorical variable for sig. change in utility rates 2. Trend variable
8 Bad debt expense—account-time analysis	1. Sales 2. Accounts receivable	1. Categ. var. for change in customer mix	1. Interest rates 2. Index of economic growth	1. Trend variable 2. Categorical variable for change in credit/collections policies
9 General expenses—office salaries and supplies, telephone, printing and duplicating, repairs, etc. multiple location analysis	1. Sales 2. Total expenses 3. Net fixed assets	1. Store type 2. Store size 3. Number of employee	1. Index of local price level	1. Age of store 2. Categorical variable for differences in office management—automation, etc.

Source: ANSWERS User's Manual, Financial Audit Systems (1986) (reprinted with permission).

The evaluation criteria identified above, precision and reliability, refer to two distinct attributes of the regression model. The *reliability* of the model is measured by the objective probability that there actually is a strong relationship between the projected and predictor variables, and that the calculated equation is therefore truly valid. The *precision* of the model is measured by the degree of error in its predictions. Both precision and reliability are important measures of the model's ability to reasonably estimate the projected variable.

There are two key measures of model precision and reliability.

1.   R-squared, the reliability measure, also called the *coefficient of determination*
2.   SE, the precision measure, also called the *standard error of the estimate*, or simply, *standard error*

R-squared is a direct measure of the reliability of the regression model and is often described as a measure of the "explanatory" power of the model. It measures the degree to which unexpected changes in the projected variable can be predicted by known or estimated changes in the predictor variable. The predictor variables "explain" changes in the projected variable, and R-squared measures this explanatory power. R-squared is a number between zero and one. A number close to one indicates a relatively reliable model, and a number close to zero indicates a relatively unreliable model. Most regression analyses involving financial data have R-squared values in excess of .5, with values in the range of .8 to .95 being most common.

The precision measure (SE) is a direct measure of the accuracy of the model's projections. The regression line gives the best prediction for the projected variable. It is, however, just an estimate. The actual points lie somewhere near the line. The SE value is a measure of the range around the regression line in which the auditor can be reasonably sure the actual points will fall. For example, if the auditor projects sales for the period to be $5000, and the SE is $100, then the auditor can estimate with reasonable confidence that actual sales will fall between $4900 and $5100.

How does the auditor determine if the SE is satisfactory (see also §11.09)? First, consider the average size of the projected variable, and compare the standard error to that. For example, consider a situation in which the standard error is $1400 and the mean of the projected variable is $35,000. The percentage relationship is 1,400/35,000, or 4%. If a range of 5% accuracy is acceptable, then the auditor can conclude that the standard error of the model in this case is reasonably good. The key is to compare the standard error to the mean of the projected variable.

Figure 11-7 illustrates situations in which the R-squared and SE values are relatively good and relatively poor. Recall that a good R-squared value is near one, while a poor R-squared is near zero. Also, a poor standard error is a relatively large amount, while a good standard error is a relatively small amount. This figure can help to explain these two concepts. At the top of the figure, low and high R-squared situations are shown as they would appear on a graph of the data with the regression line drawn in. Note how the low R-squared situation has data points scattered about widely, while the high R-squared situation has the data points clustered around the regression line. Thus, the model is a better "fit" in the latter case, and can be expected to be more reliable.

Looking to the lower part of the figure, note how a poor standard error value is associated with a relatively wide prediction range around the regression line. That is, the auditor cannot be confident that a prediction from the model is very accurate, but rather that the (unknown) true value might lie somewhat of a distance from the line. In contrast, with a relatively small standard error, as in the right hand illustration, the auditor can be more confident that a predicted value is not too far off from the true value. As before, the model is best when the R-squared value is high and the standard error is relatively small. Often, a given model will have R-squared and standard error values which are either both good or both poor, so that the proper interpretation of the model is relatively straightforward. Occasionally, the two measures will tell a different story. This generally happens when there is some other unusual characteristic of the model, such as a very large or a very small number of data points. When the number of data points is greater than 20, the two measures will generally be consistent. We recommend that 20 or more data points be used with the multiple-location application, and that 36 or more data points be used with the account-time application.

Evaluating the Regression Output

In addition to evaluating the precision and reliability of the regression model, it is useful to consider other direct measures of the quality of the model by reviewing the regression output. The two most important such measures are a review of the data plot for extremely unusual observations and an examination of the coefficients for each of the predictors to assess their reasonableness. While the review for extreme observations applies only to account-time models, the examination of coefficients applies to both multiple-location and to account-time models.

For the first measure, review the data plot of the model and identify

Figure 11-7 Comparative R-Squared and Standard Error
Values

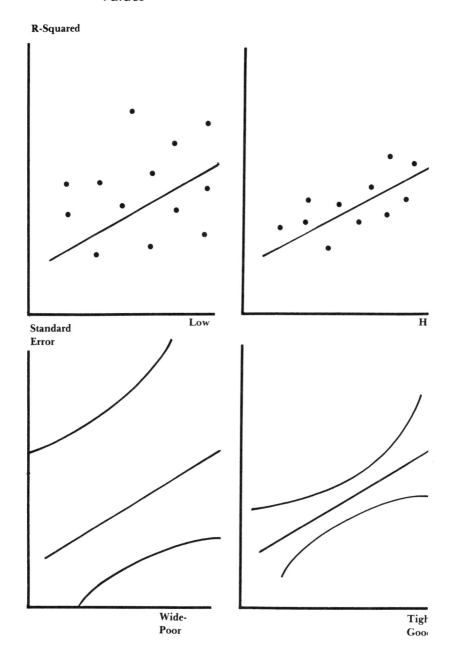

any extreme observations during the base period. The model is developed from data in the base period only, so it is not necessary to review the projection period for these extreme observations to evaluate the model. *Extreme* observations are ones which are larger than approximately four or more standard error (SE) distances.

For any observation that is extreme, the auditor should consider whether the observation is due to an error or irregularity, an undetected shift in the relationships underlying the data (for example, a significant price increase which occurred during the base period which caused an upward shift in the relationship between the predictor and projected variable), an unusual operating or financial event during the period represented by this observation, an error in data entry, or a coincidence of normal conditions which happened by chance to produce a very unusual result.

If the observation is due to an error in data entry, then the correction of the data will typically solve the problem. In cases of an undetected shift in the underlying relationships or an unusual operating or financial event, the correction of the model by means of a categorical variable is usually the best solution. However, in the cases of an error or irregularity or a coincidence of normal conditions producing an unusual result, the auditor must determine whether it is best to retain the data point as it is, to replace it with an adjusted value, or to use a categorical variable. The auditor should not simply remove the data point, as this will destroy the continuity of the time series underlying the account-time application.

For the second direct measure of the quality of the model, evaluate the reasonableness of the regression coefficient for each of the predictor variables. Each predictor variable must bear a plausible relationship to the projected variable, as determined during the model development. Now that the regression output is at hand, the auditor should review these coefficients to assess whether they bear the expected relationship to the projected variable. Specifically, the auditor should determine whether the *direction* and the *amount* of each coefficient is reasonable. For example, in a certain multiple-location analysis application, if the predictor variable were the number of beds in a hospital and the projected variable were hospital room charge revenues, the coefficient should be positive, and the amount of the coefficient should resemble the average room rate.

§11.09   Regression and the Audit Risk Model

The audit risk model for designing audit tests is as follows:

Audit Risk (A) = Inherent Risk (IR) × Control Risk (IC) × Detection Risk (D)

where:

Detection Risk (D) = Analytical Procedures Risk (AR) × Detail Test Risk (TD)

so that: A = IR × IC × AR × TD

and:

A = the risk of audit failure, the failure to detect a material misstatement

IR = the risk that a material misstatement is present

IC = the risk that the client's accounting internal control system fails to detect and correct the misstatement

D = the risk that audit procedures fail to detect the misstatement

AR = the risk of failure of analytical procedures

TD = the risk of failure of detail test procedures

Commonly, audit risk (A) is set at 5% to reflect the auditor's desire to design and perform an audit to limit audit risk to that low level. Once the level of audit risk is chosen, and the values for IR and IC are determined, then values for AR and TD can be determined so as to achieve the desired risk level.

When using regression analysis, it is important to determine the proper risk level (AR). A risk level of 1.0 would indicate no reliance on analytical procedures, while a risk level less than 50% would indicate significant reliance.

When used for an attention-directing purpose only, the auditor using regression analysis for analytical procedures should employ a risk level of 1.0 to reflect that there is no intended reliance on analytical procedures to reduce other substantive tests. On the other hand, when used for the test-reducing purpose, the auditor is often justified in using a risk level for analytical procedures somewhat less than 1.0, or even less than .5 in some cases.

The basis for determining the proper risk level is the size of the standard error of the regression model for the base period and the size of the residuals in the projection period, relative to the standard error for the projection period. Generally, the larger the standard error relative to materiality, and/or the larger the residuals relative to the standard error, the less reliance the auditor will place on analytical procedures, and thus the closer the risk level will be to 1.0.

As noted earlier, the standard error is the key measure of the predictive accuracy of the regression model. Thus, the smaller the standard error, the more accurate will be the model's predictions, so that greater reliance can be placed on the model. A value of two times the standard error is often used as a "benchmark" for comparison to the predetermined materiality level for the accounting population being examined. This value represents a distance within which the auditor can be approximately 95% confident that the (unknown) true value for the population will lie. This confidence level relates well to the 5% risk level which is commonly chosen for audit testing applications such as regression. Thus, if the model's standard error is less than one-half of materiality, the auditor can be reasonably confident that the model will provide predictions sufficiently accurate to meet the predetermined audit risk (5%) and materiality levels.

This same concept applies to the relationship between the residuals in the projection period and the standard error. The smaller the residuals are relative to the standard error, the less risk that the reported data is misstated by a material amount.

A more complete discussion of the determination of the analytical procedures risk level is beyond the scope of this book. The important concept to remember is that the greater the size of the standard error relative to materiality, and the greater the residuals in the projection period relative to the standard error, the less reliance the auditor should place on regression analysis in reducing other audit steps.

§11.10   Documenting a Regression Application

The regression application should be documented carefully to show the choice of projected and predictor variables and the results of the calculations. No additional documentation is ordinarily necessary regarding the design or statistical validity of the model. However, two important points remain to be documented.

Nature and *Purpose* of the Application

The documentation required here concerns the auditor's plan for the application. Is the objective the attention-directing or the test-reducing purpose of analytical procedures? Commonly, regression analysis will be used for the test-reducing purpose. Also, what is the objective of the application? Is it an account-time or multi-location analysis? For example, the objective could be to test revenues for understatement or overstatement (account-time analysis). Alternatively, the objective could be to select branch locations for detail inventory tests (multi-location analysis).

Relationship Between this Test and Other Substantive Tests

The required documentation here relates to the planned reliance on the regression application. This documentation can be completed in two parts. First, there should be an indication of the auditor's judgment and conclusion about whether the standard error and residuals of the model are adequate, as explained in §11.09. Second, the auditor should document a conclusion, based on the evaluation of the standard error and residuals, concerning what level of reliance will be placed on the regression application—specifically, what risk level will be used for analytical procedures in the audit risk model.

Summary

There is really nothing that different about the documentation objectives and procedures for a regression application compared to those for any other type of audit procedure. However, it is appropriate in the regression application to give particular emphasis to the documentation of the audit objective, since this can be easily lost sight of in the technical details of performing the regression application. Additionally, it is very important to provide some rationale for the selection of the predictors used in the model.

Additionally, relative to legal requirements for documentation, there has not yet been a court case which deals significantly with the issue of the use of regression analysis in auditing. However, a study of the related court decisions involving the use of statistical methods such as regression in other fields suggests that there is legal support for the use of regression analysis in auditing. Where there has been some question of the validity of the use of a statistical method, the courts have tended to focus on:

- Insufficient sample sizes
- Illogical choice of predictors (the rationale for the choice of predictors should be plausible and defensible)
- Improper handling of statistical problems

§11.11   Illustrations of Selected Regression Applications

Specific illustrations of regression applications are shown in the appendixes to this chapter and demonstrate how the ANSWERS software package calculates the regression model, and how the related regression reports are produced and interpreted.

The example in Exhibit 4 is designed to show a typical multiple-location example (the Best Value Hardware case). In this case, the audit or review objective is presented, the regression is designed and performed, and the reports are interpreted vis à vis the predetermined objective.

Exhibit 5 shows the ANSWERS reports for an application of both account-time and multiple-location analysis to the investigation of inventory spoilage for a chain of convenience stores. In this case, the multiple-location application is applied first, to determine which of the 15 stores had inventory spoilage most out-of-line with the others, based upon the relationship of the projected variable, inventory spoilage, to selected predictors, the number of employees, location type, square footage of floor space, and sales. Inventory spoilage at each of the stores should be related to these four predictor variables, and what inventory spoilage *should be* can be predicted at each of the stores using these variables in a regression model. The result of this analysis is that store number 6 is targeted for further analysis, since the actual value for inventory spoilage is far higher than the predicted amount for this store. Store number 11 and store number 13 are secondary targets, as they also have somewhat higher than expected inventory spoilage figures.

Having identified store number 6 for further investigation, we can now employ account-time analysis to identify, *for store number 6,* the specific months of this particular year in which there is the greatest chance of finding the explanation for the unexpectedly high inventory spoilage. By reviewing the Projection Report in Exhibit 5, the auditor can determine that the best months to target for initial investigation are June and July, as the actual figures exceed the expected amounts by the largest margins for these two months. Thus, in two steps, the store and the time periods which are the best targets for audit effort have been identified. In summary, the application in Exhibit 5 provides an illustration of a case in which the two types of regression application can be integrated to achieve a given audit objective.

§11.12 Summary

This chapter has provided a brief nontechnical introduction to the use of regression analysis in analytical procedures. A more technical discussion is presented in Appendix F.

The costs associated with using regression analysis are well known. They are the required expertise, additional data gathering, and unknown costs which can result from an improper use or interpretation of the analysis.

However, regression has advantages in that it objectively and systematically quantifies the evidence available to the auditor. Regression offers greater precision than can be obtained by other, nonstatistical methods. More importantly, regression analysis provides measures of reliability and precision with each regression equation, so that the auditor has a direct and objective measure of the strength of the evidence. Regression analysis can be a useful addition to the auditor's set of analytical procedures.

§11.13   References

Financial Audit Systems, Raleigh, North Carolina, *ANSWERS User's Manual* (1986).

Graham, *Analytical Review Techniques: Some Neglected Tools*, CPA J, Oct 1981, at 18-24.

Kask, *Regression and Correlation Analysis*, CPA J, Oct 1979.

Leininger & Conley, Regression Analysis in Auditing, CPA J, Oct 1980, at 43-47.

K. Stringer & T. Stewart, *Statistical Techniques for Analytical Review in Auditing* (Wiley 1986).

Wallace, *Analytical Review: Misconceptions, Applications and Experience - Part II*, CPA J, Feb 1983.

Wallace, *The Acceptability of Regression Analysis as Evidence in a Courtroom - Implications for the Auditor*, Auditing: J Prac & Theory, Spring 1983, at 66-90.

Exhibit 4

Regression Analysis Using Microcomputer Software*

To demonstrate how the ANSWERS regression software can be used for actual case situations, the example below illustrates the multiple location analysis model.

Best Value Hardware is a chain of hardware stores located throughout the southeast. There are 16 stores which are located primarily in small shopping centers. Management of Best Value is concerned about the relatively flat trend of total sales during the recent year. To analyze the problem, management has chosen to perform a regression analysis in a multiple location format to determine which of the 16 stores may be falling behind in total sales performance.

The three principal predictor variables for sales in any store are as follows:

(a) square feet of sales area in the store (variable name: SQ. FEET).

(b) advertising expenditures traceable directly to the store (variable name: ADVERTISING).

(c) the number of salespersons' hours in the store per week, on the average (variable name: SALESPERSONS).

The projected variable chosen for the application is the recent

---

* Source: ANSWERS User Manual, Financial Audit Systems (1986) (reprinted with permission).

EXHIBIT 4   251

month's sales at each location. The data for each of the 16 locations has been collected and is presented in the Data Values Report below.

REPORT DATE: 11/30/85   **Original Data Values for HARDWARE**   Page 1
PREPARED BY: **Example Client, Inc.**
REVIEWED BY: **June 30, 1985**

Loc.	SALES	SQ. FEET	ADVERTISING	SALESPERSONS
1	25,835.00	867.00	954.00	85.00
2	27,500.00	1,189.00	945.00	103.00
3	28,654.00	1,243.00	653.00	112.00
4	32,576.00	1,402.00	1,189.00	112.00
5	28,764.00	1,134.00	965.00	97.00
6	24,875.00	1,123.00	925.00	75.00
7	29,465.00	1,150.00	834.00	78.00
8	25,635.00	933.00	840.00	26.00
9	31,845.00	1,399.00	1,022.00	34.00
10	26,745.00	823.00	956.00	67.00
11	27,465.00	994.00	899.00	88.00
12	28,956.00	834.00	956.00	84.00
13	22,984.00	745.00	609.00	77.00
14	31,764.00	1,245.00	1,010.00	206.00
15	26,745.00	923.00	867.00	99.00
16	26,867.00	1,132.00	774.00	132.00

This model was run using the stepwise calculation mode. The first report to appear after a model has been run shows the results of the statistical checks. In this case, there were no statistical problems encountered in running the model.

**REPORT DATE: 11/30/85   RESULTS OF STATISTICAL
                                         CHECKS**   Page 1
PREPARED BY: **Example Client, Inc.**
REVIEWED BY: **June 30, 1985**

MODEL IS OK

The ANSWERS PROJECTION Module was able to complete a projection model for your data and relationships. No significant statistical problems were detected in the computation of the projections.

The Regression Equation Report is a compilation of the significant statistical measures and parameters of the model. This report is useful in evaluating the quality of the regression model. It is NOT directly useful for analyzing the sales performance of the different stores.

CALCULATION MODE: Stepwise Search for Best Model.

REGRESSION EQUATION:

$$SALES = 13074.378673$$
$$+ (7,792189 * SQ. FEET)$$
$$+ (7,220308 * ADVERTISING)$$

Standard Error of the Estimate =	1534.959275
F Value ("Statistical Validity") =	15.576660
Coefficient of Determination (R-Squared) =	0.705571
Durbin-Watson Statistic =	2.421794
Ratio of Standard Error to Mean of Projected Variable =	0.054983

Predictor	t-Value
SQ. FEET	3.628528
ADVERTISING	2.327761

Reviewing this report points up some key measures of the reliability of the model. Note that the R^2 value is relatively high and the ratio of the standard error of the estimate to the mean of the projected variable is relatively small. The high reliability of these measures indicates that users can have good confidence in the model, and place some reliance on its results.

This report also includes the coefficients of the predictor variables and the intercept of the regression line. These values can be used to make projections with the regression model, in addition to those already available in the Projections Report.

The Projections Report is a key report. Most of the information to be gained from the regression analysis is contained in this report.

The Projections Report shows the actual value of the projected variable for each location, and the related projected value obtained from the regression model. The amount and percentage difference is shown, together with a ranking of these differences; the locations with high ranks should be the first to be investigated. Those with projections greater than actual should be investigated to determine why their performance was not up to the standard of the others. In contrast, locations with an actual value greater than the projected value should be investigated to determine why they are so successful relative to the others.

EXHIBIT 4   253

REPORT DATE: 11/30/85   **PROJECTIONS REPORT FOR HARDWARE**   Page 1
PREPARED BY: **Example Client, Inc.**
REVIEWED BY: **June 30, 1985**

PROJECTED ACCOUNT: SALES
BASED ON RELATIONSHIPS WITH: SQ. FEET, ADVERTISING

LOCATION	PROJECTED	ACTUAL	ACTUAL OVER/ (UNDER) PROJECTED	% OVER (UNDER)	RANK
1	26,617.38	25,835.00	(883.38)	(3.31)	7
2	29,162.48	27,500.00	(1,662.46)	(5.70)	4
3	27,474.93	28,654.00	1,179.07	4.29	6
4	32,583.97	32,576.00	(7.97)	(0.02)	16
5	28,878.32	28,764.00	(114.32)	(0.40)	15
6	28,503.79	24,875.00	(3,628.79)	(12.73)	1
7	28,057.13	29,465.00	1,407.87	5.02	5
8	26,409.55	25,635.00	(774.55)	(2.930)	8
9	31,354.81	31,845.00	490.19	1.56	10
10	26,389.96	26,745.00	355.04	1.35	11
11	27,310.87	27,465.00	154.13	0.56	14
12	26,475.68	28,956.00	2,480.32	9.37	2
13	23,276.73	22,984.00	(292.73)	(1.26)	12
14	30,068.16	31,764.00	1,695.84	5.64	3
15	26,526.58	26,745.00	218.42	0.82	13
16	27,483.65	26,867.00	(616.65)	(2.24)	9
	446,674.99	446,675.00	0.01	0.00	

REPORT DATE: 11/30/85   **PROJECTIONS REPORT FOR HARDWARE**   Page 2
PREPARED BY: **Example Client, Inc.**
REVIEWED BY: **June 30, 1985**

RANGES FOR VARIOUS CONFIDENCE INTERVALS

The projected balance is the best estimate of the value for each location. Using the table below, "SALES" can be projected with 95% confidence to be the projected balance +/− 3008.52. Ranges for other confidence intervals may be found in the table below.

Confidence Level	Allowable Range
50%	1043.77 +/−
70%	1596.36 +/−
80%	1995.45 +/−
85%	2241.04 +/−
90%	2517.33 +/−
95%	3008.52 +/−
99%	4144.39 +/−

The Projections Report has two pages. The second page of the report interprets the standard error of the estimate directly in terms of a range of prediction accuracy. Remember that the projection is only an estimate, and the regression line represents the best estimate of the projected variable; the actual value should fall somewhere near the regression line. This range of possible values around the regression line is easily identifiable using the report on the second page of the Regression Equation Report. For example, the true value of a prediction will lie within a range of $3008.52 above and below the value projected by the regression line at the 95% confidence level.

Exhibit 5

Illustration of Combined Account-Time and Multiple-Location Analysis

REPORT DATE: 1/1/80 00:20   **ORIGINAL DATA VALUES FOR STORES**   Page 1
PREPARED BY: **FAST-SHOP**
REVIEWED BY: **December 31, 1987**
Dr. Edward Blocher

Loc.	INVENTORY SPOILAGE	SQUARE FOOTAGE	NUMBER OF EMPLOYEES	LOCATION	SALES
1	1,512.00	3,000.00	8.00	1.00	312,389.00
2	2,005.00	3,200.00	10.00	2.00	346,235.00
3	1,686.00	4,000.00	12.00	2.00	376,465.00
4	1,908.00	3,400.00	12.00	1.00	345,723.00
5	2,384.00	4,400.00	9.00	1.00	453,983.00
6	3,806.00	4,800.00	10.00	2.00	502,984.00
7	2,253.00	3,500.00	8.00	1.00	325,436.00
8	1,443.00	3,000.00	10.00	2.00	253,647.00
9	2,755.00	5,550.00	15.00	2.00	562,534.00
10	1,023.00	2,250.00	15.00	2.00	287,364.00
11	1,552.00	2,500.00	9.00	1.00	198,374.00
12	2,119.00	3,500.00	16.00	2.00	333,984.00
13	5,506.00	7,500.00	15.00	2.00	673,645.00
14	3,034.00	5,700.00	16.00	2.00	588,947.00
15	772.00	2,200.00	8.00	1.00	225,364.00

REPORT DATE: 1/1/80 00:22   RESULTS OF STATISTICAL CHECKS
                                         STORES   Page 1
PREPARED BY: FAST-SHOP
REVIEWED BY: December 31, 1987
Dr. Edward Blocher

MODEL IS OK

THE ANSWERS PROJECTION ANALYSIS Module was able to compute a projection model for your data and relationships. No significant statistical problems were detected in the computation of the projections.

REPORT DATE: 1/1/80 00:23   **REGRESSION EQUATION: STORES**   Page 1
PREPARED BY: **FAST SHOP**
REVIEWED BY: **December 31, 1987**
Dr. Edward Blocher

CALCULATION MODE: Stepwise Search for Best Model.

REGRESSION EQUATION:

INVENTORY SPOILAGE = -673.415749
                    + $(0.749731 * \text{SQUARE FOOTAGE})$

Standard Error of the Estimate =   463.687564
F Value ("Statistical Validity") =   79.070246
Coefficient of Determination (R-Squared) =   0.858803
Durbin-Watson Statistic =   2.101309
Ratio of Standard Error to Mean of Projected Variable =   0.206035

Predictor	t-Value
SQUARE FOOTAGE	8.892145

EXHIBIT 5   257

REPORT DATE: 1/1/80 00:24   **PROJECTIONS REPORT FOR STORES**   Page 1
PREPARED BY: **FAST-SHOP**
REVIEWED BY: **December 31, 1987**
Dr. Edward Blocher

PROJECTED ACCOUNT: INVENTORY SPOILAGE
BASED ON RELATIONSHIPS WITH: SQUARE FOOTAGE

LOCATION	PROJECTED	ACTUAL	ACTUAL OVER/ (UNDER) PROJECTED	% OVER (UNDER)	RANK
1	1,575.78	1,512.00	(63.78)	(4.05)	13
2	1,725.72	2,005.00	279.28	16.18	8
3	2,325.51	1,686.00	(639.51)	(27.50)	3
4	1,875.67	1,908.00	32.33	1.72	14
5	2,625.40	2,384.00	(241.40)	(9.19)	9
6	2,925.29	3,806.00	880.71	30.11	1
7	1,950.64	2,253.00	302.36	15.50	7
8	1,575.78	1,443.00	(132.78)	(8.43)	12
9	3,487.59	2,755.00	(732.59)	(21.01)	2
10	1,013.48	1,023.00	9.52	0.94	15
11	1,200.91	1,552.00	351.09	29.24	6
12	1,950.64	2,119.00	168.36	8.63	11
13	4,949.56	5,506.00	556.44	11.24	5
14	3,600.05	3,034.00	(566.05)	(15.72)	4
15	975.99	772.00	(203.99)	(20.90)	10
	33,758.01	33,758.00	(0.01)	(0.00)	

The projected balance is the best estimate of the value for each location. Using the table below, "INVENTORY SPOILAGE" can be projected with 95% confidence to be the projected balance $+/-$ 908.83. Ranges for other confidence intervals may be found in the table.

Confidence Level	Allowable Range
50%	315.31 $+/-$
70%	482.24 $+/-$
80%	602.79 $+/-$
85%	676.98 $+/-$
90%	760.45 $+/-$
95%	908.83 $+/-$
99%	1251.96 $+/-$

MODEL IS OK

THE ANSWERS PROJECTION ANALYSIS Module was able to compute a projection model for your data and relationships. No significant statistical problems were detected in the computation of the projections.

EXHIBIT 5   259

REPORT DATE: 1/1/80 00:10   ORIGINAL DATA VALUES FOR STORE6   Page 1
PREPARED BY: **FAST-SHOP**
REVIEWED BY: **December 31, 1987**
Dr. Edward Blocher

MO/YR	INVENTORY SPOILAGE	SALES
Jan 83	450.00	65,354.00
Feb 83	243.00	34,756.00
Mar 83	219.00	34,985.00
Apr 83	376.00	76,298.00
May 83	374.00	64,539.00
Jun 83	287.00	45,873.00
Jul 83	345.00	52,834.00
Aug 83	254.00	26,736.00
Sep 83	288.00	42,984.00
Oct 83	356.00	39,587.00
Nov 83	219.00	36,578.00
Dec 83	687.00	98,746.00
Jan 84	387.00	45,673.00
Feb 84	288.00	45,029.00
Mar 84	213.00	36,546.00
Apr 84	412.00	57,934.00
May 84	464.00	67,354.00
Jun 84	289.00	48,756.00
Jul 84	385.00	57,648.00
Aug 84	465.00	76,384.00
Sep 84	338.00	41,983.00
Oct 84	413.00	47,823.00
Nov 84	462.00	36,782.00
Dec 84	587.00	87,645.00
Jan 85	367.00	56,735.00
Feb 85	214.00	36,763.00
Mar 85	456.00	66,475.00
Apr 85	385.00	44,985.00
May 85	267.00	48,756.00
Jun 85	519.00	38,746.00
Jul 85	571.00	41,904.00
Aug 85	319.00	37,836.00
Sep 85	390.00	36,746.00
Oct 85	318.00	45,903.00

REPORT DATE: 1/1/80 00:16   **REGRESSION EQUATION: STORE 6**   Page 1
PREPARED BY: **FAST-SHOP**
REVIEWED BY: **December 31, 1987**
Dr. Edward Blocher

CALCULATION MODE: Stepwise Search for Best Model.

REGRESSION EQUATION:

    INVENTORY SPOILAGE = 82.636990
                 + (0.005373 * SALES)

Standard Error of the Estimate =	64.286978
F Value ("Statistical Validity") =	53.687132
Coefficient of Determination (R-Squared) =	0.709330
Durbin-Watson Statistic =	1.329877
Ratio of Standard Error to Mean of Projected Variable =	0.175308

Predictor	t-Value
SALES	7.327150

REPORT DATE: 1/1/80 00:17   **PROJECTIONS REPORT FOR STORE 6**   Page 1
PREPARED BY: **FAST-SHOP**
REVIEWED BY: **December 31, 1987**
Dr. Edward Blocher

PROJECTED ACCOUNT: INVENTORY SPOILAGE
BASED ON RELATIONSHIPS WITH: SALES

PERIOD	PROJECTED	ACTUAL	ACTUAL OVER/ (UNDER) PROJECTED	% OVER (UNDER)	RANK
Jan 85	387.49	367.00	(20.49)	(5.29)	8
Feb 85	280.17	214.00	(66.17)	(23.62)	5
Mar 85	439.82	456.00	16.18	3.68	9
Apr 85	324.35	385.00	60.65	18.70	6
May 85	344.61	267.00	(77.61)	(22.52)	4
Jun 85	290.83	519.00	228.17	78.46	2
Jul 85	307.80	571.00	263.20	85.51	1
Aug 85	285.94	319.00	33.06	11.56	7
Sep 85	280.08	390.00	109.92	39.24	3
Oct 85	329.28	318.00	(11.28)	(3.43)	10
	3,270.37	3,806.00	535.63	16.38	-

EXHIBIT 5   261

REPORT DATE: 1/1/80
00:18   RANGES FOR VARIOUS CONFIDENCE
                                     INTERVALS STORE 6   Page 2
PREPARED BY: FAST-SHOP
REVIEWED BY: December 31, 1987
Dr. Edward Blocher

The projected balance is the best estimate of the value for each period. Using the table below, "INVENTORY SPOILAGE" can be projected with 95% confidence to be the projected balance $+/-$ 126.00. Ranges for other confidence intervals may be found in the table.

Confidence Level	Allowable Range
50%	43.72 $+/-$
70%	66.86 $+/-$
80%	83.57 $+/-$
85%	93.86 $+/-$
90%	105.43 $+/-$
95%	126.00 $+/-$
99%	173.57 $+/-$

Analytical Procedures and Expert Systems 12

§12.01 Introduction

Among the most promising of all auditing technologies now on the horizon is the application of expert systems. Expert systems provide a direct means to enhance audit productivity, quality, and competitiveness. This technology is also one of the most exciting and challenging fields to influence audit practice in many years. In the future, major audit firms will be deeply invested in expert systems throughout the audit, from engagement selection and planning to the writing of the auditor's report. Also, a major focus of the development of expert systems in coming years will be in the area of analytical procedures. The reason is twofold. Analytical procedures are key audit functions, which can be very effective in identifying risk areas and in detecting errors and irregularities, and, though widely used, many auditors think that analytical procedures are not used as effectively as they could be, and user support aids, such as expert systems, are needed.

In this chapter, we describe the general nature of expert systems and where they are most productively employed and illustrate specific applications of these systems to analytical procedures. The software system ANSWERS, is useful in performing analytical procedures. We begin with some background on expert systems, which is one type of application of *artificial intelligence.*

§12.02 Artificial Intelligence

The term *artificial intelligence* (AI) is used to describe any type of mechanical device, usually a computer, which can perform tasks that, if performed by a person, would require some thought (intelligence). The adjective *artificial* is used to indicate that the task is being performed in a human way, but by a machine of some type. The ability to replace human effort with less expensive and more consistent machines is a strong incentive for development of artificial intelligence, and many audit firms and United States corporations, including KMG Peat Marwick Main, Coopers and Lybrand, Arthur Andersen, Price Waterhouse, CIGNA, XEROX, IBM, Westinghouse, and General Motors, among others, are actively involved in artificial intelligence research and application. There are three areas of research and application within the broad area of artificial intelligence:

1. *Robotics*—the use of machines to replace skilled human labor in manufacturing and other applications

2. *Natural Language*—the use of a machine to exchange information between a person and another machine. An example of natural language programming is the HAL software which is an add-on to the LOTUS 1-2-3 spreadsheet software. HAL enables users to type 1-2-3 commands in plain English.

3. *Expert Systems*—the use of computer-based systems to emulate human problem solving and expert decision making

Of the three areas of artificial intelligence, expert systems is the area which is most promising for application in auditing and analytical procedures.

§12.03 Expert Systems

In this section, we present a brief general description of expert systems—what judgments they are designed to facilitate, how they are designed, and the features, strengths, and weaknesses of the systems. While not directed specifically to analytical procedures, this section is important because of the novelty of expert systems, and the lack at this time of a common vocabulary and widely accepted set of concepts to describe their use and application. For two reasons, our focus in this discussion is on those systems which have been developed for the microcomputer. First, microcomputers have become widely available to audit staff in the field, so that microcomputer systems can be widely and extensively used. For this reason, the microcomputer-based systems have potentially a much broader and more significant impact within accounting and auditing practice, and the development of expert systems is generally heading in the direction of microcomputer systems. Second, the mainframe and minicomputer types of systems are relatively expensive, typically are custom-designed for a particular company or a particular large-scale application, and relatively little is written about them in the accounting and auditing professional journals.

Figure 12-1 gives an overview of the components of an expert system. The two principal components are a *knowledge base* and set of *decision rules* for extracting decisions from the knowledge base. Sometimes the set of decision rules is called the *inference engine* to indicate that it applies logic and inference to the facts, observations, and descriptions in the knowledge base in arriving at the desired decision. The knowledge base and the decision rules are thus both essential ingredients in the use of the expert system.

The third component of the expert system is the *user interface*, which is the set of screens the user views and responds to in using the system. The proper design of the interface is crucial for effective use of the system by non-experts, since the non-expert is not expected to be very familiar with the knowledge base or decision rules. Usually, the interface has a question and answer format through which the system queries the user for the relevant facts needed to specify the decision context before arriving at the desired solution or decision.

The Nature of Expertise

Since an expert system is said to emulate or replace a human behavior, it is useful at this point to specify a list of intelligent human behaviors. Davis provides the following list:[1]

- Solve a problem
- Explain the result

---

[1] R. Davis, *Amplifying Expertise with Expert Systems*, in The AI Business (MIT Press, P. H. Winston & K. A. Pendergast eds 1984).

Figure 12-1 An Overview of an Expert System

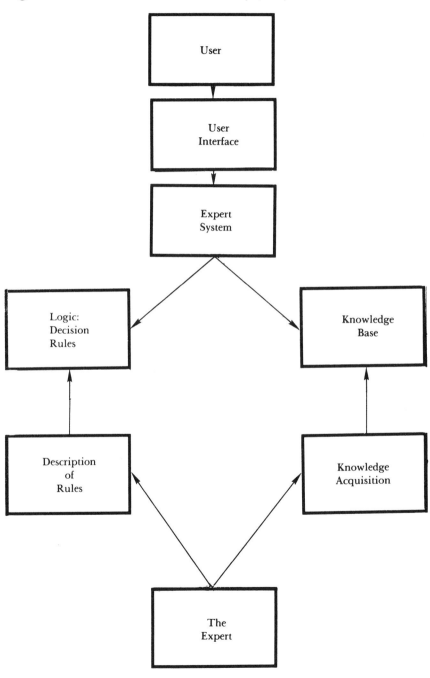

- Learn
- Restructure knowledge
- Determine relevance
- Degrade gracefully (that is, to know when you have reached the limit of your expertise)

The expert systems now available have aimed primarily at achieving the first behavior, to solve a problem. Many of the systems also include an explanation facility which tells the user why certain questions are asked (determining the relevance of the fact or description which is queried) and explains in simple terms the rationale for the decision. In summary, most expert systems will go through the following sequence of steps in solving the decision problem:

1. Ask questions of the user to elicit relevant facts, observations, and descriptions

2. Explain why a question is asked, if the user wishes

3. Make a decision based on the user's input and reference to the expert knowledge base and decision rules

4. Justify the decision and interpret it for the user

As Sviokla notes,[2] some expert systems have developed a "rudimentary learning capability" as well, but expert systems generally are not able to restructure knowledge, to degrade gracefully, to handle inconsistent knowledge, or to handle common sense matters not specifically within the domain of the expert system's decision rules and knowledge base. Thus, expert systems appear to be best at solving specific problems, but are not effective at broader intelligent activities such as learning and creating new knowledge or handling matters not specifically anticipated in the design of the system.

To further consider the nature of expert decision making, review these characteristics of human expert decision makers.

(1) A highly developed *Perceptual/Attention* ability—experts can "see" what others cannot.

(2) An awareness of the difference between *Relevant and Irrelevant* information—experts know how to concentrate on what's important.

---

[2] Sviokla, *Business Implications of Knowledge-Based Systems,* Data Base, Summer 1986, at 6.

(3)   An ability to *Simplify* complexities—experts can "make sense out of chaos."

(4)   A highly developed *Content Knowledge* about their area—experts know a lot and stay up with the latest developments.

(5)   A greater *Consistency* of cognitive processes—experts can do habitually what others have to work at.

(6)   An ability to *Tolerate Stress*—experts can work effectively under adverse conditions.

(7)   A strong set of *Communication Skills*—experts know how to demonstrate their expertise to others.

(8)   A knowledge of when to make *Exceptions*—experts know when to and when *not* to follow decision rules.

(9)   A strong sense of *Responsibility* for their choices—experts are not afraid to stand behind their decisions.

(10) A *Selectivity* about which problems to solve—experts know when to make decisions and when not to.

(11) An outward *Confidence* in their decisions—experts believe in themselves and their abilities.

(12) An ability to *Adapt* to changing task conditions—experts avoid rigidity in decision strategies.

(13) A capability to be more *Creative*—experts are better able to find novel solutions to problems.

(14) An inability to *Articulate* their decision processes—experts make decisions "on experience."

(15) A tendency for early hypotheses generation and late closure.

*Source: J. Shanteau, Psychological Characteristics of Expert Decision Makers, Presented at the University of Southern California Symposium, Audit Judgment and Expert Systems, Los Angeles (Feb 1986) (reprinted with permission).

These characteristics are derived from research on the nature of expertise by Shanteau and others. Notice that many of these characteristics relate to perhaps more uniquely human (and, therefore, more difficult to mechanize) behaviors such as creativity, communication skill, and a sense of responsibility. Items 1 through 6 on this list appear to be those characteristics which can be usefully mechanized, while the remaining characteristics may be difficult or impossible to mechanize. Again, it is apparent that the expert system has a limited but important role in emulating or replacing expert decision making as we know it today.

Types of Problems for Expert Systems

We have considered the nature of expert decision making and the types of expert behaviors that expert systems can emulate. Now we consider the different types of decision contexts and how these can be supported by expert systems. It turns out that certain decision contexts are better candidates for expert systems application than others.

More than 30 years ago, AI researchers focused on developing *general purpose* decision-making systems, which were based upon broad general principles of problem solving. More recently, development efforts have focused on specialized expert systems designed for rather narrow problem domains. The reason is that the more specialized systems have been more effective in replicating human expert decision making. The thinking now is that general problem solvers are too shallow to be effective, and that there is relatively little transfer of expertise between different types of special decision areas.[3] Thus, expert systems developers now typically choose rather narrow decision areas which focus on very specialized types of expertise. This focus on specialization is particularly appropriate for accounting and auditing applications, as Elliott and Kielich note:

> [T]he complexity of modern accounting practice leads to specialization which, in turn, leads to the concentration of expertise in specialized areas. No one can be expert at everything. Experts in each area know which factors to consider and combine in order to formulate proper conclusions. Because this is so, the demands on an expert's time can become enormous, resulting in unfilled client commitments or, worse, in errors. By capturing such a person's knowledge in an expert system, that knowledge can be made available to everyone in the firm. The firm also protects itself in the event that the expert leaves unexpectedly. And, finally, the firm can deliver more consistent quality if its experts' reasoning can be brought to bear in a greater number of decisions.[4]

The thrust of current development, then, is to create a number of specialized systems which enhance decision making in critical specialized decision-making areas, where the decision-making process is complex and the available expertise is limited. This applies particularly

---

[3] Feigenbaum, Buchanan & Lederberg, *On Generality and Problem Solving: A Case Study Using the DENDRAL Program,* in 6 Machine Intelligence (Edinburgh University Press 1971).

[4] Elliott & Kielich, *Expert Systems for Accountants,* J Accountancy, Sept 1985, at 126-34.

well to the area of analytical procedures, in that it is an area in which the decision-making process is somewhat complex, and the common perception is that, though most auditors use analytical procedures regularly, relatively few auditors are able to perform analytical procedures very effectively.

Up to this point, we have considered the generality/specificity of the decision context and how that influences the effectiveness of an expert systems application. Now we turn our attention to the issue of the degree of *structure* in the decision problem. These two dimensions of the decision context are somewhat independent. A decision problem is structured if it is relatively "programmed," that is, the decision maker follows certain well-defined steps to reach a decision.[5] Examples include decisions which can be reached using a quantitative model such as linear programming or some other optimization technique. In a sense, the optimization model provides the expert system for these decision contexts, and the decision problem can be simplified so that the use of the model alone is sufficient for effective decision making. Whether or not one would call such a model an expert system is an argument we do not address here. Our interest, however, is in the types of expert systems described above, which involve a knowledge base and set of decision rules, in contrast to the pure optimization model application.

A decision problem is unstructured if little is known about the steps of analysis required to achieve an effective solution. Examples of unstructured decision problems are decisions such as the hiring of top managers, strategic planning, and research and development evaluation. A completely unstructured decision context will be difficult to emulate with an expert system because the knowledge base and set of decision rules are not clearly defined. The current thinking is that expert systems are best suited for decision contexts which are semistructured, that is, they lie somewhere between the extremes of fully structured and completely unstructured decision contexts.[6] In other words, the decision problem is well enough understood that it is possible to describe and explain the nature of the underlying expertise. In summary, the discussions of generality/specificity and structured/unstructured dimensions give us a similar result—the more effective expert systems will be designed for relatively narrow, well-defined decision contexts.

---

[5] H. Simon. The New Science of Management Decision, (Harper and Row 1960).

[6] Sviokla, *Business Implications of Knowledge-Based Systems*, Data Base, Summer 1986, at 5-19.

The above conclusion, that expert systems will evolve around a number of relatively narrow decision contexts, has implications for the size of the expert systems we will see. As noted in the AICPA report on expert systems,[7] most business decisions are not extremely complex, but, rather, they require a small specialized knowledge base and a relatively simple set of decision rules. As a result, there will be an emphasis on relatively small expert systems applications in business.[8] The inference is that this applies also to the systems in accounting and auditing, particularly in analytical procedures.

Design Methodologies of Expert Systems

The common approach for the design of a large-scale mainframe or minicomputer-based expert system is to employ an "AI language" such as LISP or PROLOG. LISP tends to be more popular in this country, while PROLOG is more widely used in Europe and Japan. Our interest is in the small systems, and these are most often developed from an expert system "tool" or "shell." An expert system shell is a software system which can be used to develop small expert systems. The use of the shell does not require expertise in artificial intelligence languages. These shells make it possible for accountants and auditors with little additional training to become involved in the design of expert systems. This is particularly important in accounting and auditing, since, as noted above, our expectation is that many of the applications will be in small, specialized decision contexts.

There are two widely recognized types of expert system shells which employ two quite different methods for the design of an expert system—the *rule-based* approach and the *example-based* approach. In a sense, the rule-based approach focuses on one of the two components of the expert system, the set of decision rules, whereas the example-based approach focuses on the knowledge base component of the system. That is, the rule-based shell allows the designer to build an expert system through the development of a series of interrelated rules which are usually IF/THEN statements of the type, "If current ratio is less

---

[7] American Institute of CPAs, An Introduction to Artificial Intelligence and Expert Systems 18 (Management Advisory Services Special Report 1987).

[8] American Institute of CPAs, An Introduction to Artificial Intelligence and Expert Systems (Management Advisory Services Special Report 1987). This report refers to these small systems as "knowledge systems" to distinguish them from the large mainframe or mini-computer based systems. The vocabulary is not well-defined on this matter, and we will use the term "expert system" more broadly to refer to the smaller systems described above.

than 1.0 and loan default equals YES, then financial distress level equals HIGH."[9]

In contrast, the expert can design an expert system using the example-based shell inserting a number of examples of relevant decision cases. The system advises the developer if any example is inconsistent with another example. Then, the example-based shell extracts a many-part decision rule from the expert's examples, and this decision rule becomes the expert system for that application.[10]

An evaluation of the two types of shells reveals that the example-based system is often preferred for the most simple decision contexts, in which there are a small number of easily identifiable decision-relevant factors. In these situations, it is relatively convenient for the expert-developer to identify cases (that is, "examples") which would specify the expert's decision for each combination of the decision-relevant factors. Also, these shells are often easier to use, and, therefore, are preferred by nonprogrammers. However, the use of these shells requires that the decision context can be described by a number (usually, 15-30 or more) of example decision contexts.

In contrast, the rule-based shells tend to be preferred when the decision context is broader in scope and the decision-relevant factors are not as easily identified. In this situation, it is relatively convenient to build the expert system from a variety of related decision-relevant rules, that is, IF/THEN statements. Also, this approach is preferred when an expert with a history of "examples" is not available.

Benefits of Expert Systems

The potential benefits of expert systems can be summarized in the following points:

1. Better quality decision making; the decisions will reflect less bias and greater rationality, performance, and expertise

2. More consistent decision making; decision making will be more consistent among users of the system, and the decisions will be more stable over time for each user of the system

3. More clearly explained and communicated decisions; decisions are better understood because of the consistency noted above, and because of the explanation facility contained in the system

---

[9] The M.1 system from Teknowledge, Palo Alto, CA, and VP-EXPERT, Paperback Software, Berkeley, CA, are examples of rule-based shells.

[10] Commonly cited example-based systems include EXPERT-EASE, Human Edge Software, Palo Alto, CA, and Ist-CLASS, Programs in Motion, Wayland, MA.

4. Decision makers will have more time to concentrate on other elements of the task

5. Specialized expertise will become more widely available to others whose decisions require this expertise

6. The improved quality of decision making and freed-up time will contribute to greater productivity and competitiveness

7. Expert systems can be used in training, as a benchmark for performance, and as a tool for case exercises requiring identification of expert-like decision rules. Also, the involvement of expert systems in training can help focus training efforts by drawing attention to training objectives in a new way. Perhaps rote memorization objectives will have less focus, and more attention will be placed on the more analytical aspects of job performance

Each of these benefits is a strong motivation for accounting and auditing applications of expert systems. In particular, expert systems seem to be a natural application to deal with the increasing competitiveness of audit practice and the increasing complexity and need for specialization in accounting and auditing generally.

Obstacles to Effective Use of Expert Systems

The following can lead to the failure of an expert system application.

1. The decision context is not sufficiently narrow

2. The decision context is not sufficiently well-defined

3. The goal of the application is not clearly distinguished as either a practice application (a short-term focus) or a research project (long-term focus)

4. Lack of high level support

5. The decision context is not sufficiently stable

6. Expectations for the expert system are set too high or for too soon a delivery

§12.04   The Role of Expert Systems in Analytical Procedures

It is useful in discussing expert systems for analytical procedures to start with some distinctions. We categorize expert systems and decision support systems into three areas in which the judgment of the auditor can be aided. These areas are derived from the three-step judgment process of an auditor performing analytical procedures, as illustrated in Figure 12-2. The three steps are prediction, comparison, and judgment. In the prediction phase, the auditor develops predicted balances from which forecasted trends and ratio values are obtained. In the second step, these forecasted trends and ratios are compared to the actual values to develop an *exception listing* of unusual trends and relationships. We call this exception list a list of *insights,* which are the basis of the auditor's judgment in the third and final step—the ultimate assessment of audit risk based upon the analytical procedures.

There are three categories of expert systems and decision support systems corresponding to these three steps in the analytical procedures judgment process. The three categories are:

- Insight facilitating
- Decision facilitating
- Decision making

Insight Facilitating Systems

The systems which are *insight-facilitating* have the objective of producing relevant trends and ratios, facilitating the auditor's analysis and development of insights. These systems do not typically contain materiality levels or exception limits which would produce the insights. In effect, they provide a useful and more refined data base for the auditor

Figure 12-2   Auditor's Decision Process When Using
Analytical Review

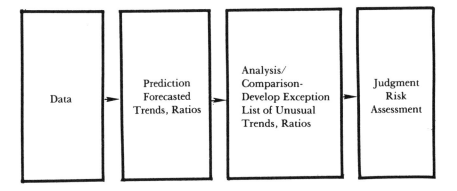

to use in developing his or her own exceptions and insights. In effect, these systems provide the first step of the three-step process outlined in Figure 12-2.

These systems are not usually referred to as expert systems, in that they do not actually embody the expertise of a given expert or group of experts. Their objective is more simply to prepare and refine data so that the auditor-expert will be relieved of some of the pencil-pushing aspects of analytical procedures.

Examples of insight-facilitating systems include spreadsheet systems, audit working paper systems, integrated accounting systems, and RAM-based database systems.

Decision-Facilitating Systems

The decision-facilitating system is a more advanced and more comprehensive type of system than the insight-facilitating system described above. In addition to the trends, ratios, and graphs produced by the insight-facilitating type of system, these systems perform the exception determination function—that is, they actually go one step further to produce the insights.

The only widely available system of this type is ANSWERS, Financial Audit Systems, Raleigh, NC. This system combines the features of both the insight facilitating and the decision-facilitating types of systems. It provides reports of trend and ratio calculations and graphic capability, but in addition it contains decision rules which "trigger" relevant insights about the data under analysis. The trigger points are pre-determined by the auditor using the system, and they can be changed as the auditor moves from one audit engagement to another.

Decision-Making Systems

The role of a decision-making type expert system for analytical procedures is to integrate the insights of the auditor into a summary judgment about audit risk for the account or item under investigation. This risk level is then used within the audit risk model in the auditor's overall planning process—to set the scope for other substantive audit procedures.

The links between insights and risk levels are not now sufficiently well-defined and understood. Therefore, auditors are reluctant to determine and specify the link between insights and risk levels due to their relatively low confidence in the effectiveness of analytical procedures.

Though no widely available systems now exist, one such system is now in use by the firm, KMG Peat Marwick, Main. This system uses

Figure 12-3 Types of Systems for Analytical Procedures

Type of System	Input to System	Output of System	Role of the Auditor Using the system
Insight-Facilitating	Financial, Operating, and External Data	* Trends * Ratios * Graphs	Develop Insights
Assessment-Facilitating	Financial, Operating, and External Data	* Trends * Ratios * Graphs * Insights	Make Risk Assessment
Assessment-Making-	Determined by Query of the System	Recommended Risk Assessment	Implement Risk Assessment-Audit Planning and Audit Scope

the M.1 shell and knowledge obtained from the firm's experts to evaluate loan loss reserves in financial institutions. The three types of systems discussed in this section are outlined and summarized in Figure 12-3.

§12.05 An Illustration

To observe a particular application of the decision-facilitating system, ANSWERS, start with a review of the data in Figure 12-4. This data is taken from the summary financial data for an actual retail company. After a brief review, consider the financial condition of the company. Is this a risky engagement? How would you assess the company's liquidity, profitability, and capital structure? Would the company have difficulty obtaining additional long-term debt or equity financing? What areas would you target for additional audit testing?

Did you recognize the company? This is the financial data for the W.T. Grant Co, which filed for bankruptcy in 1975 (the data shown are actually for the years 1968-1973). Figure 12-5 shows a selected portion of the trends and ratios produced by ANSWERS for this company, and selected insights triggered by the data are shown in Figure 12-6. A unique aspect of this case is that the commonly used financial ratios for analyzing liquidity, profitability, and capital structure did not

Figure 12-4   Example Company Selected Financial Data

Account Description	1982	1983	1984	1985	1986	1987
Cash	25,141	25,639	32,977	34.009	49,851	30,943
Accounts Receivable	272,450	312,776	368,267	419,731	477,324	542,751
Prepaids	3,982	4,402	5,037	5,246	5,378	6,648
Inventories	183,722	208,623	222,128	260,492	298,696	399,533
Property & Equipment (net)	47,578	49,931	55,311	61,832	77,173	91,420
Other Assets	18,734	20,738	23,075	26,318	36,248	39,403
Total Assets	551,607	622,109	706,795	807,628	944,670	1,110,698
Accounts Payable	49,831	64,321	70,853	80,861	94,677	78,789
Accrued Expenses	86,087	102,650	113,732	131,899	143,159	164,243
Notes Payable	99,539	118,305	182,132	246,420	237,741	390,034
Long-Term Debt	62,622	43,251	35,407	32,310	128,432	126,672
Deferred Taxes Payable	7,551	7,941	8,286	8,518	9,664	11,926
Other Liabilities	5,279	5,521	5,697	5,593	5,252	4,695
Total Liabilities	310,909	341,989	416,107	505,592	618,925	776,359
Capital Stock	73,253	87,581	79,009	71,601	81,238	73,186
Retained Earnings	167,445	192,539	211,679	230,435	244,507	261,153
Total Stockholders Equity	240,698	280,120	290,688	302,036	325,745	334,339
Total Liabilities & Equity	551,607	622,109	706,795	807,628	944,670	1,110,698
Net Sales	982,244	1,095,083	1,214,666	1,259,116	1,378,251	1,648,500
Cost of Goods Sold	669,560	739,459	817,671	843,192	931,237	1,125,261
Depreciation Expense	8,303	8,380	8,972	9,619	10,577	12,004
Interest Expense	11,248	13,146	14,919	18,874	16,562	21,128
Income Tax Expense	26,650	34,000	38,000	32,800	26,500	25,750
Dividends Paid	13,805	17,160	19,280	20,426	20,794	20,807
Net Income	32,563	37,895	41,809	39,577	35,212	37,787
Number of common shares outstanding at year-end	12,817	13,714	13,728	13,684	14,023	13,993
Market price per share	38	43	55	65	43	31

change significantly over this time frame and, therefore, would not have ordinarily revealed the extent of the problem facing W.T. Grant. In fact, many analysts were apparently surprised at the bankruptcy of W.T. Grant.[11] However, the thorough analysis available in this system uncovered the key signal of failure, the consistently decreasing and negative cash flows over the period shown. This case shows that a ratio analysis approach can be incomplete and prone to error. A comprehensive analysis such as provided by this system provides a complete and consistent set of insights for the auditor to use in forming his or her risk assessments. The expert system is particularly useful in those difficult cases such as the W.T. Grant Co. This example illustrates the

---

[11] See the article by Largay & Stickney, *Cash Flows, Ratio Analysis and the W. T. Grant Company Bankruptcy,* Fin Analysts J, July-Aug 1980, at 43-48 for a full discussion of the use of ratio analysis in the W. T. Grant case.

enhanced abilities of the user to identify potential financial difficulties by utilizing an expert system approach.

The appendix to this chapter provides a more detailed example of the potential uses of the ANSWERS expert system in completing analytical procedures.

Figure 12-5   Example Company Financial Data Summary (Partial Report)

DESCRIPTION	1983 % chng.	1984 % chng.	1985 % chng.	1986 % chng.	1987 % chng.
		LIQUIDITY/PROFITS/CAPITAL Ratios			
A/R Turnover	3.74	3.57	3.20	3.07	3.23
	–	– 4.54%	– 10.36%	– 4.06%	5.21%
Altman Z-Score (Private Corp.)	3.10	2.97	2.66	2.45	2.34
	–	– 4.19%	– 10.43%	– 7.89%	– 4.49%
Altman Z-Score (Publicly Held)	4.53	4.44	4.07	3.39	2.99
	–	– 1.98%	– 8.33%	– 16.70%	– 11.79%
Cash Flow to Total Debt	3.65%	– 0.06%	– 2.42%	– 3.84%	– 14.04%
	–	– 101.64%	– 3,933.33%	– 58.67%	– 265.62%
Cash Flow From Operations	12,491.00	– 256.00	– 12,225.00	– 23,786.00	– 109,015.00
	–	– 102.04%	– 4,675.39%	– 94.56%	– 358.31%

Figure 12-6 Trend Observations and Comments— Example Company (Partial Report)

Liquidity/Profits/Capital-Trend Decisions

Based on the materiality limits specified, the following trends and/or relationships were noted as possibly significant. You should review and evaluate the applicability of each observation and comment.

Observations	*Comments*
1. CASH FLOW TO TOTAL DEBT DECREASED	A significant decline generally indicates a weakening of the Company's liquidity. This can be a signal of increasing financial risk.
	Is this change consistent with changes throughout the industry?
	What steps are being taken by management to address the increased financial distress?
	Does the Company have the ability to respond effectively to increased financial distress?
	Has the Company recently entered into significant debt-financed plant or equipment expansion?
	Could debt be restructured to help reduce current maturities?
2. CASH FLOW FROM OPERATIONS DECREASED	Often, one way to improve cash flow is to arrange more favorable credit terms. Restructuring the arrangements with both suppliers and customers can be equally advantageous.
	If the Company has income, but little or no positive cash flow, perhaps there are overvalued assets which can be written down to provide income tax benefits.
	Perhaps a review of investments and other assets would reveal resources that could be converted to cash without significantly affecting the Company's financial position.
	Is there some way the Company could reduce or restructure its debt to help relieve the related interest cost?

§12.06 References

Akers, Porter, Blocher, & Mister, *Expert Systems for Management Accountants,* Management Account, Mar 1986, at 30-34.

American Institute of CPAs, An Introduction to Artificial Intelligence and Expert Systems (Management Advisory Services Special Report 1987).

Chandler, *Expert Systems in Auditing: The State of the Art,* Auditor's Report, Summer 1985, at 1-3.

Davis, *Amplifying Expertise with Expert Systems,* in *The AI Business,* The MIT Press, P.H. Winston & K.A. Pendergast eds, 1984).

Elliott & Kielich, *Expert Systems for Accountants,* J Accountancy, Sept 1985, at 126-34.

Feigenbaum, Buchanan & Lederberg, *On Generality and Problem Solving: A Case Study Using the DENDRAL Program,* in 6 *Machine Intelligence* (Edinburgh University Press 1971).

P. Harmon & D. King, *Expert Systems* (Wiley 1985).

Largay & Stickney, *Cash Flows, Ratio Analysis and the W.T. Grant Company Bankruptcy,* Fin Analysts J, July-Aug 1980, at 43-48.

McKee, *Expert Systems: The Final Frontier?* CPA J, July 1986, at 42-46.

J. Shanteau, Psychological Characteristics of Expert Decision Makers, Presented at the University of Southern California Symposium, Audit Judgment and Expert Systems, Los Angeles (Feb 1986).

H. Simon, *The New Science of Management Decision,* (Harper and Row 1960).

Sviokla, *Business Implications of Knowledge-Based Systems,* Data Base, Summer 1986, at 5-19.

Exhibit 6

Blue Water Sailboats
A Sample Case

The case illustration begins with some brief background about Blue Water Sailboats and presents a current set of financial statements for the company. Blue Water Sailboats is owned by a partnership of five business people and has recently been incorporated for tax benefits and other reasons. At present, the five principal stockholders are interested in expanding the business, and have invited you to make a substantial investment in the company by buying several thousand dollars worth of stock. The objective of your financial analysis, then, is to determine if the proposed investment is sound.

Blue Water Sailboats sells approximately 100 to 150 sailboats each year, ranging from 14-foot dinghies to 35-foot cruising sailboats. The sales prices range from $2,000 to over $60,000. Blue Water has a limited inventory of boats, consisting primarily of one or two boats from each of the four manufacturers who supply Blue Water.

The company operates from one location, a large building with offices, storage, and a sales area for some of the smaller sailboats. The larger sailboats are in a fenced area adjacent to the main building. An ample parking area is nearby. This year Blue Water expanded with the purchase of a boat lift, which is used for hauling boats. In addition to the revenue from these hauls, the lift has brought in revenues for boat repairs, hull painting, and related services.

The balance sheet and income statement for Blue Water Sailboats for 1983 through 1987, and for the first 11 months of 1988, are shown in Figures A and B. The increase in net fixed assets in the recent two

EXHIBIT 6   281

years is due to improvements in the building, paving of the parking area, and purchase of the lift.

Blue Water obtains its debt financing from two sources. The principal source of short-term funds is a small savings and loan. An additional source of short-term loans and the principal source of long-term debt comes from a larger, commercial bank. The terms of the loan agreement with the larger bank include certain restrictions—the current ratio must remain greater than 1.5, the debt-to-equity ratio must remain below 1.0, and the ratio of long-term debt to equity must remain less than 0.4. The loans are secured by liens on the assets of the company.

Figures C-F show reports from the ANSWERS system for the analysis of Blue Water Sailboats. A careful review of the balances for each data item in Figures A and B provides insight into the trends of the balances for the periods shown. The ratio listing for Blue Water Sailboats, shown in Figures C and D, presents a valuable source of information for evaluating profitability, liquidity, and capital structure. The "Observations" Report in Figure E shows specific comments and suggestions drawn from ANSWERS' knowledge-base regarding the entity's accounts receivable balance. The "Simple Projection" Report in Figure F provides a useful means to analyse changes in the accounts shown.

A review of Figure C shows a relatively positive profitability picture for Blue Water Sailboats. Except for a low year in 1987, the trend and level of profitability has been quite good, as shown by relatively high figures for return on assets, return on equity, gross margin percentage, and the ratio of income to sales.

Consider the basis for the company's success, especially the improvement in 1988 over the prior year. Perhaps this is due to the purchase of the boat lift. A detailed analysis of the source of revenues would indicate whether hauling fees, hull painting, and repair charges have increased substantially as a result of the boat lift. The strong improvement from 1987 to 1988 might indicate a need for further testing.

A review of the ratios shows mixed signals for the liquidity position of Blue Water sailboats. Working capital and accounts receivable turnover have increased. However, inventory turnover has been declining over the last few years and, while the current ratio and the quick ratio have been increasing in recent years, there was a sharp drop for each of these ratios in 1988. These changes may indicate a need for further investigation.

The report also includes a number of ratios which are useful for analyzing capital structure. Two important ratios to consider are total

Figure A   Balance Sheet for Blue Water Sailboats

Blue Water Sailboats
Summary Financial Data
1983-1988

	1983	1984	1985	1986	1987	1988 (11 mo.)
ASSETS						
CASH	23,260	21,966	18,735	28,166	43,692	31,264
ACCOUNTS REC	99,463	102,834	112,903	125,663	104,388	142,009
LESS ALLOW. FOR B/D	(9,304)	(8,786)	(9,424)	(11,266)	(7,282)	(12,506)
INVENTORY	35,009	56,784	61,992	67,884	58,994	93,774
OTHER CURR. ASSETS	11,894	12,894	9,424	11,266	18,923	22,903
PROPERTY & EQUIP.	262,195	282,008	299,278	369,032	405,736	499,092
ACCUM. DEPRECIAT'N	(65,984)	(93,442)	(122,892)	(158,099)	(187,227)	(226,307)
TOTAL ASSETS	356,535	374,258	370,017	432,646	437,224	552,229
LIAB & EQUITIES						
ACCOUNTS PAYABLE	82,635	78,126	63,346	56,256	40,189	49,544
FED INC TAX PAY	11,630	10,983	11,780	14,083	3,738	15,632
SHORT TERM LOANS	59,876	56,980	37,583	41,093	49,594	76,962
ACCURED PAYROLL	5,227	4,598	3,649	4,224	4,775	4,779
LONG TERM DEBT	41,873	55,439	61,690	74,167	80,526	105,938
	201,241	206,126	178,048	189,823	178,822	252,855
COMMON STOCK	116,300	116,950	117,800	140,830	148,945	136,320
RETAINED EARNINGS	38,994	51,182	74,169	101,993	109,457	143,054
TOTAL LIAB + EQUITY	356,535	374,258	370,017	432,646	437,224	552,229

debt to equity and long-term debt to equity. Both of these ratios show substantial increases over the last few years. Additionally, both the ratios are coming somewhat close to the debt restrictions imposed by the commercial lender. This suggests that further expansion will require equity financing. Perhaps this is why the original partners have sought your investment in the business. If the profitability and sales growth continue, future expansion is likely, and some equity funds will be necessary.

The Accounts Receivable/Sales Report Group, shown in Figure D, can be analyzed in a similar fashion. The table lists the data item and ratio changes which have exceeded the predetermined decision threshold. This report uses exception reporting; it presents only those changes which are significant. Additionally, the report includes a set of comments which guide your interpretation of the results by pointing

EXHIBIT 6   283

Figure B   Income Statement for Blue Water Sailboats

Blue Water Sailboats
Summary Financial Data
1983-1988

	1983	1984	1985	1986	1987	1988 (11 mo.)
GROSS SALES	767,580	724,878	777,480	929,478	764,610	938,857
RETURNS & ALLOW.	38,379	35,645	40,334	45,998	32,887	46,380
NET SALES	729,201	689,233	737,146	883,480	731,723	892,477
COST OF SALES	473,908	441,298	458,013	545,778	453,669	530,597
GROSS MARGIN	255,293	247,935	279,131	337,702	278,034	361,880
SELLING EXPENSE						
SALARIES & WAGES	81,923	73,664	77,846	95,764	92,903	99,447
OTHER	9,304	8,786	9,424	11,266	13,108	11,380
ADMIN EXPENSE						
SALARIES & WAGES	79,666	75,234	80,693	96,469	87,995	97,441
OTHER	12,630	18,927	15,763	22,903	18,934	22,662
DEPRECIATION EXPENSE	29,075	27,458	29,450	35,208	29,128	35,563
INTEREST EXPENSE	10,465	9,857	11,234	9,456	14,313	16,229
PRETAX INCOME	32,230	34,010	54,721	66,636	21,674	79,158
INCOME TAX EXPENSE	10,776	12,946	23,889	29,845	6,453	36,985
NET INCOME	21,454	21,064	30,832	36,791	15,221	42,173

out important implications and suggesting further analysis to investigate the nature of the change.

A Trend Observations and Comments Report for Accounts Receivable/Sales is illustrated in Figure E. This report indicates an increase in the bad debt allowance while receivables collectability is actually improving.

Figure C Liquidity / Profits / Capital Data Items (Partial Listing)

REPORT DATE: **FINANCIAL DATA SUMMARY**
PREPARED BY: **BLUE WATER SAILBOATS**
REVIEWED BY: **December 31, 1988**

TAG DESCRIPTION	1983	1984 % chg.	1985 % chg.	1986 % chg.	1987 % chg.	Annualized 1988 % chg.
LIQUIDITY / PROFITS / CAPITAL Data Items						
ACCOUNTS PAYABLE		Current Y-T-D Balance =			49,554	
	82,635	78,126	63,346	56,256	40,189	49,554
		−5.46%	−18.92%	−11.19%	−28.56%	23.28%
ACCOUNTS RECEIVABLE		Current Y-T-D Balance =			142,009	
	99,465	102,834	112,903	125,663	104,388	142,009
		3.39%	9.79%	11.30%	−16.93%	36.04%
CURRENT ASSETS		Current Y-T-D Balance =			279,444	
	160,324	185,692	193,630	221,713	218,715	279,444
		15.82%	4.27%	14.50%	−1.35%	27.77%
CURRENT LIABILITIES		Current Y-T-D =			146,917	
	159,368	150,688	116,358	115,655	98,295	146,917
		−5.45%	−22.78%	−0.60%	−15.01%	49.47%
COST OF SALES		Current Y-T-D Balance =			530,597	
	473,908	441,298	458,015	545,778	453,669	578,833
		−6.88%	3.79%	19.16%	−16.88%	27.59%
TOTAL DEBT		Current Y-T-D Balance =			252,855	
	201,241	206,127	178,048	189,822	178,821	252,855
		2.43%	−13.62%	6.61%	−5.80%	41.40%

EXHIBIT 6   285

Figure D   Liquidity / Profits / Capital Ratios (Partial Listing)

REPORT DATE: **FINANCIAL DATA SUMMARY**
PREPARED BY: **BLUE WATER SAILBOATS**
REVIEWED BY: December 31, 1988

TAG DESCRIPTION						Annualized
	1983	1984 % chg.	1985 % chg.	1986 % chg.	1987 % chg.	1988 % chg.
LIQUIDITY / PROFITS / CAPITAL RATIOS						
A/R TURNOVER	– **	7.17 –	7.21 0.56%	7.79 8.04%	6.65 – 14.63%	8.31 24.96%
CURRENT RATIO	1.01	1.23 21.78%	1.66 34.96%	1.92 15.66%	2.23 16.15%	1.90 – 14.80%
GROSS MARGIN %	38.26%	39.12% 2.25%	41.09% 5.04%	41.28% 0.46%	40.67% – 1.48%	43.46% 6.86%
INVENTORY TURNOVER	– **	9.62 –	7.71 – 19.85%	8.40 8.95%	7.15 – 14.88%	7.48 4.62%
LONG TERM DEBT TO EQUITY	26.96%	32.97% 22.29%	32.14% – 2.52%	30.54% – 4.98%	31.16% 2.03%	35.39% 13.58%
NET INCOME TO SALES	2.80%	2.91% 3.93%	3.97% 36.43%	3.96% – 0.25%	1.99% – 49.75%	4.49% 125.63%
QUICK RATIO (ACID TEST)	0.71	0.77 8.45%	1.05 36.36%	1.23 17.14%	1.43 16.26%	1.09 – 23.78%
RETURN ON TOTAL ASSETS	– **	0.12 –	0.18 50.00%	0.19 5.56%	0.08 – 57.89%	0.21 162.50%
RETURN ON EQUITY	– **	0.13 –	0.17 30.77%	0.17 0.00%	0.06 – 64.71%	0.16 166.67%
TOTAL DEBT TO EQUITY	129.59%	122.60% – 5.39%	92.75% – 24.35%	78.17% – 15.72%	69.20% – 11.47%	84.46% 22.05%
WORKING CAPITAL	956.00	35,004.00 3,561.51%	77,272.00 120.75%	106,058.00 37.25%	120,420.00 13.54%	132,527.00 10.05%

**Cannot print - no data available for prior year or incomplete data.

Figure E   —Sample Trend Observations and Comments Report (Partial Report)

REPORT DATE:	FINANCIAL DATA SUMMARY
PREPARED BY:	BLUE WATER SAILBOATS
REVIEWED BY:	December 31, 1988

ACCOUNTS RECEIVABLE / SALES—TREND DECISIONS

Based on the materiality limits specified, the following trends and/or relationships were noted as possibly significant. You should review and evaluate the applicability of each observation and comment.

OBSERVATIONS	COMMENTS
1. ALLOWANCE FOR BAD DEBTS INCREASED WHILE # OF DAYS SALES IN RECEIVABLES INCREASED	Are A/R writeoffs and the allowance account being accounted for consistently from year to year?
	Has the allowance account been reviewed relative to the current receivables accounts? Could the allowance account be excessive, given current and historical collections?
	Review subsequent collections on accounts previously written off to assure that they have been properly recorded.
2. A/R TURNOVER INCREASED	This could represent positive or improved receivables management.
	This could represent possible cutoff problems (i.e., sales recorded but invoices not yet mailed).
	This could reflect improper use of credit memos or unauthorized write-offs.

Since the allowance generally decreases or remains stable as the collectibility of receivables improves, this result is unusual and requires further investigation and/or explanation.

EXHIBIT 6   287

ANALYSIS OF INVENTORY/COST OF SALES

The Inventory/Cost of Sales Report Group can be analyzed through the same set of reports as explained above. For example, the Financial Data Summary Report (Figure D) contains the key ratios, inventory turnover, and inventory to current assets. A review of these ratios might indicate obsolete or unsalable inventory, changes in inventory management policy, errors in pricing, etc. In addition, the Trend Observations and Comments Report for Inventory/Cost of Sales would show which inventory relationships have changed significantly from the prior periods.

Another way to analyze inventory would be to obtain the Simple Projection Report (Figure F) and review this report for significant differences between the actual (reported) amount, and the amount which is projected based upon prior year trends and relationships. The Simple Projection Report is a useful way of finding out whether an account should have changed, rather than to observe the degree of change. The Financial Data Summary Report and the Trend Observations and Comments Report focus on the degree of change present in the reported data. They are useful for detecting large changes in this data. However, these reports are not intended to show cases in which the account balance did not change much, when it *should have changed* significantly. The Simple Projection Report would detect these cases. Notice how the balance of accounts payable is projected to be much smaller than the actual balance. Based upon historical trends, the accounts payable account should have decreased in 1985. In contrast, the balance increased slightly. Note also that the historical trend for inventory has projected a much smaller balance than the actual balance. These differences are an indication of changes in the trend with these data items during the current year. It will be necessary to review these balances further to obtain proper clarification of the unexpected differences.

Figure F   Simple Projection Report for Inventory (Partial
Listing)

REPORT DATE: **SIMPLE PROJECTION REPORT**
PREPARED BY: **BLUE WATER SAILBOATS**
REVIEWED BY: **December 31, 1988**

INVENTORY / COST OF SALES

Current Year balances have been
projected based on the average change from
period to period using all available prior years.

DESCRIPTION	ACTUAL/ ANNUALIZED 1988	PROJECTED 1988	ACTUAL OVER/(UNDER) PROJECTED	% DIFFERENCE
ACCOUNTS PAYABLE	49,544	29,577	19,967	67.50%
BUDGETED SALES	818,182	837,500	− 19,318	− 2.30%
CURRENT ASSETS	279,444	233,312	46,132	19.77%
COST OF SALES	578,833	448,609	130,224	29.02%
INVENTORY	95,774	64,990	30,784	47.36%
SALES	44,774	12,944	31,830	245.90%

Appendix A

Statement on Auditing Standards, Analytical
Procedures (Supercedes Statement on Auditing
Standards No. 23, AICPA, Professional Services, vol. 1, AU
sec. 318.)

STATEMENT ON AUDITING STANDARDS
Analytical Procedures
(Supersedes Statement on Auditing Standards No. 23,
AICPA, Professional Standards, vol. 1, AU sec. 318.)*

1. This Statement provides guidance on the use of analytical procedures and requires the use of analytical procedures in the planning and overall review stages of all audits.

2. Analytical procedures are an important part of the audit process and consist of evaluations of financial information made by a study of plausible relationships among both financial and nonfinancial data. Analytical procedures range from simple comparisons to the use of complex models involving many relationships and elements of data. A basic premise underlying the application of analytical procedures is that plausible relationships among data may reasonably be expected to exist and continue in the absence of known conditions to the contrary. Particular conditions that can cause variations in these relationships include, for example, specific unusual transactions or events, accounting changes, business changes, random fluctuations, or misstatements.

3. Understanding financial relationships is essential in planning and evaluating the results of analytical procedures, and generally requires knowledge of the client and the industry or industries in which the client operates. An understanding of the purposes of analytical procedures and the limitations of those procedures is also important. Accordingly, the identification of the relationships and types of data used, as well as conclusions reached when recorded amounts are compared to expectations, requires judgment by the auditor.

4. Analytical procedures are used for various purposes:

a. To assist the auditor in planning the nature, timing, and extent of other auditing procedures

b. As a substantive test to obtain evidential matter about particular assertions related to account balances or classes of transactions

c. As an overall review of the financial information in the final review stage of the audit

*Copyright © 1988 by American Institute of Certified Public Accountants, Inc. Reprinted with permission.

Analytical procedures should be applied to some extent for the purposes referred to in (a) and (c) above for all audits of financial statements made in accordance with generally accepted auditing standards. In addition, in some cases analytical procedures can be more effective or efficient than tests of details for achieving particular substantive testing objectives.

5. Analytical procedures involve comparisons of recorded amounts, or ratios developed from recorded amounts, to expectations developed by the auditor. The auditor develops such expectations by identifying and using plausible relationships that are reasonably expected to exist based on the auditor's understanding of the client and of the industry in which the client operates. Following are examples of sources of information for developing expectations:

a. Financial information for comparable prior period(s) giving consideration to known changes

b. Anticipated results - for example, budgets or forecasts including extrapolations from interim or annual data

c. Relationships among elements of financial information within the period

d. Information regarding the industry in which the client operates - for example, gross margin information

e. Relationships of financial information with relevant nonfinancial information

Analytical Procedures in Planning the Audit

6. The purpose of applying analytical procedures in planning the audit is to assist in planning the nature, timing, and extent of auditing procedures that will be used to obtain evidential matter for specific account balances or classes of transactions. To accomplish this, the analytical procedures used in planning the audit should focus on (a) enhancing the auditor's understanding of the client's business and the transactions and events that have occurred since the last audit date, and (b) identifying areas that may represent specific risks relevant to the audit. Thus, the objective of the procedures is to identify such things as the existence of unusual transactions and events, and amounts, ratios and trends that might indicate matters that have financial statement and audit planning ramifications.

7. Analytical procedures used in planning the audit generally use data aggregated at a high level. Furthermore, the sophistication, extent and timing of the procedures, which are based on the auditor's judgment, may vary widely depending on the size and complexity of the client. For some entities, the procedures may consist of reviewing changes in account balances from the prior to the current year using the general ledger or the auditor's preliminary or unadjusted working trial balance. In contrast, for other entities, the procedures might involve an extensive analysis of quarterly financial statements. In both cases, the analytical procedures, combined with the auditor's knowledge of the business, serve as a basis for additional inquiries and effective planning.

8. Although analytical procedures used in planning the audit often use only financial data, sometimes relevant nonfinancial information is considered as well. For example, number of employees, square footage of selling space, volume of goods produced, and similar information may contribute to accomplishing the purpose of the procedures.

Analytical Procedures Used as Substantive Tests

9. The auditor's reliance on substantive tests to achieve an audit objective related to a particular assertion[1] may be derived from tests of details, from analytical procedures, or from a combination of both. The decision about which procedure or procedures to use to achieve a particular audit objective is based on the auditor's judgment about the expected effectiveness and efficiency of the available procedures.

10. The auditor considers the level of assurance, if any, he wants from substantive testing for a particular audit objective and decides, among other things, which procedure, or combination of procedures, can provide that level of assurance. For some assertions, analytical procedures are effective in providing the appropriate level of assurance. For other assertions, however, analytical procedures may not be as effective or efficient as tests of details in providing the desired level of assurance.

---

[1] Assertions are representations by management that are embodied in financial statement components. See SAS No. 31, *Evidential Matter* (AICPA *Professional Standards*, vol 1, AU sec. 326).

11.   The expected effectiveness and efficiency of an analytical procedure in identifying potential misstatements depends on, among other things, (a) the nature of the assertion, (b) the plausibility and predictability of the relationship, (c) the availability and reliability of the data used to develop the expectation, and (d) the precision of the expectation.

Nature of Assertion

12.   Analytical procedures may be effective and efficient tests for assertions in which potential misstatements would not be apparent from an examination of the detailed evidence or in which detailed evidence is not readily available. For example, comparisons of aggregate salaries paid with the number of personnel may indicate unauthorized payments that may not be apparent from testing individual transactions. Differences from expected relationships may also indicate potential omissions when independent evidence that an individual transaction should have been recorded may not be readily available.

Plausibility and Predictability of the Relationship

13.   It is important for the auditor to understand the reasons that make relationships plausible because data sometimes appear to be related when they are not, which could lead the auditor to erroneous conclusions. In addition, the presence of an unexpected relationship can provide important evidence when appropriately scrutinized.

14.   As higher levels of assurance are desired from analytical procedures, more predictable relationships are required to develop the expectation. Relationships in a stable environment are usually more predictable than relationships in a dynamic or unstable environment. Relationships involving income statement accounts tend to be more predictable than relationships involving only balance sheet accounts since income statement accounts represent transactions over a period of time, whereas balance sheet accounts represent amounts as of a point in time. Relationships involving transactions subject to management discretion are sometimes less predictable. For example, management may elect to incur maintenance expense rather than replace plant and equipment, or they may delay advertising expenditures.

Availability and Reliability of Data

15.   Data may or may not be readily available to develop expectations for some assertions. For example, to test the completeness assertion, expected sales for some entities might be developed from production statistics or square feet of selling space. For other entities, data relevant to the assertion of completeness of sales may not be readily available, and it may be more effective or efficient to use the details of shipping records to test that assertion.

16.   The auditor obtains assurance from analytical procedures based upon the consistency of the recorded amounts with expectations developed from data derived from other sources. The reliability of the data used to develop the expectations should be appropriate for the desired level of assurance from the analytical procedure. The auditor should assess the reliability of the data by considering the source of the data and the conditions under which it was gathered, as well as other knowledge the auditor may have about the data. The following factors influence the auditor's consideration of the reliability of data for purposes of achieving audit objectives:

- Whether the data was obtained from independent sources outside the entity or from sources within the entity
- Whether sources within the entity were independent of those who are responsible for the amount being audited
- Whether the data was developed under a reliable system with adequate controls
- Whether the data was subjected to audit testing in the current or prior year
- Whether the expectations were developed using data from a variety of sources

Precision of the Expectation

17.   The expectation should be precise enough to provide the desired level of assurance that differences that may be potential material misstatements, individually or when aggregated with other misstatements, would be identified for the auditor to investigate (see paragraph 20). As expectations become more precise, the range of expected differences becomes narrower and, accordingly, the likelihood increases that significant differences from the expectations are due to misstatements. The precision of the expectation depends on, among other things, the auditor's identification and consideration of factors that significantly affect the amount being audited and the level of detail of data used to develop the expectation.

18.   Many factors can influence financial relationships. For example, sales are affected by prices, volume and product mix. Each of these, in turn, may be affected by a number of factors, and offsetting factors can obscure misstatements. More effective identification of factors that significantly affect the relationship is generally needed as the desired level of assurance from analytical procedures increases.

19. Expectations developed at a detailed level generally have a greater chance of detecting misstatement of a given amount than do broad comparisons. Monthly amounts will generally be more effective than annual amounts and comparisons by location or line of business usually will be more effective than company-wide comparisons. The level of detail that is appropriate will be influenced by the nature of the client, its size and its complexity. Generally, the risk that material misstatement could be obscured by offsetting factors increases as a client's operations become more complex and more diversified. Disaggregation helps reduce this risk.

Investigation and Evaluation of Significant Differences

20. In planning the analytical procedures as a substantive test, the auditor should consider the amount of difference from the expectation that can be accepted without further investigation. This consideration is influenced primarily by materiality and should be consistent with the level of assurance desired from the procedures. Determination of this amount involves considering the possibility that a combination of misstatements in the specific account balances or class of transactions or other balances or classes could aggregate to an unacceptable amount.[2]

21. The auditor should evaluate significant unexpected differences. Reconsidering the methods and factors used in developing the expectation and inquiry of management may assist the auditor in this regard. Management responses, however, should ordinarily be corroborated with other evidential matter. In those cases when an explanation for the difference cannot be obtained, the auditor should obtain sufficient evidence about the assertion by performing other audit procedures or he should consider the difference as a likely misstatement[3]. In designing such other procedures, the auditor should consider that unexplained differences may indicate an increased risk of material misstatement. (See SAS No. 53, *The Auditor's Responsibility to Detect and Report Errors and Irregularities* [AICPA, *Professional Standards*, vol. 1, AU sec. 316.)

---

[2] See SAS No. 47, *Audit Risk and Materiality in Conducting an Audit*, paragraphs 17 through 19 (AICPA, *Professional Standards*, vol. 1, AU sec. 312).

[3] See SAS No. 47, paragraph 28.

Analytical Procedures Used in the Overall Review

22.   The objective of analytical procedures used in the overall review stage of the audit is to assist the auditor in assessing the conclusions reached and in the evaluation of the overall financial statement presentation. A wide variety of analytical procedures may be useful for this purpose. The overall review would generally include reading the financial statements and notes and considering (a) the adequacy of evidence gathered in response to unusual or unexpected balances identified in planning the audit or in the course of the audit and (b) unusual or unexpected balances or relationships that were not previously identified. Results of an overall review may indicate that additional evidence may be needed.

Effective Date

23.   This Statement is effective for audits of financial statements for periods beginning on or after January 1, 1989. Early application of the provisions of this Statement is permissible.

Appendix B

Selected Paragraphs from SSARS No 1, "Compilation and Review of Financial Statements"*

Review of Financial Statements

.24 The accountant should possess a level of knowledge of the accounting principles and practices of the industry in which the entity operates and an understanding of the entity's business that will provide him, through the performance of inquiry and analytical procedures, with a reasonable basis for expressing limited assurance that there are no material modifications that should be made to the financial statements in order for the statements to be in conformity with generally accepted accounting principles. (. . ., reference to generally accepted accounting principles in this statement includes, where applicable, another comprehensive basis of accounting.)

.25 The requirement that the accountant possess a level of knowledge of the accounting principles and practices of the industry in which the entity operates does not prevent an accountant from accepting a review engagement for an entity in an industry with which the accountant has no previous experience. It does, however, place upon the accountant a responsibility to obtain the required level of knowledge. He may do so, for example, by consulting AICPA guides, industry publications, financial statements of other entities in the industry, textbooks and periodicals, or individuals knowledgeable about the industry.

*Copyright © 1978 by American Institute of Certified Public Accountants, Inc. Reprinted with permission.

.26   The accountant's understanding of the entity's business should include a general understanding of the entity's organization, its operating characteristics, and the nature of its assets, liabilities, revenues, and expenses. This would ordinarily involve a general knowledge of the entity's production, distribution, and compensation methods, types of products and services, operating locations, and material transactions with related parties. An accountant's understanding of an entity's business is ordinarily obtained through experience with the entity or its industry and inquiry of the entity's personnel.

.27   The accountant's inquiry and analytical procedures should ordinarily consist of the following:

a.   Inquiries concerning the entity's accounting principles and practices and the methods followed in applying them.
b.   Inquiries concerning the entity's procedures for recording, classifying, and summarizing transactions, and accumulating information for disclosure in the financial statements.
c.   Analytical procedures designed to identify relationships and individual items that appear to be unusual. For the purposes of this statement, analytical procedures consist of (1) comparison of the financial statements with statements for comparable prior period(s), (2) comparison of the financial statements with anticipated results, if available (for example, budgets and forecasts), and (3) study of the relationships of the elements of the financial statements that would be expected to conform to a predictable pattern based on the entity's experience. In applying these procedures, the accountant should consider the types of matters that required accounting adjustments in preceding periods. Examples of relationships of elements in financial statements that would be expected to conform to a predictable pattern may be the relationships between changes in sales and changes in accounts receivable and expense accounts that ordinarily fluctuate with sales, and between changes in property, plant, and equipment and changes in depreciation expense and other accounts that may be affected, such as maintenance and repairs.
d.   Inquiries concerning actions taken at meetings of stockholders, board of directors, committees of the board of directors, or comparable meetings that may affect the financial statements.
e.   Reading the financial statements to consider, on the basis of information coming to the accountant's attention, whether the financial statements appear to conform with generally accepted accounting principles.
f.   Obtaining reports from other accountants, if any, who have been

engaged to audit or review the financial statements of significant components of the reporting entity, its subsidiaries, and other investees.
g. Inquiries of persons having responsibility for financial and accounting matters concerning (1) whether the financial statements have been prepared in conformity with generally accepted accounting principles consistently applied, (2) changes in the entity's business activities or accounting principles and practices, (3) matters as to which questions have arisen in the course of applying the foregoing procedures, and (4) events subsequent to the date of the financial statements that would have a material effect on the financial statements.

.28 Knowledge acquired in the performance of audits of the entity's financial statements, compilation of the financial statements, or other accounting services may result in modification of the review procedures described in the preceding paragraph. However, such modification would not reduce the degree of responsibility the accountant assumes with respect to the financial statements he has reviewed.

.29 A review does not contemplate a study and evaluation of internal accounting control, tests of accounting records and of responses to inquiries by obtaining corroborating evidential matter, and certain other procedures ordinarily performed during an audit. Thus, a review does not provide assurance that the accountant will become aware of all significant matters that would be disclosed in an audit. However, if the accountant becomes aware that information coming to his attention is incorrect, incomplete or otherwise unsatisfactory, he should perform the additional procedures he deems necessary to achieve limited assurance that there are no material modifications that should be made to the financial statements in order for the statements to be in conformity with generally accepted principles.

.30 Although it is not possible to specify the form or content of the working papers that an accountant should prepare in connection with a review of financial statements because of the different circumstances of individual engagements, the accountant's working papers should describe:

a. The matters covered in the accountant's inquiry and analytical procedures.
b. Unusual matters that the accountant considered during the performance of the review, including their disposition.

Appendix C

Selected Paragraphs from Statements on Auditing Standards No 36, Review of Interim Financial Statements*

Objective of a Review of Interim Financial Information

.03 The objective of a review of interim financial information is to provide the accountant, based on objectively applying his knowledge of financial reporting practices to significant accounting matters of which he becomes aware through inquiries and analytical review procedures, with a basis for reporting whether material modifications should be made for such information to conform with generally accepted accounting principles. The objective of a review of interim financial information differs significantly from the objective of an examination of financial statements in accordance with generally accepted auditing standards. The objective of an audit is to provide a reasonable basis for expressing an opinion regarding the financial statements taken as a whole. A review of interim financial information does not provide a basis for the expression of such an opinion, because the review does not contemplate a study and evaluation of internal accounting control: tests of accounting records and of responses to inquiries by obtaining corroborating evidential matter through inspection, observation, or confirmation; and certain other procedures ordinarily performed during an audit. A review may bring to the accountant's attention significant matters affecting the interim financial

*Copyright © 1981 by American Institute of Certified Public Accountants, Inc. Reprinted with permission.

information, but it does not provide assurance that the accountant will become aware of all significant matters that would be disclosed in an audit.

Procedures for a Review of Interim Financial Information

.04 The characteristics of interim financial information necessarily affect the nature, timing, and extent of procedures that the accountant may apply in making a review of that information. Timeliness is an important element of interim financial reporting. Interim financial information customarily is made available to investors and others more promptly than is annual financial information. Timely reporting of interim financial information ordinarily precludes the development of information and documentation underlying interim financial information to the same extent as that underlying annual financial information. Therefore, a characteristic of interim financial information is that many costs and expenses are estimated to a greater extent than for annual financial reporting purposes. Another characteristic of interim financial information is its relationship to annual financial reporting purposes. Deferrals, accruals, and estimates at the end of each interim period are affected by judgments made at interim dates concerning anticipated results of operations for the remainder of the annual period.

.05 The procedures for a review of interim financial information are described in the following paragraphs concerning the (a) nature of procedures (paragraph **.06**), (b) timing of procedures (paragraph **.07**), and (c) extent of procedures (paragraphs **.08** through **.15**).

Nature of Procedures

.06 Procedures for making a review of interim financial information consist primarily of inquiries and analytical review procedures concerning significant accounting matters relating to the financial information to be reported. The procedures that the accountant ordinarily should apply are:

a. Inquiry concerning (1) the accounting system, to obtain an understanding of the manner in which transactions are recorded, classified, and summarized in the preparation of interim financial information, and (2) any significant changes in the system of internal accounting control, to ascertain their potential effect on the preparation of interim financial information.

b.   Application of analytical review procedures to interim financial information to identify and provide a basis for inquiry about relationships and individual items that appear to be unusual. Analytical review procedures, for purposes of this section, consist of (1) comparison of the financial information with comparable information for the immediately preceding interim period and for corresponding previous period(s), (2) comparison of the financial information with anticipated results, and (3) study of the relationships of elements of financial information that would be expected to conform to a predictable pattern based on the entity's experience. In applying these procedures, the accountant should consider the types of matters that in the preceding year or quarters have required accounting adjustments.

c.   Reading the minutes of meetings of stockholders, board of directors, and committees of the board of directors to identify actions that may affect the interim financial information.

d.   Reading the interim financial information to consider, on the basis of information coming to the accountant's attention, whether the information to be reported conforms with generally accepted accounting principles.

e.   Obtaining reports from other accountants, if any, who have been engaged to make a review of the interim financial information of significant components of the reporting entity, its subsidiaries, or other investees.

f.   Inquiry of officers and other executives having responsibility for financial and accounting matters concerning (1) whether the interim financial information has been prepared in conformity with generally accepted accounting principles consistently applied, (2) changes in the entity's business activities or accounting practices, (3) matters as to which questions have arisen in the course of applying the foregoing procedures, and (4) events subsequent to the date of the interim financial information that would have a material effect on the presentation of such information.

g.   Obtaining written representations from management concerning its responsibility for the financial information, completeness of minutes, subsequent events, and other matters for which the accountant believes written representations are appropriate in the circumstances.

Timing of Procedures

.07   Adequate planning by the accountant is essential to the timely completion of a review of interim financial information. Performance of some of the work before the end of the interim period may permit the work to be carried out in a more efficient manner and to be completed at an earlier date. Performing some of the work earlier in the interim period also permits early consideration of significant accounting matters affecting the interim financial information.

Extent of Procedures

.08   The extent to which the procedures referred to in paragraph .06 are applied depends on the considerations described in paragraphs .09 through .15.

The Accountant's Knowledge of Accounting and Reporting Practices

.09   Knowledge of a client's accounting and financial reporting practices is an important factor in the performance of a review of interim financial information. An understanding of a client's practices in preparing its most recent annual financial statements provides a practical basis for the inquiry and other procedures of a review. Such an understanding can be expected to have been acquired by the accountant who has audited a client's financial statements for one or more annual periods.

The Accountant's Knowledge of Weaknesses in Internal Accounting Control

.10   An accountant who has previously made an audit of his client's financial statements will have acquired knowledge concerning his client's system of internal accounting control relating to the preparation of financial statements, generally for an annual period. In these circumstances, the primary objective of the accountant's inquiries should be to identify and consider the effect of (a) changes in the system subsequent to his examination and (b) accounting control procedures used in the preparation of interim financial information that differ from those used in the preparation of annual financial statements. If the system of internal accounting control appears to contain weaknesses that do not permit preparation of interim financial information in conformity with generally accepted accounting principles, and, as a consequence, it is impracticable for the accountant to effectively apply his knowledge of financial reporting practices to the interim financial information, he should consider whether the weaknesses represent a restriction on the scope of his engagement sufficient to preclude completion of such a review. The accountant should also advise senior management and the board of directors or its audit committee of the circumstances; he may also wish to submit suggestions regarding other weaknesses in the system of internal accounting control, recommendations for improvement of interim reporting practices, and any other matters of significance that come to his attention.

The Accountant's Knowledge of Changes in Nature or Volume of Activity or Accounting Changes

.11   A review of interim financial information may bring to the accountant's attention changes in the nature or volume of the client's business activities or accounting changes. Examples of changes that could affect the interim financial information to be reported include business combinations: disposal of a segment of the business; extraordinary, unusual, or infrequently occurring transactions; initiation of litigation or the development of other contingencies; trends in sales or costs that could affect accounting estimates relating to the valuations of receivables and inventories, realization of deferred charges, provisions for warranties and employee benefits, and unearned income; and changes in accounting principles or in the methods of applying them. If any such changes come to the accountant's attention, he should inquire about the manner in which the changes and their effects are to be reported in the interim financial information.

Issuance of Accounting Pronouncements

.12   The accountant's knowledge of financial reporting practices is expected to include an awareness of new pronouncements on financial accounting standards. In performing a review of interim financial information he should consider the applicability of any such new pronouncements to his client's interim financial reporting practices. The accountant should also consider the applicability of existing pronouncements to new types of transactions or events that come to his attention.

Accounting Records Maintained at Multiple Locations

.13   In performing a review of interim financial information, considerations concerning locations to be visited for a client whose general accounting records are maintained at multiple locations ordinarily are similar to those involved in making an examination of the client's financial statements in accordance with generally accepted auditing standards. Usually this involves application of the foregoing procedures at both corporate headquarters and other locations selected by the accountant.

Questions Raised in Performing Other Procedures

.14   If, in performing a review of interim financial information, information comes to the accountant's attention that leads him to question whether the interim financial information to be reported conforms with generally accepted accounting principles, he should make additional inquiries or employ other procedures he considers appropriate to permit him to report on the interim financial information.

Modification of Review Procedures

.15   The procedures for a review of interim financial information may be modified, as appropriate, to take into consideration the results of auditing procedures applied in performing an examination in accordance with generally accepted auditing standards.

Appendix D

Statement on Auditing Standards, The Auditor's Consideration of an Entity's Ability to Continue as a Going Concern (Supercedes Statement on Auditing Standards No. 34, AICPA, Professional Standards, Vol. 1, AU sec. 340.)

THE AUDITOR'S CONSIDERATION OF AN ENTITY'S ABILITY TO CONTINUE AS A GOING CONCERN
(Supersedes Statement on Auditing Standards No. 34, AICPA, Professional Standards, Vol. 1, AU sec. 340.)*

1. This Statement provides guidance to the auditor in conducting an audit of financial statements in accordance with generally accepted auditing standards with respect to evaluating whether there is substantial doubt about the entity's ability to continue as a going concern.[1],[2] Continuation of an entity as a going concern is assumed in financial reporting in the absence of significant information to the contrary. When an entity has the ability to continue in operations and meet its obligations, only through substantial disposal of assets outside the ordinary course of business, or the forbearance of creditors, such circumstances should raise doubts about whether the entity is a going concern. Ordinarily, information that significantly contradicts the going concern assumption relates to the entity's inability to continue to meet its obligations as they become due without substantial disposition of assets, restructuring debt, externally forced revisions of its operations, or similar actions.

The Auditor's Responsibility

2. The auditor has a responsibility to evaluate whether there is substantial doubt about the entity's ability to continue as a going concern

---

*Copyright © 1988 by American Institute of Certified Public Accountants, Inc. Reprinted with permission.

[1] This Statement does not apply to an audit of financial statements based on the assumption of liquidation (for example, when (a) an entity is in the process of liquidation, (b) the owners have decided to commence dissolution or liquidation, or (c) legal proceedings, including bankruptcy, have reached a point at which dissolution or liquidation is probable). See Auditing Interpretation, *Reporting on Financial Statements Prepared on a Liquidation Basis of Accounting,* (AICPA *Professional Standards,* vol. 1, AU sec. 9509.33.38)

[2] The guidance provided in this Statement applies to audits of financial statements prepared either in accordance with generally accepted accounting principles or in accordance with a comprehensive basis of accounting other than generally accepted accounting principles. References in this Statement to generally accepted accounting principles are intended to include a comprehensive basis of accounting other than generally accepted accounting principles (excluding liquidation basis).

for a reasonable period of time, not to exceed one year beyond the date of the financial statements being audited (hereinafter referred to as "a reasonable period of time"). The auditor's evaluation is based on his knowledge of relevant conditions and events that exist at or have occurred prior to the completion of field work. Information about such conditions or events is obtained from the application of auditing procedures planned and performed to achieve audit objectives that are related to management's assertions embodied in the financial statements being audited, as described in SAS No.31, *Evidential Matter* (AICPA, *Professional Standards,* vol.1, AU sec. 326).

3.   The auditor should evaluate whether there is substantial doubt about the entity's ability to continue as a going concern for a reasonable period of time in the following manner:

a.   The auditor considers whether the results of his procedures performed in planning, gathering evidence relative to the various audit objectives, and completing the audit identify conditions and events that, when considered in the aggregate, indicate there could be substantial doubt about the entity's ability to continue as a going concern for a reasonable period of time. In making that consideration, it may be necessary to obtain additional information about such conditions and events, and to obtain appropriate evidence to support information that mitigates the auditor's doubt.

b.   If the auditor believes there is substantial doubt about the entity's ability to continue as a going concern for a reasonable period of time, he should (1) obtain information about management's plans that are intended to mitigate the effect of such conditions or events, and (2) assess the likelihood that such plans can be effectively implemented.

c.   After the auditor has evaluated management's plans, he concludes whether he has substantial doubt about the entity's ability to continue as a going concern for a reasonable period of time. If the auditor concludes there is substantial doubt, he should (1) consider the adequacy of disclosure about the entity's possible inability to continue as a going concern for a reasonable period of time, and (2) include an explanatory paragraph (following the opinion paragraph) in his audit report to reflect his conclusion. If the auditor concludes that substantial doubt does not exist, he should consider the need for disclosure.

4. The auditor is not responsible for predicting future conditions or events. The fact that the entity may cease to exist as a going concern subsequent to receiving a report from the auditor that does not refer to substantial doubt, even within one year following the date of the financial statements, does not, in itself, indicate inadequate performance by the auditor. Accordingly, the absence of reference to substantial doubt in an auditor's report should not be viewed as providing assurance as to an entity's ability to continue as a going concern.

Audit Procedures

5. It is not necessary to design audit procedures solely to identify conditions and events that, when considered in the aggregate, indicate there could be substantial doubt about the entity's ability to continue as a going concern for a reasonable period of time. The results of auditing procedures designed and performed to achieve other audit objectives should be sufficient for that purpose. The following are examples of procedures that may identify such conditions and events:

- Analytical procedures
- Review of subsequent events
- Review of compliance with the terms of debt and loan agreements
- Reading of minutes of meetings of stockholders, board of directors, and important committees of the board
- Inquiry of an entity's legal counsel about litigation, claims, and assessments
- Confirmation with related and third parties of the details of arrangements to provide or maintain financial support

Consideration of Conditions and Events

6. In performing audit procedures such as those presented in paragraph 5, the auditor may identify information about certain conditions or events that, when considered in the aggregate, indicate there could be substantial doubt about the entity's ability to continue as a going concern for a reasonable period of time. The significance of such conditions and events will depend on the circumstances, and some may have significance only when viewed in conjunction with others. The following are examples of such conditions and events.

- *Negative trends* - for example, recurring operating losses, working capital deficiencies, negative cash flows from operating activities, adverse key financial ratios

- *Other indications of possible financial difficulties* - for example, default on loan or similar agreements, arrearages in dividends, denial of usual trade credit from suppliers, restructuring of debt, noncompliance with statutory capital requirements, need to seek new sources or methods of financing or to dispose of substantial assets
- *Internal matters* - for example, work stoppages or other labor difficulties, substantial dependence on the success of a particular project, uneconomic long-term commitments, need to significantly revise operations
- *External matters that have occurred* - for example, legal proceedings, legislation, or similar matters that might jeopardize an entity's ability to operate; loss of a key franchise, license, or patent; loss of a principal customer or supplier; uninsured or underinsured catastrophe such as a drought, earthquake, or flood

Appendix E

Statement on Auditing Standards, Auditing
Accounting Estimates

Auditing Accounting Estimates*

1. This Statement provides guidance to auditors on obtaining and evaluating sufficient competent evidential matter to support significant accounting estimates in an audit of financial statements in accordance with generally accepted auditing standards. For purposes of this Statement, an accounting estimate is an approximation of a financial statement element, item, or account. Accounting estimates are often included in historical financial statements because -

    a.   The measurement of some amounts or the valuation of some accounts is uncertain pending the outcome of future events.

    b.   Relevant data concerning events that have already occurred cannot be accumulated on a timely, cost-effective basis.

2. Accounting estimates in historical financial statements measure the effects of past business transactions or events or the present status of an asset or liability. Examples of accounting estimates include net realizable values of inventory and accounts receivable, property and casualty insurance loss reserves, revenues from contracts accounted for by the percentage-of-completion method, and pension and warranty expenses.[1]

3. Management is responsible for making the accounting estimates included in the financial statements. Estimates are based on subjective as well as objective factors and, as a result, judgment is required to estimate an amount at the date of the financial statements. Management's judgment is normally based on its knowledge and experience about past and current events and its assumptions about conditions it expects to exist and courses of action it expects to take.

4. The auditor is responsible for evaluating the reasonableness of accounting estimates made by management in the context of the financial statements taken as a whole. As estimates are based on subjective as well as objective factors, it may be difficult for management to establish controls over them. Even when management's estimation process involves competent personnel using relevant and reliable data, there is potential for bias in the subjective factors. Accordingly, when plan-

---

*Copyright © 1988 by American Institute of Certified Public Accountants, Inc. Reprinted with permission.

   [1] Additional examples of accounting estimates included in historical financial statements are presented in the Appendix.

ning and performing procedures to evaluate accounting estimates, the auditor should consider, with an attitude of professional skepticism, both the subjective and objective factors.

Developing Accounting Estimates

5. Management is responsible for establishing a process for preparing accounting estimates. Although the process may not be documented or formally applied, it normally consists of -

a. Identifying situations for which accounting estimates are required.

b. Identifying the relevant factors that may affect the accounting estimate.

c. Accumulating relevant, sufficient, and reliable data on which to base the estimate.

d. Developing assumptions that represent management's judgment of the most likely circumstances and events with respect to the relevant factors.

e. Determining the estimated amount based on the assumptions and other relevant factors.

f. Determining that the accounting estimate is presented in conformity with applicable accounting principles and that disclosure is adequate.

The risk of material misstatement of accounting estimates normally varies with the complexity and subjectivity associated with the process, the availability and reliability of relevant data, the number and significance of assumptions that are made, and the degree of uncertainty associated with the assumptions.

Internal Control Structure Related to Accounting Estimates

6. An entity's internal control structure may reduce the likelihood of material misstatements of accounting estimates. Specific relevant aspects of that structure include the following:

a. Management communication of the need for proper accounting estimates

b. Accumulation of relevant, sufficient, and reliable data on which to base an accounting estimate

c. Preparation of the accounting estimate by qualified personnel

d.   Adequate review and approval of the accounting estimates by appropriate levels of authority including-

   1.   Review of sources of relevant factors

   2.   Review of development of assumptions

   3.   Review of reasonableness of assumptions and resulting estimates

   4.   Consideration of the need to use the work of specialists

   5.   Consideration of changes in previously established methods to arrive at accounting estimates

e.   Comparison of prior accounting estimates with subsequent results to assess the reliability of the process used to develop estimates

f.   Consideration by management of whether the resulting accounting estimate is consistent with the operational plans of the entity

Evaluating Accounting Estimates

7.   The auditor's objective when evaluating accounting estimates is to obtain sufficient competent evidential matter to provide reasonable assurance that -

a.   All accounting estimates that could be material to the financial statements have been developed.

b.   Those accounting estimates are reasonable in the circumstances.

c.   The accounting estimates are presented in conformity with applicable accounting principles[2] and are properly disclosed.[3]

Identifying Circumstances That Require Accounting Estimates

8.   In evaluating whether management has identified all accounting estimates that could be material to the financial statements, the auditor

---

[2] SAS No. 5, *The Meaning of "Present Fairly in Conformity With Generally Accepted Accounting Principles" in the Independent Auditor's Report* (AICPA, *Professional Standards*, vol. 1, AU section 411), discusses the auditor's responsibility for evaluating conformity with generally accepted accounting principles.

[3] SAS No. 32, *Adequacy of Disclosure in Financial Statements* (AICPA, *Professional Standards*, vol. 1, AU section 431), discusses the auditor's responsibility to consider whether the financial statements include adequate disclosures of material matters in light of the circumstances and facts of which he is aware.

considers the circumstances of the industry or industries in which the entity operates, its methods of conducting business, new accounting pronouncements, and other external factors. The auditor should consider performing the following procedures:

a. Consider assertions embodied in the financial statements to determine the need for estimates. (See the Appendix for examples of accounting estimates included in financial statements.)

b. Evaluate information obtained in performing other procedures, such as -

 (1) Information about changes made or planned in the entity's business, including changes in operating strategy, and the industry in which the entity operates that may indicate the need to make an accounting estimate. (SAS No. 22, *Planning and Supervision* (AICPA, *Professional Standards*, vol. 1, AU section 311).)

 (2) Changes in the methods of accumulating information.

 (3) Information concerning identified litigation, claims, and assessments (SAS No. 12, *Inquiry of a Client's Lawyer Concerning Litigation, Claims, and Assessments* (AICPA, *Professional Standards*, vol. 1, AU section 337)), and other contingencies.

 (4) Information from reading available minutes of meetings of stockholders, directors, and appropriate committees.

 (5) Information contained in regulatory or examination reports, supervisory correspondence, and similar materials from applicable regulatory agencies.

c. Inquire of management about the existence of circumstances that may indicate the need to make an accounting estimate.

Evaluating Reasonableness

9. In evaluating the reasonableness of an estimate, the auditor normally concentrates on key factors and assumptions that are -

a. Significant to the accounting estimate.

b. Sensitive to variations.

c. Deviations from historical patterns.

d. Subjective and susceptible to misstatement and bias.

The auditor normally should consider the historical experience of the entity in making past estimates as well as the auditor's experience in the industry. However, changes in facts, circumstances, or client procedures may cause factors different from those considered in the past to become significant to the accounting estimate.[4]

10. In evaluating reasonableness, the auditor should obtain an understanding of how management developed the estimate. Based on that understanding, the auditor should use one or a combination of the following approaches:

a. Review and test the process used by management to develop the estimate.

b. Develop an independent expectation of the estimate to corroborate the reasonableness of management's estimate.

c. Review subsequent events or transactions occurring prior to completion of fieldwork.

11. *Review and test management's process.* In many situations, the auditor assesses the reasonableness of an accounting estimate by performing procedures to test the process used by management to make the estimate. The following are procedures the auditor may consider performing when using this approach:

a. Identify whether there are controls over the preparation of accounting estimates and supporting data that may be useful in the evaluation.

b. Identify the sources of data and factors that management used in forming the assumptions and consider whether such data and factors are relevant, reliable, and sufficient for the purpose based on information gathered in other audit tests.

c. Consider whether there are additional key factors or alternative assumptions about the factors.

d. Evaluate whether the assumptions are consistent with each other, the supporting data, relevant historical data, and industry data.

e. Analyze historical data used in developing the assumptions to assess whether the data is comparable and consistent with data of the period under audit, and consider whether such data is sufficiently reliable for the purpose.

---

[4] In addition to other evidential matter about the estimate, in certain instances, the auditor may wish to obtain written representation from management regarding the key factors and assumptions.

f. Consider whether changes in the business or industry may cause other factors to become significant to the assumptions.

g. Review available documentation of the assumptions used in developing the accounting estimates and inquire about any other plans, goals, and objectives of the entity, as well as consider their relationship to the assumptions.

h. Consider using the work of a specialist regarding certain assumptions (SAS No. 11, *Using the Work of a Specialist* [AICPA, *Professional Standards*, vol. 1, AU section 336]).

i. Test the calculations used by management to translate the assumptions and key factors into the accounting estimate.

12. *Develop an expectation.* Based on the auditor's understanding of the facts and circumstances, he may independently develop an expectation as to the estimate by using other key factors or alternative assumptions about those factors.

13. *Review subsequent events or transactions.* Events or transactions sometimes occur subsequent to the date of the balance sheet, but prior to the completion of fieldwork, that are important in identifying and evaluating the reasonableness of accounting estimates or key factors or assumptions used in the preparation of the estimate. In such circumstances, an evaluation of the estimate or of a key factor or assumption may be minimized or unnecessary as the event or transaction can be used by the auditor in evaluating their reasonableness.

14. As discussed in SAS No. 47, *Audit Risk and Materiality in Conducting an Audit*, paragraph 29 (AICPA, *Professional Standards*, vol. 1, AU section 312.29), the auditor evaluates the reasonableness of accounting estimates in relationship to the financial statements taken as a whole:

> Since no one accounting estimate can be considered accurate with certainty, the auditor recognizes that a difference between an estimated amount best supported by the audit evidence and the estimated amount included in the financial statements may be reasonable, and such difference would not be considered to be a likely error. However, if the auditor believes the estimated amount included in the financial statements is unreasonable, he should treat the difference between that estimate and the closest reasonable estimate as a likely error and aggregate it with other likely errors. The auditor should also consider whether the difference between estimates best supported by the audit evidence and

the estimates included in the financial statements, which are individually reasonable, indicate a possible bias on the part of the entity's management. For example, if each accounting estimate included in the financial statements was individually reasonable, but the effect of the difference between each estimate and the estimate best supported by the audit evidence was to increase income, the auditor should reconsider the estimates taken as a whole.

Effective Date

15. This Statement is effective for audits of financial statements for periods beginning on or after January 1, 1989. Early application of the provisions of this Statement is permissible.

Auditing Standards Board (1986-1987)

JERRY D. SULLIVAN, Chairman
BARRY BARBER
JOHN F. BARNA
THOMAS P. BINTINGER
JAMES L. BROWN
PATRICK S. CALLAHAN
JAMES CLANCY
JOHN C. COMPTON
PHILLIP W. CRAWFORD
DONALD B. DODSON
JOHN E. ELLINGSEN
BARBARA HUTSON GONZALES

SAMUEL P. GUNTHER
RICHARD D. JOHNSON
CONRAD A. KAPPEL
JAMES K. LOEBBECKE
HAROLD L. MONK, JR.
DONALD L. NEEBES
ROBERT S. ROUSSEY
ROBERT H. TEMKIN
ERNEST L. TEN EYCK

DAN M. GUY
Vice President, Auditing
MARK S. BEASLEY
Practice Fellow, Auditing
Standards

Note: Statements on Auditing Standards are issued by the Auditing Standards Board, the senior technical body of the Institute designated to issue pronouncements on auditing matters. Rule 202 of the Institute's Code of Professional Conduct requires compliance with these standards.

Appendix

Examples of Accounting Estimates

The following are examples of accounting estimates that are included in financial statements. The list is presented for information only. It should not be considered all-inclusive.

Receivables:
Uncollectible
receivables
Allowance for loan
losses
Uncollectible
pledges

Inventories:
Obsolete
inventory
Net realizable
value of
inventories
where future
selling prices
and future costs
are involved
Losses on
purchase
commitments

Financial instruments:
Valuation of
securities
Trading versus
investment
security
classification
Probability of high
correlation of a
hedge
Sales of securities
with puts and
calls

Productive facilities, natural resources and intangibles:
Useful lives and
residual values
Depreciation and
amortization
methods
Recoverability of
costs
Recoverable
reserves

Accruals:
Property and
casualty
insurance
company loss
reserves
Compensation in
stock option
plans and
deferred plans
Warranty claims
Taxes on real and
personal
property
Renegotiation
refunds
Actuarial
assumptions in
pension costs

Revenues:
Airline passenger
revenue
Subscription
income
Freight and cargo
revenue
Dues income
Losses on sales
contracts

Contracts:
Revenue to be earned
Costs to be incurred
Percent of completion

Leases:
Initial direct costs
Executory costs
Residual values

Litigation:
Probability of loss
Amount of loss

Rates:
Annual effective
tax rate in
interim
reporting
Imputed interest
rates on
receivables and
payables
Gross profit rates
under program
method of
accounting

Other:
Losses and net
realizable value
on disposal of
segment or
restructuring of
a business
Fair values in
nonmonetary
exchanges
Interim period
costs in interim
reporting
Current values in
personal
financial
statements

Appendix F

Regression Analysis in Analytical Procedures

The objective of this appendix is to present a brief, nontechnical reference for auditors who are using regression analysis. Also, the auditor can study this material to obtain a better understanding of the benefits, limitations, and assumptions which are involved. There are a number of good references for a more complete, technical presentation, for example, J. Johnson, *Econometric Methods*, 2d ed., McGraw-Hill, New York, 1972. A good illustration of the use of regression analysis in auditing is presented in Alex W. Kask, "Regression and Correlation Analysis," *CPA Journal*, October 1979, pp. 35-41.

How Regression Works

Simple regression analysis is a statistical method for finding the best-fitting line for an equation of the form $y = a + bx + E$ through a given set of data points. The variable y is called the dependent variable, x is the independent variable, b is the coefficient of the independent variable, a is the intercept, and E is the error term.

We now show how regression works in a simple illustration involving only three data points in which direct labor hours (x) is used to predict maintenance expense (y). We use only three data points for simplicity. Usually a regression will require 10 or more points to have satisfactory reliability, as we will see in the following section.

Maintenance Expense (y)	Direct Labor Hours (x)
$ 8.00	10
12.00	20
13.00	30

Regression analysis finds the unique straight line which minimizes the sum of the squared "errors," where an error is the difference between the actual value for the dependent variable and the predicted value from the regression model. This is shown in Figure AF-1, which plots the above data and shows the regression line which is derived from these data. The distances marked E in the figure are the error terms which, when squared, are minimized through the analysis to determine the best-fitting line. Note that the line cannot be shifted in any manner without increasing the sum of the squared errors. For this reason, the regression line is sometimes called the "least squares" regression line.

The distances indicated by T and M in the figure refer, respectively, to the "total" distance to be explained, and to the portion of the total distance which is explained by the model. In statistical language, the sum of E^2 is called the "error sum of squares," the sum of M^2 is called the "model sum of squares," and the sum of T^2 is referred to as the "total sum of squares." By construction, and as is apparent in Figure AF-1, the sum of M^2 + the sum of E^2 = the sum of T^2.

The three components of the "sum of squares" identified above are important in regression analysis. They form the basis for determining the measures of precision and reliability for the regression model. Here, we are using these terms in a sense which is familiar to auditors. *Precision* refers to the width of the interval around an estimate within which the auditor can be confident the unknown true value will be. *Reliability* refers to the probability that the regression equation is not a quirk or accident, that is, the relationship between the dependent and independent variable or variables which is reflected in the equation exists in the real world.

Figure AF-1   Illustration of hypothetical regression model to predict maintenance expense.

Key to figure: asterisked coordinates (*) = actual values; circled coordinates = predicted values (on regression line); T = "total" distance = | actual value − mean |; E = "error" distance = | predicted value − actual value |; M = proportion of the distance "explained" by the model = | predicted value − mean |.

Table AF-1   Analysis of Variance Table for Data in Figure AF-1

Source of Sum of Squares	Sum of Squares	Degrees of Freedom	Mean Square	F
Model (M)	$12.5 = (2.5)^2 + (0)^2 + (2.5)^2$	1*	$12.5 = \dfrac{12.5}{1}$	$8.33 = \dfrac{12.5}{1.5}$
Error (E)	$1.5 = (.5)^2 + (1)^2 + (.5)$	1†	$1.5 = \dfrac{1.5}{1}$	
Total (T)	14.0	2‡		

$$R^2 = \frac{12.5}{14.0} = .893$$

$$SE = \sqrt{1.5} = 1.225$$

*Model degrees of freedom equal the number of independent variables, in this case 1.
†Error degrees of freedom are equal to total degrees of freedom minus model degrees of freedom.
‡Total degrees of freedom equal the number of data points minus 1, in this case, $3 - 1 = 2$.

Measures of Precision and Reliability

In this section we describe six of the most important statistical measures provided by regression analysis:

1. R^2, the coefficient of determination
2. F, the F value
3. SE, the standard error of the estimate
4. SE_c, the standard error of the coefficient for the independent variable
5. t, the t value
6. DW, the Durbin-Watson statistic

Regression analysis is often accompanied by additional statistics, but the six measures above capture the most significant aspects of precision and reliability.

In order to explain these measures, we find the concept of the M, E, and T sum of squares to be useful. Reconsider the example in Figure AF-1. We compute the three components of the sum of squares and summarize the results in what is called an "analysis of variance table," as is shown in Table AF-1. This is a common format in which computer programs for regression present the output of the analysis.

The first column of Table AF-1 indicates the type of sum of squares. Any regression model, no matter how many data points or independent variables it has, will have the same three elements. Next, the sum of squares is computed as shown, based on the "distances" observed in Figure AF-1. The next column shows the "degrees of freedom," which represent the number of potential independent choices that can be made. The model degrees of freedom are always equal to the number of independent variables, in this case 1. The total degrees of freedom are always equal to the number of data points minus 1, in this case 2. And, the error degrees of freedom are the residual, the total degrees of freedom less the model degrees of freedom.

The next column, mean square, is simply the ratio of the sum of squares to the degrees of freedom. And in the final column, the F value is the ratio of the mean square term for the model to the mean square error.

Now we are ready to see whence our six measures are derived and how they are interpreted. The first two, R^2 and F, address the reliability question.

$$R^2 = \frac{\text{sum of squares (model)}}{\text{sum of squares (total)}} = \frac{12.5}{14} = 0.893$$

R^2 is a direct measure of the explanatory power of the regression equation. In a sense, the regression "captures" or "explains" the variability in the dependent variable. If a change in the dependent variable can be explained or associated with a corresponding change in the independent variable by means of the regression line, then both the model sum of squares and R^2 should be relatively high. Values for R^2 range from 0 to 1; the closer R^2 is to 1, the better is the regression's explanatory power.

$$F = \frac{\text{mean square (model)}}{\text{mean square (error)}} = \frac{12.5}{1.5} = 8.33$$

The F value is a measure of the statistical validity of the model. Statistical validity can be interpreted as follows. Does the relationship between variables depicted in the model really exist? Or, is the regression result an artifact of a chance pattern to the data, in which R^2 is really near zero? A large F value gives comfort that such is not the case. The actual size of F needed for the auditor to conclude that the regression is not an artifact depends on the auditor's desired confidence level (usually 95 per cent) and the number of degrees of freedom for the model and error mean square terms. These values are readily available in tabular form in statistics textbooks and reference books and are often included in the computer output of the regression model.

The F value and R^2 will usually be consistent and tell us the same thing. However, if the number of data points is very large (several hundred or more), then the model might have good statistical validity (high F) and at the same time have low explanatory power (low R^2). This effect is caused by the sample size having an influence on the denominator of the F value, while having no effect necessarily on the two components of R^2. The reverse would be true for very small samples. In both these situations the auditor must interpret the results carefully. Are both explanatory power and statistical validity acceptable for the model?

Together, the R^2 and F measures given the auditor an objective basis for judging the reliability of the regression model. If the model scores satisfactorily, the auditor can go ahead with the use of the model for prediction. If not, the auditor will want to modify the model or build a new one. At this time, the auditor should consider the following matters as a guide to developing a new model:

1. Have I modeled the underlying relationships properly? Are they linear or nonlinear? Additive or multiplicative?

2. Have I included all relevant independent variables in the model? Is the model complete?

3. Have I studied the data to identify any unusual data points or

patterns to the data? Are the data clustered in an unusual manner? Are one or more points far removed from the others?

Each of the above potential problems can be addressed in the regression analysis to improve the fit of the model.

The next two of the six measures, SE and SE_c, can be used to evaluate the precision of the regression model. How accurate are its predictions?

$$SE = \sqrt{\text{Mean square error}} = \sqrt{1.5} = 1.225$$

The SE value is interpreted as the range of values around the prediction, using the model, in which the auditor is approximately 67 per cent confident that the unknown true value of the dependent variable lies. When SE is doubled, the value reflects an interval, both plus and minus around the model's prediction, in which the auditor can be 95 per cent confident that the unknown true value will lie.

The above interpretation is most appropriate when the auditor's prediction is near the mean of the independent variable. The reason for this is that the total sum of squares, which is used in regression analysis, is measured from the mean of the independent variable. This means that the precision associated with predictions from the regression model is best when the value of the independent variable is near its mean, and worst when the independent variable is far from its mean. The formula to correct SE when predicting far from the mean is given as follows:

$$SE\,(\text{corrected}) = SE \sqrt{1 + \frac{1}{n} + \frac{(\hat{x} - \bar{x})^2}{SS_x}}$$

where $n =$ number of data points
$\hat{x} =$ value of independent variable for which
prediction is desired
$SS_x =$ sum of squares for independent variable

$$= \sum_{i=1}^{n} (x_i - \bar{x})^2$$

Note from the above equation that the corrected SE is minimized when x is near to x, as you would expect. The effect of the difference between x and x on precision should not be overlooked, since to neglect it could cause the auditor to be substantially overconfident in the precision of a given prediction.

Another type of standard error, SE_c, is interpreted in a similar manner, but it applies to the coefficient of the independent variable rather than the prediction from the regression equation. SE_c is commonly provided in the output of regression analysis. A large SE_c value relative to the coefficient often indicates that the independent variable does not have a particularly close relationship to the dependent variable. In a simple regression with one independent variable, a large SE_c will ordinarily mean also a large SE value, with the result that the regression precision is low.

The final two of the six measures, t and the Durbin-Watson statistic (DW), provide information concerning the reliability of the model. The t value addresses the issue of whether the independent variable is a significant predictor, while DW is a signal of a potential nonlinear relationship in the data.

$$t = \frac{\text{coefficient of the independent variable}}{SE_c}$$

The t value is a measure of the statistical validity of the independent variable and, as such, is interpreted in much the same way as the F value. A t value larger than approximately 2.0 is an indication that the independent variable has a significant statistical relationship with the dependent variable. Lower values suggest the relationship may not exist for these variables.

The DW statistic is a useful measure of the potential for a nonlinear relationship between the dependent and independent variable. Since regression is a linear method, it is important to know the extent of nonlinearity which might exist. If a nonlinear relationship is not detected, the SE values produced by the linear regression analysis will underestimate the true level of the standard error. As a result, the auditor will conclude there is greater precision of prediction than is warranted.

The DW statistic ranges from 0 to 4. A value between 1 and 3 would indicate no significant problem as described above. But, when DW is outside the 1 to 3 range, the auditor should reexamine the data to eliminate the nonlinearity by either adding independent variables, dropping variables, or transforming variables. A method which is often used for time-series data is to use the "first differences" in the variables, rather than the original data. The *first difference* is the amount of the change from period to period. First differences often eliminate the nonlinearity. We discuss transforming variables in more detail later.

Illustrative Regression Model

This section presents a complete numerical illustration for a small regression problem. Those looking only for an overview of regression analysis may prefer to skip now to the next section.

The illustration we have chosen is the use of regression to predict maintenance expense on the basis of square feet of floor space. The analysis is done for seven retail outlets for which we have current maintenance expense and floor space data. These data are shown in the first three columns of Table AF-2. The audit objective might be to use the error terms from the regression as a basis for identifying problem outlets for further investigation.

Table AF-2 summarizes the computational aspects of the analysis. In this simple problem it is possible to show all the necessary arithmetic in a single table. For more complex problems involving more data or additional independent variables, the computer would be used to make these calculations.

The best way to understand Table AF-2 is to read it from the bottom up. The regression equation obtained from the data is

$$\text{Maintenance expense} = -\$10.454 + .368 \times \text{square feet}$$

The negative intercept looks suspicious, but is not a problem so long as we are using the regression to analyze the seven outlets only and do not extend our analysis beyond these outlets. More on this matter later.

Directly above the equation are the calculations needed to derive the intercept a and coefficient b of the equation. The data supporting these computations are at the top of the table.

The information in Table AF-2 can be used to develop an analysis of variance table. This is done in Table AF-3. The statistical measures are shown at the bottom of the table. These measures indicate a relatively reliable and precise model. R^2 and F are high, and the SE is low relative to the mean of the dependent variable. The auditor may then conclude that the planned use of the model will give meaningful results.

Since the audit objective is to identify outlets with potentially excessive maintenance expense, the best approach would be to select outlet 7 on the basis of its high error term. Maintenance expense is $1.054 greater than predicted by the regression model. Of course, a variety of other types of information would also be brought to bear in making this judgment—audit history, age or configuration of the outlets, and so on.

Table AF-2   Results for Illustrative Regression Analysis

Outlet	Maintenance Expense (y)	Square Feet of Floor Square (x)	x^2	xy	Regression Prediction $(\hat{y})$	Error (E)	E^2
1	12	61	3721	732	11.994	.006	.0000
2	16	72	5184	1152	16.042	.042	.0018
3	18	75	5625	1350	17.146	.854	.7293
4	22	89	7921	1958	22.298	.298	.0888
5	19	80	6400	1520	18.986	.014	.0002
6	8	54	2916	432	9.418	1.418	2.0107
7	9	50	2500	450	7.946	1.054	1.1109
	y = 104	x = 481	x^2 = 34,267	xy = 7594			3.9417

$$(\ x)^2 = (481)^2 = 231,361$$

$$a = \frac{(\ y)(\ x^2) - (\ x)(\ xy)}{n(\ x^2) - (\ x)^2} = \frac{(104)(34,267) - (481)(7594)}{(7)(34,267) - 231,361} = -\$10.454$$

$$b = \frac{(n)(\ xy) - (\ x)(\ y)}{(n)(\ x^2) - (\ x)^2} = \frac{(7)(7594) - (481)(104)}{(7)(34,267) - 231,361} = .368$$

Regression equation: $y = -\$10.454 + .368x$

Multiple Regression (two or more independent variables)

Though we have discussed only the simple regression case thus far, the concepts we have developed apply also to the multiple regression case. One unique and important characteristic of the multiple regression model is the potential problem of multicollinearity between independent variables. Multicollinearity reflects the situation in which two or more of the independent variables are not truly independent. The effect, like that of an unfavorable DW statistic, is that the auditor is likely to overestimate the degree of precision actually present in the model.

Nonlinear Regression

The auditor is not likely to encounter pure linear relationships in the real world. The common approach is to use a tight range of values for

Table AF-3   Analysis of Variance Table for Illustrative Regression Analysis

Source of Sum of Squares	Sum of Squares	Degrees of Freedom	Mean Square	F
Model (M)	164.912	1	164.912	209.3
Error (E)	3.942	5	0.788	
Total (T)	168.854	6		

$$R^2 = \frac{164.912}{168.854} = .977$$

$$SE = \quad 0.788 \quad = 0.888$$

$$SE_c = \sqrt{\sum_{i=1}^{7} (x_i - \bar{x})^2} = \sqrt{\frac{SE}{1209.83}} = \frac{0.888}{\sqrt{1209.83}} = 0.026$$

$$t = \frac{.368}{0.026} = 14.15$$

the independent variables, so that within the given small range approximate linearity can be assumed. Alternatively, the auditor can add polynomial terms (x^2, x^3, xy, . . .) as new independent variables to capture the nonlinearity. Another option is to transform the data using a log transform, a power function, or an exponential function.

In some cases, the auditor wishes to build a model with two or more independent variables which are not additively (and therefore not linearly) related. For example, the auditor wishing to predict payroll expense P from data about hours worked per employee H, number of employees E, and average wage rate W is dealing with a multiplicative rather than an additive model.

$$P = H \times E \times W$$

To use regression on these data properly, the auditor must transform it to a linear form. A common approach is to use the log transform, which is additive.

$$\log P = \log H + \log E + \log W$$

The regression equation would be fitted using transformed data, and predictions would be obtained by applying the antilog to the regression predictions.

Assumptions

We close this discussion of regression analysis with an identification of the most important assumptions involved in using it properly. The auditor should carefully evaluate each assumption in each regression application. Failure to do so will generally lead to overconfidence in the precision of predictions from the model, as noted above.

1. *Accurate data.* The data used to fit the model must be accurate, or the model and its statistics will be misspecified. Research has shown that even small errors can have a significant effect on the achieved precision of the model.

2. *Relevant range.* The auditor should not use the regression model outside the range of values which were used to fit it. The coefficients and statistics of the model are relevant only in that range. Additionally, to avoid the effects of nonlinearity, the auditor, in fitting the model, should pick a range of data that is reasonably tight.

3. *Linearity.* The auditor should evaluate whether the relationship under examination is linear and whether the independent variables truly combine in an additive or multiplicative manner.

There are a variety of means for dealing with nonlinearity if it is present.

4. *Trend effect.* When using time-series data, the auditor should be alert to separate the following two aspects of the model—the relationship between dependent and independent variable and the trend effect influencing both variables. The significant effect of trend on most accounting data means that care should be taken in time-series regression. When using time-series data, the auditor should consider the following suggestions:

   a. Use monthly rather than annual data, and use no more than 36 periods or so.

   b. The effect of trend might be captured by adding additional independent variables to the model.

   c. Using "first differences" on the data may eliminate the trend effect.

5. *Inclusion of all relevant variables.* Is the model complete? Are there additional explanatory variables which can be used to help predict the dependent variable?

6. *Statistical properties of the errors.* The proper interpretation of the regression statistics requires that the error terms (E) be distributed in a certain manner. In statistical language, the errors must be independent, distributed normally, and show constant variance.

Appendix G

Industry Ratio Data

Key to Appendix G

The data in this appendix is taken from the Industrial Compustat File, which is a large database of publicly-held firms. Within each industry, firms are split into two groups—small firms and large firms. A firm is classified as small if its total assets (for non-financial firms) or total revenues (for financial firms) fall below the median value for the related industry. A firm is classified as large if the appropriate total is greater than or equal to the industry median.

The column heading "P25" means that 25% of the firms in the industry have ratio values as low or lower than this amount. The headings "P50" and "P75" are interpreted in a similar fashion. The value for "P50" is also called the median.

The 25 ratios in each table are defined as in Table 3-2 in §3.04. The 25th ratio is the Altman-Z score, as described in Chapter 3, §3.04. The abbreviations for the 25 ratios are as follows.

Operating Ratios

1. ROS—return on sales
2. ROA—return on total assets

3. ROTNW—return on tangible net worth
4. PPC—percentage profit change
5. PSC—percentage sales change
6. STA—sales to total assets
7. CVNI—coefficient of variation of net income

Leverage ratios

8. LTDC—long-term debt to capitalization
9. NTALTD—net tangible assets to long-term debt
10. WCLTD—working capital to long-term debt
11. FCC—fixed-charge coverage
12. CFTD—cash flow to total debt
13. TDTA—total debt to total assets
14. MVEBVD—market value of equity to book value of debt
15. IC—interest coverage
16. LTDE—long-term debt to equity
17. TNWTD—tangible net worth to total debt

Liquidity ratios

18. WCTA—working capital to total assets
19. CR—current ratio
20. QR—quick- (acid test) ratio
21. LR—liquidity ratio
22. WCT—working capital turnover
23. ART—accounts receivable turnover
24. IT—inventory turnover
25. ALTZ—Altman Z-score

Other factors to remember when consulting the tables are:

1. Industry groups are determined on the basis of 2-digit SIC codes, shown in these tables behind each industry name
2. The ratios are calculated using the data available through the end of fiscal year 1985
3. Wherever possible, the minority interest is excluded from the financial variables

4. Profit before tax and extraordinary items excludes the effects of discontinued operations

5. After-tax net income includes the effects of both extraordinary items and discontinued operations

6. A multiplication by 100 is included in computing the various returns that stand alone.

7. The coefficient of variation of net income is calculated using annual income for each of the last 10 years

8. Deferred taxes are treated as including investment tax credits

9. In determining the market value of equity, the redemption value of preferred stock is used as a surrogate for the market value of preferred stock

Table 1 Agriculture Production—Crops (10)

	Small Firms			Large Firms			All Firms		
	P25	P50	P75	P25	P50	P75	P25	P50	P75
1. ROS	-9.199	4.640	31.818	-33.747	6.740	10.445	-10.913	6.740	13.172
2. ROA	-2.550	12.354	18.851	-8.046	5.202	6.734	-4.518	5.321	9.478
3. ROTNW	-5.719	9.846	27.518	-28.747	6.378	13.945	-10.092	6.378	19.744
4. PPC	-178.051	-24.903	11.688	-284.133	-22.187	132.240	-186.585	-23.198	18.415
5. PSC	-11.813	-1.447	5.327	-13.128	1.535	20.205	-13.128	1.496	6.979
6. STA	0.381	0.475	0.672	0.329	0.405	0.563	0.355	0.442	0.578
7. CVNI	68.090	139.422	504.284	81.484	176.835	1122.002	81.484	176.835	751.946
8. LTDC	0.000	0.003	0.430	0.179	0.328	0.481	0.002	0.231	0.471
9. NTALTD	1.998	2.490	267.222	2.173	3.768	6.380	2.166	2.777	6.484
10. WCLTD	0.318	0.703	44.165	0.175	0.544	0.948	0.178	0.588	1.315
11. FCC	4.094	4.094	4.094	-1.545	1.120	3.786	-1.545	3.786	4.094
12. CFTD	-0.115	0.081	0.300	-0.067	0.144	0.214	-0.056	0.128	0.188
13. TDTA	0.152	0.302	0.552	0.349	0.491	0.614	0.219	0.392	0.602
14. MVEBVD	1.642	6.303	16.647	0.745	1.198	5.152	0.947	2.426	8.460
15. IC	-44.719	0.682	2.598	-1.118	2.930	3.786	-1.555	1.141	3.759
16. LTDE	0.000	0.003	0.755	0.218	0.507	0.928	0.002	0.301	0.891
17. TNWTD	0.849	2.498	5.625	0.553	0.712	1.815	0.585	1.210	3.348
18. WCTA	0.102	0.150	0.347	0.049	0.090	0.197	0.067	0.128	0.207
19. CR	1.886	2.597	4.565	1.389	1.839	2.658	1.508	2.102	3.448
20. QR	1.177	1.867	2.517	0.595	0.984	1.474	0.768	1.401	2.049
21. LR	1.029	4.201	29.757	1.972	3.660	11.706	1.718	4.197	17.394
22. WCT	1.764	3.422	4.281	2.137	3.331	10.773	2.137	3.331	5.500
23. ART	4.337	16.636	23.605	5.587	6.568	14.451	5.557	6.687	18.673
24. IT	1.843	3.939	5.344	2.499	3.386	4.485	2.267	3.515	4.554
25. ALTZ	2.143	5.699	9.977	0.407	1.910	3.044	1.350	2.385	6.019

Table 2 Airlines (45)

	Small Firms			Large Firms			All Firms		
	P25	P50	P75	P25	P50	P75	P25	P50	P75
1. ROS	-4.303	2.903	5.684	0.500	4.192	7.751	-1.490	2.993	5.684
2. ROA	2.877	8.256	10.844	5.135	9.052	12.022	3.239	8.256	11.652
3. ROTNW	-40.757	15.050	35.063	-0.000	16.179	28.326	0.423	15.716	26.205
4. PPC	-216.459	-15.418	6.598	-118.967	-10.367	38.613	-127.074	-13.792	24.087
5. PSC	7.926	13.026	19.783	3.489	10.099	31.738	7.926	10.548	19.783
6. STA	0.760	1.170	1.260	0.917	1.086	1.329	0.811	1.145	1.292
7. CVNI	94.798	142.446	406.076	85.836	148.905	501.626	89.349	142.446	461.569
8. LTDC	0.490	0.717	0.913	0.369	0.565	0.804	0.450	0.605	0.838
9. NTALTD	1.082	1.453	1.718	1.793	2.311	3.188	1.376	1.732	2.339
10. WGLTD	-0.258	0.029	0.137	-0.128	0.167	0.489	-0.246	0.060	0.306
11. FCC	0.687	1.185	1.498	0.877	1.546	1.880	0.791	1.205	1.572
12. CFTD	0.033	0.113	0.159	0.116	0.206	0.293	0.089	0.149	0.216
13. TDTA	0.682	0.775	0.938	0.645	0.740	0.876	0.647	0.772	0.896
14. MVEBVD	0.216	0.329	0.560	0.311	0.474	0.652	0.249	0.431	0.598
15. IC	0.412	1.346	2.301	1.108	2.067	3.547	0.984	1.811	2.558
16. LTDE	0.818	1.575	3.073	0.593	1.312	4.463	0.807	1.473	3.073
17. TNWTD	0.080	0.213	0.317	0.085	0.302	0.542	0.101	0.215	0.477
18. WCTA	-0.098	0.013	0.097	-0.060	0.051	0.139	-0.068	0.029	0.118
19. CR	0.672	1.033	1.400	0.814	1.152	1.629	0.793	1.139	1.629
20. QR	0.524	0.948	1.288	0.576	0.874	1.314	0.560	0.948	1.288
21. LR	3.030	5.080	8.925	3.119	6.312	14.545	3.073	6.178	13.884
22. WCT	-11.278	6.871	30.711	-30.771	-4.573	9.423	-16.388	4.821	20.129
23. ART	9.229	13.335	17.986	7.717	9.650	12.784	8.773	11.918	15.251
24. IT	29.951	54.102	83.304	23.602	27.937	37.087	24.523	36.249	57.575
25. ALTZ	1.160	1.697	2.116	1.422	1.760	2.141	1.297	1.712	2.116

Table 3 Apparel (23)

	Small Firms			Large Firms			All Firms		
	P25	P50	P75	P25	P50	P75	P25	P50	P75
1. ROS	-6.620	-1.522	5.759	4.442	7.124	10.547	-4.036	5.207	8.716
2. ROA	-6.930	0.825	11.480	11.308	14.210	19.467	-2.890	11.474	17.598
3. ROTNW	-18.974	1.277	33.795	14.928	20.868	29.408	-14.707	15.246	30.634
4. PPC	-168.727	-64.766	14.648	-29.518	7.614	22.910	-95.497	-14.213	16.600
5. PSC	-10.739	-4.121	-0.111	-8.134	-3.054	15.733	-9.073	-3.404	8.430
6. STA	1.415	1.769	1.883	1.578	1.787	2.244	1.483	1.771	2.033
7. CVNI	115.378	217.809	387.665	29.495	56.101	167.910	39.650	93.060	321.407
8. LTDC	0.003	0.093	0.263	0.121	0.183	0.310	0.037	0.142	0.271
9. NTALTD	3.665	8.248	125.840	3.899	6.749	10.777	3.801	7.852	16.618
10. WCLTD	2.179	5.508	50.867	1.828	3.437	6.057	1.944	4.395	7.416
11. FCC	-0.597	0.564	1.753	1.889	2.585	4.555	0.525	1.916	3.142
12. CFTD	-0.185	-0.018	0.213	0.146	0.246	0.576	-0.061	0.187	0.324
13. TDTA	0.334	0.552	0.610	0.333	0.381	0.515	0.334	0.461	0.509
14. MVEBVD	0.527	1.056	2.289	0.990	2.226	3.306	0.630	2.065	2.590
15. IC	-0.982	0.496	2.857	2.698	4.290	8.284	-0.026	2.932	5.101
16. LTDE	0.003	0.103	0.357	0.138	0.224	0.452	0.039	0.165	0.372
17. TNWTD	0.705	0.868	2.241	0.906	1.552	1.920	0.776	1.460	1.932
18. WCTA	0.278	0.369	0.518	0.415	0.542	0.576	0.338	0.460	0.565
19. CR	1.506	2.109	3.042	2.745	3.843	4.254	1.974	2.811	4.047
20. QR	0.628	0.988	1.432	1.110	1.495	1.991	0.819	1.343	1.738
21. LR	1.072	1.643	4.075	5.313	22.471	62.918	1.505	4.718	29.424
22. WCT	3.043	3.729	5.395	3.050	3.694	5.003	3.053	3.711	5.078
23. ART	4.554	6.184	6.876	5.876	7.219	9.338	5.206	6.469	8.815
24. IT	2.338	2.919	3.369	2.821	3.287	3.911	2.777	3.178	3.645
25. ALTZ	2.250	2.844	3.989	3.063	4.260	5.113	2.589	3.655	4.630

Table 4 Banking (60)

	Small Firms			Large Firms			All Firms		
	P25	P50	P75	P25	P50	P75	P25	P50	P75
1. ROS	7.057	9.811	12.195	7.004	9.500	11.322	7.048	9.562	11.687
2. ROA	6.024	6.587	7.059	6.365	6.757	7.412	6.277	6.699	7.245
3. ROTNW	8.010	20.814	25.456	17.354	21.917	26.383	16.299	21.411	25.874
4. PPC	−0.253	19.235	35.375	10.039	28.884	44.719	4.793	21.573	39.045
5. PSC	1.356	5.743	11.793	−1.498	5.597	15.920	−0.076	5.658	13.610
6. STA	0.095	0.101	0.104	0.094	0.099	0.107	0.095	0.101	0.106
7. CVNI	34.128	41.772	51.503	37.268	52.691	71.800	35.395	46.248	68.600
8. LTDC	0.122	0.174	0.247	0.205	0.278	0.388	0.154	0.228	0.319
9. NTALTD	.	.	.	.	.	.	.	.	.
10. WCLTD	.	.	.	.	.	.	.	.	.
11. FCC	1.103	1.147	1.181	1.088	1.137	1.166	1.097	1.143	1.175
12. CFTD	.	.	.	.	.	.	.	.	.
13. TDTA	.	.	.	.	.	.	.	.	.
14. MVEBVD	.	.	.	.	.	.	.	.	.
15. IC	1.110	1.156	1.195	1.093	1.144	1.176	1.101	1.150	1.184
16. LTDE	0.139	0.211	0.329	0.258	0.385	0.633	0.181	0.295	0.469
17. TNWTD	.	.	.	.	.	.	.	.	.
18. WCTA	.	.	.	.	.	.	.	.	.
19. CR	.	.	.	.	.	.	.	.	.
20. QR	.	.	.	.	.	.	.	.	.
21. LR	.	.	.	.	.	.	.	.	.
22. WCT	.	.	.	.	.	.	.	.	.
23. ART	.	.	.	.	.	.	.	.	.
24. IT	.	.	.	.	.	.	.	.	.
25. ALTZ	.	.	.	.	.	.	.	.	.

Table 5   Building Materials, Hardware, Garden Supply, Mobile Home Dealers (52)

	Small Firms			Large Firms			All Firms		
	P25	P50	P75	P25	P50	P75	P25	P50	P75
1. ROS	−3.609	5.432	7.644	1.638	1.767	5.173	1.638	4.349	5.980
2. ROA	−0.807	12.199	14.339	6.388	8.818	16.296	6.388	10.485	14.810
3. ROTNW	−40.899	15.804	18.966	11.526	21.125	28.375	10.392	18.072	22.199
4. PPC	−353.882	−26.236	−11.607	−30.478	1.086	64.282	−43.365	−8.315	2.167
5. PSC	−0.027	7.063	8.596	−0.595	18.222	42.321	1.966	7.316	20.475
6. STA	1.452	1.522	2.035	0.969	1.843	2.355	1.324	1.683	2.195
7. CVNI	24.324	43.361	238.072	57.695	73.560	4005.863	43.361	60.006	188.503
8. LTDC	0.137	0.234	0.565	0.288	0.446	0.598	0.222	0.352	0.551
9. NTALTD	1.958	4.381	8.395	1.514	2.648	3.647	1.711	3.222	4.809
10. WCLTD	0.667	1.993	3.128	0.482	1.050	1.397	0.507	1.153	2.056
11. FCC	−0.532	1.549	4.087	1.360	1.467	2.933	1.336	1.508	3.210
12. CFTD	0.164	0.264	0.365	0.066	0.193	0.259	0.115	0.193	0.312
13. TDTA	0.308	0.473	0.697	0.488	0.631	0.773	0.419	0.539	0.769
14. MVEBVD	0.616	1.044	3.013	0.742	1.080	2.066	0.785	1.062	2.294
15. IC	−0.169	4.002	8.956	1.606	1.735	3.681	1.606	2.130	5.153
16. LTDE	0.163	0.305	1.731	0.405	0.806	1.630	0.287	0.548	1.323
17. TNWTD	0.403	1.379	2.202	0.239	0.581	1.019	0.286	0.816	1.740
18. WCTA	0.205	0.286	0.344	0.152	0.280	0.352	0.194	0.283	0.340
19. CR	1.734	2.130	3.339	1.561	2.124	2.251	1.802	2.127	2.240
20. QR	0.335	0.504	1.209	0.289	0.762	0.847	0.353	0.651	0.888
21. LR	0.586	1.840	34.075	3.116	3.458	14.467	1.605	3.406	13.950
22. WCT	4.812	6.254	9.524	5.221	7.882	10.269	5.085	6.878	10.230
23. ART	13.664	25.929	91.506	4.416	18.429	133.109	8.109	24.876	76.801
24. IT	2.380	3.837	5.200	3.209	4.344	4.966	2.636	4.344	5.085
25. ALTZ	2.067	3.605	4.664	1.773	2.903	4.630	1.839	2.903	4.624

Table 6   Chemicals and Drugs (28)

	Small Firms			Large Firms			All Firms		
	P25	P50	P75	P25	P50	P75	P25	P50	P75
1. ROS	3.809	7.069	13.438	4.834	10.952	16.594	4.134	8.771	15.743
2. ROA	9.023	14.776	18.626	9.180	13.966	18.331	9.141	14.240	18.618
3. ROTNW	9.775	25.934	34.386	8.693	25.793	35.106	9.041	25.882	34.386
4. PPC	−34.030	−0.171	47.462	−49.846	1.990	9.211	−40.350	0.482	14.826
5. PSC	−4.895	1.237	14.021	−3.829	2.679	6.001	−4.191	2.539	8.227
6. STA	1.030	1.440	1.854	0.882	1.039	1.260	0.914	1.188	1.556
7. CVNI	33.697	54.362	125.635	28.811	38.684	56.242	30.522	44.697	79.388
8. LTDC	0.051	0.176	0.341	0.119	0.222	0.311	0.090	0.215	0.328
9. NTALTD	2.401	4.344	9.629	3.120	4.639	8.884	3.004	4.469	9.139
10. WCLTD	1.019	1.814	7.052	0.657	1.447	3.637	0.833	1.699	3.960
11. FCC	1.380	2.428	4.345	1.333	2.664	3.703	1.368	2.455	3.720
12. CFTD	0.138	0.237	0.465	0.159	0.286	0.422	0.145	0.262	0.424
13. TDTA	0.324	0.444	0.581	0.400	0.488	0.575	0.388	0.485	0.579
14. MVEBVD	1.078	2.057	5.811	1.122	1.766	4.306	1.118	1.995	4.354
15. IC	1.542	3.302	8.454	1.766	3.474	6.094	1.666	3.408	7.574
16. LTDE	0.050	0.191	0.497	0.135	0.285	0.451	0.093	0.271	0.483
17. TNWTD	0.530	1.106	1.894	0.637	0.960	1.347	0.575	1.000	1.466
18. WCTA	0.199	0.304	0.425	0.148	0.205	0.285	0.158	0.261	0.368
19. CR	1.663	2.170	2.679	1.510	1.876	2.176	1.613	2.007	2.456
20. QR	0.994	1.241	1.883	0.801	1.051	1.362	0.878	1.147	1.550
21. LR	4.540	8.675	23.424	3.311	5.428	8.984	3.613	6.537	16.014
22. WCT	2.981	4.603	6.442	3.623	5.172	6.904	3.257	4.993	6.776
23. ART	5.092	6.157	7.123	5.092	6.258	7.008	5.092	6.225	7.008
24. IT	2.343	3.772	6.130	2.334	3.684	4.836	2.340	3.754	5.296
25. ALTZ	2.628	3.950	6.541	2.388	3.102	4.664	2.416	3.674	5.125

Table 7 Communication and Television (48)

	Small Firms			Large Firms			All Firms		
	P25	P50	P75	P25	P50	P75	P25	P50	P75
1. ROS	5.551	13.734	17.815	4.512	15.794	20.830	5.373	14.735	19.210
2. ROA	7.640	11.433	16.038	8.306	11.788	12.963	8.108	11.748	12.995
3. ROTNW	8.409	28.659	65.302	6.981	23.626	27.287	10.163	24.182	31.695
4. PPC	-9.417	17.848	60.803	-9.087	11.375	17.994	-6.172	11.670	42.666
5. PSC	11.000	16.459	25.795	4.850	8.618	12.649	6.146	12.649	22.982
6. STA	0.293	0.431	0.869	0.435	0.526	0.590	0.407	0.498	0.600
7. CVNI	35.775	57.641	195.220	8.201	29.679	55.690	19.977	42.503	74.852
8. LTDC	0.381	0.635	0.837	0.377	0.405	0.534	0.380	0.456	0.667
9. NTALTD	1.080	1.605	2.507	1.933	2.496	2.784	1.363	2.067	2.713
10. WCLTD	-0.002	0.104	0.177	-0.063	-0.006	0.064	-0.040	0.033	0.137
11. FCC	1.064	1.347	2.650	1.156	2.101	2.407	1.123	1.907	2.418
12. CFTD	0.093	0.148	0.423	0.156	0.241	0.258	0.112	0.237	0.259
13. TDTA	0.538	0.641	0.801	0.592	0.614	0.707	0.580	0.614	0.739
14. MVEBVD	0.577	0.931	1.391	0.684	0.863	1.011	0.621	0.909	1.158
15. IC	1.075	1.579	2.920	1.256	2.720	3.119	1.154	2.331	3.108
16. LTDE	0.560	1.191	3.301	0.606	0.682	1.147	0.596	0.767	1.798
17. TNWTD	0.019	0.285	0.769	0.395	0.575	0.662	0.233	0.447	0.666
18. WCTA	0.001	0.043	0.110	-0.016	-0.002	0.015	-0.013	0.010	0.067
19. CR	1.009	1.258	1.983	0.894	0.988	1.089	0.921	1.067	1.370
20. QR	0.747	0.878	1.536	0.671	0.724	0.862	0.696	0.792	0.975
21. LR	3.387	5.227	23.036	2.831	3.733	6.866	2.973	4.403	7.656
22. WCT	2.428	5.481	30.685	-47.212	-14.632	18.826	-26.952	5.120	27.137
23. ART	4.385	5.591	7.088	5.171	5.832	6.552	5.035	5.820	6.691
24. IT	5.521	13.995	28.911	7.740	14.717	23.942	7.724	14.717	27.460
25. ALTZ	1.059	1.407	2.206	1.372	1.546	1.826	1.259	1.481	1.998

Table 8   Construction—Building Contractors (15)

	Small Firms			Large Firms			All Firms		
	P25	P50	P75	P25	P50	P75	P25	P50	P75
1. ROS	-3.851	2.543	7.466	0.630	1.006	6.419	-0.230	1.775	6.252
2. ROA	-1.998	8.623	19.064	3.752	5.432	12.252	2.152	7.028	14.539
3. ROTNW	-9.490	33.738	45.946	6.744	18.087	27.428	6.744	27.273	35.529
4. PPC	-31.680	37.464	273.641	-50.930	22.965	223.324	-29.827	31.000	166.874
5. PSC	8.429	13.326	83.781	-2.673	17.448	32.262	3.540	15.387	29.583
6. STA	0.900	1.859	3.056	1.577	1.798	2.684	1.508	1.829	2.863
7. CVNI	91.186	178.760	561.843	38.237	45.797	112.781	45.296	91.186	226.310
8. LTDC	0.121	0.404	0.724	0.103	0.150	0.469	0.105	0.235	0.634
9. NTALTD	0.855	4.031	10.326	2.619	6.660	10.238	1.512	6.437	10.238
10. WCLTD	0.208	3.023	7.157	0.758	4.518	7.821	0.300	4.518	6.743
11. FCC	-5.732	0.347	1.988	1.295	1.527	1.759	-2.688	1.527	1.903
12. CFTD	0.091	0.091	0.091	0.028	0.109	0.196	0.034	0.091	0.188
13. TDTA	0.577	0.777	0.874	0.609	0.722	0.851	0.609	0.722	0.863
14. MVEBVD	0.486	1.257	7.175	0.256	0.408	0.839	0.386	0.525	1.447
15. IC	-20.734	2.176	10.086	-2.474	2.644	4.361	-2.577	2.410	4.969
16. LTDE	0.139	0.679	2.785	0.114	0.177	1.059	0.118	0.321	1.741
17. TNWTD	0.191	0.383	0.806	0.196	0.458	0.653	0.191	0.383	0.692
18. WCTA	0.072	0.130	0.531	0.089	0.136	0.394	0.082	0.136	0.394
19. CR	1.149	1.227	3.927	1.155	1.314	2.248	1.172	1.249	2.248
20. QR	0.787	1.090	1.128	0.621	0.960	1.198	0.789	1.043	1.120
21. LR	19.423	19.423	19.423	2.045	9.343	31.808	2.148	14.383	25.721
22. WCT	5.470	15.520	32.642	4.452	14.970	31.791	5.110	14.970	29.636
23. ART	2.591	7.885	73.998	4.394	5.428	11.290	4.377	5.428	13.963
24. IT	2.961	9.936	24.920	3.142	10.276	41.986	3.142	10.276	28.077
25. ALTZ	1.191	4.105	4.981	2.658	3.113	3.205	2.658	3.199	4.105

Table 9   Fabricated Metal Products (34)

	Small Firms			Large Firms			All Firms		
	P25	P50	P75	P25	P50	P75	P25	P50	P75
1. ROS	-5.148	3.725	11.950	2.600	8.016	11.063	-0.260	5.351	11.350
2. ROA	-2.405	10.416	15.234	7.385	11.766	17.392	2.703	11.232	16.486
3. ROTNW	-19.887	15.198	29.368	8.266	22.134	33.383	-0.564	17.736	30.857
4. PPC	-38.397	5.237	93.226	-46.348	5.117	31.894	-39.789	5.214	34.178
5. PSC	-8.356	-0.616	11.851	0.960	5.666	13.422	-4.951	3.918	13.163
6. STA	1.112	1.280	1.668	0.929	1.305	1.553	1.067	1.281	1.636
7. CVNI	42.914	113.820	266.313	40.606	67.286	98.733	41.169	81.439	181.542
8. LTDC	0.112	0.288	0.555	0.181	0.314	0.391	0.178	0.309	0.508
9. NTALTD	1.656	2.812	6.843	2.197	2.921	4.851	1.825	2.921	5.312
10. WCLTD	0.598	1.265	2.754	0.796	1.446	2.592	0.689	1.388	2.604
11. FCC	-0.017	1.377	5.708	1.303	2.239	2.938	0.964	1.988	3.633
12. CFTD	0.044	0.389	0.506	0.059	0.154	0.291	0.061	0.212	0.435
13. TDTA	0.289	0.489	0.744	0.424	0.524	0.660	0.383	0.519	0.672
14. MVEBVD	0.487	1.125	3.479	0.739	1.121	2.208	0.645	1.123	2.913
15. IC	-0.253	3.173	16.595	1.397	2.779	5.391	1.057	2.801	6.895
16. LTDE	0.105	0.382	1.207	0.221	0.458	0.641	0.208	0.406	1.025
17. TNWTD	0.381	0.988	2.377	0.424	0.673	0.963	0.424	0.727	1.603
18. WCTA	0.192	0.401	0.510	0.213	0.320	0.391	0.202	0.342	0.461
19. CR	1.447	3.056	4.376	1.700	2.251	2.723	1.677	2.468	3.481
20. QR	0.774	1.477	2.976	0.902	1.171	1.375	0.864	1.268	1.900
21. LR	2.098	10.836	30.027	3.443	7.199	20.688	2.789	9.683	22.839
22. WCT	2.471	3.998	6.884	3.386	4.422	6.907	3.124	4.397	6.890
23. ART	5.238	6.679	7.804	5.038	6.242	7.111	5.167	6.341	7.465
24. IT	2.993	4.530	6.445	3.409	4.393	7.203	3.406	4.517	6.602
25. ALTZ	1.807	2.953	5.032	2.156	2.606	3.818	1.963	2.673	4.480

Table 10 Financial Services—Other Than Banking (61)

	Small Firms			Large Firms			All Firms		
	P25	P50	P75	P25	P50	P75	P25	P50	P75
1. ROS	3.955	11.501	20.159	3.315	7.244	9.884	3.799	8.242	14.808
2. ROA	2.547	4.768	10.875	2.581	3.395	5.326	2.581	3.590	7.991
3. ROTNW	5.583	18.908	44.740	12.748	32.792	69.650	7.988	27.187	59.958
4. PPC	-6.689	25.684	70.630	-33.224	58.100	160.428	-13.546	32.374	137.150
5. PSC	4.302	17.872	37.498	3.867	16.375	26.030	4.302	17.872	31.175
6. STA	0.109	0.138	0.182	0.109	0.119	0.144	0.109	0.123	0.177
7. CVNI	34.210	81.460	137.769	36.829	66.872	225.217	37.375	78.030	166.104
8. LTDC	0.363	0.612	0.749	0.613	0.751	0.848	0.494	0.700	0.798
9. NTALTD	0.861	1.306	2.974	-0.338	1.022	18.455	0.575	1.127	3.885
10. WCLTD	.	.	.	.	.	.	.	.	.
11. FCC	1.216	1.333	1.604	1.126	1.214	1.363	1.171	1.265	1.464
12. CFTD	0.068	0.069	0.069	0.004	0.004	0.004	0.004	0.068	0.069
13. TDTA	0.656	0.793	0.953	0.814	0.928	0.989	0.731	0.854	0.956
14. MVEBVD	0.087	0.446	0.693	0.019	0.174	0.311	0.029	0.289	0.451
15. IC	1.231	1.448	1.634	1.134	1.293	1.447	1.177	1.300	1.524
16. LTDE	0.570	1.578	2.988	1.600	3.009	5.646	0.975	2.332	3.949
17. TNWTD	0.014	0.360	0.487	-0.032	0.018	0.158	-0.019	0.108	0.425
18. WCTA	.	.	.	.	.	.	.	.	.
19. CR	.	.	.	.	.	.	.	.	.
20. QR	13.136	13.136	13.136	2.449	2.449	2.449	2.449	7.792	13.136
21. LR	2.226	5.619	23.181	2.908	4.671	4.968	2.678	4.819	13.368
22. WCT	.	.	.	.	.	.	.	.	.
23. ART	0.180	0.198	0.901	0.110	0.326	0.358	0.175	0.202	0.358
24. IT	1.183	8.096	44.883	2.953	19.125	82.398	2.953	12.569	55.655
25. ALTZ	.	.	.	.	.	.	.	.	.

Table 11   Food Products (20)

	Small Firms			Large Firms			All Firms		
	P25	P50	P75	P25	P50	P75	P25	P50	P75
1. ROS	1.253	4.284	8.619	4.736	7.291	11.494	2.644	6.448	11.150
2. ROA	7.343	10.401	18.276	11.363	15.378	17.659	8.083	13.901	18.097
3. ROTNW	7.163	23.003	36.417	24.013	34.590	42.792	14.354	28.014	39.741
4. PPC	−80.371	7.064	40.277	0.304	11.362	19.083	−13.298	10.847	26.070
5. PSC	−3.834	5.035	21.145	3.271	7.097	13.821	0.340	7.033	14.611
6. STA	1.128	1.688	2.251	1.312	1.623	1.919	1.279	1.659	2.124
7. CVNI	50.843	87.083	254.142	28.301	38.940	57.342	36.450	53.525	104.789
8. LTDC	0.123	0.306	0.447	0.180	0.270	0.388	0.177	0.291	0.402
9. NTALTD	2.230	2.934	5.486	2.318	3.607	5.256	2.289	3.181	5.315
10. WCLTD	0.305	0.733	2.097	0.446	1.161	1.965	0.384	1.030	2.027
11. FCC	1.324	1.888	3.879	1.770	2.522	3.241	1.619	2.237	3.411
12. CFTD	0.110	0.207	0.453	0.176	0.252	0.333	0.126	0.235	0.335
13. TDTA	0.404	0.550	0.578	0.441	0.544	0.629	0.429	0.545	0.614
14. MVEBVD	0.821	1.219	3.423	1.094	1.848	2.322	0.906	1.586	2.774
15. IC	1.398	3.370	7.709	2.804	3.519	5.158	2.140	3.380	5.617
16. LTDE	0.140	0.441	0.810	0.219	0.370	0.635	0.215	0.411	0.672
17. TNWTD	0.618	0.735	1.384	0.429	0.584	0.913	0.533	0.722	1.082
18. WCTA	0.080	0.242	0.354	0.103	0.181	0.251	0.093	0.199	0.293
19. CR	1.270	2.082	2.467	1.382	1.655	2.120	1.319	1.802	2.344
20. QR	0.700	1.044	1.459	0.655	0.891	1.070	0.666	0.950	1.289
21. LR	2.561	10.381	23.280	3.483	6.974	16.158	3.066	7.643	21.377
22. WCT	4.406	6.081	14.251	6.072	9.812	14.930	5.042	7.936	14.173
23. ART	9.402	12.044	14.313	8.921	11.346	14.723	9.094	11.711	14.301
24. IT	4.747	7.800	11.625	4.644	6.943	8.303	4.722	7.026	9.615
25. ALTZ	2.603	3.696	5.404	3.226	3.742	4.548	3.007	3.737	4.785

Table 12 Food Stores (54)

	Small Firms			Large Firms			All Firms		
	P25	P50	P75	P25	P50	P75	P25	P50	P75
1. ROS	0.356	1.611	2.396	1.724	2.280	3.202	1.433	1.935	2.518
2. ROA	3.803	9.034	12.976	10.373	11.909	15.996	8.284	11.348	14.705
3. ROTNW	-4.085	9.602	23.507	24.330	31.810	39.944	17.432	25.661	32.399
4. PPC	-117.843	8.358	79.679	-11.455	9.661	20.557	-28.413	9.661	27.278
5. PSC	-3.481	-0.533	12.527	5.605	6.853	13.427	-0.840	6.202	13.427
6. STA	3.519	4.309	5.200	2.895	3.976	4.570	3.315	4.060	4.943
7. CVNI	35.565	101.208	284.509	33.308	51.286	61.361	36.084	56.434	132.489
8. LTDC	0.265	0.345	0.494	0.290	0.367	0.457	0.278	0.351	0.457
9. NTALTD	2.684	3.533	13.434	1.766	2.426	3.616	2.248	3.059	3.981
10. WCLTD	0.146	0.523	0.831	0.234	0.377	0.614	0.230	0.473	0.798
11. FCC	1.243	1.625	2.054	1.485	1.881	2.059	1.450	1.723	2.051
12. CFTD	0.027	0.125	0.232	0.160	0.191	0.336	0.146	0.184	0.290
13. TDTA	0.505	0.574	0.688	0.552	0.635	0.697	0.535	0.610	0.690
14. MVEBVD	0.548	0.815	1.260	0.748	0.994	2.021	0.698	0.836	1.533
15. IC	1.784	2.829	3.260	2.053	3.115	4.446	1.962	2.909	3.329
16. LTDE	0.361	0.527	0.985	0.411	0.579	0.842	0.386	0.541	0.842
17. TNWTD	0.377	0.811	1.113	0.341	0.629	0.932	0.402	0.674	1.023
18. WCTA	0.042	0.099	0.153	0.064	0.105	0.195	0.059	0.105	0.172
19. CR	1.123	1.380	1.698	1.167	1.334	1.638	1.156	1.337	1.638
20. QR	0.280	0.474	0.502	0.184	0.248	0.618	0.223	0.417	0.538
21. LR	3.067	4.661	8.361	1.921	3.269	17.130	1.959	4.141	8.361
22. WCT	11.689	29.732	46.863	22.325	34.227	57.735	16.236	33.955	51.138
23. ART	50.346	63.829	138.786	85.945	107.580	166.778	58.434	96.694	159.054
24. IT	10.853	13.916	16.186	9.579	10.606	12.774	9.850	11.961	14.546
25. ALTZ	4.625	5.763	6.699	4.450	5.214	6.428	4.493	5.623	6.597

Table 13   Furniture (25)

	Small Firms			Large Firms			All Firms		
	P25	P50	P75	P25	P50	P75	P25	P50	P75
1. ROS	-1.796	5.433	7.286	5.825	9.252	10.978	4.379	6.508	9.768
2. ROA	-1.251	10.831	16.777	11.515	14.150	18.058	10.544	12.319	17.294
3. ROTNW	-14.597	25.101	31.967	17.929	19.663	30.147	7.386	20.499	31.967
4. PPC	-59.162	-13.926	30.314	-28.396	-13.206	26.145	-32.061	-13.926	24.225
5. PSC	-10.552	3.718	8.331	1.349	6.203	15.573	-1.175	4.334	11.111
6. STA	1.266	1.722	2.299	1.268	1.603	1.804	1.315	1.603	1.933
7. CVNI	32.038	52.819	283.050	21.148	51.216	63.772	26.033	51.216	79.561
8. LTDC	0.071	0.372	0.493	0.012	0.168	0.299	0.037	0.237	0.440
9. NTALTD	1.906	2.696	21.460	4.348	7.614	287.258	2.281	4.701	52.106
10. WCLTD	0.889	1.748	14.561	1.450	3.044	114.649	1.185	2.183	26.728
11. FCC	1.341	1.721	3.399	1.900	2.145	2.958	1.683	2.121	2.927
12. CFTD	0.187	0.215	0.244	0.224	0.355	0.486	0.197	0.234	0.425
13. TDTA	0.272	0.524	0.673	0.221	0.356	0.501	0.264	0.433	0.616
14. MVEBVD	0.542	1.362	3.977	1.321	3.740	6.468	0.880	2.379	4.674
15. IC	0.911	2.082	15.899	3.187	4.045	10.084	2.081	3.743	4.798
16. LTDE	0.078	0.611	0.977	0.012	0.207	0.448	0.039	0.311	0.785
17. TNWTD	0.348	0.584	2.752	1.331	2.316	6.852	0.513	2.183	2.752
18. WCTA	0.282	0.469	0.522	0.308	0.352	0.454	0.317	0.384	0.494
19. CR	1.877	2.849	3.935	2.362	2.727	3.990	2.241	2.741	3.656
20. QR	0.933	1.118	2.242	1.050	1.441	2.725	1.028	1.217	2.126
21. LR	2.457	14.300	52.690	6.132	18.324	141.770	3.169	18.324	37.883
22. WCT	3.172	4.558	7.847	3.228	4.400	5.244	3.347	4.558	5.023
23. ART	4.681	6.414	7.875	5.928	6.280	7.456	5.653	6.280	7.064
24. IT	3.002	3.584	4.073	3.434	5.377	5.509	3.115	3.981	5.410
25. ALTZ	1.977	3.927	5.117	3.217	4.727	5.266	2.986	4.371	5.198

Table 14   Hotels and Motels (70)

	Small Firms			Large Firms			All Firms		
	P25	P50	P75	P25	P50	P75	P25	P50	P75
1. ROS	-10.493	-1.637	2.977	5.547	12.428	16.894	-1.906	4.501	12.536
2. ROA	-1.050	7.871	8.674	8.768	14.690	17.476	7.045	8.768	15.062
3. ROTNW	-49.489	-2.873	7.055	8.943	17.706	27.785	-7.756	7.452	20.365
4. PPC	-157.118	-55.458	-39.570	-29.258	-2.401	27.574	-64.002	-35.301	4.711
5. PSC	2.184	14.389	31.954	4.136	11.940	130.534	3.884	13.165	29.671
6. STA	0.483	0.669	0.784	0.377	0.558	0.888	0.430	0.657	0.766
7. CVNI	61.754	85.269	1398.654	29.582	43.497	74.648	41.223	64.898	133.687
8. LTDC	0.556	0.689	0.792	0.326	0.621	0.730	0.466	0.653	0.760
9. NTALTD	1.319	1.449	1.878	1.508	2.276	3.270	1.359	1.601	2.688
10. WCLTD	-0.041	-0.025	0.328	-0.170	-0.019	0.665	-0.070	-0.022	0.468
11. FCC	-0.330	1.091	1.357	1.292	1.668	2.758	0.956	1.339	1.753
12. CFTD	0.013	0.054	0.095	0.079	0.089	0.099	0.029	0.087	0.098
13. TDTA	0.623	0.748	0.834	0.469	0.729	0.764	0.581	0.739	0.784
14. MVEBVD	0.457	0.675	1.032	0.610	1.731	2.686	0.500	0.842	1.941
15. IC	-0.444	1.122	1.399	1.384	1.917	4.173	0.950	1.399	2.464
16. LTDE	1.284	2.211	3.947	0.485	1.642	2.816	0.900	1.903	3.179
17. TNWTD	0.155	0.287	0.531	0.294	0.751	1.081	0.240	0.383	0.954
18. WCTA	-0.026	-0.014	0.151	-0.077	-0.012	0.165	-0.038	-0.013	0.142
19. CR	0.803	0.925	1.921	0.679	0.825	2.508	0.765	0.875	1.959
20. QR	0.490	0.636	1.376	0.518	0.723	2.255	0.516	0.680	1.498
21. LR	1.617	1.681	11.049	1.066	2.116	51.621	1.580	1.899	16.363
22. WCT	-43.661	2.441	65.555	-38.460	-15.183	5.986	-33.529	-6.371	9.194
23. ART	3.810	8.630	14.671	8.033	12.003	19.458	6.659	10.316	14.984
24. IT	7.563	13.620	31.231	29.753	32.609	53.326	11.331	28.967	33.741
25. ALTZ	1.066	1.515	1.743	1.482	2.272	3.205	1.250	1.743	2.456

Table 15   Instruments, Photographic Equipment, Clocks and Watches (38)

	Small Firms			Large Firms			All Firms		
	P25	P50	P75	P25	P50	P75	P25	P50	P75
1. ROS	2.513	5.549	11.097	0.747	6.296	10.445	2.325	6.100	10.446
2. ROA	6.424	9.356	16.501	3.601	9.866	15.138	5.181	9.356	15.876
3. ROTNW	4.012	13.972	26.289	4.709	20.559	30.086	4.373	16.042	29.584
4. PPC	−45.361	−12.815	33.598	−70.319	−7.695	20.945	−60.707	−10.420	23.029
5. PSC	−1.934	11.889	20.150	−0.704	1.686	11.787	−0.704	7.321	16.713
6. STA	0.800	1.076	1.442	0.908	1.014	1.211	0.860	1.037	1.310
7. CVNI	48.386	78.159	110.398	39.404	67.143	121.522	41.004	70.891	114.697
8. LTDC	0.061	0.245	0.484	0.128	0.219	0.369	0.111	0.238	0.439
9. NTALTD	1.767	4.185	13.080	2.655	4.567	7.193	1.955	4.300	8.131
10. WCLTD	1.112	2.336	7.497	1.109	2.351	4.337	1.118	2.336	5.826
11. FCC	1.264	1.662	2.323	1.291	2.163	2.960	1.305	1.880	2.744
12. CFTD	0.132	0.202	0.293	0.121	0.213	0.335	0.123	0.206	0.312
13. TDTA	0.308	0.441	0.612	0.333	0.454	0.568	0.333	0.451	0.583
14. MVEBVD	1.095	2.009	2.979	1.296	1.886	2.925	1.117	2.009	2.895
15. IC	1.426	2.844	3.744	1.507	2.940	6.503	1.521	2.853	5.776
16. LTDE	0.052	0.282	0.832	0.147	0.281	0.584	0.122	0.282	0.719
17. TNWTD	0.432	1.190	2.117	0.633	1.147	1.828	0.532	1.168	1.989
18. WCTA	0.350	0.446	0.546	0.279	0.402	0.455	0.339	0.424	0.499
19. CR	2.191	2.758	3.938	2.163	2.493	3.464	2.177	2.724	3.593
20. QR	1.000	1.393	1.997	0.979	1.464	2.205	0.983	1.448	2.150
21. LR	2.368	5.576	26.953	3.829	7.075	22.476	3.551	6.146	23.905
22. WCT	1.539	2.726	3.440	2.337	2.874	4.246	1.962	2.860	3.651
23. ART	3.900	4.731	5.478	4.230	4.941	5.628	4.037	4.882	5.528
24. IT	1.641	2.053	2.995	2.005	2.669	3.720	1.826	2.271	3.317
25. ALTZ	2.456	3.170	3.937	2.246	2.974	3.886	2.314	3.026	3.878

Table 16   Insurance (63)

	Small Firms			Large Firms			All Firms		
	P25	P50	P75	P25	P50	P75	P25	P50	P75
1. ROS	3.759	7.438	11.578	−0.217	5.114	8.635	1.327	6.046	10.062
2. ROA	1.107	3.109	4.961	0.872	3.140	4.286	1.033	3.109	4.713
3. ROTNW									
4. PPC	−49.627	6.785	92.850	3.779	23.371	128.402	−24.590	18.790	99.601
5. PSC	3.036	10.219	22.602	8.795	16.275	23.039	5.853	13.086	22.775
6. STA	0.212	0.367	0.501	0.318	0.362	0.418	0.292	0.362	0.424
7. CVNI	32.850	37.794	77.839	27.178	39.273	55.287	31.562	38.664	69.817
8. LTDC	0.000	0.098	0.205	0.071	0.149	0.246	0.015	0.116	0.228
9. NTALTD									
10. WCLTD									
11. FCC									
12. CFTD									
13. TDTA									
14. MVEBVD									
15. IC	3.234	7.474	15.441	3.342	4.698	7.589	3.529	6.010	9.320
16. LTDE	0.000	0.068	0.203	0.076	0.175	0.327	0.012	0.124	0.265
17. TNWTD									
18. WCTA									
19. CR									
20. QR									
21. LR	0.991	4.742	15.232	4.154	7.500	178.280	2.234	6.135	24.818
22. WCT									
23. ART	3.877	7.930	11.253	2.776	4.496	6.766	2.920	6.149	9.738
24. IT									
25. ALTZ									

Table 17   Leather Goods (31)

	Small Firms			Large Firms			All Firms		
	P25	P50	P75	P25	P50	P75	P25	P50	P75
1. ROS	3.623	6.886	10.850	-0.951	2.199	6.329	1.498	6.305	8.603
2. ROA	4.279	13.520	18.651	3.162	5.533	14.446	4.000	12.265	18.346
3. ROTNW	4.699	25.488	34.882	-4.171	5.617	22.716	3.010	15.877	30.999
4. PPC	-125.111	-28.305	-5.323	-67.147	1.498	195.718	-81.638	-14.862	95.300
5. PSC	-14.497	-5.942	19.276	-12.866	-4.323	-3.153	-13.274	-5.132	-0.291
6. STA	1.166	1.857	1.940	1.484	1.702	2.004	1.463	1.827	1.956
7. CVNI	37.605	63.476	125.681	44.587	62.118	178.536	42.841	62.797	138.895
8. LTDC	0.000	0.029	0.109	0.137	0.195	0.440	0.023	0.123	0.235
9. NTALTD	7.496	10.458	116.315	2.485	5.516	7.577	3.493	6.732	10.266
10. WCLTD	3.262	6.204	104.007	1.341	4.034	5.071	2.421	4.495	7.975
11. FCC	1.228	2.268	5.314	0.413	1.270	1.518	0.925	1.512	2.540
12. CFTD	0.172	0.273	0.552	0.102	0.241	0.299	0.150	0.257	0.325
13. TDTA	0.125	0.278	0.476	0.385	0.433	0.574	0.260	0.420	0.498
14. MVEBVD	1.698	2.935	5.887	0.854	1.493	2.220	0.858	1.895	3.510
15. IC	2.546	4.134	12.955	0.669	1.901	6.614	1.448	4.132	6.614
16. LTDE	0.000	0.030	0.122	0.159	0.242	0.786	0.024	0.140	0.319
17. TNWTD	0.906	2.564	7.116	0.663	1.452	1.523	0.853	1.478	2.854
18. WCTA	0.302	0.577	0.743	0.477	0.594	0.598	0.380	0.586	0.654
19. CR	1.847	4.766	8.647	3.300	3.589	3.967	2.519	3.693	5.272
20. QR	0.452	3.600	6.156	1.139	1.594	2.159	0.896	1.728	3.763
21. LR	0.792	5.996	241.995	5.326	10.584	41.673	3.594	8.290	111.464
22. WCT	1.496	2.718	6.915	2.584	3.247	3.792	2.565	2.982	4.751
23. ART	4.288	9.238	10.974	5.565	6.688	9.573	5.361	7.256	9.745
24. IT	1.690	4.014	8.044	2.495	2.723	3.842	2.103	2.963	4.996
25. ALTZ	3.313	4.923	6.988	2.669	3.230	3.808	3.090	3.738	5.187

Table 18 Machinery—Electrical (36)

	Small Firms			Large Firms			All Firms		
	P25	P50	P75	P25	P50	P75	P25	P50	P75
1. ROS	-2.264	4.729	10.774	-0.093	7.042	11.739	-1.369	6.251	11.154
2. ROA	0.559	8.472	12.634	3.928	10.962	15.441	1.935	9.587	14.493
3. ROTNW	-4.845	12.966	22.180	-3.371	18.238	28.471	-4.448	14.748	27.079
4. PPC	-92.151	-29.882	18.117	-72.101	-7.296	10.464	-82.752	-16.404	12.328
5. PSC	-11.424	-0.146	11.701	-5.673	6.154	16.991	-9.413	3.771	13.811
6. STA	0.879	1.113	1.470	0.963	1.113	1.317	0.926	1.113	1.417
7. CVNI	64.313	104.825	358.211	40.192	61.868	124.517	48.747	85.803	214.246
8. LTDC	0.037	0.156	0.371	0.052	0.166	0.300	0.044	0.165	0.331
9. NTALTD	2.197	4.730	15.982	3.566	6.117	21.544	2.750	5.583	16.634
10. WCLTD	1.129	2.394	8.665	1.329	2.548	7.801	1.189	2.519	8.179
11. FCC	0.186	1.301	3.079	0.693	2.081	3.613	0.397	1.956	3.330
12. CFTD	0.047	0.138	0.306	0.113	0.256	0.405	0.064	0.211	0.368
13. TDTA	0.326	0.429	0.576	0.339	0.452	0.551	0.334	0.447	0.562
14. MVEBVD	1.025	1.900	3.222	1.175	2.129	3.894	1.103	1.984	3.513
15. IC	-0.339	2.484	8.500	0.808	3.922	9.190	0.128	3.114	8.932
16. LTDE	0.030	0.175	0.547	0.054	0.199	0.428	0.042	0.190	0.473
17. TNWTD	0.663	1.236	1.986	0.823	1.145	1.823	0.767	1.196	1.904
18. WCTA	0.308	0.414	0.526	0.230	0.333	0.451	0.270	0.375	0.498
19. CR	2.149	2.793	4.082	1.768	2.383	3.263	1.918	2.563	3.547
20. QR	1.032	1.538	2.308	0.890	1.288	1.945	0.939	1.423	2.088
21. LR	3.149	8.153	31.727	4.594	10.264	34.073	3.702	9.316	32.204
22. WCT	2.012	2.789	4.019	2.363	3.840	5.162	2.208	3.127	4.575
23. ART	4.065	5.164	6.299	4.050	4.898	6.376	4.051	5.061	6.361
24. IT	2.108	3.061	4.190	2.430	3.319	4.151	2.279	3.254	4.170
25. ALTZ	1.989	2.803	4.220	2.368	3.132	4.773	2.122	3.089	4.596

Table 19   Machinery—Non Electrical (35)

	Small Firms			Large Firms			All Firms		
	P25	P50	P75	P25	P50	P75	P25	P50	P75
1. ROS	-2.442	3.359	8.233	-0.697	3.472	7.793	-1.341	3.440	7.903
2. ROA	-0.241	7.509	15.082	2.606	6.613	12.501	1.695	6.783	14.234
3. ROTNW	-32.085	6.453	21.621	0.765	8.958	21.720	-4.192	7.670	21.416
4. PPC	-85.390	-9.341	46.692	-116.304	-25.132	8.190	-98.174	-17.015	20.074
5. PSC	-5.258	3.504	15.469	-2.888	3.801	11.204	-4.659	3.801	12.003
6. STA	0.968	1.247	1.500	1.018	1.193	1.313	1.004	1.219	1.438
7. CVNI	55.840	121.285	359.015	47.192	74.182	209.626	49.352	90.669	259.015
8. LTDC	0.107	0.273	0.490	0.169	0.257	0.341	0.140	0.262	0.371
9. NTALTD	1.914	3.169	8.991	3.062	3.782	5.781	2.260	3.541	6.259
10. WCLTD	0.861	2.032	4.703	1.088	1.748	2.544	1.060	1.804	3.019
11. FCC	0.614	1.764	2.874	0.274	1.514	2.413	0.475	1.654	2.637
12. CFTD	0.048	0.194	0.352	0.082	0.167	0.274	0.069	0.187	0.336
13. TDTA	0.408	0.512	0.665	0.464	0.523	0.615	0.434	0.518	0.640
14. MVEBVD	0.652	1.276	2.083	0.779	1.053	1.691	0.706	1.147	1.870
15. IC	0.110	2.189	4.819	0.789	1.732	4.160	0.662	2.034	4.489
16. LTDE	0.070	0.307	0.832	0.197	0.344	0.511	0.144	0.342	0.567
17. TNWTD	0.431	0.725	1.367	0.534	0.817	1.099	0.497	0.813	1.119
18. WCTA	0.300	0.393	0.468	0.234	0.293	0.340	0.240	0.322	0.426
19. CR	1.845	2.407	3.127	1.687	2.027	2.344	1.760	2.202	2.846
20. QR	0.919	1.208	1.822	0.806	0.996	1.270	0.830	1.078	1.440
21. LR	2.635	6.059	18.430	4.941	7.183	17.149	3.338	7.115	17.149
22. WCT	2.531	3.411	4.708	3.179	4.140	5.011	2.769	3.870	4.880
23. ART	3.639	4.420	6.187	4.477	5.239	6.979	3.948	5.017	6.303
24. IT	2.383	3.023	4.226	2.568	3.509	4.414	2.517	3.181	4.360
25. ALTZ	1.842	2.591	3.832	1.881	2.431	3.083	1.881	2.511	3.452

Table 20 Newspapers, Books, and Periodicals (27)

	Small Firms			Large Firms			All Firms		
	P25	P50	P75	P25	P50	P75	P25	P50	P75
1. ROS	6.532	11.713	16.385	11.453	13.439	19.798	9.075	12.379	17.714
2. ROA	14.034	18.691	25.721	14.528	19.077	22.770	14.050	19.077	23.690
3. ROTNW	25.302	32.901	46.307	29.675	50.273	73.051	26.930	37.621	55.658
4. PPC	−1.923	15.423	25.592	0.619	12.065	26.617	0.796	12.906	25.252
5. PSC	5.487	11.145	17.756	6.197	8.724	12.528	5.949	9.155	13.046
6. STA	1.175	1.405	1.667	0.857	1.076	1.195	0.988	1.175	1.470
7. CVNI	31.537	47.422	64.810	33.584	44.914	57.144	33.579	46.273	59.718
8. LTDC	0.085	0.170	0.324	0.188	0.316	0.445	0.109	0.278	0.378
9. NTALTD	2.784	4.299	10.071	1.752	2.413	5.154	2.069	3.152	8.365
10. WCLTD	0.630	1.788	5.724	0.144	0.602	2.092	0.349	1.136	4.779
11. FCC	1.745	3.071	5.265	2.222	2.969	3.878	2.020	2.969	4.383
12. CFTD	0.199	0.385	0.548	0.223	0.259	0.372	0.223	0.303	0.393
13. TDTA	0.325	0.427	0.558	0.448	0.546	0.612	0.374	0.493	0.605
14. MVEBVD	1.199	3.896	6.539	1.664	2.807	4.005	1.524	3.028	4.972
15. IC	2.889	7.655	11.244	3.990	6.069	12.877	3.980	6.140	12.409
16. LTDE	0.093	0.205	0.479	0.235	0.463	0.801	0.122	0.385	0.608
17. TNWTD	0.538	1.136	1.923	0.337	0.484	0.923	0.370	0.702	1.545
18. WCTA	0.142	0.361	0.425	0.055	0.142	0.275	0.085	0.217	0.404
19. CR	1.730	2.533	3.555	1.307	1.775	2.366	1.438	2.013	2.987
20. QR	1.081	1.707	2.888	0.807	1.130	1.634	0.908	1.490	2.051
21. LR	5.041	29.561	71.555	6.066	10.324	74.090	5.859	14.933	66.425
22. WCT	3.549	4.251	8.261	3.341	7.016	11.883	3.605	6.159	9.665
23. ART	4.574	5.687	7.656	5.646	7.302	8.543	5.148	6.843	7.963
24. IT	4.673	7.059	11.487	4.377	12.337	21.451	4.676	8.877	18.822
25. ALTZ	3.464	5.153	6.993	2.743	3.925	4.946	3.103	4.411	5.709

Table 21   Paper and Related Products (26)

	Small Firms			Large Firms			All Firms		
	P25	P50	P75	P25	P50	P75	P25	P50	P75
1. ROS	2.192	5.815	8.679	3.530	6.166	10.491	3.525	5.815	9.906
2. ROA	6.724	9.681	13.174	6.897	9.927	11.763	8.878	9.681	12.683
3. ROTNW	7.721	15.608	20.151	9.414	13.673	20.960	8.426	14.444	20.503
4. PPC	−60.866	−28.009	16.654	−56.857	−12.333	12.993	−55.434	−15.496	15.997
5. PSC	−9.610	−1.225	11.604	−1.730	1.506	5.235	−4.226	0.385	7.821
6. STA	0.850	1.217	1.481	0.862	1.063	1.236	0.854	1.143	1.322
7. CVNI	32.510	61.061	121.826	30.112	40.785	66.545	30.244	46.206	86.516
8. LTDC	0.150	0.235	0.585	0.237	0.330	0.395	0.196	0.311	0.399
9. NTALTD	1.812	3.478	5.450	2.962	3.086	4.428	2.513	3.138	4.769
10. WCLTD	0.289	1.234	2.472	0.210	0.459	0.832	0.257	0.661	1.851
11. FCC	1.043	1.389	2.582	1.634	1.965	2.753	1.229	1.779	2.625
12. CFTD	0.074	0.116	0.250	0.184	0.212	0.319	0.112	0.195	0.281
13. TDTA	0.353	0.456	0.656	0.458	0.522	0.562	0.408	0.513	0.568
14. MVEBVD	0.628	1.438	1.654	0.841	1.134	1.520	0.757	1.138	1.652
15. IC	1.297	2.822	5.333	1.928	2.472	4.270	1.829	2.573	4.296
16. LTDE	0.177	0.307	1.410	0.310	0.492	0.652	0.244	0.451	0.663
17. TNWTD	0.541	1.116	1.642	0.626	0.905	0.971	0.588	0.912	1.247
18. WCTA	0.141	0.271	0.308	0.044	0.106	0.177	0.075	0.153	0.276
19. CR	1.891	2.207	2.525	1.206	1.597	2.059	1.473	1.939	2.455
20. QR	0.969	1.090	1.728	0.668	0.893	1.091	0.798	0.998	1.418
21. LR	3.916	6.577	20.498	3.987	6.818	16.075	3.987	6.601	17.951
22. WCT	4.251	4.904	7.906	5.759	10.066	14.304	4.415	7.351	10.421
23. ART	6.490	8.604	11.546	8.577	9.480	10.681	7.577	9.411	11.160
24. IT	4.290	6.287	7.283	5.211	7.250	8.118	4.593	6.748	7.939
25. ALTZ	1.804	3.142	3.632	2.252	2.527	2.693	2.085	2.580	3.382

Table 22   Real Estate Development (65)

	Small Firms			Large Firms			All Firms		
	P25	P50	P75	P25	P50	P75	P25	P50	P75
1. ROS	-1.816	8.131	30.936	4.408	9.350	14.853	3.639	8.883	19.559
2. ROA	1.079	7.699	10.947	8.776	11.803	16.674	4.751	9.626	14.002
3. ROTNW	0.717	6.735	21.944	9.722	25.571	40.630	5.303	18.381	35.431
4. PPC	-61.081	-28.188	91.112	-50.551	24.043	56.486	-56.987	6.539	59.768
5. PSC	-21.291	-1.199	41.078	-6.837	25.333	38.402	-8.907	11.139	37.296
6. STA	0.127	0.188	0.337	0.472	0.684	0.908	0.188	0.387	0.740
7. CVNI	80.334	132.510	329.409	65.010	81.210	136.834	69.258	96.997	187.777
8. LTDC	0.077	0.524	0.768	0.390	0.556	0.691	0.268	0.548	0.733
9. NTALTD	1.441	1.918	13.105	1.535	2.450	2.897	1.513	1.970	3.802
10. WCLTD	0.127	0.341	0.778	0.173	0.993	1.876	0.146	0.430	1.798
11. FCC	0.433	1.049	2.172	1.231	1.443	2.234	1.090	1.384	2.234
12. CFTD	0.030	0.096	2.430	0.030	0.134	0.183	0.031	0.098	0.176
13. TDTA	0.325	0.657	0.774	0.610	0.653	0.767	0.463	0.655	0.768
14. MVEBVD	0.301	0.850	1.673	0.344	0.686	1.159	0.335	0.791	1.182
15. IC	0.863	1.538	2.191	1.256	1.831	2.681	1.149	1.582	2.372
16. LTDE	0.050	0.638	2.581	0.642	1.252	2.239	0.300	1.127	2.355
17. TNWTD	0.272	0.595	2.806	0.221	0.474	0.605	0.246	0.544	1.021
18. WCTA	0.046	0.106	0.315	0.062	0.141	0.462	0.048	0.127	0.408
19. CR	1.458	1.943	2.353	1.164	1.641	2.952	1.365	1.720	2.665
20. QR	0.431	1.098	1.783	0.507	0.672	0.862	0.468	0.709	1.360
21. LR	1.004	4.130	21.373	0.683	1.869	2.628	0.943	2.360	5.043
22. WCT	0.072	1.594	4.183	2.173	4.654	11.436	1.289	3.109	5.705
23. ART	1.310	5.496	52.582	6.665	13.608	19.982	4.904	10.132	25.104
24. IT	0.285	1.027	3.297	0.874	1.351	3.429	0.803	1.312	3.297
25. ALTZ	0.817	1.447	2.366	1.605	1.958	3.130	1.374	1.782	2.829

Table 23   Real Estate Investment (67)

	Small Firms			Large Firms			All Firms		
	P25	P50	P75	P25	P50	P75	P25	P50	P75
1. ROS	33.483	62.490	91.513	35.381	53.614	91.152	35.167	54.874	91.214
2. ROA	8.618	11.802	13.815	8.368	12.140	23.516	8.599	12.140	19.043
3. ROTNW	5.612	12.743	16.381	8.996	15.354	23.017	7.879	13.632	20.742
4. PPC	-48.103	-6.397	27.130	-13.120	2.183	36.868	-21.692	0.908	36.853
5. PSC	-13.397	4.192	36.006	-3.823	6.086	25.573	-11.198	4.813	26.757
6. STA	0.080	0.123	0.164	0.119	0.171	0.361	0.106	0.149	0.247
7. CVNI	40.220	84.652	358.857	24.695	55.830	76.857	38.790	61.595	89.463
8. LTDC	0.000	0.025	0.286	0.000	0.095	0.412	0.000	0.032	0.382
9. NTALTD	1.635	4.271	29.656	1.769	2.330	5.914	1.728	3.654	8.949
10. WCLTD	33.830	33.830	33.830	7.297	13.960	20.623	7.297	20.623	33.830
11. FCC	1.215	1.699	2.182	1.802	5.225	8.648	1.362	1.992	7.031
12. CFTD	0.070	0.494	3.494	0.095	0.492	11.844	0.093	0.493	4.999
13. TDTA	0.031	0.155	0.664	0.045	0.338	0.540	0.044	0.219	0.597
14. MVEBVD	1.378	6.975	26.744	1.246	3.981	75.308	1.417	5.754	38.372
15. IC	1.208	2.071	5.751	1.836	3.099	6.928	1.711	2.312	6.832
16. LTDE	0.000	0.025	0.401	0.000	0.105	0.703	0.000	0.033	0.618
17. TNWTD	0.458	4.026	11.766	0.484	1.613	21.905	0.484	3.136	14.756
18. WCTA	0.002	0.306	0.617	-0.000	0.030	0.181	0.002	0.051	0.378
19. CR	1.878	5.173	8.521	0.299	2.480	5.628	1.010	3.102	7.671
20. QR	1.085	3.323	7.914	0.299	2.333	5.628	1.029	3.039	6.200
21. LR	3.838	3.995	9.741	0.000	0.426	350.344	0.320	3.916	94.891
22. WCT	0.172	1.140	130.429	-3.188	2.236	11.987	0.140	2.189	9.810
23. ART	0.757	5.334	78.744	2.778	4.928	23.072	1.788	4.928	39.269
24. IT	0.000	0.000	0.000	15.598	15.598	15.598	0.000	7.799	15.598
25. ALTZ	1.979	4.822	18.094	5.038	44.423	174.545	4.111	11.566	76.954

Table 24 Retail—Apparel (56)

	Small Firms			Large Firms			All Firms		
	P25	P50	P75	P25	P50	P75	P25	P50	P75
1. ROS	-4.629	5.954	12.212	4.002	7.452	10.141	1.869	6.712	10.487
2. ROA	-9.983	18.990	31.130	9.497	16.540	24.985	9.242	17.180	24.985
3. ROTNW	2.360	26.602	44.209	12.775	29.278	45.978	9.356	28.781	44.770
4. PPC	-79.135	0.213	4.522	-25.814	18.703	49.862	-35.204	0.630	23.787
5. PSC	1.672	5.345	35.282	-0.742	12.582	24.703	2.738	8.499	32.657
6. STA	1.577	2.450	2.705	1.751	2.026	2.290	1.720	2.185	2.517
7. CVNI	22.566	60.325	289.534	32.032	47.735	73.483	24.032	53.188	123.329
8. LTDC	0.026	0.087	0.229	0.107	0.289	0.493	0.077	0.156	0.430
9. NTALTD	6.252	11.162	13.332	2.157	4.501	10.027	2.555	6.509	11.440
10. WCLTD	1.988	5.043	6.608	0.575	1.892	5.351	1.097	2.757	6.418
11. PCC	0.437	1.536	2.230	1.233	1.598	1.900	1.233	1.598	2.046
12. CFTD	-0.258	0.225	0.569	0.228	0.291	0.338	0.214	0.248	0.408
13. TDTA	0.291	0.373	0.576	0.434	0.463	0.608	0.347	0.440	0.581
14. MVEBVD	1.265	2.250	11.542	1.756	2.287	4.460	1.617	2.250	4.587
15. IC	-1.680	8.466	20.304	2.887	4.807	12.746	2.880	5.033	19.492
16. LTDE	0.027	0.095	0.335	0.120	0.414	0.971	0.084	0.185	0.754
17. TNWTD	0.870	1.774	2.456	0.538	1.082	1.239	0.660	1.212	1.907
18. WCTA	0.211	0.360	0.562	0.236	0.324	0.478	0.236	0.348	0.499
19. CR	1.789	2.424	3.973	1.798	2.342	3.331	1.906	2.342	3.513
20. QR	0.191	0.762	1.478	0.358	0.645	1.122	0.236	0.645	1.280
21. LR	0.572	13.485	26.176	10.372	15.370	43.439	4.922	13.690	29.760
22. WCT	3.642	6.232	11.711	3.964	7.230	9.990	4.039	7.126	8.987
23. ART	27.093	44.750	78.685	14.420	44.210	90.409	19.004	44.210	81.938
24. IT	2.183	3.758	4.764	2.602	3.513	4.864	2.441	3.670	4.411
25. ALTZ	3.394	5.010	11.590	3.613	4.354	6.303	3.395	4.670	6.756

Table 25   Retail—Eating Places (58)

	Small Firms			Large Firms			All Firms		
	P25	P50	P75	P25	P50	P75	P25	P50	P75
1. ROS	-5.687	3.354	9.558	2.551	6.678	12.127	0.481	4.931	10.200
2. ROA	-1.809	10.720	16.155	7.065	11.600	20.249	5.312	11.462	17.179
3. ROTNW	-38.663	11.310	37.736	17.859	30.676	40.160	-3.141	21.197	39.208
4. PPC	-112.909	-35.386	60.378	-50.321	-2.006	21.970	-52.728	-6.359	27.039
5. PSC	-6.007	3.753	14.449	1.270	10.309	17.147	-0.247	7.433	15.593
6. STA	1.160	1.641	2.220	1.158	1.356	1.712	1.159	1.590	1.763
7. CVNI	36.213	80.372	212.122	31.587	48.749	63.394	35.580	58.440	195.401
8. LTDC	0.282	0.504	0.689	0.201	0.294	0.584	0.223	0.369	0.608
9. NTALTD	1.189	1.589	12.560	2.162	3.095	4.222	1.442	2.643	4.098
10. WCLTD	-0.326	0.032	0.101	-0.367	-0.179	0.163	-0.335	-0.038	0.105
11. FCC	0.472	0.963	1.770	1.248	1.617	2.963	0.874	1.486	2.643
12. CFTD	0.030	0.467	0.919	0.191	0.299	0.427	0.121	0.331	0.525
13. TDTA	0.456	0.593	0.790	0.407	0.453	0.659	0.421	0.567	0.773
14. MVEBVD	0.448	0.830	3.152	1.007	1.610	3.472	0.708	1.165	3.232
15. IC	-0.080	0.930	3.083	1.651	3.766	9.501	0.724	2.560	6.117
16. LTDE	0.049	0.604	1.606	0.153	0.333	0.730	0.151	0.437	1.227
17. TNWTD	0.139	0.364	1.176	0.326	0.835	1.190	0.238	0.612	1.173
18. WCTA	-0.096	0.010	0.042	-0.085	-0.038	0.029	-0.080	-0.019	0.033
19. CR	0.589	1.050	1.197	0.425	0.798	1.197	0.491	0.922	1.180
20. QR	0.382	0.560	0.871	0.278	0.423	0.686	0.321	0.528	0.763
21. LR	1.403	3.989	9.614	2.154	5.265	16.674	1.912	4.944	11.290
22. WCT	-13.565	26.297	89.446	-27.707	-6.723	36.271	-15.950	-1.812	43.503
23. ART	19.499	26.285	65.211	18.349	37.531	60.853	19.570	32.217	58.529
24. IT	19.583	39.855	58.416	23.254	31.702	58.765	20.405	34.104	57.955
25. ALTZ	1.833	2.714	5.500	2.521	3.422	4.698	2.293	3.189	4.510

Table 26　Retail—General Merchandise (53)

	Small Firms			Large Firms			All Firms		
	P25	P50	P75	P25	P50	P75	P25	P50	P75
1. ROS	1.877	2.483	5.702	3.996	5.349	7.142	2.186	4.920	6.860
2. ROA	8.049	10.635	18.980	11.673	13.755	15.807	8.323	12.470	16.195
3. ROTNW	13.218	17.204	42.554	14.850	23.750	31.101	13.698	19.739	32.669
4. PPC	−37.542	16.928	50.286	−6.924	9.291	20.377	−21.504	9.363	24.462
5. PSC	3.686	10.591	22.831	4.011	6.667	9.793	4.044	8.185	12.459
6. STA	1.859	2.137	2.512	1.476	1.780	2.250	1.697	1.933	2.360
7. CVNI	58.319	81.594	99.764	31.524	39.620	49.348	33.948	49.088	84.503
8. LTDC	0.058	0.361	0.474	0.284	0.341	0.465	0.270	0.351	0.467
9. NTALTD	2.146	2.732	2.910	2.159	2.783	4.333	2.150	2.732	3.587
10. WCLTD	0.754	1.098	1.693	0.975	1.258	1.649	0.851	1.235	1.621
11. FCC	1.247	1.506	2.037	1.455	1.888	2.665	1.358	1.734	2.462
12. CFTD	0.082	0.137	0.244	0.157	0.202	0.226	0.131	0.187	0.238
13. TDTA	0.462	0.590	0.683	0.534	0.559	0.631	0.525	0.579	0.662
14. MVEBVD	0.589	1.491	4.070	0.658	1.181	1.817	0.613	1.269	2.372
15. IC	1.561	2.002	3.093	1.555	3.330	4.168	1.555	2.551	4.077
16. LTDE	0.062	0.565	0.902	0.396	0.518	0.870	0.370	0.541	0.875
17. TNWTD	0.450	0.649	0.819	0.469	0.616	0.898	0.455	0.624	0.820
18. WCTA	0.224	0.254	0.435	0.228	0.256	0.303	0.229	0.256	0.384
19. CR	1.651	2.176	2.742	1.676	1.797	2.120	1.670	1.830	2.298
20. QR	0.264	0.379	0.609	0.280	0.785	1.335	0.270	0.500	1.042
21. LR	1.545	5.603	6.315	5.088	10.214	37.386	4.540	6.112	25.959
22. WCT	6.295	7.252	10.331	4.731	7.963	10.268	5.318	7.377	10.217
23. ART	16.746	44.754	110.379	4.522	7.442	36.289	6.330	17.759	48.690
24. IT	2.904	3.759	5.665	3.539	4.380	4.969	3.340	3.839	4.956
25. ALTZ	2.709	4.130	4.733	2.610	3.487	4.317	2.644	3.605	4.500

Table 27   Retail—Miscellaneous (59)

	Small Firms			Large Firms			All Firms		
	P25	P50	P75	P25	P50	P75	P25	P50	P75
1. ROS	1.419	3.811	6.115	0.609	2.823	5.493	1.325	3.205	5.581
2. ROA	4.293	9.499	15.452	5.602	9.556	19.097	4.993	9.505	16.021
3. ROTNW	8.758	13.975	21.999	-0.556	14.947	30.155	5.460	14.062	26.099
4. PPC	-78.631	-35.598	65.638	-80.384	-33.111	6.596	-79.135	-33.531	9.408
5. PSC	-13.333	4.293	14.998	-0.452	7.637	15.205	-1.281	5.846	15.010
6. STA	1.834	2.198	2.635	1.130	1.714	2.821	1.249	1.987	2.709
7. CVNI	39.195	57.637	525.733	48.593	70.010	136.518	42.012	60.455	153.347
8. LTDC	0.000	0.196	0.355	0.108	0.400	0.508	0.067	0.234	0.482
9. NTALTD	2.183	4.510	6.320	1.899	2.763	8.734	1.946	3.326	7.994
10. WCLTD	1.029	1.622	3.514	0.848	1.345	2.140	0.854	1.525	3.417
11. TCC	1.085	1.407	1.936	1.195	1.552	2.030	1.144	1.479	1.954
12. CFTD	0.123	0.154	0.306	0.094	0.119	0.275	0.104	0.139	0.288
13. TDTA	0.394	0.476	0.545	0.431	0.593	0.607	0.397	0.498	0.636
14. MVEBVD	0.988	2.077	4.826	0.700	1.269	2.531	0.914	1.326	3.590
15. IC	1.487	3.811	4.843	1.823	2.727	3.858	1.657	2.781	4.723
16. LTDE	0.000	0.244	0.551	0.122	0.672	1.034	0.072	0.306	0.931
17. TNWTD	0.638	1.065	1.472	0.518	0.795	1.326	0.566	1.013	1.399
18. WCTA	0.297	0.432	0.519	0.155	0.283	0.364	0.178	0.324	0.491
19. CR	1.841	2.289	2.774	1.523	1.970	2.511	1.715	2.088	2.522
20. QR	0.302	0.875	1.619	0.319	0.595	0.988	0.315	0.736	1.059
21. LR	0.782	2.809	9.610	2.534	5.496	23.117	1.431	3.887	13.183
22. WCT	2.914	4.884	5.842	3.972	8.542	13.206	3.578	5.612	9.388
23. ART	6.781	19.723	43.046	6.296	31.620	79.497	6.674	22.399	50.595
24. IT	2.120	3.682	5.291	2.757	4.071	6.003	2.339	4.071	5.688
25. ALTZ	3.325	4.010	5.538	2.571	3.691	5.495	3.103	3.953	5.327

Table 28   Rubber and Plastic Products (30)

	Small Firms			Large Firms			All Firms		
	P25	P50	P75	P25	P50	P75	P25	P50	P75
1. ROS	-5.113	4.948	10.586	3.081	4.763	10.618	1.720	4.921	10.594
2. ROA	-1.033	10.320	16.014	7.795	10.885	17.292	5.305	10.603	16.660
3. ROTNW	-16.364	19.041	44.319	12.407	20.011	28.650	7.435	19.800	34.010
4. PPC	-163.305	-12.853	13.551	-32.927	1.351	18.480	-48.794	-6.559	15.815
5. PSC	-12.239	3.134	16.398	-5.897	2.259	10.328	-7.643	2.753	11.253
6. STA	0.748	1.266	1.930	1.134	1.390	1.542	1.054	1.353	1.808
7. CVNI	52.068	123.387	437.866	39.329	51.869	94.011	45.719	64.135	291.279
8. LTDC	0.081	0.239	0.341	0.144	0.211	0.430	0.129	0.216	0.374
9. NTALTD	3.191	4.194	9.899	2.230	3.100	5.149	2.511	3.727	5.532
10. WCLTD	0.865	2.312	5.369	0.974	1.547	3.101	0.964	1.669	3.824
11. FCC	0.742	2.391	3.528	1.629	2.096	3.334	1.589	2.313	3.343
12. CFTD	0.037	0.205	0.562	0.122	0.227	0.382	0.108	0.215	0.454
13. TDTA	0.327	0.471	0.693	0.372	0.523	0.630	0.363	0.481	0.679
14. MVEBVD	0.784	1.401	4.829	0.502	1.161	3.165	0.563	1.292	3.243
15. IC	0.522	4.510	10.358	1.898	3.361	7.207	1.886	4.042	7.434
16. LTDE	0.089	0.314	0.517	0.162	0.239	0.752	0.107	0.253	0.525
17. TNWTD	0.400	0.800	1.627	0.487	0.647	1.051	0.470	0.729	1.190
18. WCTA	0.130	0.271	0.438	0.208	0.315	0.374	0.206	0.284	0.415
19. CR	1.353	2.387	2.817	1.677	2.338	2.926	1.607	2.362	2.844
20. QR	0.730	1.259	2.371	0.874	1.323	1.945	0.793	1.284	2.108
21. LR	2.977	11.556	43.693	7.210	10.589	34.840	5.468	10.589	35.472
22. WCT	4.015	5.409	7.078	4.440	5.116	8.361	4.400	5.252	7.188
23. ART	5.655	6.507	8.116	5.862	6.835	8.167	5.684	6.816	8.128
24. IT	3.604	5.534	8.134	5.412	5.654	6.304	4.461	5.632	7.246
25. ALTZ	2.049	3.556	5.825	2.294	3.306	4.596	2.238	3.431	4.788

Table 29   Security and Commodity Brokers (62)

	Small Firms			Large Firms			All Firms		
	P25	P50	P75	P25	P50	P75	P25	P50	P75
1. ROS	4.610	10.078	14.436	3.177	8.298	18.878	3.380	9.361	17.028
2. ROA	4.977	7.617	11.336	5.626	6.514	10.096	5.770	6.581	11.296
3. ROTNW	12.039	20.398	39.225	15.452	35.892	49.681	15.378	33.923	46.845
4. PPC	-179.453	-8.524	144.680	5.566	47.667	340.483	-29.705	38.655	172.884
5. PSC	-15.266	27.525	49.455	9.905	20.411	22.071	7.326	21.351	30.203
6. STA	0.258	0.376	0.525	0.114	0.196	0.439	0.164	0.304	0.498
7. CVNI	46.815	52.920	134.575	52.242	84.897	110.593	50.259	56.265	115.150
8. LTDC	0.000	0.051	0.391	0.000	0.314	0.407	0.000	0.134	0.405
9. NTALTD	10.263	10.263	10.263	2.448	5.369	8.290	2.448	8.290	10.263
10. WCLTD				0.377	1.174	1.971	0.377	1.174	1.971
11. FCC	1.137	1.484	1.732	1.047	1.146	3.582	1.079	1.384	1.866
12. CFTD	0.048	0.048	0.048	0.099	0.853	1.608	0.048	0.099	1.608
13. TDTA	0.708	0.755	0.861	0.296	0.453	0.810	0.428	0.706	0.839
14. MVEBVD	0.363	0.510	0.658	0.324	1.061	13.955	0.363	0.658	6.710
15. IC	1.222	1.760	2.328	1.060	1.151	3.345	1.096	1.295	2.328
16. LTDE	0.000	0.054	0.646	0.000	0.457	0.686	0.000	0.155	0.681
17. TNWTD	0.242	0.309	0.377	0.277	1.120	2.437	0.242	0.536	1.142
18. WCTA				0.093	0.148	0.352	0.093	0.148	0.352
19. CR				1.289	1.395	3.187	1.289	1.395	3.187
20. QR				0.646	0.923	1.200	0.646	0.923	1.200
21. LR				1.204	1.442	1.681	1.204	1.442	1.681
22. WCT				2.207	2.982	12.552	2.207	2.982	12.552
23. ART				1.234	5.009	8.785	1.234	5.009	8.785
24. IT	1.191	2.562	4.404	0.065	0.405	2.317	0.354	1.224	3.248
25. ALTZ				1.219	2.990	15.251	1.219	2.990	15.251

Table 30   Services—Business (73)

	Small Firms			Large Firms			All Firms		
	P25	P50	P75	P25	P50	P75	P25	P50	P75
1. ROS	-1.007	2.423	11.486	3.122	9.430	15.056	0.683	6.988	14.073
2. ROA	2.157	7.666	22.605	5.419	10.608	17.761	4.797	10.251	19.987
3. ROTNW	-14.312	11.100	40.377	20.330	27.053	51.351	1.990	24.671	41.020
4. PPC	-73.565	18.822	91.370	-43.082	4.158	55.315	-64.088	11.957	60.656
5. PSC	-2.527	10.128	27.833	6.361	13.442	24.392	1.050	12.259	25.989
6. STA	0.970	1.524	2.427	0.540	0.939	1.250	0.757	1.154	2.043
7. CVNI	56.528	115.036	350.463	44.721	66.059	112.402	50.177	77.749	183.586
8. LTDC	0.005	0.199	0.404	0.040	0.155	0.398	0.032	0.173	0.399
9. NTALTD	1.605	4.600	27.168	2.264	4.450	11.926	2.052	4.589	20.821
10. WCLTD	0.682	1.741	8.328	0.946	3.329	6.786	0.701	2.139	7.122
11. FCC	0.580	1.509	2.798	1.287	1.701	2.670	1.003	1.639	2.702
12. CFTD	0.094	0.304	0.501	0.086	0.167	0.410	0.086	0.226	0.479
13. TDTA	0.410	0.593	0.692	0.362	0.524	0.690	0.377	0.588	0.689
14. MVEBVD	0.673	1.757	4.474	0.686	1.772	5.389	0.680	1.772	4.883
15. IC	-1.548	1.765	7.602	1.462	4.666	11.860	0.572	2.840	11.651
16. LTDE	0.002	0.247	0.636	0.042	0.184	0.661	0.028	0.190	0.642
17. TNWTD	0.382	0.664	1.958	0.257	0.521	0.837	0.286	0.637	1.335
18. WCTA	0.128	0.270	0.530	0.146	0.219	0.301	0.141	0.242	0.400
19. CR	1.317	1.529	3.024	1.303	1.682	2.405	1.314	1.604	2.592
20. QR	1.175	1.376	2.665	1.209	1.453	1.984	1.175	1.420	2.179
21. LR	4.627	20.371	84.169	9.137	28.769	45.430	5.209	24.130	59.914
22. WCT	2.286	4.911	9.856	2.791	5.533	8.953	2.769	5.338	9.589
23. ART	3.337	4.541	6.245	2.838	4.310	6.595	3.101	4.447	6.437
24. IT	4.557	6.388	20.375	4.786	9.226	33.297	4.565	6.812	25.098
25. ALTZ	1.601	3.583	5.461	1.743	3.252	5.364	1.729	3.457	5.454

Table 31 Services—Electric, Gas, and Sanitary (49)

	Small Firms			Large Firms			All Firms		
	P25	P50	P75	P25	P50	P75	P25	P50	P75
1. ROS	5.106	8.254	16.645	11.671	19.700	23.918	6.406	14.820	21.569
2. ROA	9.437	12.101	13.673	10.588	11.814	12.988	9.931	11.973	13.181
3. ROTNW	4.322	27.959	41.225	8.564	14.621	24.604	9.376	21.504	34.548
4. PPC	-14.616	-1.594	12.239	-9.425	2.411	10.487	-11.638	-0.044	10.649
5. PSC	-5.697	0.337	8.031	-2.772	2.418	7.146	-3.650	1.344	7.463
6. STA	0.484	0.877	1.215	0.311	0.429	0.586	0.382	0.538	0.979
7. CVNI	29.522	37.916	54.068	35.774	44.986	50.850	33.309	41.088	51.577
8. LTDC	0.385	0.453	0.532	0.442	0.485	0.522	0.424	0.470	0.524
9. NTALTD	1.656	2.145	4.482	1.752	2.023	2.317	1.705	2.023	2.934
10. WCLTD	-0.205	-0.064	0.142	-0.059	0.014	0.072	-0.130	-0.006	0.123
11. FCC	0.830	2.831	3.821	1.009	1.153	1.318	1.037	1.535	2.890
12. CFTD	0.123	0.151	0.184	0.133	0.158	0.183	0.130	0.156	0.183
13. TDTA	0.595	0.650	0.695	0.584	0.611	0.648	0.590	0.625	0.678
14. MVEBVD	0.527	0.821	4.379	0.323	0.501	0.675	0.461	0.601	1.179
15. IC	1.901	2.355	2.927	1.923	2.348	2.615	1.910	2.351	2.768
16. LTDE	0.626	0.829	1.135	0.793	0.941	1.092	0.737	0.886	1.100
17. TNWTD	0.363	0.458	0.899	0.273	0.385	0.529	0.338	0.447	0.614
18. WCTA	-0.058	-0.019	0.049	-0.025	0.005	0.025	-0.042	-0.002	0.089
19. CR	0.747	0.895	1.388	0.828	1.043	1.309	0.775	0.985	1.322
20. QR	0.816	1.193	1.481	0.515	0.707	0.975	0.599	0.937	1.206
21. LR	3.227	9.577	23.339	1.826	2.809	4.482	2.423	4.431	11.540
22. WCT	-21.209	-6.511	14.492	-12.069	8.835	24.455	-15.976	6.327	20.140
23. ART	5.220	6.911	8.529	6.138	6.942	8.721	5.872	6.926	8.474
24. IT	30.156	54.752	179.175	7.378	14.008	23.327	9.055	23.327	52.261
25. ALTZ	1.289	1.901	4.483	1.497	1.612	1.963	1.462	1.803	2.459

Table 32 Services—Engineering and Architectural (89)

	Small Firms			Large Firms			All Firms		
	P25	P50	P75	P25	P50	P75	P25	P50	P75
1. ROS	-3.320	4.428	5.744	1.875	4.841	7.178	1.383	4.551	5.878
2. ROA	-1.875	11.180	14.207	6.368	11.601	17.971	5.012	11.180	14.736
3. ROTNW	-77.625	22.104	29.683	12.758	19.170	60.825	2.838	22.088	29.870
4. PPC	-105.599	53.163	117.676	-122.131	-33.651	-1.674	-118.654	-20.086	-1.674
5. PSC	18.858	34.622	59.243	5.739	7.144	16.139	6.369	16.824	33.838
6. STA	1.064	1.528	2.262	1.393	1.952	2.732	1.342	1.647	2.265
7. CVNI	130.335	240.401	380.865	47.739	55.040	172.037	52.056	124.977	249.413
8. LTDC	0.029	0.136	0.680	0.061	0.264	0.400	0.054	0.222	0.418
9. NTALTD	1.513	5.503	21.941	3.162	8.372	32.039	2.551	5.805	21.277
10. WCLTD	1.077	2.523	21.844	1.097	1.678	5.060	1.077	2.405	11.882
11. FCC	0.772	1.546	1.712	1.134	1.738	2.131	1.203	1.628	1.863
12. CFTD	0.023	0.075	0.280	0.086	0.236	0.300	0.078	0.212	0.286
13. TDTA	0.401	0.545	0.801	0.494	0.548	0.690	0.486	0.545	0.709
14. MVEBVD	0.936	1.138	2.257	0.810	1.470	1.802	0.936	1.232	1.819
15. IC	-3.842	3.505	15.437	2.061	3.833	6.025	1.736	3.833	7.993
16. LTDE	0.030	0.158	2.124	0.065	0.364	0.670	0.057	0.285	0.718
17. TNWTD	0.291	0.702	1.004	0.310	0.620	0.973	0.314	0.685	0.906
18. WCTA	0.259	0.309	0.415	0.170	0.234	0.330	0.196	0.274	0.377
19. CR	1.626	2.034	2.140	1.431	1.585	2.523	1.457	1.681	2.140
20. QR	1.589	1.925	2.082	1.076	1.558	1.731	1.258	1.621	1.937
21. LR	4.563	46.050	86.979	3.773	25.182	44.377	4.317	34.731	60.940
22. WCT	5.334	6.782	8.021	4.820	10.439	18.081	5.669	7.684	12.163
23. ART	2.182	3.309	4.015	3.858	4.364	6.415	2.968	3.905	5.086
24. IT	13.797	52.918	88.622	7.620	14.837	43.365	12.660	17.014	52.918
25. ALTZ	1.681	2.963	4.030	2.738	3.110	5.260	2.452	3.110	4.622

Table 33 Services—Health (80)

	Small Firms			Large Firms			All Firms		
	P25	P50	P75	P25	P50	P75	P25	P50	P75
1. ROS	−3.798	2.532	7.176	4.505	11.261	14.184	2.352	6.100	12.400
2. ROA	−0.507	7.650	14.936	11.740	13.153	18.866	9.798	12.942	16.428
3. ROTNW	−3.550	23.755	38.701	28.929	37.684	44.876	16.641	28.966	43.045
4. PPC	−203.000	10.546	44.751	−17.401	13.198	25.165	−17.401	13.198	25.165
5. PSC	3.301	29.851	91.756	14.913	18.666	51.231	11.585	19.060	57.357
6. STA	1.073	1.377	1.654	0.659	0.773	0.880	0.738	0.907	1.392
7. CVNI	32.176	80.246	512.667	77.733	87.397	92.374	52.686	87.397	97.355
8. LTDC	0.164	0.279	0.676	0.570	0.613	0.791	0.202	0.572	0.676
9. NTALTD	1.396	2.999	5.951	1.194	1.548	2.087	1.393	1.657	4.451
10. WCLTD	0.040	1.780	4.557	0.104	0.141	0.197	0.098	0.184	1.890
11. FCC	0.458	1.321	1.764	1.179	1.548	2.013	1.116	1.323	1.991
12. CFTD	−0.052	0.240	0.405	0.087	0.155	0.238	0.087	0.155	0.292
13. TDTA	0.404	0.507	0.754	0.666	0.705	0.824	0.490	0.668	0.754
14. MVEBVD	1.004	2.074	2.928	0.434	0.778	1.670	0.731	1.402	2.329
15. IC	0.103	1.983	3.430	1.518	2.060	2.354	1.202	2.027	3.317
16. LTDE	0.196	0.388	2.083	1.324	1.585	4.209	0.254	1.335	2.083
17. TNWTD	0.156	0.791	0.881	0.208	0.322	0.487	0.208	0.361	0.856
18. WCTA	0.021	0.310	0.459	0.059	0.067	0.095	0.058	0.078	0.310
19. CR	1.097	1.793	2.691	1.433	1.477	1.678	1.427	1.615	2.107
20. QR	0.939	1.643	2.329	1.225	1.293	1.489	1.224	1.407	1.886
21. LR	4.783	10.826	13.656	7.752	12.263	23.182	6.327	11.754	19.077
22. WCT	2.363	7.794	11.923	8.954	11.716	21.447	6.089	10.260	16.889
23. ART	4.289	5.416	11.550	4.719	6.587	7.694	4.719	5.746	7.900
24. IT	6.418	12.008	208.928	32.881	42.280	49.148	17.888	37.345	61.001
25. ALTZ	1.847	2.901	3.581	1.762	1.941	2.847	1.762	2.440	3.129

Table 34 Stone, Clay, Glass, and Concrete Products (32)

	Small Firms			Large Firms			All Firms		
	P25	P50	P75	P25	P50	P75	P25	P50	P75
1. ROS	0.796	6.286	9.653	2.521	5.825	8.343	2.167	6.221	8.806
2. ROA	3.746	10.058	17.472	5.728	9.764	12.789	5.776	9.833	13.222
3. ROTNW	-0.106	13.518	33.863	3.461	11.832	19.218	5.871	12.585	24.422
4. PPC	-64.053	17.164	146.515	-42.646	16.515	27.721	-37.179	16.515	69.469
5. PSC	-0.995	10.600	15.200	-1.638	3.582	9.071	-1.177	4.295	12.903
6. STA	0.804	1.051	1.360	0.755	1.032	1.431	0.795	1.051	1.390
7. CVNI	86.984	186.785	257.916	41.682	55.291	112.531	48.230	92.688	207.923
8. LTDC	0.252	0.370	0.541	0.212	0.316	0.409	0.221	0.326	0.448
9. NTALTD	1.879	2.448	3.524	2.490	3.048	4.476	2.216	2.752	3.524
10. WCLTD	0.441	0.861	1.388	0.351	0.777	1.452	0.382	0.859	1.348
11. FCC	0.964	1.728	2.313	1.165	1.522	2.085	1.216	1.656	2.212
12. CFTD	0.107	0.144	0.445	0.159	0.200	0.220	0.135	0.173	0.225
13. TDTA	0.464	0.560	0.694	0.479	0.514	0.589	0.480	0.546	0.605
14. MVEBVD	0.573	0.859	1.506	0.594	0.935	1.575	0.639	0.903	1.490
15. IC	1.317	2.203	3.521	1.341	2.138	4.106	1.426	2.138	3.702
16. LTDE	0.339	0.593	1.185	0.269	0.462	0.693	0.283	0.484	0.811
17. TNWTD	0.492	0.730	1.190	0.630	0.822	1.065	0.627	0.730	1.109
18. WCTA	0.143	0.232	0.303	0.107	0.149	0.235	0.119	0.200	0.279
19. CR	1.644	1.960	3.317	1.591	1.827	2.266	1.615	1.911	2.336
20. QR	0.607	1.070	1.771	0.900	0.983	1.256	0.769	1.026	1.441
21. LR	2.253	5.980	23.198	3.334	7.713	17.790	3.156	6.896	20.202
22. WCT	3.451	5.233	9.867	4.924	6.797	9.133	4.105	5.736	9.514
23. ART	6.285	8.049	10.529	6.164	7.069	8.672	6.314	7.342	9.351
24. IT	3.947	5.193	8.705	4.687	6.411	8.126	4.248	5.657	8.193
25. ALTZ	1.586	2.395	2.960	1.779	2.288	3.361	1.696	2.377	3.209

Table 35   Textiles (22)

	Small Firms			Large Firms			All Firms		
	P25	P50	P75	P25	P50	P75	P25	P50	P75
1. ROS	-0.678	1.856	6.782	-0.480	3.931	8.271	-0.532	2.975	7.381
2. ROA	3.077	8.928	11.630	4.327	8.731	15.040	3.510	8.766	14.243
3. ROTNW	-0.825	12.531	24.077	9.035	20.958	25.786	5.769	15.741	25.081
4. PPC	-151.405	-57.532	43.604	-116.191	-39.188	23.737	-129.348	-44.110	23.787
5. PSC	-8.219	2.468	20.839	-9.593	4.058	13.190	-8.811	2.659	14.129
6. STA	1.304	1.614	2.081	1.211	1.491	1.593	1.246	1.559	1.993
7. CVNI	50.889	153.670	326.081	40.134	59.931	148.190	43.633	100.468	203.014
8. LTDC	0.130	0.301	0.501	0.238	0.320	0.476	0.178	0.320	0.497
9. NTALTD	1.921	3.279	8.106	2.588	3.219	4.447	1.987	3.219	6.167
10. WCLTD	1.180	2.338	4.745	1.000	1.742	2.222	1.183	1.881	3.072
11. FCC	0.909	1.560	2.265	0.936	1.879	3.340	0.968	1.826	2.349
12. CFTD	0.016	0.078	0.259	-0.005	0.181	0.387	0.017	0.139	0.326
13. TDTA	0.345	0.514	0.641	0.454	0.530	0.620	0.405	0.530	0.635
14. MVEBVD	0.514	1.141	1.737	0.641	0.903	1.978	0.598	0.948	1.820
15. IC	0.792	2.005	3.166	0.985	2.513	5.076	0.935	2.407	3.792
16. LTDE	0.149	0.441	1.006	0.313	0.472	0.938	0.217	0.472	0.988
17. TNWTD	0.523	0.899	1.611	0.646	0.934	1.245	0.608	0.934	1.456
18. WCTA	0.379	0.458	0.555	0.285	0.382	0.414	0.337	0.394	0.482
19. CR	2.400	3.213	4.084	2.352	2.721	2.884	2.352	2.860	3.478
20. QR	0.804	1.373	2.068	1.122	1.420	1.705	1.017	1.413	1.898
21. LR	2.814	5.710	22.030	4.119	6.127	21.706	3.639	6.127	21.706
22. WCT	2.536	3.816	4.661	3.324	4.031	5.631	3.214	3.897	5.023
23. ART	5.771	6.588	8.219	5.030	5.781	7.550	5.577	6.474	7.768
24. IT	2.943	3.797	4.746	3.906	4.777	5.662	3.516	4.368	5.241
25. ALTZ	2.336	3.267	3.846	2.111	2.777	4.390	2.181	2.892	3.851

Table 36   Transportation Equipment (37)

	Small Firms			Large Firms			All Firms		
	P25	P50	P75	P25	P50	P75	P25	P50	P75
1. ROS	0.021	4.995	8.459	5.085	7.337	9.400	2.230	6.696	9.321
2. ROA	3.739	11.262	18.528	11.211	13.729	18.357	6.634	12.994	18.108
3. ROTNW	6.009	21.096	34.038	21.417	27.328	50.053	16.219	25.844	39.142
4. PPC	-44.457	-2.327	62.930	-26.287	-0.831	20.377	-29.135	-2.327	43.171
5. PSC	-3.984	10.329	23.762	-5.285	3.316	17.838	-4.775	5.015	19.185
6. STA	1.245	1.565	2.090	1.252	1.528	1.865	1.255	1.542	1.950
7. CVNI	63.117	137.139	225.914	41.506	74.268	150.909	46.918	84.081	169.050
8. LTDC	0.044	0.217	0.432	0.067	0.223	0.383	0.049	0.221	0.423
9. NTALTD	2.258	4.172	10.218	3.074	4.572	12.714	2.373	4.531	11.949
10. WCLTD	0.793	1.836	5.254	0.485	0.808	2.417	0.585	1.202	3.480
11. FCC	0.560	1.865	4.388	1.658	2.660	4.085	1.083	2.476	4.166
12. CFTD	0.054	0.183	0.397	0.226	0.290	0.351	0.137	0.265	0.363
13. TDTA	0.372	0.510	0.669	0.465	0.595	0.666	0.404	0.576	0.666
14. MVEBVD	0.610	1.588	2.592	0.635	1.125	1.921	0.610	1.240	2.153
15. IC	1.050	3.466	6.860	3.128	6.176	13.332	2.003	5.160	10.987
16. LTDE	0.046	0.277	0.762	0.072	0.287	0.628	0.051	0.284	0.732
17. TNWTD	0.418	0.799	1.593	0.414	0.641	0.918	0.417	0.649	1.348
18. WCTA	0.208	0.331	0.417	0.058	0.185	0.312	0.104	0.259	0.376
19. CR	1.705	2.235	2.607	1.121	1.642	2.035	1.265	1.876	2.296
20. QR	0.867	1.123	1.519	0.633	0.775	1.180	0.693	0.934	1.281
21. LR	3.488	7.451	44.226	3.760	10.880	29.709	3.636	9.632	30.862
22. WCT	3.110	5.578	7.498	4.249	6.142	23.532	3.862	6.089	9.608
23. ART	5.411	7.061	10.384	6.734	7.875	12.778	5.951	7.667	11.515
24. IT	3.250	5.187	6.883	3.699	7.170	10.534	3.326	5.964	9.739
25. ALTZ	2.059	3.491	4.585	2.738	3.325	4.004	2.285	3.370	4.302

Table 37 Trucking (42)

	Small Firms			Large Firms			All Firms		
	P25	P50	P75	P25	P50	P75	P25	P50	P75
1. ROS	-1.476	3.950	4.951	0.191	4.159	6.653	-0.124	3.950	6.301
2. ROA	-0.347	13.092	13.809	3.238	7.487	12.224	2.342	9.244	13.428
3. ROTNW	-148.327	2.765	30.220	5.630	13.561	21.235	-3.536	9.914	25.875
4. PPC	-10.274	12.011	20.572	-103.698	-32.155	22.979	-76.306	-1.022	20.572
5. PSC	4.375	11.643	13.319	1.412	7.085	10.766	2.139	9.690	12.284
6. STA	1.565	2.095	2.414	1.206	1.620	1.860	1.389	1.800	2.095
7. CVNI	73.838	177.589	687.460	36.225	54.077	125.811	52.150	73.838	260.815
8. LTDC	0.323	0.375	0.511	0.113	0.367	0.605	0.171	0.375	0.511
9. NTALTD	2.050	2.755	7.462	1.446	2.031	3.284	1.976	2.449	3.236
10. WCLTD	0.144	0.299	1.491	0.005	0.035	0.712	0.013	0.293	0.680
11. FCC	-0.875	1.225	3.158	0.158	1.471	1.821	0.501	1.329	2.453
12. CFTD	0.089	0.203	0.290	0.159	0.352	0.421	0.116	0.290	0.354
13. TDTA	0.577	0.659	0.688	0.480	0.584	0.730	0.520	0.599	0.688
14. MVEBVD	0.304	0.804	1.295	0.547	1.304	2.440	0.477	0.804	1.944
15. IC	-3.677	2.406	3.705	-2.514	2.328	6.397	-1.126	2.328	3.983
16. LTDE	0.000	0.580	0.901	0.129	0.582	1.583	0.104	0.580	1.003
17. TNWTD	0.246	0.490	0.639	0.309	0.624	1.336	0.353	0.490	0.734
18. WCTA	0.060	0.068	0.191	0.003	0.049	0.173	0.006	0.068	0.186
19. CR	1.140	1.212	2.142	1.009	1.266	1.678	1.015	1.212	1.718
20. QR	0.746	0.994	1.837	0.758	1.064	1.320	0.746	0.994	1.334
21. LR	2.995	5.637	86.362	3.757	7.447	34.983	3.271	7.447	28.031
22. WCT	9.451	24.164	48.170	-16.927	11.696	21.373	6.929	14.053	32.242
23. ART	7.700	8.640	12.337	7.081	8.118	11.339	7.635	8.362	11.898
24. IT	17.797	53.929	88.984	16.162	41.211	91.151	16.682	50.311	79.309
25. ALTZ	2.838	3.268	3.641	2.311	2.476	3.917	2.344	3.250	3.710

Table 38   Wholesale Trade—Durable Goods (50)

	Small Firms			Large Firms			All Firms		
	P25	P50	P75	P25	P50	P75	P25	P50	P75
1. ROS	-1.974	2.458	6.216	0.994	3.007	5.567	-0.662	2.704	6.091
2. ROA	0.745	6.670	13.518	4.697	9.064	12.422	2.173	8.510	13.159
3. ROTNW	-6.019	9.345	24.670	7.426	14.834	23.934	0.118	14.317	24.115
4. PPC	-116.907	-47.689	16.283	-71.943	-12.048	7.778	-106.513	-36.377	13.483
5. PSC	-13.920	3.049	21.356	-7.644	0.644	9.120	-12.959	1.499	11.436
6. STA	1.089	1.518	2.097	1.444	1.798	2.185	1.293	1.665	2.156
7. CVNI	66.311	174.135	620.155	37.942	60.192	180.685	43.387	92.554	343.615
8. LTDC	0.233	0.371	0.484	0.130	0.215	0.445	0.159	0.265	0.457
9. NTALTD	2.089	2.464	3.716	2.176	4.553	10.103	2.115	2.893	5.366
10. WCLTD	1.034	1.585	2.105	1.047	2.824	4.550	1.035	1.857	3.052
11. FCC	0.409	1.554	2.310	1.105	2.129	3.023	0.876	1.821	2.574
12. CFTD	0.075	0.147	0.231	0.099	0.159	0.360	0.088	0.154	0.271
13. TDTA	0.509	0.641	0.738	0.302	0.458	0.622	0.406	0.565	0.718
14. MVEBVD	0.458	0.752	2.130	0.685	1.271	3.345	0.524	1.128	2.463
15. IC	-0.004	1.999	3.318	1.056	3.037	6.136	0.592	2.350	4.593
16. LTDE	0.258	0.575	0.910	0.108	0.268	0.779	0.167	0.328	0.819
17. TNWTD	0.253	0.559	1.374	0.476	1.127	2.327	0.386	0.678	2.029
18. WCTA	0.223	0.349	0.553	0.355	0.396	0.552	0.247	0.390	0.551
19. CR	1.487	2.159	3.072	1.930	2.797	3.858	1.755	2.394	3.407
20. QR	0.667	0.899	1.646	0.907	1.242	1.635	0.766	1.164	1.623
21. LR	1.908	3.084	6.613	4.124	17.307	44.241	2.495	6.333	17.615
22. WCT	2.274	3.779	6.395	3.237	3.773	5.503	2.954	3.776	5.894
23. ART	5.260	5.962	7.565	5.433	6.997	8.029	5.409	6.532	7.855
24. IT	2.006	3.429	4.072	2.970	3.533	4.873	2.788	3.481	4.438
25. ALTZ	1.820	2.922	3.706	2.385	3.667	5.010	2.006	3.289	4.292

Table 39 Wholesale Trade—Non Durable Goods (51)

	Small Firms			Large Firms			All Firms		
	P25	P50	P75	P25	P50	P75	P25	P50	P75
1. ROS	-0.947	1.214	8.036	1.268	1.920	3.429	0.233	1.760	4.943
2. ROA	2.640	5.806	15.813	6.081	10.476	14.830	3.819	10.360	15.311
3. ROTNW	-4.947	11.084	31.505	14.236	27.667	36.717	4.032	22.740	33.780
4. PPC	-81.937	-27.162	24.595	-101.451	4.038	29.201	-74.189	-19.851	23.686
5. PSC	-8.091	7.281	21.240	-0.877	13.187	28.318	-4.959	8.278	21.879
6. STA	0.922	2.188	3.939	1.754	2.879	3.862	1.446	2.519	3.858
7. CVNI	95.563	253.270	760.336	45.077	67.119	136.327	58.188	118.923	451.327
8. LTDC	0.149	0.414	0.587	0.229	0.449	0.570	0.189	0.417	0.569
9. NTALTD	0.969	2.066	2.813	1.783	2.207	4.497	1.727	2.090	3.733
10. WCLTD	0.395	1.205	3.206	0.671	1.091	2.103	0.505	1.093	2.103
11. FCC	0.832	1.643	3.241	1.273	1.656	2.264	1.097	1.643	2.303
12. CFTD	0.027	0.126	0.172	0.103	0.148	0.241	0.090	0.145	0.183
13. TDTA	0.490	0.583	0.777	0.586	0.667	0.755	0.544	0.649	0.754
14. MVEBVD	0.445	0.781	2.338	0.558	0.805	1.182	0.489	0.783	1.629
15. IC	0.688	1.803	3.393	1.415	1.989	3.380	1.011	1.846	3.365
16. LTDE	0.122	0.497	0.940	0.299	0.815	1.324	0.159	0.705	0.972
17. TNWTD	-0.069	0.519	0.846	0.245	0.465	0.613	0.200	0.467	0.772
18. WCTA	0.151	0.262	0.555	0.152	0.219	0.301	0.153	0.249	0.349
19. CR	1.392	2.140	3.170	1.390	1.583	1.932	1.400	1.666	2.687
20. QR	0.642	0.914	2.128	0.601	0.818	1.221	0.630	0.883	1.253
21. LR	2.299	5.828	22.377	2.618	19.458	52.736	2.698	8.551	33.797
22. WCT	2.062	4.471	14.203	7.886	10.281	18.895	4.471	9.488	15.424
23. ART	5.387	8.758	14.194	7.286	11.536	15.264	7.006	11.184	14.872
24. IT	2.075	7.165	16.749	5.877	8.800	15.061	4.609	8.541	16.459
25. ALTZ	2.150	3.050	5.360	2.235	4.042	5.398	2.161	3.860	5.249

Table 40 Wood Products (24)

	Small Firms			Large Firms			All Firms		
	P25	P50	P75	P25	P50	P75	P25	P50	P75
1. ROS	-8.037	-3.885	1.778	2.434	3.436	6.314	-3.885	2.434	5.218
2. ROA	-14.656	-4.849	5.353	5.373	9.761	13.682	-4.849	5.373	11.322
3. ROTNW	-52.104	-16.190	14.397	4.013	13.648	26.057	-16.674	4.034	20.422
4. PPC	-221.705	-50.268	191.490	-59.378	-16.715	-4.657	-149.568	-16.715	30.624
5. PSC	-8.916	0.178	10.353	-3.523	1.613	12.028	-5.415	1.138	10.770
6. STA	1.240	1.845	2.785	1.104	1.457	2.147	1.216	1.533	2.327
7. CVNI	92.028	229.563	796.537	36.489	51.894	84.229	47.456	85.152	279.899
8. LTDC	0.195	0.421	0.474	0.127	0.218	0.353	0.144	0.290	0.456
9. NTALTD	2.264	2.672	6.056	1.778	3.614	6.633	2.264	3.073	6.056
10. WCLTD	0.606	0.991	2.043	0.452	0.922	3.274	0.517	0.991	2.088
11. FCC	-1.658	-1.024	0.148	1.388	2.718	5.068	-1.378	1.306	2.718
12. CFTD	-0.207	-0.089	0.104	0.054	0.229	0.247	-0.125	0.054	0.235
13. TDTA	0.557	0.612	0.644	0.439	0.516	0.557	0.464	0.557	0.629
14. MVEBVD	0.486	0.720	0.970	1.091	1.166	1.720	0.604	1.047	1.286
15. IC	-2.971	-0.843	1.875	1.475	2.436	4.805	-1.299	1.543	3.104
16. LTDE	0.242	0.726	0.902	0.145	0.278	0.546	0.168	0.408	0.840
17. TNWTD	0.545	0.811	1.139	0.541	0.896	1.232	0.592	0.851	1.229
18. WCTA	0.155	0.244	0.387	0.096	0.135	0.571	0.113	0.221	0.483
19. CR	1.438	1.744	2.487	1.398	1.693	4.235	1.448	1.706	3.342
20. QR	0.606	0.938	1.399	0.532	0.810	1.955	0.598	0.810	1.410
21. LR	1.477	3.223	8.735	2.063	4.378	16.559	1.882	3.990	13.999
22. WCT	5.296	6.802	11.017	3.182	10.590	13.033	3.811	7.912	12.076
23. ART	5.986	9.579	14.644	10.087	11.939	18.726	6.966	10.594	17.736
24. IT	3.742	5.301	8.276	4.324	7.430	8.358	4.135	6.112	8.340
25. ALTZ	1.874	2.790	3.158	2.668	2.976	3.705	2.310	2.842	3.447

Index